Power and Governance in a Partially Globalized World

Robert O. Keohane has been one of the most innovative and influential thinkers in international relations for more than three decades. His groundbreaking work in institutional theory has redefined our understanding of international political economy. This book is a selection of his most recent essays, which address such core issues as interdependence, institutions, the development of international law, globalization, and global governance. The essays are placed in historical and intellectual context by a substantial new introduction outlining the developments in Keohane's thought. In an original afterword (Chapter 12), the author offers a challenging interpretation of the September 11th attacks and their aftermath.

Power and Governance in a Partially Globalized World is essential reading for anyone with an interest in international relations.

Robert O. Keohane is James B. Duke Professor of Political Science at Duke University. He has also taught at Swarthmore College, Stanford, Brandeis, and Harvard. His publications include *After Hegemony* (Princeton University Press 1984), *International Institutions and State Power* (Westview 1989), *Ideas and Foreign Policy*, co-edited with Judith Goldstein (Cornell University Press 1993), and *Power and Interdependence*, co-authored with Joseph S. Nye, Jr. (third edition: Addison Wesley Longman 2001).

Power and Governance in a Partially Globalized World

Robert O. Keohane

London and New York

First published 2002
by Routledge
11 New Fetter Lane, London EC4P 4EE

Simultaneously published in the USA and Canada
by Routledge
29 West 35th Street, New York, NY 10001

Routledge is an imprint of the Taylor & Francis Group

© 2002 Robert O. Keohane

Typeset in Times by RefineCatch Ltd, Bungay, Suffolk
Printed and bound in Great Britain by St Edmundsbury Press,
Bury St Edmunds, Suffolk

British Library Cataloguing in Publication Data
A catalogue record for this book is available from the British Library

Library of Congress Cataloging in Publication Data
A catalog record for this book has been requested

ISBN 0–415–28818–5 (hbk)
ISBN 0–415–28819–3 (pbk)

To Nan: Partner, Lover and Friend

Contents

Preface

The essays in this book were first published between 1990 and 2001 and indicate the development of my thinking during those years. They form a sequel to my previous volume of essays, *International Institutions and State Power* (Boulder: Westview, 1989). The new introduction to this volume describes the conception of world politics that informs them all, as well as the evolution of my thinking during the last decade of the Millennium. Since that introduction combines intellectual with personal history, it leaves little for this preface except acknowledgements of my debts to others.

This book was first imagined not by me but by my editor, Craig Fowlie. Craig approached me with the idea for a book of essays a couple of years ago, and eventually the seed he planted germinated. I am grateful to him for his confidence and persistence, and for his efficiency in securing reviews and managing the editorial process. The previously published chapters appear as they did originally, with a few minor editorial changes and corrections of points of fact, but without changes in interpretation or argument.

The manuscript was completed while I was on leave from Duke University in the fall of 2001. Chapters 1 and 12 were written then. Duke has been a rewarding place to teach and to do research – not to speak of watching basketball! I wish to express my appreciation to Duke University and in particular to the chair of the Department of Political Science, Michael Munger, for providing me with the leave that made this volume possible at this time. I also wish to thank my assistant, Doris Cross, for her help in making the final arrangements for sending this work to the publisher.

Chapters 3, 4, 6 and part of Chapter 5 were written while I was on the faculty of the Department of Government of Harvard University. Harvard always treated me very well, and it is difficult to imagine that I would have written this book without the opportunities offered by this great university. Dean Jeremy Knowles was particularly kind and generous to me when I decided to leave Harvard for Duke, and I wish to record here my thanks to him for his thoughtfulness and consideration.

My "turn toward law" was facilitated not only by the intellectual interests and personal friendships discussed in the introduction, but also by a Frank Kenan Fellowship at the National Humanities Center, Research Triangle

Park, North Carolina, in 1995–96. Frank Kenan was a great benefactor of many fine institutions, whom it was an honor to know. The National Humanities Center is a wonderful place for reflection and writing, and I am grateful to its Director, Robert Connor, and its Associate Director, Kent Mullikin.

One of my most important debts is to the co-authors of five of the papers in this volume: Kenneth Abbott, Andrew Moravcsik, Joseph S. Nye, Duncan Snidal, Anne-Marie Slaughter, and Celeste A. Wallander. I learned from all of these colleagues and friends, who have generously agreed to allow me to reprint our co-authored work here. I must particularly acknowledge the contributions to my thinking of Anne-Marie Slaughter, since without her prodding and her friendship, my turn toward international law is hard to imagine. And if it were not so important, it would go without saying that my greatest debt to a co-author is to Joseph S. Nye. Joe and I have been working together, off and on, for over 33 years – more than half our lives. Joe taught me more than I can convey – probably more than I am aware. He certainly taught me how to bring otherwise inchoate ideas together into sustained published form. Our friendship has also reminded me often of the pleasures of linking intellectual with personal comradeship.

The person with the greatest impact on my life is my wife, Nannerl Overholser Keohane. Her own career as a political theorist, college president, and university president, is an inspiration to me, as it has been to others. Her thinking about political philosophy has enriched my own perspectives, and her criticisms and suggestions on my writings are always trenchant. She cares deeply about the institutions she leads and the people within them, never letting her own ego drive her decisions. She manages stress and tension, at a level never experienced by mere faculty members, with remarkable grace, humor, and resilience. And she seizes the joys and opportunities of life with incomparable zest. Living with her is an enriching experience, and most of the time, it is really *fun*! I therefore dedicate *Power and Governance in a Partially Globalized World* to Nan Keohane.

Durham, North Carolina
December 14, 2001

Acknowledgments

The author and publishers would like to thank the following copyright holders for granting permission to reproduce material in this work:

'International Institutions: Can Interdependence Work?' reproduced with permission from *Foreign Policy* #110 (Spring 1998). Copyright 1998 by Carnegie Endowment for International Peace.

Cambridge University Press for permission to reproduce 'International Liberalism Reconsidered' from John Dunn ed., *Economic Limits to Modern Politics* (1990), pp. 165–194.

'Hobbes's Dilemma and Institutional Change in World Politics: Sovereignty in International Society' from *Whose World Order?* by Hans-Henrick Holm and Georg Sørensen. Copyright 1995 by Westview Press, Inc. Reprinted by permission of Westview Press, a member of Perseus Books, L.L.C.

Oxford University Press for permission to reproduce 'Risk, Threat, and Security Institutions' by Robert O. Keohane and Celeste Wallander from Helga Haftendorn, Robert O. Keohane and Celeste Wallander, eds, *Imperfect Unions: Security Institutions over Time and Space* (1999), pp. 21–47.

Harvard International Law Journal for permission to reproduce 'International Relations and International Law: Two Optics' from *Harvard International Law Journal* **38–1** (Spring 1997), pp. 487–502. Copyright 1997 by the President and Fellows of Harvard College and the Harvard Civil Rights–Civil Liberties Law Review.

Massachusetts Institute of Technology Press Journals for permission to reproduce 'The Concept of Legalization' by Robert O. Keohane, Kenneth Abbot, Andrew Moravcsik, Anne-Marie Slaughter and Duncan Snidal from *International Organization* **54–3** (Summer 2000), pp. 401–419. Copyright 2000 by the IO Foundation and the Massachusetts Institute of Technology.

Massachusetts Institute of Technology Press Journals for permission to reproduce 'Legalized Dispute Resolution: Interstate and Transnational' by Robert O. Keohane, Andrew Moravcsik and Anne-Marie Slaughter from *International Organization* **54-3** (Summer, 2000), pp. 457–488. Copyright 2000 by the IO Foundation and the Massachusetts Institute of Technology.

Reprinted by permission of the Brookings Institution Press, Washington DC, 'Governance in a Globalizing World' by Robert O. Keohane and J. S. Nye from Joseph S. Nye and John D. Donahue, eds, *Governance in a Globalizing World* (Brookings: 2000), pp. 1–41.

Reprinted by permission of the Brookings Institution Press, Washington DC, 'The Club Model of Multilateral Cooperation and Problems of Democratic Legitimacy' by Robert O. Keohane and J. S. Nye from Roger B. Porter *et al.*, eds, *Efficiency, Equity and Legitimacy: The Multilateral Trading System at the Millennium* (Brookings: 2001), pp. 264–307.

American Political Science Association for permission to reproduce 'Governance in a Partially Globalized World' from *American Political Science Review* (March 2001), pp. 1–13.

1 Introduction: from interdependence and institutions to globalization and governance[1]

Robert O. Keohane

(2002)

This volume contains essays written (several in conjunction with co-authors) between 1990 and 2001. All of them revolve around issues of interdependence, institutions, and governance in world politics. They address a wide variety of different problems, but they do so, I believe, from the standpoint of a consistent analytical framework. That is, there is a view of how the world works embedded in these essays, each of which reveals a different aspect of this multifaceted understanding of world politics.

The purpose of this introduction is, first of all, to elucidate this conception of how the world works. It is both individualist and institutionalist, regarding institutions both as created by human action and as structuring that action. The principal motor of action in this view is self-interest, guided by rationality, which translates structural and institutional conditions into payoffs and probabilities, and therefore incentives. But my conceptions of self-interest and rationality are broad ones. Self-interest is not simply material; on the contrary, it encompasses one's interest in being thought well of, and in thinking well of oneself. One's self-interest is not divorced from one's principled ideas or identity but closely connected with them. Furthermore, not all action is necessarily self-interested: actions such as those of firemen rushing into the burning World Trade Center on September 11, 2001, reflect commitment and courage rather than interest.

The resulting conception of how the world works is complex, seeking to take into account subjectivity as well as objectivity, primal urges for power as well as institutional constraints, principled beliefs and worldviews that cannot be validated as well as rational calculation. It therefore lacks parsimony. The core of my contribution to this view of the world has been to explore how international institutions operate, in the context of interdependence. But my exploration of institutions and interdependence has taken place in the context of an awareness of how they are affected by other, broader factors. Hence, I do not assume that institutions and interdependence are the most important aspects of contemporary world politics, that they somehow contain the unique key to history. Indeed, they only make sense if they are fit into the larger puzzle.

What follows is part intellectual autobiography, part elaboration of con-nections among views, and presumably part rationalization of arguments that I now see as more closely connected than they may have originally been.[2] After all, to a considerable extent we invent the past. Nevertheless, I believe that this reconstruction is not pure invention; and it can be at least partially tested by reference to the essays that appear, with minor stylistic or grammatical changes but without substantive changes, in this volume.

I begin with the concept of interdependence, as discussed and elaborated by Joseph S. Nye and myself in 1977. I next discuss what I call "institutional theory" and its research program, then turn to its implications for the study of international law. From there, I move to the two key buzzwords of our own day – globalization and governance – and try to show how, in discussing those concepts, I used and elaborated the framework of analysis developed earlier in the study of institutions and interdependence. At the end of this introduction, I refer to an essay that illustrates how my way of understanding world politics can be applied to contemporary events. Shortly after September 11 I set myself the task of asking about the implications of that attack for theories of world politics, in particular for the theories with which my own work is associated. My response was not meant to be comprehensive, since scholars with other specialties would respond from their own distinctive perspectives. But since this essay should illuminate both the value and the limitations of my own approach, it is included as Chapter 12 of this volume.

From interdependence to institutional theory

Over thirty years ago, astute observers of the world political economy began to comment on striking increases in economic connections among societies and the growing role of multinational corporations (Cooper 1968; Vernon 1971). Meanwhile, the literature on the European Community, pioneered by Ernst B. Haas, focused on how economic interdependence affected arrange-ments for governance (Haas 1958). Nye and I picked up on these themes, beginning with our edited special issue of *International Organization* on transnational relations (Keohane and Nye 1972), a term that we did not invent but that we did insert into the literature on world politics.

At that time the buzzword for these changes was "interdependence". In the 1970s, Nye and I built a theory elucidating the notion of "complex inter-dependence," an ideal type for analyzing situations of multiple transnational issues and contacts in which force is not a useful instrument of policy. We defined interdependence itself more broadly, to encompass strategic issues involving force as well as economic ones. In our analysis, interdependence is frequently asymmetrical and highly political: indeed, asymmetries in interdependence generate power resources for states, as well as for non-state actors. *Power and Interdependence*, published first in 1977, elaborated this theory and applied it to fifty years of history (1920–1970) in two issue-areas (oceans and money) and two country relationships (US–Australia and

US–Canada). There were a number of gaps in our analysis, some of which we acknowledged a decade later,[3] but the analysis of the relationship between asymmetrical interdependence and power continues to be useful, as illustrated by Chapter 12.

Power and Interdependence contained an incipient theory of institutions, in the form of what Nye and I called an international organization model of regime change (Keohane and Nye 1977, 54–58). But this theory was not well-developed. What preoccupied me for seven years after the publication of *Power and Interdependence* was the puzzle of why states establish international regimes – rule-oriented institutions that limit their Members' legal freedom of action. In *After Hegemony: Cooperation and Discord in the World Political Economy* (1984), I presented a theory of international institutions based on rationalist theory, in particular economic theories of the firm and of imperfect markets. I argued that institutions perform important tasks for states, enabling them to cooperate. In particular, institutions reduce the costs of making, monitoring, and enforcing rules – transaction costs – provide information, and facilitate the making of credible commitments. In this theory, the principal guarantors of compliance with commitments are reciprocity (including both threats of retaliation and promises of reciprocal cooperation) and reputation. A brief summary of the major arguments of this theory, and a discussion of its evolution, is contained in Chapter 2 below.

My formulation of institutional theory has often been referred to as "liberal institutionalism" or "neo-liberal institutionalism." These labels do not appeal to me, not just because they are awkward. My theory does have its roots in liberalism, as Chapters 3 and 11 demonstrate. But the connotations of liberalism are multiple and misleading. My theory has nothing to do with the view that commerce leads necessarily to peace; that people are basically good; or that progress in human history is inevitable – all propositions sometimes associated with liberalism. Nor is it connected with the view that liberty should have priority over equality and social justice, much less with the "neo-liberalism" of the past decade: the so-called "Washington Consensus" that dictated the dismantling of much governmental regulation of markets in developing countries. My liberalism is more pessimistic about human nature and more cautious about causal connections running from economics to politics than some versions of classical liberalism; and I have never been a supporter of the "Washington Consensus" in its strong neo-liberal form. Since attaching a "liberal label" to my perspective generates such a need for explication, it seems better to leave it off entirely.

"Institutionalist" is descriptive of my work, since it emphasizes the significance of institutions and seeks to explain them. Using this term is not meant as a claim to intellectual hegemony. Indeed, there are many other institutionalist theories, often with quite different concepts, and implications, than my own (March and Olsen 1995, Chapter 2; March and Olsen 1999; Ruggie 1998; Ruggie 1999). However, I regard my own formulation as having as good a claim to the adjective "institutionalist" as any of its competitors. When I refer below to "institutionalist theory," I refer to my own version of institutionalism.

The theory in *After Hegemony* was rather stylized: as in *Power and Interdependence*, differences in domestic politics were deliberately overlooked for purposes of simplification. This is not to say that the importance of domestic politics was denied: quite the contrary. But the theory did not encompass domestic politics. Indeed, the theoretical gap created by the omission from the theory of domestic politics was sufficiently wide to drive many dissertations through it. Some of my former students have been leaders in this effort. They have analyzed the impact of domestic politics on world politics, in the context of a sophisticated understanding of interstate politics and the roles played by international institutions and non-state actors.[4]

The fact that my former students have written over a dozen books linking domestic politics and international relations is not only gratifying to me personally; it illustrates a broader aspect of American graduate education that is often overlooked. The resumés of scholars normally include only their own work. But the puzzles that they recognize but fail to address may be as important to their own students, and to their field as a whole, as their own contributions. Paths that lead through open doors may beckon more strongly to aspiring scholars than imposing intellectual edifices, no matter how impressive. And the explorations of graduate students instruct their professors. Graduate education is a process of interchange, not merely of transmission.

The theory developed in *After Hegemony* and closely related writings (e.g. Keohane 1986b) was strongly affected by my research on trade, monetary, and energy issues – all questions of material self-interest in which reciprocity played a substantial role. On the whole, the same framework fits environmental issues quite well (Haas, Keohane and Levy 1993; Keohane and Levy 1996). Perhaps this congruity should not be surprising, since similar questions arise of cross-border externalities and economic competition. On both sets of issues, monitoring of agreements is important and is carried out largely under the auspices of international institutions, while enforcement takes place through state action, legitimated through such institutions.

Environmental issues do have a moral dimension that is largely missing from the economic questions emphasized in *After Hegemony*. Principled ideas, concerned with right and wrong, play a significant role in mobilizing publics on issues such as ozone depletion, pollution of the oceans, and global warming. Such principled ideas play an even more prominent role on questions of human rights. And causal ideas, specifying connections between cause and effect, are important in policy debates in both issue-areas, as well as in other arenas of world politics.

Intrigued by the role of ideas, and their connections to rationalistic frameworks of analysis, Judith Goldstein and I began to explore the role of ideas on policy in the early 1990s (Goldstein and Keohane 1993). The role of ideas, of course, has been a long-standing theme in the work of a number of distinguished students of international relations, including my own mentor, Stanley Hoffmann (1987), Hedley Bull (1978), and Martin Wight (1992). Goldstein and I, however, were particularly interested in reconciling theories of rational choice, with which we were sympathetic, with our view that ideas are significant in world politics. We distinguished among three types of beliefs: worldviews, principled beliefs, and causal beliefs. Worldviews are illustrated by religion, principled beliefs by doctrines of human rights, and causal beliefs by Keynesian or monetarist theories of macroeconomics. All three types of belief affect policy, but they do so differently.

Goldstein and I went on to suggest that ideas exert effects along three causal pathways: (1) as "roadmaps," (2) as focal points where there is no unique equilibrium, and (3) as embedded elements of institutions. Our essay is not reprinted here both because it is well-known and easily accessible, and because it forms an integral part of an edited volume to which it served as an introduction. But my thinking since the early 1990s has been deeply affected by my appreciation, heightened by work on this project, of the role of ideas in world politics. As noted below, my recent work on international law seeks to explore how the ideas incorporated in legal thinking affect persuasion and practice in world politics.

As these remarks imply, I disagree with the frequently-heard criticism that the role of ideas is necessarily de-emphasized by a view of the world that is based on an individualist ontology and a neo-positivist epistemology. It is individuals who have beliefs, although of course these beliefs are formed through social processes, and are perpetuated through societies that outlive individuals. As social scientists, we can investigate the impact of these beliefs through theoretical and empirical work, exploring how variations in ideas – between individuals and between groups – help to account for variations in behavior. Of course we have to be alert to the operation of social norms and practices, and shared memories – so we should not adopt an unsocialized, atomistic notion of human beings. Man, as Aristotle pointed out, is a social animal. But in my view we should focus on individuals as the principal unit of analysis, as long as we keep in mind their interactions in society, and the historical and cultural contexts within which they live. This means that the analyst goes back and forth between individual and society, regarding both seriously, but always seeking to explain individual behavior, and aggregate it upward, rather than to theorize about society without considering whether the resulting propositions are consistent with patterns of individual behavior. In this way, we can give our theories micro-foundations and avoid the reification of abstract concepts or the positing of a collective consciousness for which there seems to be little scientific evidence.

The most important work on the role of ideas in world politics has been done not by me but others. The politics of human rights are not well-explained by the reciprocity-based logic of institutionalist theory: states do not retaliate for human rights violations by others by abridging human rights themselves (Hathaway 2001). On other issues, such as the use of weapons of mass destruction, principled ideas and organizational cultures seem to have played an important a role in accounting for behavior (Katzenstein (ed.) 1996; Legro 1995). "Constructivist" writing on world politics has emphasized, as did work drawing on psychology earlier (Jervis 1976), the importance of subjectivity: the beliefs by which our images of the world are constructed in shaping world politics (Wendt 1999). Major work on the role of ideas has also been done by such scholars as Goldstein, Martha Finnemore, Margaret Keck, Friedrich Kratochwil, Henry R. Nau, my former student Daniel Philpott, Thomas Risse, John Gerard Ruggie, and Kathryn Sikkink.[5]

Institutional and realist theory

It should be clear from this discussion that I do not claim that institutional theory is a comprehensive theory of world politics. I still believe it to be superior to a crude realism that fails to incorporate international institutions as important entities (Mearsheimer 1994/95; Keohane and Martin 1995). But as Peter Katzenstein, Stephan Krasner and I have argued (Katzenstein *et al.* 1999b), a stylized competition between realism and institutionalism is not particularly conducive to new insights, now, in our field. Sophisticated versions of realism – both of the classical and structural varieties – share a great deal with my version of institutionalism, epistemologically and ontologically. They are all concerned with issues of power, including state power (Keohane 1983). Indeed, it is one of the silliest criticisms of my own work that it ignores power, as the titles of my major works from the 1970s and 1980s make clear.[6] Realism and institutionalism, in my formulation, are actor-oriented, individualist theories whose practitioners follow neo-positivist standards of evidence. They are by no means incommensurate paradigms; rather they are labels for loosely grouped interpretations that differ along a variety of dimensions. These dimensions include the intensity of competition in world politics, the role of rules and norms, the nature of information available to actors, and the linkages and separations between issue-areas.

Realism is a useful "first cut" at understanding world politics, but its vision of the field is too limited to make it a good comprehensive doctrine. Too much is left out: not only institutions, but also transnational relations, domestic politics and the role of ideas. Realism is long on structure, short on process.

Due to its limitations, realism is a poor candidate to correct the flaws in much institutionalist work that have been noted above: failure to theorize domestic politics, and an under-emphasis on the role of ideas. Realist cannot correct these flaws because it shares them, even in a more pronounced way. Waltz's *Theory of International Politics* (1979) abstracts away from domestic politics, just as my own book of the mid-1980s, *After Hegemony* (1984) does. This is not to say that either Professor Waltz or I were unaware of its importance: Waltz, for instance, wrote a whole book on the subject before developing his system-oriented theory (Waltz 1967). But it is difficult to construct a theory that simultaneously takes into account relations between states and relations within them, and that remains parsimonious.[7]

Classical realism – as in the hands of Carr (1946) and Morgenthau (1948) – has discussed the role of ideas, but more recent structural realism, as notably developed by Waltz and Robert Gilpin (1981), has omitted it. The lack of extensive and sophisticated understanding of the role of ideas in world politics – which would have to include Nazism, communism and fundamentalism as well as human rights thinking and environmental awareness – hampers us particularly now in the wake of the September 11, 2001 attacks on the United States. These attacks illustrate the role of religion – overlooked by both of these secular approaches – in world politics. What Nye labeled "soft power" in the 1990s is not a monopoly of secular society, much less of the United States. Chapter 12 of this volume emphasizes this point.

The implication of these remarks is that two major trends in the study of world politics during the 1990s need to be continued and extended: the analysis of how domestic and world politics interact, and the investigation of the role of ideas in world politics. The brand of liberalism represented by the work of Andrew Moravcsik (1997) and Anne-Marie Slaughter (1995) is a valuable way to analyze the former; constructivist theory offers promise in understanding how ideas matter (Finnemore and Sikkink 1999).

In breaking into the theoretically complacent world of realist thinking, it was expedient to emphasize the distinctive value of institutionalist theory, even while recognizing the contributions of realism (Keohane 1983). And in the heat of subsequent controversy, it has been all too easy to overstate differences between institutional and realist theory, and perhaps to over-emphasize the superiority of the former (Keohane 1989, Ch. 1; Keohane 1993). No perspective has a monopoly on wisdom: realism, theories focusing on domestic politics, and theories emphasizing subjective beliefs all have a role to play. Contestation between different approaches can play a positive role in social science scholarship, pushing advocates to sharpen their theories and to test them in more convincing ways. But if the contending approaches become conflicting schools of warring scholars, with graduate students signed up as in one camp or another, they become what Albert Hirschman (1970) once called "paradigms as hindrances to understanding."[8]

Institutionalism and the puzzle of compliance

The institutionalist theory that I developed in *After Hegemony* created only a promissory note on a major issue: that of compliance. In a world without centralized government, why should states comply with obligations that had become inconvenient? One set of problems might arise from deliberate deception, although prudence on the part of others could limit those dangers. A more pervasive set of problems could arise as a result of time: events may adversely change the cost-benefit calculus of state compliance. Why, one asks, should states guided by rational self-interest comply with obligations that have become inconvenient?

I sought in the late 1980s and 1990s to explore these questions in an historically-oriented inquiry focused on United States foreign policy. I learned a great deal in the process, but failed to come up with either a comprehensive theory or satisfactory systematic evidence. On the theoretical side, my initial hunch was that concerns about reputation would ensure fairly regular compliance. In the record of United States foreign policy I did indeed find much concern with reputation, but I also found a consistent pattern, when commitments were inconvenient, of ingenious attempts to design policies to avoid reputational constraints.

US policy-makers in the late eighteenth century made the Jay Treaty with Britain (1795), which effectively abrogated a treaty of alliance with France, dating from 1778, while, in the text of the treaty, denying any such abrogation. In 1810 the United States seized West Florida from a weak Spain, concocting the tale that West Florida had actually been ceded to the United States in the Louisiana Purchase. Such an account required, as Henry Adams later wrote, "that Spain had retroceded West Florida to France without knowing it, that France had sold it to the United States without suspecting it, that the United States had bought it without paying for it, and that neither France nor Spain, although the original contracting parties, were competent to decide the meaning of their own contract" (Adams 1986: 468). In 1814, United States negotiators with Britain distinguished between agreements with "European nations" and "savages." A provision in the treaty providing that the United States restore to the Indians the rights and privileges that they had before the War of 1812 was dismissed by US negotiator Albert Gallatin as "nominal," and it became a dead letter.[9] In the 1880s the United States reneged on Chinese immigration treaties, and in the years before 1901 it successfully pressured Britain into renegotiating an 1850 treaty on Central America, on threat of violation. After World War II, the United States broke a UN embargo of Southern Rhodesia, failed for fifteen years to pay its UN dues, threatened unilaterally to reinterpret the 1972 ABM treaty with the Soviet Union, and defied United Nations General Assembly resolutions in the 1980s condemning US interventions in Latin America.

Of course it would be wrong to generalize from these violations of commitments, since many other commitments were kept. In other words, focusing on broken commitments creates severe selection bias (Achen and Snidal 1989; King, Keohane and Verba 1994). The strategy I tried, of examining commitments that were politically contested, also introduced selection bias, since contestation of commitments was obviously correlated with the dependent variable: whether commitments were kept or broken. Yet including all commitments would have created an unmanageable number of commitments, the vast majority of which would not only never have been questioned, but which would be theoretically irrelevant since they would have remained convenient. That is, maintaining them continued to be in the interest of the United States as interpreted by its leaders; hence it could not be inferred that the commitment itself had any effect on observed behavior.

More progress on this subject has been made by other scholars. Ronald Mitchell (1994) studied oil pollution by tankers at sea and showed that attempts to limit discharges failed, since tanker captains had strong incentives to violate the rules and the capacity to do so; but that standards for new equipment succeeded by changing both incentives and capacity. Beth Simmons (2000) has provided the most telling evidence for the efficacy of treaty commitments by focusing on Article VIII of the IMF agreements, which enables states voluntarily to commit themselves not to restrict payments on current account. She finds that accepting the legal commitment to maintain current account openness helps to explain subsequent behavior, after controlling for a variety of other relevant factors. Her interpretation of her findings points strongly to reputation as the key motivation for maintaining such commitments even in times of economic difficulty.

Although I am naturally somewhat chagrined by my own failure to solve the puzzle of compliance with commitments, I gain considerable satisfaction from the fact that at least for some issues it is being analyzed successfully within the framework of a rational-institutionalist theory. What matters for the fruitfulness of a theory is not the work of an individual, but the effort of a research community that is sufficiently intrigued or inspired by the theory to develop it creatively and test its implications systematically. There emerges a division of labor within this community among those who create the original theoretical intuitions, who specify the theory, who test it systematically, and who explore the wider implications of the findings that emerge. Since these capabilities are rarely all found in a single person, it is shortsighted to make any one of them the litmus test for productive scholarship. It is clear from my career that I am better at proposing new explanations, beginning to specify them as a theory, and exploring their wider implications, than at formalizing or testing hypotheses systematically. In a sense, then, my contributions can only be validated by others, which makes me very grateful to them for their creativity, intelligence, and effort. The fact that many of the major contributors to the institutionalist research program are former students of mine, naturally imbues this gratitude with feelings of pride.

If pride in one's own accomplishments and those of one's colleagues increases over time, even more does humility. Humility is probably not a positive attribute for a young scholar: one has to believe that one's own ideas are superior to conventional wisdom in certain areas, which requires, for an untested scholar, a certain arrogance. Certainly few colleagues who encountered me during my 30s would have listed humility as one of my virtues. Over time, however, one's personal failure to solve certain problems or keep up with certain technical advances does induce humility. So does the broader recognition that one's own theory – in my case, institutional theory – is only a partial approach to world politics, which needs to be combined with other perspectives.

Liberalism, sovereignty and security

One way of thinking about institutions and interdependence is to view interdependence as the context within which international institutions operate. Institutions are, in this view, a response to interdependence. The tradition of modern thought that is most conducive to this framing of the issue is that of liberalism, discussed in Chapter 3. Liberalism as an approach to international relations emphasizes individuals, seeks to understand collective decisions, and, in an ethical sense, promotes human rights and validates attempts to ameliorate the human condition. Sophisticated liberalism combines strands of commercialism, republicanism and regulatory politics. Attempts to regulate transnational activity occur as a response to economic interdependence, in the context of pluralistic democracy. Liberalism reaffirms the attempt of institutionalists to seek to understand politics for the sake of designing institutions that will promote cooperation, welfare, and human rights.

As I indicated above, liberalism has many variants, not all of which are consistent with one another. Hence as a general perspective, it does not offer specific normative guidance. My own form of liberalism is discussed in greater detail in Chapter 11. It emphasizes that interdependence among human beings produces discord, which generates a need for institutions. But it also stresses that institutions can be oppressive. My brand of liberalism is therefore hardly the naively overoptimistic doctrine caricatured by Voltaire in *Candide*, whose hero goes from disaster to disaster proclaiming that he is in "the best of all possible worlds." My liberalism recognizes the arguments of Judith Shklar's "liberalism of fear," while still holding out hope for progress. My intellectual heroes include James Madison, for his recognition that institutions must be designed to check one another, and John Rawls, for his construction of a moral theory based on adopting a standpoint of impartiality. I believe that institutions, including international institutions, should be accountable to those they govern. It is also desirable that they rest insofar as possible on honest persuasion rather than on coercion or bargaining based on asymmetrical resources; and that they encourage public participation. My own liberalism, while resolutely anti-utopian, nevertheless offers normative as well as positive guidance for public policy.

Sovereignty is important from this perspective because it illuminates a central tension in contemporary liberalism. Commercial liberalism emphasizes the benefits of the division of labor, hence favors greater openness and the institutions needed to assure openness. Republican liberalism, on the contrary, stresses the importance of self-determination and democracy within well-defined boundaries, so that the public can exercise effective control over self-seeking private actors. From the standpoint of commercial liberalism, sovereignty is a problem; from the standpoint of republican liberalism, it is an essential guarantee. It is therefore not surprising that contemporary debates about openness often pit proponents of sovereignty against opponents of it, and divide the traditional right as well as the traditional left.

During the 1980s, theories of world politics were rather sharply sub-divided into those dealing with security and those concerned with issues of political economy. In fact, the field virtually bifurcated into two specialties, which were often seen as having little relationship to one another. In *After Hegemony* I even defended "abstracting from military issues" as a way of focusing more clearly on "the economic origins of change" (Keohane 1984: 41).

Even during the Cold War, this view was quite problematic, as the impact of Ronald Reagan's military buildup on Soviet power, and indirectly on the world economy, was soon to demonstrate. The end of the Cold War made this separation between political-military issues and political-economic ones even more untenable. In *Bound to Lead* (1990), Nye developed a persuasive argument about the centrality of American power, which linked security tightly to political economy.[10] Some work I did with colleagues at Harvard on international institutions after the Cold War (Keohane, Hoffmann and Nye 1993) reinforced my interest in explaining how institutional theory could illuminate security issues.

Two results of my renewed interest in security affairs, beginning in the early 1990s, appear as Chapters 4 and 5. Chapter 4 reprints an essay on sovereignty and institutional change, written in 1992–93 and published in 1995. This essay delineates what I call "Hobbes's Dilemma": that concentrating power to create order at a domestic level can create predatory, oppressive states that are a danger to world order. The historic liberal solution – institutions founded not on idealism but on an understanding of self-interest – is, in my view, relevant not only to domestic constitutionalism but to the creation of international regimes. Locke and Madison are the intellectual heroes of this essay. Sovereignty is an institution created for international society; like other institutions, it undergoes change in response to environmental conditions. In the OECD area, characterized by what Nye and I called complex interdependence (Keohane and Nye 1977), sovereignty is changing from a territorially-defined barrier to a bargaining resource.

Writing when western action in the former Yugoslavia was at its weakest and most vacillating, I distinguished sharply – probably too sharply – between the situation under conditions of complex interdependence and that in "zones of conflict." Since I did not anticipate the terrorist threat, I expected that after the collapse of the Soviet Union the United States would, in these areas, "be reluctant to intervene, except where this can be done at low cost" (p. 78). Even before the events of September 11 invalidated this forecast, armed intervention by NATO in Bosnia and Kosovo showed that in conflicted areas of the world, sovereignty was becoming less of a barrier to action than I had anticipated.

The second article on security issues, reprinted here as Chapter 5, is "risk, threat and security institutions," with Celeste A. Wallander. According to both this chapter and the previous one, the transaction costs–informational theories of international institutions developed in *After Hegemony* also pertain to security issues in which the participants have common or complementary interests. States that seek to cooperate on security issues also need to devise institutions that facilitate cooperation by making promises credible, providing information, and reducing other costs of agreement. Once successful institutions have been developed, it is easier to adapt them to respond to change than to create entirely new ones, particularly if the institutions have a "hybrid" quality, with practices that can be transferred at relatively low cost to new situations. The claim of Chapter 5, written in 1997–98 and published in 1999, is that NATO, as such a hybrid institution, is "changing from an exclusive alliance focused on threats to an inclusive security management institution concerned chiefly with risks" (p. 108). From the perspective of 2002, such a transformation seems to be occurring with breathtaking speed, as Russia is drawn more closely into NATO decision making. The events of September 11 have pushed NATO much more rapidly down a path that, according to Professor Wallander and myself, it was already following earlier.

From institutions to law

In the later 1980s and early 1990s a few innovative legal scholars began to use institutionalist theory. Kenneth Abbott (1989) systematically reviewed and commented on institutionalist theory in a major law review article. Anne-Marie Slaughter (1993), writing under her former name of Burley, essentially argued that political scientists were speaking legal prose without recognizing it: that we were theorizing about institutions that generations of legal scholars had described, though not explained.[11] At about the same time the General Agreement on Tariffs and Trade (GATT) was being transformed from a non-binding system into the legally binding system that became the World Trade Organization (WTO) in 1995. Both in the world of ideas and in the real world of international institutions, the separation between institutions and law seemed more and more tenuous.

My own aversion to international law had been forged in graduate school, when the "world peace through world law" work of Louis Sohn and Grenville Clark and Louis B. Sohn (Clark and Sohn 1960) had seemed utterly divorced from Cold War reality. More influential in my own training were the critiques of legalism by the realists E.H. Carr (1946) and George F. Kennan (1951). Perhaps as a reaction to my own tendency toward personal moralism, I have always been allergic to preaching as a substitute for analysis. But by the early 1990s I had recognized that international law did not have to be textual, formalistic and separated from real political problems and ethnical dilemmas. Friendship with Abram and Antonia Chayes, and with Anne-Marie Slaughter (a student of Abe Chayes) had helped to teach me that, as had my acquaintance with the ideas and arguments of Ken Abbott, Tom Franck, and Harold Koh.[12]

The immediate occasion for studying law was provided by the invitation to give the Sherrill Lecture at Yale Law School in 1996. I used time on leave the preceding fall to read in the legal literature for that lecture, which appears as Chapter 6 below. From the lecture it was a short step to collaboration on a special issue of *International Organization* focusing on legalization in world politics, which appeared in the journal in 2000 and in book form in 2001 (Goldstein *et al.*, 2001). The conceptual paper for that volume, and a chapter on legalized dispute resolution, appear as Chapters 7 and 8 below.

I think that the analysis of legalization undertaken by my colleagues and myself is consistent with my overall framework for the analysis of world politics. I begin with actors – individuals and organizations – pursuing their interests as they see them, and guided by the values they internalize. These actors use resources at their disposal, including force, material capabilities, and persuasive ideas, to seek to achieve their objectives. The actors are located in structures of power that provide incentives for action, by affecting the payoffs of various strategies; they are also located within organizations, which delegate authority to various agents. Individuals respond to incentives in a broadly rational way; organizations may do so also, depending on how they are structured. Rationality does not mean full information, or the ability to calculate perfectly; instead, it is the "bounded rationality" of Herbert Simon (1996). In contemporary world politics, states are usually the most important actors, although they are by no means alone. They have to contend with transnational actors, and with structures of transnational as well as interstate relationships. Both sets of actors, state and non-state, also deal with institutions in two important senses: as inherited patterns of rules and relationships that can affect beliefs and expectations, and as potential tools for the pursuit of their own objectives.

To understand politics within this framework, one first looks for the key bargains that create policies and establish coalitions. One can think of these bargains as reflecting the equilibria of games, which create institutions, which then, in turn, establish or solidify equilibria so that these institutions, and particular policies, persist (Shepsle 1986). The viability of these institutionalized agreements, however, depends not merely on the interests, capacities, and beliefs of the participants, and on the nominal rules of the institutions, but also on their consistency with broader sets of beliefs and expectations held by other actors or coalitions that control political resources.

Legalized institutions, with precise obligations interpreted by third parties, often impose particularly strong constraints on political actors, as well as providing opportunities for innovative strategies that involve legal action. The success of these strategies is frequently dependent on whether implicit coalitions can be formed, and bargains made, among actors playing well-defined legal roles, including judges. Strategic interaction is central both to politics and to law. Beliefs and institutions, as well as material capabilities, are crucial to strategic interaction. Indeed, the outcomes of strategic inter-actions may depend as much on how rules are interpreted – a key focus of international legal scholarship – as on the wording of the rules themselves. World politics and the processes of international law can only be understood, therefore, from multiple perspectives, which encompass issues of state power, non-state action, domestic politics, institutions, processes of interpretation, coalitions and bargaining, and the persuasiveness of competing sets of ideas. Understanding how international legal scholars work helps one see issues of interpretation and persuasion in a more subtle way.

From interdependence to globalism

These articles do not make reference to "globalization" or "globalism." However, my recent work is cast in those terms. What explains the shift?

The cavalier answer to this question would be that when a new buzzword comes to our faddish field, it is more effective to redefine and reinterpret it than to ignore it. Interdependence was the buzzword of the 1970s, but it had been used in sloppy ways that limited thought. In *Power and Inter-dependence*, Nye and I sought to redefine and reinterpret it as an analytically useful concept. We disparaged "rhetorical" uses of the phrase and defined interdependence as referring to situations characterized by reciprocal costly effects among actors. We explicitly rejected the view that interdependence was necessarily benign and declared our skepticism about the naïve view that "rising interdependence is creating a brave new world of cooperation to replace the bad old world of international conflict" (Keohane and Nye 1977: 10). We therefore sought to make interdependence into a useful analytical tool that did not prejudge conclusions.

When globalization became the buzzword of the 1990s, my first reaction was to regard it as journalistic hype: interdependence in flashier but less revealing garb. Indeed, Helen Milner and I entitled a book that we edited in 1996, "internationalization and domestic politics," rather than "globalization and domestic politics," since "globalization" seemed to imply an answer to the question we were asking about convergence or divergence of national policies (Keohane and Milner, eds, 1996). But it is frustrating to try to row against a strong tide, or to sail directly into the wind. To be heard, the scholar has to speak to the concerns of his era in the language of his era. Doing so gets people hooked; then one can proceed to the analysis that may increase their understanding, or at least raise questions about their preconceptions.

At one level, then, "interdependence" was simply overtaken by "globaliza-tion" as the fashionable language to describe increases in economic open-ness and integration. But at a deeper level, changes in terminology reflect changes in reality. The most comprehensive work on globalization of which I am aware defines it as a set of processes that embody "a transformation in the spatial organization of social relations and transactions" generating transcontinental flows and networks. This book distinguishes four aspects of globalization: extensity (the stretching of space), intensity, velocity, and impact (Held *et al.* 1999: 16). Globalization moves beyond linkages between separate societies to the reorganization of social life on a transnational basis. As John Ruggie commented on an earlier version of this introduction: globalization is to interdependence as Federal Express is to the exchange of letters between separate national post offices.

We should notice, however, the semantic differences between these two terms. Interdependence refers to a *state of the world*, whereas globalization describes a *trend* of increasing transnational flows and increasingly thick networks of interdependence. For the terms to be comparable, we need to use a different term: "globalism," which describes a state of the world. Both interdependence and globalism can be viewed as matters of degree; both can increase or decline over time. Globalization, by contrast, implies increases in globalism. It makes more sense to speak of a "decline in globalism" (as, for instance, with economic globalism between 1914 and 1945) than a "decline in globalization."

Despite the differences, the complexities of interdependence, as Nye and I and others had worked them out in the 1970s, are crucial to a coherent and realistic understanding of globalism and globalization. In particular, interdependence was not just economic, but also strategic, environmental, and ideational. Globalism, as Nye and I define it in Chapter 9, is also multi-dimensional. We differentiate economic, social, environmental and military globalization, each of which has political dimensions. Globalism involves thick networks of interdependence, organized on a transnational basis. Each strand of interdependence involves specific actors, whereas globalism refers to the aggregate pattern produced by all of these strands, and by their organization on a global scale.

From institutions to governance

Finally, how does "governance" enter this picture? As one reviewer of a draft table of contents for this volume asked, what explains the apparent shift in my emphasis from institutions to governance? The answer to this question parallels my answer to the last one. As networks of interdependence intensify, they become more important to domestic publics. And as they thicken into globalism, the connections between them also become more intense. It is less and less feasible to regard issues of trade, finance, environment, and security as separable, each with its own institution devoted to it. The world system looks more and more like a polity. Successful polities have governance structures in which the institutions are well-articulated with one another; but the world polity, if one can call it that, has disarticulated and fragmented institutions. Hence the problem arises of governance, which is defined in Chapter 9 as "the processes and institutions, both formal and informal, that guide and restrain the collective activities of a group." Globally, the question of governance is one of how the various institutions and processes of global society could be meshed more effectively, in a way that would be regarded as legitimate by attentive publics controlling access to key resources.

In this context, what Nye and I in Chapter 10 call the "club model" of international organizations becomes less and less tenable. In the half-century after World War II, a practice developed by which a limited set of elites from different countries came together within the confines of an international organization to bargain over a limited set of issues. These clubs were not very transparent and they kept outsiders at arms' length, but they often succeeded, as in trade or in the European Union, in negotiating important agreements that promoted openness. Yet with the growth in sophistication and activism of both developing countries and non-governmental actors, and in the context of a democratic political culture in their leading members, the club model has lost legitimacy. In particular, demands have been raised for accountability within the organizations – demands that are inconsistent with club practices, as well as with the interests of the developing countries as they perceive them. Legitimacy in terms of outputs – liberalized trade, widely beneficial to all, including the poor – may be inconsistent with legitimacy in terms of inputs, involving transparency and accountability. It is still unclear what form of governance on issues related to trade could be developed that would be sufficiently transparent and participatory to be legitimate, yet effective enough to solve pressing problems of inefficiency and the poverty that is accentuated by inefficiency.

The key issues, in my view, involve governance in a partially globalized world, as outlined by the title essay, which appears as Chapter 11. A partially globalized world is a world of thick networks of interdependence, in which boundaries, and states, nevertheless matter a great deal. Even the quite open US–Canadian border has a strong impact on economic activity (Helliwell 1998). And as much work has demonstrated, globalization has not produced convergence of national welfare-state policies.[13]

To understand governance in such a world, we have to understand institutions, which arise in the first instance from demands by political actors and from bargaining. To an extent they are the product of rational egoism; but simple functional theories that derive outcomes from need or purpose overlook both a variety of perverse incentives that often stand in the way, and the potential for public-spirited action. Institutions have paradoxical effects: they are essential for the good life, but they may also institutionalize bias in ways that make the good life impossible to attain for many people.

One response is to recognize that even if most people behave in self-interested ways most of the time, self-interest can be defined in more or less enlightened ways, and many people are not purely egotistical. Another response is to stress the role of prevailing expectations and beliefs in structuring even self-interested behavior. If just principles are generally accepted in a society, even self-interested people may have more incentives to act justly. Normatively, thinking about institutionalized governance raises issues of institutional design: in particular, fostering accountability, participation and persuasion by providing incentives for those practices to flourish. In the face of globalization, the essay concludes, our challenge is similar to that of the founders of the United States: "to design working institutions for a polity of unprecedented size and diversity."

Such institutions can only operate smoothly in a world free from threats of terror, just as threats of terror are only likely to be minimized in a world of well-functioning global institutions. What Nye and I referred to as "complex interdependence" in 1977 – a world of multiple interactions in which recourse to force is excluded – is a condition for deep cooperation, which creates potential vulnerabilities as societies become intertwined. Relationships in which terror is employed involve interdependence, but are obviously not relationships of "complex interdependence." Hence, the attacks on the United States of September 11, 2001, reinforce the caution that Nye and I have consistently expressed about the spread of complex interdependence. As Nye likes to say, "security is like oxygen." You are only aware of it when it is absent. Global governance during the next decades will have to deal with threats of force as well as with economic interdependence.

The impact of September 11 will depend heavily on the *responses* of the United States and other countries to those attacks. As of the late fall of 2001, it appears that both progressive and retrogressive responses are possible. Americans, in particular, could combine a praiseworthy resolve to stop terrorism with reflection about the role of the United States in the world. They could try to understand more about world politics, to become both less arrogant toward other cultures and political systems, and more resolved to play a positive role in improving the often horrible conditions of life that contribute to support for terrorism and other forms of violence. Or the American public could seek to cut itself off from the ills of troubled societies, to emphasize barriers to attacks and the ability to counterattack, but to overlook more fundamental conditions and policies that promote hatred against the United States. In my opinion, military and police responses to the attacks of September 11 were essential. But to be successful in the long run, they need to be only part of a more fundamental reorientation of the American, and western, view of the world – an orientation that accepts responsibility for more far-reaching action against poverty and injustice, without accepting the responsibility to govern other societies. Such an orientation will require more openness toward information – even, or especially, information that makes us uncomfortable, such as information about the negative views of American policy held by many people elsewhere in the world, and not only in the Middle East.

The importance of this choice of response makes it appropriate to publish, as Chapter 12 to this volume, an essay that I wrote between October 2001 and February 2002 on "The globalization of informal violence, theories of world politics, and 'the liberalism of fear.'" This essay illustrates my approach to world politics in the context of some events involving the use of force. In the first instance, the attacks on the United States of September 11 did not focus on the world political economy, nor were international institutions directly involved. Perspectives from realism and political philosophy shed light on these events, but so do approaches with their origins in the study of interdependence and institutions. I do not claim that my perspectives on these issues are more important than other perspectives, but I do believe that theories linking asymmetrical interdependence to power, and institutional analysis, both contribute productively to the analysis of the globalization of informal violence.

We students of world politics did not choose our subject because it is aesthetically pleasing, nor because clear propositions about it can be developed and tested easily, using scientific methods. We should aspire to be scientific in the best sense; but neither the experimental nor statistical methods are easy to apply to a world of strategic interactions, by a limited number of players, that are not subject to our control. We chose our subject because it is vitally important: a matter of life and death, wealth and poverty. Surely the events of September 11 indicate anew its crucial significance. We face a moral imperative to understand world politics better. Better understanding should enable people to design better policies and institutions, although it is no guarantee of such improvements. Better institutions would enable ordinary human beings to live lives of their own choosing, free from fear. Under such conditions, people could devise their own ways to love and respect other people and to value the natural world on which we all depend.

Notes

1 I am indebted to Nannerl O. Keohane, Joseph S. Nye, and John Gerard Ruggie for comments on an earlier version of this introduction, and to my editor, Craig Fowlie, both for encouraging me to write this introduction and for comments on an earlier draft.

2 For my earlier intellectual autobiography, see Chapter 2 of Keohane (1989), originally published in Kruzel and Rosenau, 1989: 403–415.

3 See Keohane and Nye (1987), reprinted in the second and third editions of *Power and Interdependence*, 1989 and 2001.

4 I have had so many able students that I would hesitate to create an exhaustive list, for fear of omitting some important work by people I respect very much. Books by former students of mine that discuss connections between domestic politics and world politics include DeSombre 2000, Gilligan 1997, Karl 1997, Martin 2000, Moravcsik 1998, Milner 1988 and 1997, Owen 1997, Simmons 1994, Stone 1996, Tickner 1987, Yoffie 1983, and Zakaria 1998.

5 See especially Goldstein 1993, Finnemore 1996, Keck and Sikkink 1998, Kratochwil 1989, Nau 1990, Philpott 2001, Risse, Ropp and Sikkink 1999, Ruggie 1998.

6 *Power and Interdependence* (1977), *After Hegemony* (1984), *International Institutions and State Power* (1989).

7 For an interesting effort in this direction, see Evans *et al.*, 1993. See also the works listed in note 4.

8 The volume that I edited in 1986a, *Neorealism and Its Critics*, has been widely used and is still in print, but I have mixed feelings about it. It helpfully brought

together Kenneth Waltz's seminal statements of neo-realist thinking, together with some of the major early critiques of his work. But it probably contributed to the "us versus them" tone of the discussion for much of the following decade.

9 For the quotation see *American State Papers*, vol. III, p. 810. For a discussion, see Horsman 1969: 258.

10 Robert Gilpin (1975) had been the leader, in the post-1970 literature, in connecting political–military with political–economic issues.

11 See also Slaughter *et al.*,1998.

12 See Franck 1990; Chayes and Chayes 1995; Koh 1998.

13 There is an enormous literature on this subject. For some excellent work, see Garrett 1998, Kitschelt *et al.* 1999, Iversen 1999, Mosley 2000, and Hall and Soskice 2001.

References

Abbott, Kenneth W. 1989. Modern International Relations Theory: a Prospectus for International Lawyers. *14 Yale Journal of International Law* 335.

Achen, Christopher H. and Duncan Snidal. 1989. Rational Deterrence Theory and Comparative Case Studies. *World Politics*, vol. 41, no. 2 (January): 143–169.

Adams, Henry. 1986 (originally published 1891). *The History of the United States during the Administrations of Thomas Jefferson*. New York: Library of America.

Baldwin, David A., ed. 1994. *Neorealism and Neoliberalism: the Contemporary Debate*. New York: Columbia University Press.

Bull, Hedley. 1977. *The Anarchical Society: A Study of Order in World Politics*. New York: Columbia University Press.

Burley, Anne-Marie Slaughter. 1993. International Law and International Relations Theory: A Dual Agenda. 87 *American Journal of International Law* 205.

Carr, E. H. 1946. *The Twenty Years' Crisis: An Introduction to International Relations*. 2nd edition. London: Macmillan.

Chayes, Abram and Antonia Handler Chayes. 1995. *The New Sovereignty: Compliance with International Regulatory Agreements*. Cambridge: Harvard University Press.

Clark, Grenville, and Louis B. Sohn. 1960. *World Peace through World Law*. Cambridge: Harvard University Press.

Cooper, Richard N. 1968. *The Economics of Interdependence*. New York: McGraw Hill for the Council on Foreign Relations.

DeSombre, Elizabeth R. 2000. *Domestic Sources of International Environmental Policy: Industry, Environmentalists and US Power*. Cambridge: MIT Press.

Evans, Peter B., Harold K. Jacobson, and Robert D. Putnam, eds. 1993. *Double-Edged Diplomacy: International Bargaining and Domestic Politics*. Berkeley: University of California Press.

Finnemore, Martha. 1996. *National Interests in International Society*. Ithaca: Cornell University Press.

Finnemore, Martha and Kathryn Sikkink. 1999. International Norm Dynamics and Political Change. In Katzenstein *et al.* 1999a: 247–277.

Franck, Thomas. 1990. *The Power of Legitimacy Among Nations*. Oxford: Oxford University Press.

Garrett, Geoffrey. 1998. *Partisan Politics in the Global Economy*. Cambridge: Cambridge University Press.

Gilligan, Michael J. 1997. *Empowering Exporters: Reciprocity, Delegation and Collective Action in American Trade Policy*. Ann Arbor: University of Michigan Press.

Gilpin, Robert. 1975. *US Power and the Multinational Corporation: the Political Economy of Foreign Direct Investment*. New York: Basic Books.

Gilpin, Robert. 1981. *War and Change in World Politics*. Cambridge: Cambridge University Press.

Goldstein, Judith. 1993. *Ideas, Interests and American Trade Policy*. Ithaca: Cornell University Press.

Goldstein, Judith, and Robert O. Keohane. 1993. Ideas and Foreign Policy: an Analytical Framework. In Goldstein and Keohane, eds, *Ideas and Foreign Policy: Beliefs, Institutions and Political Change*. Ithaca: Cornell University Press.

Goldstein, Judith, Miles Kahler, Robert O. Keohane, and Anne-Marie Slaughter. 2001. *Legalization and World Politics*. Cambridge: MIT Press. This book is a reprint of the Summer 2000 issue of *International Organization* (vol. 54, no. 3).

Haas, Ernst B. 1958. *The Uniting of Europe: Political, Economic and Social Forces, 1950–1957*. Stanford: Stanford University Press.

Haas, Peter M., Robert O. Keohane, and Marc L. Levy. 1993. *Institutions for the Earth: Sources of Effective International Environmental Protection*. Cambridge: MIT Press.

Hall, Peter A. and David Soskice. 2001. *Varieties of Capitalism: The Institutional Foundations of Comparative Advantage*. Oxford: Oxford University Press.

Hathaway, Oona. 2001. Do Treaties Make a Difference? Human Rights Treaties and the Problem of Compliance. *111 Yale Law Journal* June Issue 8 (June 2002).

Held, David, Anthony McGrew, David Goldblatt, and Jonathan Perraton. 1999. *Global Transformations: Politics, Economics and Culture*. Stanford: Stanford University Press.

Helliwell, John. 1998. *How Much do National Borders Matter?* Washington: Brookings.

Hirschman, Albert O. 1970. The Search for Paradigms as a Hindrance to Understanding. *World Politics* 22–3 (April): 329–343.

Hoffmann, Stanley. 1987. *Janus and Minerva: Essays in the Theory and Practice of International Politics*. Boulder: Westview Press.

Horsman, Reginald. 1969. *The War of 1812*. New York: Knopf.

Iversen, Torben. 1999. *Contested Economic Institutions: The Politics of Macroeconomics and Wage Bargaining in Advanced Democracies*. Cambridge: Cambridge University Press.

Jervis, Robert. 1976. *Perception and Misperception in International Politics*. Princeton: Princeton University Press.

Karl, Terry. 1997. *The Paradox of Plenty: Oil Booms and Petro-States*. Berkeley: University of California Press.

Katzenstein, Peter J., ed. 1996. *The Culture of National Security*. New York: Columbia University Press.

Katzenstein, Peter J., Robert O. Keohane and Stephen D. Krasner, eds. 1999a. *Exploration and Contestation in the Study of World Politics*. Cambridge: MIT Press. This book is a reprint of the fall 1998 issue of *International Organization* (volume 52, no. 4).

Katzenstein, Peter J., Robert O. Keohane and Stephen D. Krasner. 1999b.

International Organization and the Study of World Politics. In Katzenstein *et al.*, 1999: 5–45.

Keck, Margaret and Kathryn Sikkink. 1998. *Activists Beyond Borders: Advocacy Networks in International Politics*. Ithaca: Cornell University Press.

Kennan, George F. 1951. *American Diplomacy 1900–1950*. Chicago: University of Chicago Press.

Keohane, Robert O. 1983. Theory of World Politics: Structural Realism and Beyond. In Ada Finifter, ed., *Political Science: The State of the Discipline* (Washington, DC: American Political Science Association): 503–540. Reprinted in Keohane 1989, Ch. 3.

Keohane, Robert O. 1984. *After Hegemony: Cooperation and Discord in the World Political Economy*. Princeton: Princeton University Press.

Keohane, Robert O., ed. 1986a. *Neorealism and Its Critics*. New York: Columbia University Press.

Keohane, Robert O. 1986b. Reciprocity in International Relations. *International Organization* **27–1** (winter): 1–27.

Keohane, Robert O. 1989. *International Institutions and State Power*. Boulder: Westview Press.

Keohane, Robert O. 1993. Institutionalist Theory and the Realist Challenge after the Cold War. In Baldwin, ed., 1993: 269–300.

Keohane, Robert O. and Marc L. Levy. 1996. *Institutions for Environmental Aid: Pitfalls and Promise*. Cambridge: MIT Press.

Keohane, Robert O. and Lisa L. Martin. 1995. The Promise of Institutionalist Theory. *International Security* **20–1** (summer): 39–51.

Keohane, Robert O. and Helen V. Milner. 1996. *Internationalization and Domestic Politics*. New York: Cambridge University Press.

Keohane, Robert O. and Joseph S. Nye, Jr. 1972. *Transnational Relations and World Politics*. Cambridge: Harvard University Press.

Keohane, Robert O. and Joseph S. Nye, Jr. 1977. *Power and Interdependence: World Politics in Transition*. Boston: Little Brown. 2nd Edition, 1989 (Glenview, IL: Scott Foresman and Co.). 3rd edition, 2001 (New York: Addison-Wesley Longman).

Keohane, Robert O. and Joseph S. Nye, Jr. 1987. Power and Interdependence Revisited. *International Organization* **41–4** (autumn): 725–753.

Keohane, Robert O., Joseph S. Nye, and Stanley Hoffmann. 1993. *After the Cold War: International Institutions and State Strategies in Europe, 1989–1991*. Cambridge: Harvard University Press.

King, Gary, Robert O. Keohane and Sidney Verba. 1994. *Designing Social Inquiry: Scientific Inference in Qualitative Research*. Princeton: Princeton University Press.

Kitschelt, Herbert, Peter Lange, Gary Marks and John Stephens, eds. 1999. *Continuity and Change in Contemporary Capitalism*. Cambridge: Cambridge University Press.

Koh, Harold Honju. 1998. Bringing International Law Home. 35 *Houston Law Review*: 623.

Kratochwil, Friedrich V. 1989. *Rules, Norms and Decisions: On the Conditions of Practical and Legal Reasoning in International Relations and Domestic Affairs*. Cambridge: Cambridge University Press.

Kruzel, Joseph and James N. Rosenau, eds. 1989. *Understanding World Politics*. Lexington, Mass: Lexington Books: 403–415.

Legro, Jeffrey. 1995 *Cooperation Under Fire: Anglo-German Restraint During World War II*. Ithaca, NY: Cornell University Press.

March, James G. and Johan Olsen. 1995. *Democratic Governance*. New York: Free Press.

March, James G. and Johan Olsen. 1999. The Institutional Dynamics of International Political Orders. In Katzenstein *et al.* 1999: 303–329.

Martin, Lisa L. 2000. *Democratic Commitments: Legislatures and International Cooperation*. Princeton: Princeton University Press.

Mearsheimer, John J. 1994/95. The False Promise of International Institutions. *International Security* **19–3** (winter): 5–49.

Milner, Helen V. 1988. *Resisting Protectionism: Global Industries and the Politics of International Trade*. Princeton: Princeton University Press.

Milner, Helen V. 1997. *Interests, Institutions and Information: Domestic Politics and International Relations*. Princeton: Princeton University Press.

Mitchell, Ronald B. 1994. *Intentional Oil Pollution at Sea: Environmental Policy and Treaty Compliance*. Cambridge: MIT Press.

Moravcsik, Andrew. 1997. Taking Preferences Seriously: A Liberal Theory of International Politics. *International Organization* **51–4**: 513–553.

Moravcsik, Andrew. 1998. *The Choice for Europe: Social Purpose and State Power from Messina to Maastricht*. Ithaca: Cornell University Press.

Morgenthau, Hans J. 1948. *Politics Among Nations: The Struggle for Power and Peace*. New York: Knopf. Many subsequent editions of this book have appeared.

Mosley, Layna. 2000. Room to Move: International Financial Markets and National Welfare States. *International Organization* **54–1** (autumn): 737–773.

Nau, Henry R. 1990. *The Myth of America's Decline: Leading the World Economy into the 1990s*. Oxford: Oxford University Press.

Nye, Joseph S. 1990. *Bound to Lead: The Changing Nature of American Power*. New York: Basic Books.

Owen, John Malloy. 1997. *Liberal Peace, Liberal War: American Politics and International Security*. Ithaca, NY: Cornell University Press.

Philpott, Daniel. 2001. *Revolutions in Sovereignty: How Ideas Shaped Modern International Relations*. Princeton: Princeton University Press.

Risse, Thomas, Stephen C. Ropp and Kathryn Sikkink, eds. 1999. *The Power of Human Rights: International Norms and Domestic Change*. Cambridge: Cambridge University Press.

Ruggie, John Gerard. 1998. *Constructing the World Polity: Essays on International Institutionalization*. London: Routledge.

Ruggie, John Gerard. 1999. What Makes the World Hang Together? Neo-Utilitarianism and the Social Constructivist Challenge. In Katzenstein *et al.* 1999: 215–245.

Shepsle, Kenneth A. 1986. Institutional Equilibrium and Equilibrium Institutions. In Herbert F. Weisberg ed., *Political Science: The Science of Politics*. New York: Agathon: 51–81.

Simmons, Beth A. 1994. *Who Adjusts? Domestic Sources of Foreign Economic Policy During the Interwar Years*. Princeton: Princeton University Press.

Simmons, Beth A. 2000. International Law and State Behavior: Commitment and Compliance in International Monetary Affairs. *American Political Science Review* **94–4** (December): 819–836.

Simon, Herbert A. 1996. *The Sciences of the Artificial*. Cambridge: MIT Press.

Slaughter, Anne-Marie. 1995. Law in a World of Liberal States. *European Journal of International Law* 6 (December): 503–38.

Slaughter, Anne-Marie, Andrew S. Tulumello and Stepan Wood. 1998. International Law and International Relations Theory: A New Generation of Interdisciplinary Scholarship. **92** *American Journal of International Law* 367.

Stone, Randall W. 1996. *Satellites and Commissars: Strategy and Conflict in the Politics of Soviet Bloc Trade*. Princeton: Princeton University Press.

Tickner, J. Ann. 1987. *Self-Reliance versus Power Politics: The American and Indian Experiences in Building Nation States*. New York: Columbia University Press.

Vernon, Raymond. 1971. *Sovereignty at Bay: The Multinational Spread of US Enterprises*. New York: Basic Books.

Waltz, Kenneth N. 1967. *Foreign Policy and Democratic Politics: the American and British Experience*. Boston: Little-Brown.

Waltz, Kenneth N. 1979. *Theory of International Politics*. Reading, MA: Addison-Wesley.

Wendt, Alexander. 1999. *Social Theory of International Politics*. Cambridge: Cambridge University Press.

Wight, Martin. 1992. *International Theory: the Three Traditions*. New York: Holmes and Meier.

Yoffie, David B. 1983. *Power and Protectionism: Strategies of the Newly Industrializing Countries*. New York: Columbia University Press.

Zakaria, Fareed. 1998. *From Wealth to Power: the Unusual Origins of America's World Role*. Princeton: Princeton University Press.

Part I

Interdependence and institutions

2 International institutions: can interdependence work?

Robert O. Keohane
(1998)

To analyze world politics in the 1990s is to discuss international institutions: the rules that govern elements of world politics and the organizations that help implement those rules. Should NATO expand? How can the United Nations Security Council assure UN inspectors access to sites where Iraq might be conducting banned weapons activity? Under what conditions should China be admitted to the World Trade Organization (WTO)? How many billions of dollars does the International Monetary Fund (IMF) need at its disposal to remain an effective "lender of last resort" for countries such as Indonesia, Korea, and Thailand that were threatened in 1997 with financial collapse? Will the tentative Kyoto Protocol on Climate Change be renegotiated, ratified, and implemented effectively? Can future United Nations peacekeeping practices – in contrast to the UN fiascoes in Bosnia and Somalia – be made more effective?

These questions help illustrate the growing importance of international institutions for maintaining world order. In 1985 (*Foreign Policy* 60: 148–67) Joseph Nye and I gave "two cheers for multilateralism," pointing out that even the administration of President Ronald Reagan, which took office ill-disposed toward international institutions, had grudgingly come to accept their value in achieving American purposes. Superpowers need general rules because they seek to influence events around the world. Even an unchallenged superpower such as the United States would be unable to achieve its goals through the bilateral exercise of influence: the costs of such massive "arm-twisting" would be too great.

International institutions are increasingly important, but they are not always successful. Ineffective institutions such as the United Nations Industrial Development Organization or the Organization of African Unity exist alongside effectual ones such as the Montreal Protocol on Substances that Deplete the Ozone Layer and the European Union. In recent years, we have gained insight into what makes some institutions more capable than others – how such institutions best promote cooperation among states and what mechanics of bargaining they use. But our knowledge is incomplete, and as the world moves toward new forms of global regulation and governance, the increasing impact of international institutions has raised new questions about how these institutions themselves are governed.

Theory and reality, 1919–89

Academic "scribblers" did not always have to pay much attention to international institutions. The 1919 Versailles Treaty constituted an attempt to construct an institution for multilateral diplomacy – the League of Nations. But the rejection of the League Covenant by the US Senate ensured that until World War II the most important negotiations in world politics – from the secret German–Russian deals of the 1920s to the 1938 Munich conference – took place on an ad hoc basis. Only after the United Nations was founded in 1945, with strong support from the United States and a multiplicity of specialized agencies performing different tasks, did international institutions begin to command substantial international attention.

Until the late 1960s, American students of international relations equated international institutions with formal international organizations, especially the United Nations. *International Organization*, the leading academic journal on the subject, carried long summaries of UN meetings until 1971. However, most observers recognized long before 1972 that the United Nations did not play a central role in world politics. Except for occasional peacekeeping missions – of which the First UN Emergency Force in the Middle East between 1956 and 1967 was the most successful – its ability to resolve hostilities was paralyzed by conflicts of interest that resulted in frequent superpower vetoes in the Security Council. Moreover, the influx of new postcolonial states helped turn the General Assembly into an arena for North–South conflict after 1960 and ensured that the major Western powers, especially the United States, would view many General Assembly resolutions as hostile to their interests and values – for example, the New International Economic Order and the Zionism is Racism resolutions of the 1970s. Analysts and policy-makers in Europe, North America, and much of Asia concluded that international institutions were marginal to a game of world politics still driven by the traditional exercise of state power. The UN – called "a dangerous place" by former US representative to the UN Daniel Patrick Moynihan – seemed more a forum for scoring points in the Cold War or North–South conflicts than an instrument for problem-solving cooperation.

In reality, however, even the most powerful states were relying increasingly on international institutions – not so much on the UN as other organizations and regimes that set rules and standards to govern specific sets of activities. From the late 1960s onward, the Treaty on the Non-Proliferation of Nuclear Weapons was the chief vehicle for efforts to prevent the dangerous spread of nuclear weapons. NATO was not only the most successful multilateral alliance in history but also the most highly institutionalized, with a secretary-general, a permanent staff, and elaborate rules governing relations among members. From its founding in 1947 through the Uruguay Round that concluded in 1993, the General Agreement on Tariffs and Trade (GATT) presided over a series of trade rounds that have reduced import tariffs among industrialized countries by up to 90 percent, boosting international trade. After a shaky start in the 1940s, the IMF had – by the 1960s – become the centerpiece of efforts by the major capitalist democracies to regulate their monetary affairs. When that function atrophied with the onset of flexible exchange rates in the 1970s, it became their leading agent for financing and promoting economic development in Africa, Asia, and Latin America. The sheer number of intergovernmental organizations also rose dramatically – from about 30 in 1910 to 70 in 1940 to more than 1,000 by 1981.

The exchange rate and oil crises of the early 1970s helped bring perceptions in line with reality. Suddenly, both top policymakers and academic observers in the United States realized that global issues required systematic policy coordination and that such coordination required institutions. In 1974, then secretary of state Henry Kissinger, who had paid little attention to international institutions, helped establish the International Energy Agency to enable Western countries to deal cooperatively with the threat of future oil embargoes like the 1973 OPEC embargo of the Netherlands and United States. And the Ford administration sought to construct a new international monetary regime based on flexible rather than pegged exchange rates. Confronted with complex interdependence and the efforts of states to manage it, political scientists began to redefine the study of international institutions, broadening it to encompass what they called "international regimes" – structures of rules and norms that could be more or less informal. The international trade regime, for example, did not have strong formal rules or integrated, centralized management; rather, it provided a set of interlocking institutions, including regular meetings of the GATT contracting parties, formal dispute settlement arrangements, and delegation of technical tasks to a secretariat, which gradually developed a body of case law and practice. Some international lawyers grumbled that the political scientists were merely using other terms to discuss international law. Nevertheless, political scientists were once again discussing how international rules and norms affect state behavior, even if they avoided the "L-word."

In the 1980s, research on international regimes moved from attempts to describe the phenomena of interdependence and international regimes to closer analysis of the conditions under which countries cooperate. How does cooperation occur among sovereign states and how do international institutions affect it? From the standpoint of political realism, both the reliance placed by states on certain international institutions and the explosion in their numbers were puzzling. Why should international institutions exist at all in a world dominated by sovereign states? This question seemed unanswerable if institutions were seen as opposed to, or above, the state but not if they were viewed as devices to help states accomplish their objectives.

The new research on international institutions broke decisively with legalism – the view that law can be effective regardless of political conditions – as well as with the idealism associated with the field's origins. Instead, scholars adopted the assumptions of realism, accepting that relative state power and competing interests were key factors in world politics, but at the same time drawing new conclusions about the influence of institutions on the process. Institutions create the capability for states to cooperate in mutually beneficial ways by reducing the costs of making and enforcing agreements – what economists refer to as "transaction costs." They rarely engage in centralized enforcement of agreements, but they do reinforce practices of reciprocity, which provide incentives for governments to keep their own commitments to ensure that others do so as well. Even powerful states have an interest, most of the time, in following the rules of well-established international institutions, since general conformity to rules makes the behavior of other states more predictable.

This scholarship drew heavily on the twin concepts of uncertainty and credibility. Theorists increasingly recognized that the preferences of states amount to "private information" – that absent full transparency, states are uncertain about what their partners and rivals value at any given time. They naturally respond to uncertainty by being less willing to enter into agreements, since they are unsure how their partners will later interpret the terms of such agreements. International institutions can reduce this uncertainty by promoting negotiations in which transparency is encouraged; by dealing with a series of issues over many years and under similar rules, thus encouraging honesty in order to preserve future reputation; and by systematically monitoring the compliance of governments with their commitments.

Even if a government genuinely desires an international agreement, it may be unable to persuade its partners that it will, in the future, be willing and able to implement it. Successful international negotiations may therefore require changes in domestic institutions. For instance, without "fast-track" authority on trade, the United States' negotiating partners have no assurance that Congress will refrain from adding new provisions to trade agreements as a condition for their ratification. Hence, other states are reluctant to enter into trade negotiations with the United States since they may be confronted, at the end of tortuous negotiations, with a redesigned agreement less favorable to them than the draft they initialed. By the same token, without fast-track authority, no promise by the US government to abide by negotiated terms has much credibility, due to the president's lack of control over Congress.

In short, this new school of thought argued that, rather than imposing themselves on states, international institutions should respond to the demand by states for cooperative ways to fulfill their own purposes. By reducing uncertainty and the costs of making and enforcing agreements, international institutions help states achieve collective gains.

Yesterday's controversies: 1989–95

This new institutionalism was not without its critics, who focused their attacks on three perceived shortcomings: first, they claimed that international institutions are fundamentally insignificant since states wield the only real power in world politics. They emphasized the weakness of efforts by the UN or League of Nations to achieve collective security against aggression by great powers, and they pointed to the dominant role of major contributors in international economic organizations. Hence, any effects of these international institutions were attributed more to the efforts of their great power backers than to the institutions themselves.

This argument was overstated. Of course, great powers such as the United States exercise enormous influence within international institutions. But the policies that emerge from these institutions are different from those that the United States would have adopted unilaterally. Whether toward Iraq or recipients of IMF loans, policies for specific situations cannot be entirely ad hoc but must conform to generally applicable rules and principles to be endorsed by multilateral institutions. Where agreement by many states is necessary for policy to be effective, even the United States finds it useful to compromise on substance to obtain the institutional seal of approval. Therefore, the decision-making procedures and general rules of international institutions matter. They affect both the substance of policy and the degree to which other states accept it.

The second counterargument focused on "anarchy": the absence of a world government or effective international legal system to which victims of injustice can appeal. As a result of anarchy, critics argued, states prefer relative gains (i.e., doing better than other states) to absolute gains. They seek to protect their power and status and will resist even mutually beneficial cooperation if their partners are likely to benefit more than they are. For instance, throughout the American–Soviet arms race, both sides focused on their relative positions – who was ahead or threatening to gain a decisive advantage – rather than on their own levels of armaments. Similar dynamics appear on certain economic issues, such as the fierce Euro-American competition (i.e., Airbus Industrie versus Boeing) in the production of large passenger jets.

Scholarly disputes about the "relative gains question" were intense but short-lived. It turned out that the question needed to be reframed: not, "do states seek relative or absolute gains?" but "under what conditions do they forego even mutually beneficial cooperation to preserve their relative power and status?" When there are only two major players, and one side's gains may decisively change power relationships, relative gains loom large: in arms races, for example, or monopolistic competition (as between Airbus and Boeing). Most issues of potential cooperation, however, from trade liberalization to climate change, involve multilateral negotiations that make relative gains hard to calculate and entail little risk of decisive power shifts for one side over another. Therefore, states can be expected most of the time to seek to enhance their own welfare without being worried that others will also make advances. So the relative gains argument merely highlights the difficulties of cooperation where there is tough bilateral competition; it does not by any means undermine prospects for cooperation in general.

The third objection to theories of cooperation was less radical but more enduring. Theorists of cooperation had recognized that cooperation is not harmonious: it emerges out of discord and takes place through tough bargaining. Nevertheless, they claimed that the potential joint gains from such cooperation explained the dramatic increases in the number and scope of cooperative multilateral institutions. Critics pointed out, however, that bargaining problems could produce obstacles to achieving joint gains. For instance, whether the Kyoto Protocol will lead to a global agreement is questionable in part because developing countries refused to accept binding limits on their emissions and the US Senate declared its unwillingness to ratify any agreement not containing such commitments by developing countries. Both sides staked out tough bargaining positions, hindering efforts at credible compromise. As a result of these bargaining problems, the fact that possible deals could produce joint gains does not assure that cooperative solutions will be reached. The tactics of political actors and the information they have available about one another are both key aspects of a process that does not necessarily lead to cooperation. Institutions may help provide "focal points," on which competing actors may agree, but new issues often lack such institutions. In this case, both the pace and the extent of cooperation become more problematic.

Today's debates

The general problem of bargaining raises specific issues about how institutions affect international negotiations, which always involve a mixture of discord and potential cooperation. Thinking about bargaining leads to concerns about subjectivity, since bargaining depends so heavily on the beliefs of the parties involved. And the most fundamental question scholars wish to answer concerns effectiveness: What structures, processes, and practices make international institutions more or less capable of affecting policies – and outcomes – in desired ways?

The impact of institutional arrangements on bargaining remains puzzling. We understand from observation, from game theory, and from explorations of bargaining in a variety of contexts that outcomes depend on more than the resources available to the actors or the pay-offs they receive. Institutions affect bargaining patterns in complex and nuanced ways. Who, for example, has authority over the agenda? In the 1980s, Jacques Delors used his authority as head of the European Commission to structure the agenda of the European Community, thus leading to the Single European Act and the Maastricht Treaty. What voting or consensus arrangements are used and who interprets ambiguities? At the Kyoto Conference, agreement on a rule of "consensus" did not prevent the conference chair from ignoring objections as he gaveled through provision after provision in the final session. Can disgruntled participants block implementation of formally ratified agreements? In the GATT, until 1993, losers could prevent the findings of dispute resolution panels from being implemented; but in the WTO, panel recommendations take effect unless there is a consensus not to implement them. Asking such questions systematically about international institutions may well yield significant new insights in future years.

Institutional maneuvers take place within a larger ideological context that helps define which purposes such institutions pursue and which practices they find acceptable. The Mandates System of the League of Nations depended in part on specific institutional arrangements, but more fundamental was the shared understanding that continued European rule over non-European peoples was acceptable. No system of rule by Europeans over non-Europeans could remain legitimate after the collapse of that consensus during the 15 years following World War II.

The end of the Cold War shattered a whole set of beliefs about world politics. Theories of international politics during the Cold War were overwhelmingly materialistic, reflecting a view of the world in which states pursued "national interests" shaped by geopolitical and economic realities. As Stalin once famously quipped about the pope: "How many divisions does he have?" Not only did an unarmed Pope John Paul II prevail in the contest for the allegiance of the Polish people, but after the failed 1991 coup against Gorbachev, the Soviet Union broke into its constituent parts on the basis of the norm of "self-determination," rather than along lines of military power or economic resources. State interests now depend in part on how people define their identities – as Serbs or Croats, Russians or Chechens. They also depend on the political and religious values to which their publics are committed.

Hence, the end of the Cold War made scholars increasingly aware of the importance of ideas, norms, and information – topics that some of them had already begun to explore. Some years earlier, such a reorientation might have faced fierce criticism from adherents of game theory and other economics-based approaches, which had traditionally focused on material interests. However, since the mid-1980s, bargaining theory has shown more and more that the beliefs of actors are crucially important for outcomes. To adapt economist Thomas Schelling's famous example, suppose that you and I want to meet for lunch in New York City, but you work on Wall Street and I work on the Upper West Side. Where will we get together? We have a mutual interest in meeting, but each of us would prefer not to waste time traveling. If you leave a message on my answering machine suggesting a restaurant on Wall Street and are then unreachable, I have to choose between skipping lunch with you or showing up at your preferred location. Asymmetrical information and our mutual belief that I know where you will be waiting for me have structured the situation.

The procedures and rules of international institutions create informational structures. They determine what principles are acceptable as the basis for reducing conflicts and whether governmental actions are legitimate or illegitimate. Consequently, they help shape actors' expectations. For instance, trade conflicts are increasingly ritualized in a process of protesting in the WTO – promising tough action on behalf of one's own industries, engaging in quasi-judicial dispute resolution procedures, claiming victory if possible, or complaining about defeat when necessary. There is much sound and fury, but regularly institutionalized processes usually relegate conflict to the realm of dramatic expression. Institutions thereby create differentiated information. "Insiders" can interpret the language directed toward "outsiders" and use their own understandings to interpret, or manipulate, others' beliefs.

Finally, students of international institutions continue to try to understand why some institutions are so much more effective than others. Variation in the coherence of institutional policy or members' conformity with institutional rules is partially accounted for by the degree of common interests and the distribution of power among members. Institutions whose members share social values and have similar political systems – such as NATO or the European Union – are likely to be stronger than those such as the Organization for Security and Cooperation in Europe or the Association of South East Asian Nations, whose more diverse membership does not necessarily have the same kind of deep common interests. Additionally, the character of domestic politics has a substantial impact on international institutions. The distribution of power is also important. Institutions dominated by a small number of members – for example, the IMF, with its weighted voting system – can typically take more decisive action than those where influence is more widely diffused, such as the UN General Assembly.

Overcoming the democratic deficit

Even as scholars pursue these areas of inquiry, they are in danger of overlooking a major normative issue: the "democratic deficit" that exists in many of the world's most important international institutions. As illustrated most recently by the far-reaching interventions of the IMF in East Asia, the globalization of the world economy and the expanding role of international institutions are creating a powerful form of global regulation. Major international institutions are increasingly laying down rules and guidelines that governments, if they wish to attract foreign investment and generate growth, must follow. But these international institutions are managed by technocrats and supervised by high governmental officials. That is, they are run by élites. Only in the most attenuated sense is democratic control exercised over major international organizations. Key negotiations in the WTO are made in closed sessions. The IMF negotiates in secret with potential borrowers, and it only began to become more transparent about the conditions it imposes on recipients after the world financial crisis of 1997–98.

The EU provides another case in point. Its most important decision-making body is its Council of Ministers, which is composed of government representatives who perform more important legislative functions than the members of the European Parliament. The council meets behind closed doors and until recently did not publish its votes. It also appoints members to the European Commission, which acts as the EU executive, whose ties to the public are thus very indirect indeed. The European Parliament has narrowly defined powers and little status; most national parliaments do not closely scrutinize European-level actions. How much genuine influence do German or Italian voters therefore have over the council's decisions? Very little.

The issue here is not one of state sovereignty. Economic interdependence and its regulation have altered notions of sovereignty: few states can still demand to be completely independent of external authority over legal practices within their territories. The best most states can hope for is to be able to use their sovereign authority as a bargaining tool to assure that others also have to abide by common rules and practices. Given these changes, the issue here is who has influence over the sorts of bargains that are struck? Democratic theory gives pride of place to the public role in deciding on the distributional and value tradeoffs inherent in legislation and regulation. But the practices of international institutions place that privilege in the hands of the élites of national governments and of international organizations.

Admittedly, democracy does not always work well. American politicians regularly engage in diatribes against international institutions, playing on the dismay of a vocal segment of their electorates at the excessive number of foreigners in the United Nations. More seriously, an argument can be made that the IMF, like central banks, can only be effective if it is insulated from direct democratic control. Ever since 1787, however, practitioners and theorists have explored how authoritative decision making can be combined with accountability to publics and indirect democratic control. The US Constitution is based on such a theory – the idea that popular sovereignty, though essential, is best exercised indirectly, through rather elaborate institutions. An issue that scholars should now explore is how to devise international institutions that are not only competent and effective but also accountable, at least ultimately, to democratic publics.

One possible response is to say that all is well, since international institutions are responsible to governments – which, in turn, are accountable in democracies to their own people. International regulation simply adds another link to the chain of delegation. But long chains of delegation, in which the public affects action only at several removes, reduce actual public authority. If the terms of multilateral cooperation are to reflect the interests of broader democratic publics rather than just those of narrow élites, traditional patterns of delegation will have to be supplemented by other means of ensuring greater accountability to public opinion.

One promising approach would be to seek to invigorate transnational society in the form of networks among individuals and nongovernmental organizations. The growth of such networks – of scientists, professionals in various fields, and human rights and environmental activists – has been aided greatly by the fax machine and the Internet and by institutional arrangements that incorporate these networks into decision making. For example, natural and social scientists developed the scientific consensus underlying the Kyoto Protocol through the Intergovernmental Panel on Climate Change (IPCC) whose scientific work was organized by scientists who did not have to answer to any governments. The Kyoto Protocol was negotiated, but governments opposed to effective action on climate change could not hope to renegotiate the scientific guidelines set by the IPCC.

The dramatic fall in the cost of long-distance communication will facilitate the development of many more such transnational networks. As a result, wealthy hierarchical organizations – multinational corporations as well as states – are likely to have more difficulty dominating transnational communications. Thirty years ago, engaging in prolonged intercontinental communication required considerable resources. Now individuals do so on the Internet, virtually free.

Therefore, the future accountability of international institutions to their publics may rest only partly on delegation through formal democratic institutions. Its other pillar may be voluntary pluralism under conditions of maximum transparency. International policies may increasingly be monitored by loose groupings of scientists or other professionals, or by issue advocacy networks such as Amnesty International and Greenpeace, whose members, scattered around the world, will be linked even more closely by modern information technology. Accountability will be enhanced not only by chains of official responsibility, but by the requirement of transparency. Official actions, negotiated among state representatives in international organizations, will be subjected to scrutiny by transnational networks.

Such transparency, however, represents nongovernmental organizations and networks more than ordinary people, who may be as excluded from élite networks as they are from government circles. That is, transnational civil society may be a necessary but insufficient condition for democratic accountability. Democracies should insist that, wherever feasible, international organizations maintain sufficient transparency for transnational networks of advocacy groups, domestic legislators, and democratic publics to evaluate their actions. But proponents of democratic accountability should also seek counterparts to the mechanisms of control embedded in national democratic institutions. Governors of the Federal Reserve Board are, after all, nominated by the president and confirmed by the Senate, even if they exercise great authority during their terms of office. If Madison, Hamilton, and Jay could invent indirect mechanisms of popular control in the *Federalist Papers* two centuries ago, it should not be beyond our competence to devise comparable mechanisms at the global level in the twenty-first century.

As we continue to think about the normative implications of globalization, we should focus simultaneously on the maintenance of robust democratic institutions at home, the establishment of formal structures of international delegation, and the role of transnational networks. To be effective in the twenty-first century, modern democracy requires international institutions. And to be consistent with democratic values, these institutions must be accountable to domestic civil society. Combining global governance with effective democratic accountability will be a major challenge for scholars and policymakers alike in the years ahead.

Want to know more?

The best single source for academic writings on international institutions is the quarterly journal *International Organization*, published by MIT Press. A special issue, published in Autumn 1998, reviewed the last 30 years of scholarship in the field.

The sophisticated realism of the 1970s, which largely ignored international institutions, is best represented by Kenneth Waltz's **Theory of World Politics** (Reading, MA: Addison Wesley, 1979). For data on numbers of international organizations, see Cheryl Shanks, Harold Jacobson, and Jeffrey Kaplan's **"Inertia and Change in the Constellation of International Governmental Organizations, 1981–1992"** (*International Organization*, Autumn 1996). For statements of institutionalist theory, see Robert Keohane's **After Hegemony: Cooperation and Discord in the World Political Economy** (Princeton, NJ: Princeton University Press, 1984) and Kenneth Oye, ed., **Cooperation under Anarchy** (Princeton, NJ: Princeton University Press, 1986). For a reflection on this literature by an international lawyer, see Anne-Marie Slaughter [Burley], **"International Law and International Relations Theory: A Dual Agenda"** (*American Journal of International Law*, April 1993).

On the United Nations and multilateralism, see Daniel Patrick Moynihan's **A Dangerous Place** (Boston, MA: Little, Brown and Company, 1978); Keohane and Joseph Nye, Jr.'s **"Two Cheers for Multilateralism"** (*Foreign Policy*, Fall 1985); and John Ruggie's **Winning the Peace** (New York, NY: Columbia University Press for the Twentieth Century Fund, 1996).

The "relative gains debate" is thoroughly reported in David Baldwin, ed., **Neorealism and Neoliberalism: the Contemporary Debate** (New York, NY: Columbia University Press, 1993).

On bargaining and distributional issues, see Stephen Krasner's **"Global Communications and National Power: Life on the Pareto Frontier"** (*World Politics*, April 1991); James Morrow's **"Modeling the Forms of International Cooperation: Distribution versus Information"** (*International Organization*, Summer 1994); and James Fearon's **"Bargaining, Enforcement and International Cooperation"** (*International Organization*, forthcoming).

Work on the legalization of international institutions is just beginning; my comments in this article reflect an ongoing project on this subject that I am codirecting with Judith Goldstein, Miles Kahler, and Anne-Marie Burley.

On the role of ideas, see Goldstein and Keohane, eds, *Ideas and Foreign Policy: Beliefs, Institutions, and Political Change* (Ithaca, NY: Cornell University Press, 1993) and Martha Finnemore's *National Interests in International Society* (Ithaca, NY: Cornell University Press, 1996). Finally, on transnational issue networks, see Burley's **"The Real New World Order"** (*Foreign Affairs*, September/October 1997) and Margaret Keck and Kathryn Sikkink's *Activists Beyond Borders: Advocacy Networks in International Politics* (Ithaca, NY: Cornell University Press, 1997).

3 International liberalism reconsidered[1]

Robert O. Keohane

(1990)

World politics both creates opportunities for modern governments and imposes constraints on the range of actions that it is feasible for them to pursue. One way to think about these opportunities and constraints is to analyze the operation of the contemporary international political–military system, or the world political economy, and to consider how these systems affect state action. Much of the modern study of international relations is devoted to this task. Yet another perspective on the impact of world politics on states can be gained by asking how perceptive observers of politics have reflected on these issues in the past. This approach, which looks to the history of political thought for insights into contemporary international affairs, will be pursued here.[2] Although the form and intensity of the constraints and opportunities created by the contemporary world system are different from those in earlier centuries, the impact of international politics and economics on state action has been evident for a long time, and has occasioned a great deal of sophisticated commentary.

At some risk of blurring differences between thinkers of broadly similar inclinations, three major Western schools of thought on this subject can be identified: Marxist, realist and liberal. Each has been influential, although it is probably fair to say that realism has been the creed of Continental European statesmen for centuries, and that since World War II it has been predominant in the United States as well. Marxism has remained the doctrine of a minority in Western Europe and a mere splinter group in the United States, although in the Soviet Union and elsewhere it attained the status of official truth. Liberalism has been heavily criticized as an allegedly naive doctrine with utopian tendencies, which erroneously ascribes to the conflictual and anarchic international realm properties that only pertain to well-ordered domestic societies.[3] Although the most sophisticated critics of liberalism have often borrowed important elements of it – Carr perceived a "real foundation for the Cobdenite view of international trade as a guarantee of international peace"[4] and Morgenthau put much of his faith in diplomacy[5] – self-styled realists often dismiss the insights of liberalism as naive and misleading.

This essay takes issue with this common denigration of liberalism among professional students of international relations. My argument is that liberalism – or at any rate, a certain strand of liberalism – is more sophisticated than many of its critics have alleged. Although liberalism is often caricatured, a sophisticated form of liberalism provides thoughtful arguments designed to show how open exchanges of goods and services, on the one hand, and international institutions and rules, on the other, can promote international cooperation as well as economic prosperity. Liberalism makes the positive argument that an open international political economy, with rules and institutions based on state sovereignty, provides incentives for international cooperation and may even affect the internal constitutions of states in ways that promote peace. It also makes the normative assertion that such a reliance on economic exchange and international institutions has better effects than the major politically-tested alternatives. I do not necessarily subscribe to all of these claims, but I take them seriously, and I wish to subject them to examination in this chapter.

The first section of the chapter briefly examines Marxism and realism, the principal alternative traditions to liberalism in international relations theory. I ask what answers writers in these two traditions provide to three questions, two empirical and one normative:

1. What are the "limits to modern politics" in the advanced industrial democracies imposed by the state system and the world political economy?
2. How do the state system and the global system of production and exchange shape the character of societies and states?
3. Are the patterns of exchange and of international rules and norms characteristic of contemporary capitalism morally justifiable?

Second, I consider liberalism in some detail, distinguishing three forms that liberal doctrines of international relations have taken. I argue that a combination of what I call commercial and regulatory liberalism makes a good deal of sense as a framework for interpreting contemporary world politics and for evaluating institutions and policies. Such a sophisticated liberalism emphasizes the construction of institutions that facilitate both economic exchange and broader international cooperation.

The third and final section considers the normative judgments made by liberals about the capitalist international political economy that they have fostered since World War II. I emphasize that even sophisticated liberalism is morally questionable, since the international political economy defended by liberals generates inequalities that cannot be defended according to principles of justice. Nevertheless, on balance I uphold the view of liberals themselves, that liberal prescriptions for peace and prosperity compare favorably with the politically tested alternatives.

Marxism and realism

Marxism

Contemporary Marxists and neo-Marxists hold that the external limits to modern politics result principally from the world capitalist system of production and exchange. One of the major manifestations of the impact of the capitalist system is the power of transnational capital, which is expressed both through the operation of transnational corporations and the impacts of transnational capital flows, especially capital flight. Business has a privileged position over labor not merely because of the internal characteristics of the capitalist state, but because capital is more mobile than workers: it can easily leave jurisdiction in which government policies are markedly less favorable to it than elsewhere. The mobility and power of transnational capital thus constrain the internal policies of governments, particularly their economic and social welfare policies.

Capitalist governments have created international institutions: informal arrangements for policy coordination as well as formal international organizations such as the World Bank and the International Monetary Fund. This means, according to Marxist writers, that the probusiness bias exerted by the mobility of transnational capital is reinforced by the need of governments, whether of Left or Right, for support at critical moments from other governments and from international economic institutions. As Ralph Miliband has argued:

> Capitalism is now more than ever an international system, whose constituent economies are closely related and interlinked. As a result, even the most powerful capitalist countries depend, to a greater or lesser extent, upon the good will and cooperation of the rest, and of what has become, notwithstanding enduring and profound national capitalist rivalries, an interdependent international capitalist "community."[6]

Not only does world capitalism impose limits on modern politics, the location of a society in the international division of labor profoundly affects its character as a state. Theda Skocpol declares that "all modern social revolutions must be seen as closely related in their causes and accomplishments to the internationally uneven spread of capitalist economics development and nation-state formation on a world scale."[7] Domestic class struggles are shaped in considerable part by the position of a country in the world capitalist system – this is as true for imperialist states as for dependent ones. Furthermore, global class struggle may appear as nationalist or ethnic struggle in particular countries: "The fundamental political reality of the world-economy is a class struggle which however takes constantly changing forms: over class consciousness versus ethno-national conscious-ness, classes within nations versus classes across nations."[8] Marxists argue that the political coalitions that are formed within countries cannot be understood without comprehending both how the capitalist world political economy functions and how particular countries are inserted within it.

On the normative value of capitalism, Marxist arguments are of course familiar: Capitalism is an exploitative system that oppresses poor people, especially those on the periphery of the world system, and that generates war. Its rules are designed to perpetuate exploitation and oppression, not to relieve them. The sooner they are destroyed by revolutionary action, bringing into being a vaguely defined, but assertedly superior new order, the better. Fortunately, since capitalism contains the seeds of its own destruction, its development, however exploitative, contributes to the conditions for socialism.

Realism

For realists, limits on state action result primarily from the power of other states. World politics lacks common government and is therefore an arena in which states must defend themselves or face the possibility of extinction. The necessity of self-help, however, entails competitive efforts by governments to enhance their own security, which create a "security dilemma," defined as a situation in which "many of the means by which a state tries to increase its security decrease the security of others."[9] The power that states wield is derived ultimately not only from population, natural resources and industrial capacity, but also from organizational coherence, the ability to extract resources from society, military preparedness, diplomatic skill, and national will.[10] The external limits on modern politics, for realists, operate largely through political–military competition and the threat thereof.

Such competition also forces states to rely on themselves to develop capaci-ties for self-defense.[11] By creating threats, the state system helps to create states organized for violence: the Spartas and Prussias of this world are in part results of political–military competition. Realists follow Otto Hintze, who declared around the turn of the century, "It is one-sided, exaggerated and therefore false to consider class conflict the only driving force in history. Conflict between nations has been far more important; and throughout the ages, pressure from without has been a determining influence on internal structure."[12]

Marxists would reply that in the modern era conflict among nations has resulted principally from the contradictions of the world political economy, in particular from inequality and uneven development. But for the realists, it is not inequality among states that creates conflict; indeed, a world of equal states could be expected to be particularly warlike, even if there were no capitalist exploitation. Hobbes argued that, in the state of nature, the natural equality of men leads to conflict by creating "equality of hope in the attaining of our ends," which leads to conflict when both desire the same goods. "In the condition of mere nature," he argues, "the inequality of power is not discerned but by the event of battle."[13] Hobbes implies that a virtue of establishing independent states is that this equality disappears, leading to more security as a result of the fact that unequal combat has more predictable results than combat among equals. A contemporary realist, Robert W. Tucker, has argued that trends toward greater equality are likely to lead to a "decline of power" and a more disorderly international system.[14]

From realism's standpoint, liberalism's flaw is less moral than explanatory: not its countenance of exploitation but its reliance on incentives provided by economic exchange and on rules to moderate state behavior in a condition of anarchy. A judgment on the validity of this criticism must await our exploration of liberalism's analysis of the limits imposed by the international system on state action.

The insufficiency of realism and Marxism

The insights that states are constrained by capitalism and by the state system are clearly true and profound. They are necessary elements of our understanding of the economic and military limits to modern politics. Yet the constraints pointed to by Marxist and realists, taken separately or in combination, are hardly sufficient to determine state action. If they were, realists or Marxists would have been more successful in devising accurate predictive theories of world politics. We would not observe variations in cooperation from one time period to another, or issue by issue, that were unexplained by the dynamics of capitalism or by changes in international structure.[15] Yet we do observe such variations in cooperation. And we also encounter international institutions whose actions are not well explained simply by the social forces or states on which Marxism and realism focus their attention.[16]

This suggests that any claims to theoretical closure made by Marxists or realists in moments of theoretical enthusiasm should not be taken very seriously. Neither Marxism nor realism constitutes a successful deterministic theory, and the most thoughtful Marxists and realists have always recognized this. Marx taught that "men make their own history, but they do not make it just as they please."[17] Hans J. Morgenthau devoted much of his life to instructing Americans on how they should act in world politics to attain peace as well as power; he especially stressed the role of diplomacy. Toward the end of *War and Change in World Politics*[18] Robert Gilpin argues that "states can learn to be more enlightened in their definitions of their interests and more cooperative in their behavior" (p. 227), and he calls on "statesmen in the final decades of the twentieth century to build on the positive forces of our age in the creation of a new and more stable international order" (p. 244).

Kenneth Waltz acknowledges explicitly that state behavior depends not just on international structure but on the internal characteristics of states and that the decisions of leaders also make a difference.[19]

The absence of a successful deterministic theory of international relations is fortunate for us as agents in history, since determinism is an unsatisfactory doctrine for human beings. In an era when the fates not only of our species but of the biosphere seem to depend on human decisions, it would be morally as well as intellectually irresponsible to embrace deterministic accounts of world politics. The avoidance of nuclear war is not guaranteed by the existence of capitalism or the state system, any more than its occurrence is rendered inevitable by these structures. Nor do international political and economic structures either guarantee or entirely preclude economic growth or the more equitable distribution of income in Third World countries, although, as will be seen below, they may render the latter difficult to obtain. In combating both war and poverty, there is considerable scope for the effects of conscious human action: neither Pangloss nor Cassandra provides an accurate guide to issues of war and poverty in the contemporary world.

Avoiding nuclear war and promoting equitable Third World development both require international institutions. So do such tasks as retarding nuclear proliferation and protecting the global environment. Managing economic interdependence requires an unprecedented degree of international policy coordination, which the forces of power and world capitalism hardly bring about automatically. Neither class struggle nor hegemonic rule alone offers us much hope of coping successfully with these issues.

In contrast to Marxism and realism, liberalism is not committed to an ambitious and parsimonious structural theory. Its attempts at theory often seem therefore to be vaguely stated and to yield uncomfortably indeterminate results. Yet liberalism's theoretical weakness can be a source of strength as a guide to choice. Liberalism puts more emphasis on the cumulative effects of human action, particularly institution building, than does either Marxism and realism; for liberals, people really do make their own history. Liberalism may therefore offer some clues about how we can change the economic and political limits to modern international politics.

Liberalism as a theory of international relations

As Michael Doyle points out, "there is no canonical description of Liberalism."[20] Some commentators equate liberalism with a belief in the superiority of economic arrangements relying on markets rather than on state control. This conception of liberalism identifies it with the view of Adam Smith, David Ricardo and generations of classical and neoclassical economists. Another version of liberalism associates it more generally with the principle of "the importance of the freedom of the individual."[21] From this classic political perspective, liberalism "begins with the recognition that men, do what we will, are free; that a man's acts are his own, spring from his own personality, and cannot be coerced. But this freedom is not possessed at birth; it is acquired by degrees as a man enters into the self-conscious possession of his personality through a life of discipline and moral progress."[22]

Neither the view of liberalism as a doctrine of unfettered economic exchange nor its identification with liberty for the individual puts forward an analysis of the constraints and opportunities that face states as a result of the international system in which they are embedded. Instead, the emphasis of liberalism on liberty and rights only suggests a general orientation toward the moral evaluation of world politics.

For purposes of this chapter, therefore, it is more useful to consider liberalism as an approach to the analysis of social reality rather than as a doctrine of liberty.[23]

I will therefore regard liberalism as an approach to the analysis of social reality that (1) begins with individuals as the relevant actors, (2) seeks to understand how aggregations of individuals make collective decisions and how organizations composed to individuals interact, and (3) embeds this analysis in a world view that emphasizes individual rights and that adopts an ameliorative view of progress in human affairs. In economics, liberalism's emphasis on the collective results of individual actions leads to the analysis of markets, market failure, and institutions to correct such failure; in traditional international relations theory it implies attempts to reconcile state sovereignty with the reality of strategic interdependence.

Liberalism shares with realism the stress on explaining the behavior of separate and typically self-interested units of action, but from the standpoint of international relations, there are three critical differences between these two schools of thought. First, liberalism focuses not merely on states but on privately organized social groups and firms. The transnational as well as domestic activities of these groups and firms are important for liberal analysts, not in isolation from the actions of states but in conjunction with them. Second, in contrast to realism, liberalism does not emphasize the significance of military force, but rather seeks to discover ways in which separate actors, with distinct interests, can organize themselves to promote economic efficiency and avoid destructive physical conflict, without renouncing either the economic or political freedoms that liberals hold dear.[24] Finally, liberalism believes in at least the possibility of cumulative progress, whereas realism assumes that history is not progressive.

Much contemporary Marxist and neo-Marxist analysis minimizes the significance of individuals and state organizations, focusing instead on class relations or claiming that the identities of individuals and organizations are constituted by the nature of the world capitalist system, and that the system is therefore ontologically prior to the individual. Thus, liberalism is separated from much Marxist thought by a rather wide philosophical gulf. Yet liberalism draws substantially on those aspects of Marxism that analyze relations between discrete groups, such as investigations of multinational corporations or of the political consequences of capital flows. Both schools of thought share the inclination to look behind the state to social groups. Furthermore, both liberals and Marxists believe in the possibility of progress, although the liberals' rights-oriented vision is to emerge incrementally whereas Marxists have often asserted that their more collective new world order would be brought about through revolution.

Liberalism does not purport to provide a complete account of international relations. On the contrary, most contemporary liberals seem to accept large portions of both the Marxist and realist explanations. Much of what liberals wish to explain about world politics can be accounted for by the character and dynamics of world capitalism, on the one hand, and the nature of political–military competition, on the other. The realist and Marxist explanations focus on the underlying structure of world politics, which helps to define the limits of what is feasible and therefore ensures that the intentions of actors are often not matched by the outcomes they achieve. Yet as noted above, these explanations are incomplete. They fail to pay sufficient attention to the institutions and patterns of interaction created by human beings that help to shape perceptions and expectations, and therefore alter the patterns of behavior that take place within a given structure. Liberalism's strength is that it takes political processes seriously.

Although liberalism does not have a single theory of international relations, three more specific perspectives on international relations have nevertheless been put forward by writers who share liberalism's analytic emphasis on individual action and normative concern for liberty. I label these arguments republican, commercial, and regulatory liberalism. They are not inconsistent with one another. All three variants of international liberalism can be found in Immanuel Kant's essay "Eternal Peace," and both commercial and regulatory liberalism presuppose the existence of limited constitutional states, or republics in Kant's sense. Nevertheless, these liberal doctrines are logically distinct from one another. They rest on somewhat different premises, and liberals' interpretations of world politics vary in the degree to which they rely upon each set of causal arguments.

Republican liberalism

Republican liberalism argues that republics are more peacefully inclined than are despotisms. For Kant, a principal spokesman for all three versions of liberalism, republics are constitutional governments based on the principles of freedom of individuals, the rule of law, and the equality of citizens. In republics, legislatures can limit the actions of the executive; furthermore, "the consent of the citizens is required in order to decide whether there should be war or not," and "nothing is more natural than that those who would have to decide to undergo all the deprivations of war will very much hesitate to start such an evil game."[25] Yet as Michael Doyle has pointed out, for Kant republicanism only produces caution; it does not guarantee peace.

To prevent war, action at the international as well as the national level is necessary.[26]

The association of republics with peace has often been criticized or even ridiculed. Citizens in democracies have sometimes greeted war enthusiastically, as indicated by the Crimean and Spanish–American wars and with respect to several belligerent countries, by the onset of World War I. Furthermore, many of the people affected by war have not been enfranchised in the actual republics of the last two centuries.[27] In the twentieth century, it has been difficult for legislatures to control actions of the executive that may be tantamount to war. And republics have certainly fought many and bloody wars.

Yet the historical record provides substantial support for Kant's view, if it is taken to refer to the waging of war between states founded on liberal principles rather than between these states and their illiberal adversaries. Indeed, Michael Doyle has shown on the basis of historical evidence for the years since 1800 that "constitutionally secure liberal states have yet to engage in war with one another."[28]

This is an interesting issue that could bear further discussion. But my essay concerns the impact of *international relations* on state behavior. Republican liberalism explains state behavior in the international arena on the basis of *domestic* politics and is thus not directly germane to my argument here. Furthermore, as noted above, sophisticated advocates of republican liberalism, such as Kant, acknowledge that even well-constituted republics can be warlike unless international relations are properly organized. Attention to liberalism's arguments about international relations is therefore required.[29]

Commercial liberalism

Commercial liberalism affirms the impact of international relations on the actions of states. Advocates of commercial liberalism have extended the classical economists' benign view of trade into the political realm. From the Enlightenment onward, liberals have argued, in Montesquieu's words, that "the natural effect of commerce is to lead to peace. Two nations that trade together become mutually dependent if one has an interest in buying, the other has one in selling; and all unions are based on mutual needs."[30] Kant clearly agreed: "It is the *spirit of commerce* that cannot coexist with war, and which sooner or later takes hold of every nation."[31]

This liberal insistence that commerce leads to peace has led some critical observers to define liberalism in terms of belief in "a natural harmony that leads, not to a war of all against all, but to a stable, orderly and progressive society with little need for a governmental intervention."[32] The utopianism that could be fostered by such a belief is illustrated by a statement of the American industrialist and philanthropist, Andrew Carnegie. In 1910 Carnegie established the Carnegie Endowment for International Peace, stating, as the Endowment's historian says, "that war could be abolished and that peace was in reach, and that after it was secured his trustees 'should consider what is the next most degrading remaining evil or evils whose banishment' would advance the human cause and turn their energies toward eradicating it."[33]

In its straightforward, naive form, commercial liberalism is untenable, relying as it does both on an unsubstantiated theory of progress and on a crudely reductionist argument in which politics is determined by economics. The experience of the First World War, in which major trading partners such as Britain and Germany fought each other with unprecedented intensity, discredited simplistic formulations of commercial liberalism. Yet in my judgment too much has been discredited: commentators have identified commercial liberalism with its most extreme formulations and have thus discarded it rather cavalierly. Defensible forms of commercial liberalism have been put forward in this century, most notably in the 1930s.

At the end of that decade, Eugene Staley proposed a particularly lucid statement of commercial liberalism. Staley begins, in effect, with Adam Smith's dictum that "the division of labor depends on the extent of the market." Increased productivity depends on an international division of labor, for countries not exceptionally well-endowed with a variety of resources. Economic nationalism blocks the division of labor, thus leading to a dilemma for populous but resource-poor states such as Japan: expand or accept decreased living standards.

> The widespread practice of economic nationalism is likely to produce the feeling in a country of rapidly growing population that it is faced with a terrible dilemma: either accept the miserable prospect of decreased living standards (at least, abandon hope of greatly improved living standards), or seek by conquest to seize control of more territory, more resources, larger market and supply areas.[34]

This leads to a general conclusion:

> To the extent, then, that large, important countries controlling substantial portions of the world's resources refuse to carry on economic relations with the rest of the world, they sow the seeds of unrest and war. In particular, they create a powerful dynamic of imperialism. *When economic walls are erected along political boundaries, possession of territory is made to coincide with economic opportunity* [italics added]. Imperialistic ambitions are given both a partial justification and a splendid basis for propaganda.[35]

Staley's argument does not depend on his assumption about increasing population, since increasing demands for higher living standards could lead to the same pressure for economic growth. The important point here for our purposes is that in Staley's version of commercial liberalism, incentives for peaceful behavior are provided by an open international environment characterized by regularized patterns of exchange and orderly rules. Commerce by itself does not ensure peace, but commerce on a nondiscriminatory basis within an orderly political framework promotes cooperation on the basis of enlightened national conceptions of self-interest that emphasize production over war.

Regulatory liberalism

Advocates of regulatory liberalism emphasize the importance for peace of the rules governing patterns of exchange among countries. Albert O. Hirschman points out that as people began to think about interests in the eighteenth century, they began to realize "that something was to be gained for both parties (in international politics) by the adherence to certain rules of the game and by the elimination of 'passionate' behavior, which the rational pursuit of interest implied."[36] Kant regards regulation as a central principle of perpetual peace. He proposes a "federalism" of free states, although this federation is to fall short of a world republic, since a constitutionally organized world state based on the national principle is not feasible.[37]

Kant does not go into details on how such a federation would be institutionalized, but his vision clearly presages the international organizations of the twentieth century, with their established rules, norms, and practices. A major change in the concept of regulatory liberalism, however, has taken place, since relatively few contemporary international organizations limit membership to republics. Indeed, most members of the United Nations would qualify as despotisms by Kant's criteria. Contemporary practice has created different types of international organizations. Some, such as the European Community and the Organization for Economic Cooperation and Development (OECD), are at least for the most part limited to republics, but the United Nations, a variety of global economic organizations, and regional organizations outside Europe are not. Contemporary advocates of regulatory liberalism may continue to believe that republics in Kant's sense are the best partners for international cooperation; but for a number of global problems, it would be self-defeating to refuse to seek to collaborate with autocratic states. Even autocracies may have an interest in following international rules and facilitate mutually beneficial agreements on issues such as arms control, nuclear reactor safety, and the regulation of international trade.

Kant's argument for a federation is in my view profoundly different from the conception (also found in "Eternal Peace") of the gradual emergence of peace through commerce as a natural process, implying a theory of progress. In contrast not only to Marxism and realism but also to this notion of peace deriving automatically from commerce, regulatory liberalism emphasizes discretionary human action. International rules and institutions play a crucial role in promoting cooperation; yet there is great variation in their results, depending on the human ingenuity and commitment used to create and maintain them. This emphasis of regulatory liberalism on human choices conforms with experience: the life-histories of international organizations differ dramatically. In some cases, their institutional arrangements, and the actions of their leaders, have encouraged sustained, focused work that accomplishes common purposes and maintains support for the organization: NATO, the European Community, the Association of Southeast Asian Nations (ASEAN) and the World Health Organization (WHO) are examples. Other organizations, such as UNESCO, have failed to maintain the same level of institutional coherence and political support.[38]

If we keep the insights of regulatory liberalism in mind, along with the experiences of international organizations in the twentieth century, we will be cautious about seeking to predict international behavior on the basis of "the effects of commerce." Such an inference is no more valid than purporting to construct comprehensive analyses of world politics solely on the basis of "the constraints of capitalism" or the necessary effects of anarchy. "Commerce," "capitalism," and "anarchy" can give us clues about the incentives – constraints and opportunities – facing actors, but without knowing the institutional context, they do not enable us to understand how people or governments will react. Regulatory liberalism argues that we have to specify the institutional features of world politics before inferring expected patterns of behavior. I believe that this awareness of institutional complexity is a great advantage, that it constitutes an improvement in subtlety. It improves our capacity to account for change, since change is not explained adequately by shifts in patterns of economic transactions (commercial liberalism), fundamental power distributions (realism), or capitalism (Marxism).

Nothing in regulatory liberalism holds that harmony of interest emerges automatically. On the contrary, cooperation has to be constructed by human beings on the basis of a recognition that independent governments both hold predominant power resources and command more legitimacy from human populations than do any conceivable international organizations. Neither peace nor coordinated economic and social policies can be sought on the basis of a hierarchical organizing principle that supersedes governments. Governments must be persuaded; they cannot be bypassed. This means that international institutions need to be constructed both to facilitate the purposes that governments espouse in common and gradually to alter governmental conceptions of self-interest in order to widen the scope for cooperation. International institutions provide information, facilitate communication, and furnish certain services that cannot be as easily offered by national governments: they do not enforce rules. Liberals recognize that although it is possible to cooperate on the basis of common interest, such cooperation does not derive from an immanent world community that only has to be appreciated, nor does it occur without sweat and risk.

The accomplishments of regulatory liberalism in our age are substantial. They should not be dismissed because severe dangers and dilemmas continue to face governments or because much that we would like to accomplish is frustrated by state sovereignty and conflicts of interest. The global environment would be in even greater danger in the absence of the United Nations Environmental Program (UNEP) and agreements reached under its auspices; protectionist trade wars might be rampant were it not for the General Agreement on Tariffs and Trade (GATT); starvation would have been much worse in Africa in the early 1980s without the World Food Program and other international cooperative arrangements; smallpox would not have been eradicated without the efforts of the World Health Organization. Regulatory liberalism asserts that better arrangements that constructively channel the pursuit of self-interest – or that enrich definitions of self-interest – can realistically be constructed, not that they will appear without effort. History supports both parts of its claim.

Sophisticated liberalism

Commercial liberalism stresses the benign effects of trade; in Staley's version, trade may, under the right conditions, facilitate cooperation but does not automatically produce it. Regulatory liberalism emphasizes the impact of rules and institutions on human behavior. Both versions are consistent with the premise that states make choices that are, roughly speaking, rational and self-interested; that is, they choose means that appear appropriate to achieve their own ends. Yet this premise misses an important element of liberalism, which does not accept a static view of self-interest, determined by the structure of a situation, but rather holds open the possibility that people will change their attitudes and their loyalties. As students of European political integration have shown, a combination of strengthened commercial ties and new institutions can exert a substantial impact on people's conceptions of their self-interest.[39] People cannot be expected, in general, to cease to act in self-interested ways, but their conceptions of their self-interest can change.

What I call sophisticated liberalism incorporates this sociological perspective on interests into a synthesis of commercial and regulatory liberalism. It does not posit that expanding commerce leads directly to peace but rather agrees with Staley that conditions of economic openness can provide incentives for peaceful rather than aggressive expansion. This is only likely to occur, however, within the framework of rules and institutions that promote and guarantee openness. Not just any set of commercial relationships will lead to peace: The effects of commerce depend on the institutional context – the rules and habits – within which it takes place. Furthermore, the development of commerce cannot be regarded as inevitable, since it depends on a political structure resting on interests and power.

What liberalism prescribes was to a remarkable extent implemented by the United States and its Western European allies after World War II. The United States, in conjunction with Western European governments, set about constructing a framework of rules that would promote commerce and economic growth. Consistently with the expectations of both realism and Marxism, American power was used to ensure that the rules and institutions that emerged satisfied the basic preferences of American elites. What the Europeans established differed considerably from American plans, and the construction of European institutions preceded the implementation of the global economic arrangements that had been outlined at the Bretton Woods Conference and at the negotiations leading to the General Agreement on Tariffs and Trade (GATT).[40] Yet without American prodding, it is unclear whether these European institutions would have been created; and the United States had relatively little difficulty accepting the new European institutions, which promoted basic American goals of security and prosperity within the institutional frameworks of representative government and capitalism.

Even if the European institutions were not entirely devoted to the principles of commercial liberalism – and the European Payments Union, the European Coal and Steel Community, and the European Economic Community had many restrictionist elements – they were not sharply inconsistent with the institutions of Bretton Woods and GATT, which emphasized the value of open markets and nondiscriminatory trade. The resulting arrangements, taken as a whole, epitomized a liberalism that was "embedded" in the postwar interventionist welfare state. That is, liberalism no longer required rejection of state interventionism, but rather efforts to ensure that interventionist practices were limited by joint agreements and rules, in order to maintain their broadly liberal character and to facilitate international exchange.[41] Economic growth, promoted by international trade and investment, was expected to facilitate the growth of democratic institutions within societies, and thus to reshape states in pacific directions as well as to provide incentives for peaceful economic expansion rather than military conquest. The political complications entailed by growing economic interdependence were to be managed by an increasingly complex network of formal and informal institutions, within Europe and among the advanced industrial countries.[42]

This strategy was remarkably successful. Indeed, the benign results foreseen by such writers as Staley ensued, although it might be difficult to prove decisively that they resulted principally from institutionalized patterns of interdependence more than from the looming presence of the Soviet Union. At any rate, war and threats of war were eliminated as means of economic aggrandizement for the advanced parliamentary democracies. Furthermore, as American hegemony began to wane after the mid-1960s, the value of liberalism's emphasis on rules became more evident to those who sought to avoid a return to economic warfare and generalized conflict. International regimes such as those revolving around the GATT or the International Monetary Fund have displayed remarkable staying power, even after the power constellations that brought them into being had eroded.

Liberals have used their positive theory stressing the role of institutions to bolster their normative argument that liberal orders are to be preferred to available alternatives. It is important to note here that the liberal stress on institution building is not based on naivete about harmony among people, but rather on an agreement with realists about what a world without rules or institutions would look like: a jungle in which governments seek to weaken one another economically and militarily, leading to continual strife and frequent warfare. Liberals do not believe in the soothing effects of "international community." It is precisely because they have seen the world in terms similar to those of the realists – not because they have worn rose-colored glasses – that sophisticated liberals from Kant to Staley to Stanley Hoffmann have sought alternatives. Their pessimism about world politics and human conflict makes sophisticated liberals willing to settle for less than that demanded by utopians of whatever stripe.

Evaluating liberalism: doctrine and practice

Regulatory liberalism argues for the construction of institutions to promote exchanges regarded by governments as beneficial. This is to be done without directly challenging either the sovereignty of states or the inequalities of power among them. Liberals who appreciate Marxist and realist insights are careful not to present these exchanges as unconstrained or necessarily equally beneficial to all parties concerned, much less to categories of people (such as the rural poor in less developed countries) that are unrepresented at the bargaining table. As a reformist creed, liberalism does not promise justice or equity in a setting, such as that of international relations, in which inequalities of power are so glaring and means of controlling the exercise of power so weak. It is therefore open to charges of immorality from utopians and of naivete from cynics; and depending on the context, liberals may be guilty of either charge, or of both. Liberals seek to build on what exists in order to improve it, and run the risk that their policies will either worsen the situation or help to block alternative actions that would radically improve it. Nevertheless, liberals can fairly ask their opponents to propose alternative strategies that are not merely attractive in principle, but seem likely to produce better results in practice.

Yet even if we accept the liberal argument this far, we may be reluctant to embrace liberalism as a normative theory of international affairs. Before we could do so, we would need to consider the negative as well as the positive aspects of the open international order, with its rules and institutions to guide the actions of states, that liberals favor. In particular we would need to consider the impact of such an order on two major values: peace and economic welfare. What are the effects of an open, interdependent international order on the constraints facing states, and on the ways in which states are reshaped in world politics? What is the liberal view of these constraints? How do these constraints compare with those imposed by alternative arrangements for the management of international affairs?

Liberalism and peace

As we have seen, liberalism assures states of access, on market or near-market terms, to resources located elsewhere. "In a liberal economic system," admits a critic of liberalism, "the costs of using force in pursuit of economic interests are likely to outweigh any gains, because markets and resources are already available on competitive terms."[43]

This access to markets and resources is assured by complex international political arrangements that would be disrupted by war. If the division of labor is limited by the extent of the market, as Adam Smith taught, the extent of the market is limited by the scope of international order. The more tightly intertwined and interdependent the valued interactions among states, the greater the incentives for long-term cooperation in order to avoid disrupting these ties. In international relations as in other social relations, incentives for cooperation depend on whether actors are "involved in a thick enough network of mutual interactions" and on the degree to which they benefit from these ties.[44] This does not mean that commerce necessarily leads to peace, or that entwining the Soviet Union in networks of interdependence will get the Soviets to stop fostering revolution in the Third World; but it is reasonable to assert that a calculation of costs and benefits will enter into state decision making, and that this calculation will be affected by the costs of disrupting beneficial ties. Thus we can find analytical support for the view, espoused by liberals such as Staley, that an open, rule-oriented international system provides incentives for peaceful behavior.[45]

The existence of an orderly and open international system may affect the balance of interests and power for societies poised between commercial and belligerent definitions of self-interest. Japan before and after World War II provides the outstanding example. Admittedly, the contrast between its behaviour before World War II and since is partly accounted for by the restructuring of Japanese government and society during the American Occupation and by the dependence of Japan on the United States for defense against the Soviet Union. Nevertheless, the dominance of peacefully inclined commercial rather than bellicose military elites in postwar Japanese policymaking has surely been encouraged by the opportunities provided for Japanese business by relatively open markets abroad, particularly in the United States.[46]

Yet the picture for liberalism is not so rosy as the previous paragraphs might seem to suggest. Liberalism may indeed inhibit the use of force, but it may also have the opposite effect. Whether American liberalism was in any way responsible for the massive use of violence by the United States in Southeast Asia is still unclear: Liberal moralism may have justified the use of force, although it seems from *The Pentagon Papers* that a skewed conception of geopolitics provided a more powerful motivation for action.[47] Furthermore, liberal values were crucial in providing the moral basis for the popular protests against United States military involvement in Vietnam, which eventually brought the war to an end.

Yet even if liberalism tends to be peacefully oriented, and was not responsible for the war in Vietnam, the effects of liberalism on peace may not necessarily be benign. The extension of economic interests worldwide under liberalism in search of wider markets requires the extension of political order: insofar as that order is threatened, protection of one's own economic interests may entail the use of force. Thus a global political economy may make it difficult for leaders of a peacefully oriented liberal state not to use force, precisely by making it vulnerable to the use of force against it by nonliberal states or movements. Three examples illustrate this point:

Direct foreign investment   The United States in recent decades has intervened directly or indirectly in a number of countries in which it had substantial direct foreign investments, including Guatemala (1954), Cuba (1961), and Chile (1973). Fear of the extension of Soviet influence to the Western Hemisphere seems to have been a principal motivation for American action, but in all three cases, intergovernmental conflicts were generated by the presence of US-owned companies in societies undergoing revolutionary change. In the absence of the extension of American economic interests to these countries, such interventions would, it seems, have been less likely to occur.

Control over resources   The Carter Doctrine, which raised the possibility of American intervention in the Persian Gulf, was clearly motivated by United States government concern for access to oil resources in that area. So was the movement of a large US naval task force into the gulf in the spring and summer of 1987. Such military action in defense of far-flung economic interests – of America's allies even more than of itself – created the obvious possibility of war between the United States and Iran. Soviet–American confrontation was also conceivable: indeed, the scenarios of superpower conflict arising in the Middle East seemed in many ways more plausible than the scenarios for Soviet–American military confrontation in Europe.[48] The general point is that the global economic interests of liberal states make them vulnerable to threats to their access to raw materials and to markets. Liberal states may use violence to defend access to distant resources that more autarkic states would not have sought in the first place.

Air transport   Liberal societies not only extend their economic interests worldwide, they also believe in individual freedom to travel. This means that at any given time, thousands of citizens of such societies are in airplanes around the world – potential hostages or victims of terrorists. Since socialist or mercantilist governments not only have limited foreign economic interests but often restrict travel by their people, they are not so vulnerable. Reacting to their vulnerability, powerful republics may escalate the use of force, as the United States did, in April 1986, against Libya. The global extension of international activity fostered by liberalism's stress on economic openness and political rights not only creates opportunities for terrorists but also provides incentives for powerful republics to use force – even if its use is justified as defensive and protective rather than aggressive.

How do incentives for the use of force balance out against incentives against such use? The peaceful behaviour of liberal governments toward one another, and their reluctance to resort to force against nonliberal states in the oil crisis of the 1970s, suggest that the current interdependent international political economy may have inhibited – or at least, has not encouraged – widespread resort to force. Barry Buzan argues that, despite this success, liberalism will lead in the long run to the use of force because it is unstable and will deteriorate.[49] The recent upsurge of terrorism reminds us that this caution is well founded. A degenerating liberal system, in which commitments and vulnerabilities exceed the capacities of liberal states to deal with them, could be exceedingly dangerous – perhaps even more so than a decaying system of self-reliant mercantilist states. But this observation could just as well be taken as a justification for committing ourselves more strongly to underpinning a liberal economic system with multilateral institutions supported by power, than as an argument against a liberal international system. To regard the dangers of a decay of liberalism as an argument against an open international order is reminiscent of Woody Allen's character in *Hannah and Her Sisters* who attempts to commit suicide out of fear of death!

Liberalism and economic welfare

Conservative economists find the international order favored by liberalism congenial. The international market serves as a "reality test" for governments' economic strategies. Inefficient policies such as those overemphasizing provision of welfare and state bureaucracy will do badly.[50] Eventually, the failure of these policies will become evident in slow and distorted growth and balance-of-payments problems. From this standpoint, the constraints imposed by the world economy are not properly seen as malign constraints on autonomy, but rather as beneficial limits on governments' abilities to damage their own economies and people through foolish policies. International liberalism fosters a world economy that gives timely early warning of economic disaster, rather than enabling states to conceal crises by using controls that in the long run only make matters worse. As Locke said about law, "That ill deserves the Name of Confinement which hedges us in only from Bogs and Precipices."[51]

The international political economy of modern capitalism is viewed more critically, however, both by liberals who empathize strongly with ordinary people in the Third World and by First World supporters of social democracy. It is evident to many liberals as well as Marxists that the modern capitalist world economy exerts a bias against poor, immobile people as well as against generous welfare states. Conservative economists point this out with some glee: the McCracken Report argues that "countries pursuing equality strenuously with an inadequate growth rate" may suffer "capital flight and brain drain."[52] The existence of international capitalism improves the bargaining power of investors vis-à-vis left-wing governments. The ease with which funds can flow across national boundaries makes it difficult for any country with a market-oriented economy to institute measures that change the distribution of income against capital.

Capital flight can have catastrophic effects on the debt-ridden nations of the Third World. As Marxists emphasize, it also constrains attempts to promote equity or nibble away at the privileges of business in the advanced industrialized countries of Europe, North America, and the Pacific. When Thatcher or Reagan sought to help business and improve profits, capital flowed into their countries – at least temporarily. When Mitterand sought to expand the welfare state, stimulate demand, and nationalize selected industries, by contrast, capital flowed out, the franc declined and his social democratic policy was eventually exchanged for austerity. An open capitalist world financial system therefore tends to reinforce itself, although, even in the face of such constraints, such countries as Sweden and Austria have been able to devise effective strategies to maintain high levels of employment and social equality. Ironically, states with strong but flexible public institutions, able to manipulate the world economy when possible and to correct for its effects when necessary, seem to thrive best in an open world political economy. For countries not blessed with such institutions, the international economic order of modern capitalism manifests a pronounced bias against policies promoting equality.[53]

International liberalism: an evaluation

The international order proposed by liberalism has a number of appealing features, particularly when a substantial number of powerful states are republics. Orderly exchange, within a framework of rules and institutions, provides incentives for peaceful expansion and productive specialization. International institutions facilitate cooperation and foster habits of working together. Therefore, a realistic liberalism, premised not on automatic harmony but on prudential calculation, has a great deal to commend it as a philosophy of international relations.

Yet liberalism has several major limitations, both as a framework for analysis and as a guide for policy. It is incomplete as an explanation, it can become normatively myopic, and it can backfire as a policy prescription.

Liberalism only makes sense as an explanatory theory within the constraints pointed out by Marxism and realism. Viewed as an explanation of state action, sophisticated liberalism emphasizes the difference that international rules and institutions can make, even when neither the anarchic state system nor world capitalism can be transformed or eliminated. If major powers come into violent conflict with one another or capitalism disintegrates, the institutions on which liberalism relies will also collapse.

International liberalism is therefore only a partial theory of international relations: it does not stand on its own.

Normatively, liberalism is, as John Dunn has put it, "distressingly plastic."[54] It accommodates easily to dominant interests, seeking to use its institutional skills to improve situations rather than fundamentally to restructure them. Liberalism is also relatively insensitive to exploitation resulting from gross asymmetries of wealth and power. Liberals may be inclined to downplay values such as equality when emphasis on such values would bring them into fundamental conflict with powerful elites on whose acquiescence their institutional reformism depends. Liberalism is sometimes myopic as a normative theory, since it focuses principally on moderating "economic constraints on modern politics" in a way that facilitates governments' purposes, rather than directly on the condition of disadvantaged groups. To satisfied modern elites and middle classes, liberalism seems eminently reasonable, but it is not likely to be as appealing to the oppressed or disgruntled.

As policy advice, liberalism can backfire under at least two different sets of conditions. First, if only a few governments seek to promote social equity and welfare in an open economy, they may find their policies constrained by the more benighted policies of others. "Embedded liberalism" represents an attempt to render a liberal international order compatible with domestic interventionism and the welfare state. As we have seen, this is a difficult synthesis to maintain. Second, liberalism may have perverse effects if the global extension of interests that it fosters cannot be defended. Decaying liberal systems may be the most dangerous of all. One way to deal with this problem of decay is to use military power to uphold the liberal order. But we may also want to consider how to make ourselves less vulnerable by trimming back some of these interests, insofar as we can do so without threatening the rule-based structure of exchange that is the essence of a liberal order. It would be foolish for liberalism to commit suicide for fear of death. But perhaps we could go on a diet, reducing some of the excess weight that may make us vulnerable to disaster. Greater energy self-reliance – endangered by the mid-1980s fall in oil prices – remains one valuable way to do this.[55]

The appeal of liberalism clearly depends in part on where you sit. Liberalism can become a doctrine of the status quo; indeed, this danger is probably greater for the nonutopian liberalism that I advocate than for the utopian liberalism that E.H. Carr criticized almost half a century ago. But realism has an even greater tendency to be morally complacent, since it lacks the external standards of human rights that liberalism can use to criticize governments in power. Realism lacks the "imaginative flexibility" of liberalism about human possibilities, and is therefore missing an ethical dimension that liberals possess.[56] Marxism is anything but complacent about the capitalist status quo, although as a moral theory the weakness of orthodox Marxism is its inability to show that the alternatives it proposes *as they are likely actually to operate in practice* are morally superior to feasible reformist alternatives. Soviet

Marxists, of course, have traditionally supported the status quo in socialist states within the Soviet sphere of influence, regardless of how repressive their governments may be.

The strength of liberalism as moral theory lies in its attention to how alternative governing arrangements will operate in practice, and in particular how institutions can protect human rights against the malign inclinations of power holders. Unlike realism, liberalism strives hard for improvement; but unlike Marxism, it subjects proffered "new orders" to skeptical examination. "No liberal ever forgets that governments are coercive."[57] A liberalism that remains faithful to its emphasis on individual rights and individual welfare as the normative basis for international institutions and exchange, can never become too wedded to the status quo, which never protects those rights adequately.

In the end I return to the emphasis of liberalism on human action and choice. Liberalism incorporates a belief in the possibility of ameliorative change facilitated by multilateral arrangements. It emphasizes the moral value of prudence.[58] For all its faults and weaknesses, liberalism helps us to see the importance of international cooperation and institution building, even within the fundamental constraints set by world capitalism and the international political system. Liberalism holds out the prospect that we can affect, if not control, our fate, and thus encourages both better theory and improved practice. It constitutes an antidote to fatalism and a source of hope for the human race.

Notes

1 The author is grateful for comments on earlier drafts of this paper to Professors Vinod Aggarwal, Michael Doyle, John Dunn, Ernst B. Haas, Stanley Hoffmann, Nannerl O. Keohane, Joseph S. Nye, Susan Moller Okin, and Kenneth N. Waltz. Further valuable suggestions were received when such a draft was presented to the Harvard-MIT study group on international institutions and cooperation during the fall of 1986 and to a discussion group at the Center for Advanced Study in the Behavioral Sciences during the fall of 1987.

2 For the classic modern work in this vein, see Kenneth N. Waltz, *Man, the State and War* (New York: Columbia University Press, 1959).

3 On British and American thinking, see Arnold Wolfers and Laurence W. Martin, eds, *The Anglo-American Tradition in Foreign Affairs: Readings from Thomas More to Woodrow Wilson* (New Haven: Yale University Press, 1956). For the most influential English-language critiques of liberalism in international relations, see E.H. Carr, *The Twenty Years' Crisis, 1919–1939* (London: Macmillan, 1st edition, 1939; 2nd edition, 1946); Hans J. Morgenthau, *Scientific Man Versus Power Politics* (Chicago: University of Chicago Press, 1946); and Waltz, *Man, the State and War*.

4 E.H. Carr, *Nationalism and After* (New York: Macmillan, 1945), p. 11.

5 See Hans J. Morgenthau, *Politics Among Nations* (New York: Knopf, 4th edition, 1967).

6 Ralph Miliband, *The State in Capitalist Society* (New York: Basic, 1969), p. 153.

7 Theda Skocpol, *States and Social Revolutions* (Cambridge University Press, 1979), p. 19.
8 Immanuel Wallerstein, *The Capitalist World-Economy* (Cambridge University Press, 1979), p. 230.
9 Robert Jervis, "Cooperation Under the Security Dilemma," *World Politics*, vol. 30, no. 2 (January 1978), p. 169.
10 For a classic listing, see Morgenthau, *Politics Among Nations*, Chap. 9.
11 For a discussion of "self-help" as a defining characteristic of world politics, see Kenneth N. Waltz, *Theory of International Politics* (Reading, Mass: Addison-Wesley, 1979), Chap. 6.
12 Felix Gilbert, ed., *The Historical Essays of Otto Hintze* (New York: Oxford University Press, 1975), p. 183.
13 Thomas Hobbes, *Leviathan* (1651, Chaps 13, 15; Library of Liberal Arts Edition, Indianapolis: Bobbs-Merrill), pp. 104, 118.
14 Robert W. Tucker, *The Inequality of Nations* (New York: Basic, 1977), p. 175.
15 International structure for neorealists such as Waltz comprises three elements: the central principle of anarchy, the similarity of the units composing the system, and the distribution of power among them. See Waltz, *Theory of International Politics*, Chap. 5.
16 For a sustained discussion of this point, see Robert O. Keohane, *After Hegemony: Cooperation and Discord in the World Political Economy* (Princeton: Princeton University Press, 1984).
17 Karl Marx, *The Eighteenth Brumaire of Louis Napoleon*, second paragraph (1852), reprinted in Lewis Feuer, ed., *Marx and Engels: Basic Writings on Politics and Philosophy* (Garden City, N.Y.: Doubleday, 1959), p. 320.
18 Cambridge: Cambridge University Press, 1981.
19 Waltz, *Theory of International Politics*, p. 122.
20 Michael W. Doyle, "Liberalism and World Politics," *American Political Science Review*, vol. 80, no. 4 (December, 1986), p. 1152.
21 Michael W. Doyle, "Kant, Liberal Legacies, and Foreign Affairs," Part I, *Philosophy and Public Affairs*, vol. 12, no. 3 (1983), p. 206. A parallel definition, focusing on political freedom, is offered by Stanley Hoffmann, "Liberalism and International Affairs," in Hoffmann, *Janus and Minerva* (Boulder: Westview Press, 1986).
22 R.G. Collingwood, "Preface" to Guido de Ruggiero, *The History of European Liberalism*, tr. R.G. Collingwood (Boston: Beacon, 1959), pp. vii–viii, quoted by John Dunn, *Rethinking Modern Political Theory* (Cambridge University Press, 1985), p. 158. The use of the word, "man," rather than "person," in this quotation reflects a limitation of the thinking of classical liberalism, with the notable exception of John Stuart Mill, as well as other schools of political thought before the late twentieth century: women are not regarded as the political equals of men, and labor and nurturing by women, which have traditionally been instrumental in the development of children's personality, are ignored.
23 For this suggestion I am indebted to Andrew Moravcsik.
24 As a large critical literature emphasizes, of course, liberalism is not power free. As E.H. Carr emphasized, liberal economic institutions have typically been undergirded by structures of power, which may be hidden by the veil of economics and therefore be more or less invisible.
25 Immanuel Kant, "Eternal Peace" (1795), in Carl J. Friedrich, ed., *The Philosophy of Kant* (New York: Modern Library, 1949), pp. 437–9.
26 Doyle, "Liberalism and World Politics," cited, p. 1160.
27 Susan Okin has pointed out to me that Kant excluded from citizenship women and day laborers. Many republics excluded people without property from voting until late in the last century, and women until early in this one.

28 Doyle, "Liberal Legacies," cited, p. 213. Doyle defines liberal states in a manner consistent with Kant's specifications.

29 Another reason for this emphasis is that recent work on liberalism and international affairs, especially that by Michael Doyle, has discussed republican liberalism with great sophistication but has paid less attention to commercial and regulatory liberalism.

30 Albert O. Hirschman, *The Passions and the Interests: Political Arguments for Capitalism Before its Triumph* (Princeton: Princeton University Press, 1977), p. 80.

31 Kant, "Eternal Peace," cited, p. 455, italics in text.

32 Kenneth N. Waltz, *Man, the State and War*, p. 86. Twenty years before Waltz's book, E.H. Carr argued that liberalism was essentially utopian in character, and that the liberal engaged in "clothing his own interest in the guise of a universal interest for the purpose of imposing it on the rest of the world." Carr, *The Twenty Years' Crisis, 1919–1939*; 2nd edition, pp. 27, 75.

33 Larry L. Fabian, *Andrew Carnegie's Peace Endowment* (New York: Carnegie Endowment for International Peace, 1985), p. 43.

34 Eugene Staley, *The World Economy in Transition* (New York: Council on Foreign Relations, 1939), p. 103.

35 Ibid.

36 Hirschman, *Passions*, cited, p. 51.

37 Kant, "Eternal Peace," pp. 441, 445.

38 For a comparative analysis of eight international organizations that substantiates the importance of institutional histories and choices, see Robert W. Cox and Harold K. Jacobson, eds, *The Anatomy of Influence: Decision Making in International Organization* (New Haven: Yale University Press, 1973).

39 The pioneering works are, Karl W. Deutsch *et al.*, *Political Community and the North Atlantic Area: International Organization in the Light of Historical Experience* (Princeton: Princeton University Press, 1957); Ernst B. Haas, *The Uniting of Europe: Political, Social and Economic Forces, 1950–1957* (Stanford: Stanford University Press, 1958.

40 For an impressive work of scholarship that emphasizes the European ability to obstruct American plans and implement their own, see Alan Milward, *The Reconstruction of Western Europe, 1945–51* (Berkeley and Los Angeles: University of California Press, 1984).

41 John Gerard Ruggie, "International Regimes, Transactions and Change: Embedded Liberalism in the Post-War Economic Order," *International Organization*, vol. 36, no. 2 (1982), pp. 379–415.

42 For a discussion, see Robert O. Keohane and Joseph S. Nye, Jr., *Power and Interdependence: World Politics in Transition* (Boston: Little, Brown, 1977).

43 Barry Buzan, "Economic Structure and International Security: The Limits of the Liberal Case," *International Organization*, vol. 38, no. 4 (1984), p. 603.

44 Russell Hardin, *Collective Action* (Baltimore: Johns Hopkins University Press, 1982), p. 228.

45 For a recent book that revives this thesis, in a not entirely consistent or persuasive form, see Richard N. Rosecrance, *The Rise of the Trading State* (New York: Basic, 1985). Rosecrance drifts too much, in my view, into seeing the "rise of the trading state" as a more or less inevitable trend, ignoring some of the qualifications that must be made to the thesis, as observed below.

46 It is hard to be more specific than this about the effects of the international system without detailed empirical investigation. In general, we must guard against the temptation to overestimate the effects of international arrangements on the propensity of governments to use force. Even sophisticated international liberalism is a systemic theory which does not probe deeply into the nature of domestic

political and social coalitions. The impact of the international system is only one of many factors – even if an important one – affecting the behavior of states.

47 For an analysis of policymaking in the Vietnam War, based principally on *The Pentagon Papers*, see Leslie H. Gelb with Richard K. Betts, *The Irony of Vietnam: The System Worked* (Washington: The Brookings Institution, 1979).

48 See Graham T. Allison, Albert Carnesale, and Joseph S. Nye, Jr., *Hawks, Doves, and Owls: An Agenda for Avoiding Nuclear War* (New York: Norton, 1985).

49 Buzan, "Economic Structure and International Security: the Limits of the Liberal Case," *International Organization*, vol. 38, no. 4 (Autumn 1984), pp. 597–624.

50 See, for instance Paul McCracken *et al.*, *Towards Full Employment and Price Stability* (Paris: OECD, 1977) for an analysis along these lines by a "blue-ribbon panel" of economists.

51 John Locke, *Second Treatise of Government* (1690), paragraph 57. Idem, *Two Treatises of Government*, edited by Peter Laslett, 2nd edition (Cambridge University Press, 1967), p. 323.

52 McCracken *et al.*, *Towards Full Employment and Price Stability*, pp. 136–7.

53 For an elaboration of this argument, see Robert O. Keohane, "The World Political Economy and the Crisis of Embedded Liberalism," in John H. Goldthorpe, ed., *Order and Conflict in Contemporary Capitalism* (Oxford: Clarendon Press, 1984), pp. 22–6. The best work on strategies of small states such as Austria for coping with constraints from the world economy is by Peter J. Katzenstein. See *Corporatism and Change: Austria, Switzerland and the Politics of Industry* (Ithaca, N.Y.: Cornell University Press, 1984); and idem, *Small States in World Markets* (Ithaca, N.Y.: Cornell University Press, 1985).

54 Dunn, *Rethinking Modern Political Theory*, cited, p. 169.

55 It could be worthwhile to ask whether there could be analogous self-protective responses to terrorism. The problem, clearly, is that the obvious solution – restricting the right of one's citizens to travel or denying them protection if they do so – conflicts with liberalism's conception that the state should protect individual rights.

56 The phrase, "imaginative flexibility," I owe to John Dunn.

57 Judith Shklar, *Ordinary Vices* (Cambridge, Mass.: Harvard University Press, 1984), p. 244.

58 Dunn, *Rethinking Modern Political Theory*, cited, p. 169.

4 Hobbes's dilemma and institutional change in world politics: sovereignty in international society[1]

Robert O. Keohane

(1995)

Any coherent attempt to understand contemporary international relations must include an analysis of the impact of two factors: long-term tendencies toward globalization – the intensification of transnational as well as inter-state relations – and the more immediate effects of the end of the Cold War and the collapse of the Soviet Union. For the United States, accustomed to being both relatively autonomous and a leader of a "free world" coalition, both of these changes have immediate impact. Indeed, the very concept of world leadership is up for grabs as it has not been since World War II. Like other contributors to this volume, I do not expect the end of the Cold War to lead to a new world order, which President George Bush sought to celebrate in 1991. Voltaire is reputed to have said that the Holy Roman Empire was neither holy, nor Roman, nor an empire, and one could say about the new world order that it is neither new, nor global in scope, nor an order. A focus on the effects of the end of the Cold War, and of globalization, is more fruitful.

As a result of the end of the Cold War, the United States is likely to reduce its global ambitions and be disinclined to enter into new alliances, although US policymakers will continue to seek to enhance the role of NATO and US leadership in it. US economic rivalry with former Cold War allies will no longer be muted by the need to remain united in the face of a Soviet threat, as Joanne Gowa anticipated on theoretical grounds before the end of the Cold War.[2] Severe competitive pressures on major US corporations, resulting both from the rapidity of technological change and from globalization, are combining with anxiety about rapid increases in Japanese (and more generally, East Asian) economic capabilities relative to those of the United States to increase policymakers' concern about the competitive position of the United States in the world economy. Economic strength is ultimately the basis for economic and military power, and the United States can no longer take its economic preponderance for granted. US domestic policies will increasingly be oriented toward maintaining competitiveness in the world economy, which in turn requires technological leadership and may also involve further attempts to organize a trade and investment bloc, as in the North American Free Trade Agreement (NAFTA). Increasing concern in the United States about its commercial competitiveness was evident before the end of the Cold War but has been accentuated by the collapse of the Soviet Union. The Soviet collapse reduces both the US need for allies against another superpower and the incentive for US commercial rivals to defer to US leadership.

During the early years of the Cold War, world politics was unusually hierarchical in structure. The United States was to a remarkable degree economically and militarily self-sufficient: at least for some time, it could have managed to be quite autarchic. However, US policymakers viewed autarchy as unattractive, since it would have forced the United States to forgo the economic benefits of foreign trade and investment, and it could have led to the creation of a coalition against the United States that included the potential power centers of China, Japan, and Western Europe. The impact of autarchy on US political institutions, Assistant Secretary of State Dean Acheson told Congress in 1945, would be severe: "If you wish to control the entire trade and income of the United States, which means the life of the people, you could probably fix it so that everything produced here would be consumed here, but that would completely change our Constitution, our relations to property, human liberty, our very conception of law."[3]

The decision by the United States in 1945 to maintain a capitalist economy with increasing openness (measured by such indicators as trade and investment as shares of gross domestic product) has been a crucial source of the globalization – the increasingly global character of social, economic, and political transactions – that we now experience. And the outward orientation of US policy clearly owes a great deal to the Soviet challenge and the Cold War. Now that the Cold War is over, globalization continues apace and has implications for sovereignty that affect the United States as well as other capitalist democracies.

Yet globalization coexists with an older feature of world politics: States are independent entities with diverse interests and have no guarantees that other states will act benignly toward them or even keep their commitments. World politics is a "self-help system," as Kenneth N. Waltz has expressed it, in which states seek to maintain and insofar as feasible expand their power and in which they are concerned about their power relative to others as well as about their own welfare.[4] One of the earliest and most powerful expressions of these assumptions about human nature and human interactions was enunciated by Thomas Hobbes in the seventeenth century. Hobbes, who was thinking principally about domestic politics and civil strife but who referred also to international relations, developed an argument for unified sovereignty and authoritarian rule that led to what I will refer to as Hobbes's dilemma. Hobbes's dilemma encapsulates the existential tragedy that results when human institutions collapse and people expect the worst from each other, whether this occurs in Somalia, Bosnia, or the Corcyrean Revolution described by Thucydides: "Death thus ranged in every shape. . . . There was no length to which violence did not go. . . . Reckless audacity came to be considered as the courage of a loyal ally; prudent hesitation, specious cowardice; moderation was seen to be a cloak for unmanliness; ability to see all sides of a question, inaptness to act on any. . . . The cause of all these evils was the lust for power arising from greed and ambition."[5]

However, Hobbes's dilemma is not a statement of immutable fact, since it can be avoided; indeed, it can be seen as an expression of the dead end to which Hobbesian assumptions can lead. Properly appreciated, it is less an insightful key to world politics than a metaphor of the "realist trap."[6] Adopting an institutionalist perspective, I suggest that one way out of the realist trap is to explore further the concept of *sovereignty*. Sovereignty is often associated with realist thinking; and globalist writers sometimes argue that its usefulness and clarity have been diminished in the modern world.[7] In contrast, I will argue that sovereign statehood is an *institution* – a set of persistent and connected rules prescribing behavioral roles, constraining activity, and shaping expectations[8] – whose rules significantly modify the Hobbesian notion of anarchy. We can understand this institution by using a rationalistic argument: Its evolution can be understood in terms of the rational interests of the elites that run powerful states, in view of the institutional constraints that they face. Our prospects for understanding the present conjuncture – globalization, the end of the Cold War, the dubious prospects for a new world order – will be enhanced if we understand the nature of sovereignty.

The first section covers Hobbes's dilemma and the failure of Hobbes's solution to it and includes a brief summary of institutionalist responses at the domestic and international levels of analysis. In the section on sovereignty under conditions of high interdependence I develop an argument about how sovereignty is changing in those areas of the world characterized by "complex interdependence," areas within which multiple channels of contact exist among pluralistic societies and between which war is excluded as a means of policy.[9] In the section on zones of peace and conflict I introduce a cautionary note by arguing that we are entering a period of great diversity in world politics, with zones of conflict as well as a zone of peace, and therefore emphasizing the limits to institutionalist solutions to Hobbes's dilemma. The section on responses to conflict is an inquiry into the relevance of institutionalist thinking in a partially Hobbesian world and returns to the theme aforementioned: the prospects for world leadership in a globalized world after the Cold War.[10] The issue of leadership, of course, is of particular relevance to the United States and of especial interest to US strategists and observers.

In this chapter I do not sketch a vision of what the world should be like – if I were to do so, I would outline a Rawlsian utopia or offer a political strategy for change. Rather, as a social scientist I seek to analyze some of the actual changes in the international system from the standpoint of the United States and the institutionalist international relations theory that I have sought to develop. Rather than speculate on current events, I have sought to identify a major institution, that of sovereign statehood, and ask in light of past experience how it is changing. Hence, I do not try to survey recent changes but to focus on sovereignty both as a lens through which to view the contemporary world and as a concept with implications for international relations theory. My hope is that what may appear idiosyncratic in my account will lead to some insights even if it does not command universal acceptance.

Hobbes's dilemma and the institutionalist response

We can summarize Hobbes's dilemma in two propositions:

1. *Since people are rational calculators, self-interested, seeking gain and glory, and fearful of one another, there is no security in anarchy.* Concentrated power is necessary to create order; otherwise, "the life of man [is] solitary, poor, nasty, brutish and short."[11]
2. *But precisely because people are self-interested and power-loving, unlimited power for the ruler implies a predatory, oppressive state.* Its leaders will have ex post incentives to renege on commitments; ex ante, therefore, they will find it difficult to persuade their subjects to invest for the long term, lend the state money, and otherwise create the basis for wealth and power. This is what Martin Wight calls "the Hobbesian paradox": "The classic Realist solution to the problem of anarchy is to concentrate power in the hands of a single authority and to hope that this despot will prove a partial exception to the rule that men are bad and should be regarded with distrust."[12]

Hobbes firmly grasped the authoritarian–predatory state horn of his dilemma. Partly because he regarded reason as the servant of the passions, he was pessimistic about prospects for cooperation among people not controlled by a centralized power. His solution is to establish "Leviathan," a centralized, unified state enabled "by terror . . . to form the wills of them all to peace at home and mutual aid against their enemies abroad."[13] Yet Hobbes's solution to the problem of domestic anarchy reproduces his dilemma at the international level: *The Hobbesian solution creates a "war of all against all."* Sovereigns, "because of their independency, are in continual jealousies and in the state and posture of gladiators."[14] Under neither general anarchy nor the Hobbesian solution to it can international trade or other forms of economic exchange flourish: property rights are in both circumstances too precarious.

For Hobbes, the fact that war is reproduced at the international level is not debilitating, since by fighting each other the sovereigns "uphold the industry of their subjects." That is, the gains from international economic exchange that are blocked by warfare are dwarfed by the gains from internal economic exchange; and the "hard shell" of the nation-state, described over 30 years ago by John Herz, protects subjects from most direct depredations of international war.[15] Since it is not necessary to overcome anarchy at the international level, the contradiction inherent in the Hobbesian paradox does not pose the problems for Hobbes's approach to international relations that it poses for his solution to problems of domestic anarchy.

In much realist thought Hobbes's international solution has been reified as if it were an essential quality of the world. Yet by his own argument about the consequences of anarchy, its implications seem morally unacceptable. Only the ad hoc assumption that rulers can protect their subjects appears superficially to save his solution from condemnation by his own argument. Even in the seventeenth century, the Hobbesian external solution – anarchy tempered by the ability to defend territory – only worked for island countries such as England. The Thirty Years' War devastated much of Germany, killing a large portion of the population; the population of the state of Wurttemberg fell from 450,000 in 1620 to under 100,000 in 1639, and the great powers are estimated to have suffered 2,000,000 battle deaths.[16] If the result of accepting realist pessimism is inevitable military conflict among the great powers, locked into a mutually destructive competition from which they cannot escape, then rather than celebrating our awareness of tragedy, we had better look for a way out of the realist trap.

Both of Hobbes's solutions to his dilemma are deficient. Indeed, their deficiencies stem from the same cause: the lack of attention to how institutions can profoundly affect self-interested action by changing constraints and incentives. Institutions are not a substitute for self-interest, but they shape self-interest, both domestically and internationally.[17]

Hobbes's internal solution is politically vitiated by the Hobbesian paradox: It is only viable if the ruler has qualities that he cannot be expected to have given the assumptions of the theory. Otherwise, absolute rule will lead to a predatory state, whose economically self-defeating nature is well explained by the political economy literature with its origins in the thought of Adam Smith. In Smith's view, economic growth depends on an institutional framework for market exchange and the provision of public goods. Improvement in productivity results from the division of labor; the division of labor "is limited by the extent of the market"; markets are defined as areas over which transactions can take place at similar prices, which implies political action to establish money and remove barriers to exchange.[18]

Hobbesian monarchs had incentives to expand internal markets, since they would capture part of the gains from trade, but their time horizons were shorter than those of the states that they controlled; thus they had incentives to capture immediate gains at the expense of long-term growth, as the repeated defaults of the Hapsburg emperors on their debts illustrate. Furthermore, they had difficulty making credible commitments that would guarantee property rights precisely because these rulers were unconstrained by law. Their predatory states could provide some order but could not credibly commit themselves. They could not create proper incentives to produce and invest. Hence at the domestic level the Hobbesian solution is fundamentally flawed.

If predatory states cannot make credible domestic commitments, they can hardly do so internationally, where lack of enforceability of promises is compounded by the ever-present danger of war. Economically, therefore, the Hobbesian solution implies that international economic exchange will be limited to balanced trade not requiring credible commitments. Neither governments nor firms will knowingly and willingly invest in specific assets subject to opportunistic expropriation by others.[19] In the contemporary world Hobbesian states will not be able to reap the vastly expanded benefits of international scientific, technological, and economic exchange, without which no state can long remain a great power. And since they are vulnerable to the security dilemma, they may well become involved in destructive military conflicts.

Hence the Hobbesian solution in the contemporary world is self-defeating: It creates internal oppression, external strife, technological backwardness, and economic decay. Indeed, its failure is illustrated by the fate of the Soviet Union. The Soviet Union chose an essentially Hobbesian path: internally, by constructing a centralized authoritarian state and externally, by seeking autarchy and being suspicious of international cooperation and its institutionalized forms. Internally, the Soviet approach failed for similar reasons to those that neoclassical economic historians have cited for the poor growth records of absolute monarchies, although the Soviet Union compounded its commitment problem by arrogating all key property rights to the state – that is, to the Communist Party elite acting collectively – and by creating a cumbersome bureaucratic structure that did not have incentives to act efficiently or to innovate. Nevertheless, many of the Soviet Union's weaknesses were inherent in its inability to make credible internal or external commitments. The collapse of the Soviet Union suggests, although it does not demonstrate, the futility of Hobbesian thinking for modern states in the contemporary world.[20]

But Hobbes's dilemma remains: How can political order be created given the nature of human beings?

Institutions: constitutional government and sovereignty

The historically successful answer to Hobbes's dilemma at the internal level – constitutional government – is very different from that proposed by Hobbes. Liberal thinkers have sought to resolve Hobbes's dilemma by building reliable representative institutions, with checks on the power of rulers, hence avoiding the dilemma of accepting either anarchy or a predatory state.[21] These institutions presuppose the establishment of a monopoly of force within a given territory; hence the emphasis of realist international relations theory on the role of state power helps to explain their existence. However, regardless of institutions' dependence on state power, liberal insights are in my view important for understanding contemporary world politics. Changes in the nature of states profoundly affect international relations, and although world politics falls short of the normative standards of liberalism, it is more highly institutionalized than realists think.

For liberals, constitutional government must be combined with a framework of stable property rights that permit markets to operate in which individual incentives and social welfare are aligned with one another. "Individuals must be lured by incentives to undertake the socially desirable activities [that constitute economic growth]. Some mechanisms must be devised to bring social and private rates of return into closer parity. . . . A discrepancy between private and social benefits or costs means that some third party or parties, without their consent, will receive some of the benefits or incur some of the costs. Such a difference occurs when property rights are poorly defined, or are not enforced. If the private costs exceed the private benefits, individuals ordinarily will not be willing to undertake the activity even though it is socially profitable."[22]

The political argument of constitutionalism is familiar: Constitutionalism is to constrain the ruler, thus creating order without arbitrariness or predation. Economically, constitutional government created institutions that could make sovereigns' promises credible, thereby reducing uncertainty, facilitating the operation of markets, and lowering interest rates for loans to sovereigns, thus directly creating power resources for states with constitutional governments.[23] Constitutionalism involved a modification of the traditional conception of sovereignty, dating to the thought of Jean Bodin and reflected in that of Hobbes. This conception linked sovereignty to will, "the idea that there is a final and absolute authority in the political community."[24] This notion, however, was challenged by theorists such as Locke and Montesquieu, whose ideas were developed and applied by the American revolutionaries. The debates between 1763 and 1775 in the American colonies over relations with Britain "brought into question the entire concept of a unitary, concentrated, and absolute governmental sovereignty."[25] As James Madison put it in a letter of 1787 to Thomas Jefferson: "The great desideratum of Government is, so to modify the sovereignty as that it may be sufficiently neutral between different parts of the Society to control one part from invading the rights of another, and at the same time sufficiently controlled itself, from setting up an interest adverse to that of the entire Society."[26] Thus internal sovereignty became pluralized and constitutionalized in liberal polities.

Externally, Hobbes's dilemma of internal anarchy versus international anarchy was traditionally dealt with, if not resolved, by the institution of sovereignty. Internationally, formal sovereignty can be defined, as Hans J. Morgenthau did, as "the supreme legal authority of the nation to give and enforce the law within a certain territory and, in consequence, independence from the authority of any other nation and equality with it under international law."[27] This doctrine is traditionally seen as an outcome of the Peace of Westphalia, although Stephen Krasner has recently argued convincingly that this "Westphalian system" was not inherent in the treaties signed in 1648.[28] As Martin Wight and the English school of international relations have shown, the function of the concept of sovereignty changed over time: "It began as a theory to justify the king being master in his new modern kingdom, absolute internally. Only subsequently was it turned outward to become the justification of equality of such sovereigns in the international community."[29] By the eighteenth and nineteenth centuries, as Hedley Bull explains, the conception of sovereignty as reflecting equality and reciprocity had become the core principle of international society. The exchange of recognition of sovereignty had become "a basic rule of coexistence within the states system," from which could be derived corollaries such as the rule of nonintervention and the rights of states to domestic jurisdiction.[30]

This is not to imply that rulers were either altruistic or that they followed norms of international society that were in conflict with their conceptions of self-interest. On the contrary, I assume that self-interest, defined in the traditional terms of maintenance of rule, extension of power, and appropriation of wealth, constitutes the best explanatory principle for rulers' behavior. However, the institution of sovereignty served their interests by restraining intervention. Intervention naturally led to attempts to foster disunion and civil war and therefore reduced the power of monarchs vis-á-vis civil society. Hence, agreement on principles of nonintervention represented a cartel-type solution to a problem of collective action: In specific situations, the dominant strategy was to intervene, but it made sense to refrain *conditional on others' restraint*. With respect to intervention, as well as logically, sovereignty and reciprocity were closely linked. Traditional sovereign statehood was an international institution prescribing fairly clear rules of behavior. Indeed, between the late seventeenth and the mid-twentieth centuries it was the central institution of international society, and it continues to be so in much of the world. It is true that world politics was "anarchic" in the specific sense that it lacked common government and states had to rely on their own strategies and resources, rather than outside authority, to maintain their status and even, in extreme situations, their existence. But this "anarchy" was institutionalized by general acceptance of the norm of sovereignty. To infer from the lack of common government that the classical Western state system lacked accepted norms and practices is to caricature reality and to ignore what Bull and Wight referred to as international society.[31]

International institutions include organizations, formal rules (regimes), and informal conventions. The broad institutional issue to which traditional sovereignty was an appropriate response is how to preserve and extend order without having such severe demands placed on the institutions that they either collapse or produce more disorder. The key question is how well a set of institutions is adapted to underlying conditions, especially the nature and interests of the interacting units. The Westphalian system was well adapted, since the essential principle of sovereignty was consistent with the demand for freedom of action by states, relatively low levels of interdependence, and the desire of rulers to limit intervention that could jeopardize their control over their populations. As reductions in the cost of transportation increased the potential benefits from international trade, adaptations in the institution of sovereign statehood were made to permit powerful states to capture these gains. Colonialism enabled European states to capture such gains in the nineteenth century, but it was premised on the assumptions that intraimperial gains from trade would outweigh losses from interimperial barriers; that resistance by colonized peoples would be minimal; and that colonialism would retain legitimacy in the metropoles. By 1945 all of these premises were being challenged, not least in the United States. Oceanic hegemony, established first by Britain, then by the United States, constituted another response to the need for a set of enforceable rules to control opportunism, but it proved to be vulnerable to the consequences of its own success: the rapid growth of other countries and their resistance to hegemonic dominance. Yet as noted earlier, the restoration of traditional sovereignty would not create the basis for large-scale economic exchange under conditions of high interdependence. Fundamental contracting problems among sovereign states therefore generate a demand for international regimes: sets of formal and informal rules that facilitate cooperation among states.[32] Such regimes can facilitate mutually beneficial agreements – even though they fall far short of instituting rules that can guarantee the ex ante credibility of commitments.

Sovereignty under conditions of high interdependence

To judge from renewed debates about the concept, traditional notions of sovereignty seem to be undergoing quite dramatic change. On issues as diverse as ratification of the Maastricht Treaty for European integration and the role of the United Nations in Iraq, sovereignty has once again become a contested concept.

One way of thinking about this process has been articulated eloquently by Alexander Wendt, who puts forward the hypothesis that interactions among states are changing their concepts of identity and their fundamental interests. States will "internalize sovereignty norms," and this process of socialization will teach them that "they can afford to rely more on the institutional fabric of international society and less on individual national means" to achieve their objectives.[33] Georg Sørensen sees this process of socialization as breaking the neorealists' automatic link between anarchy and self-help.[34]

Wendt himself has modestly and perceptively acknowledged that the force of his argument depends on "how important interaction among states is for the constitution of their identities and interests."[35] Furthermore, for rational leaders to rely more on international institutions to maintain their interests, these institutions need to be relatively autonomous – that is, not easily manipulated by other states. Yet evidence seems plentiful that in contemporary pluralistic democracies, state interests reflect the views of dominant *domestic* coalitions, which are constituted increasingly on the basis of common interests with respect to the world political economy.[36] And the history of the European Community – the most fully elaborated and authoritative multilateral institution in modern history – demonstrates that states continue to use international institutions to achieve their own interests, even at the expense of their partners.

At a more basic theoretical level, no one has yet convincingly traced the microfoundations of a socialization argument: how and why those individuals with influence over state policy would eschew the use of the state as agent for their specific interests in order to enable it to conform to norms that some self-constituted authorities proclaimed to be valid. The only major attempt in recent centuries to found an international institution on untested belief – the League of Nations – was a tragic failure. The League could only have succeeded if governments had genuinely believed that peace was indivisible and that this belief was shared sufficiently by others that it would be safe to rely "on the institutional fabric of international society." But in fact, that belief was not shared by key elites, and in light of long experience with the weakness of international institutions, it is hard to blame them.[37] Idealists hope to transmute positive beliefs into reality; but the conditions for the success of this strategy are daunting indeed.

Despite the wishful thinking that seems to creep into idealistic institutionalism, its proponents usefully remind us that sovereign statehood is an institution whose meaning is not fixed but has indeed changed over time. And they have shown convincingly that sovereignty has never been simply a reflection, at the level of the state, of international anarchy, despite Kenneth Waltz's definition, which equates sovereignty with autonomy.[38] If idealistic institutionalism does not provide an answer to questions about the evolution of sovereignty, it certainly helps open the door to a discussion of these issues.

I propose a rational-institutionalist interpretation of changes in sovereignty. Just as cooperation sometimes emerges from discord, so may intensified conflict under conditions of interdependence fundamentally affect the concept of sovereignty and its functions. The concept of sovereignty that emerges, however, may be very different in different parts of the world: no linear notion of progress seems applicable here. In this section I will just sketch the argument for changes in sovereignty under conditions of complex interdependence.

Sovereignty has been most thoroughly transformed in the European Community (EC). The legal supremacy of community over national law makes the EC fundamentally different, in juridical terms, from other international organizations. Although national governments dominate the decisionmaking process in Europe, they do so within an institutional context involving the pooling and sharing of sovereignty, and in conjunction with a commission that has a certain degree of independence. As in the United States, it is difficult to identify "the sovereign institution" in the European Community: there is no single institutional expression of the EC's will. Yet, unlike in the United States, the constituent parts retain the right to veto amendments to the constitutional document (in the EC case the Treaty of Rome), and there is little doubt that secession from the community would not be resisted by force. So the European Community is not by any means a sovereign state, although it is an unprecedented hybrid, for which the traditional conception of sovereignty is no longer applicable.[39]

Interdependence is characterized by continual discord within and between countries, since the interests of individuals, groups, and firms are often at odds with one another. As global economic competition among sectors continues to increase, so will policy contention. Indeed, such discord reflects the responsiveness of democracies to constituency interests. A stateless competitive world market economy, in which people as well as factors of production could move freely, would be extremely painful for many residents of rich countries: the quasi-rents they now receive as a result of their geographical location would disappear. Matters would be even worse for people not protected by powerful governments who had to face economic agents wielding concentrated power or supported by state policy. It is not surprising, therefore, that people around the world expect protective action from their governments – and in Europe from the European Community and its institutions – and that free trade is more a liberal aspiration than a reality. In a bargaining situation, concentrating resources is valuable, and only the state can solve the collective-action problem for millions of individuals. Hence, as global competition intensifies with technological change and the decline of natural barriers to exchange, public institutions are likely to be used in an increasing variety of ways to provide advantages for their constituents. In most of the world, the state is the key institution: the state is by no means dead. In Europe, supranational and intergovernmental institutions play a significant role, along with states. Economic conflict between the EC and other major states, and among states (within and outside the EC) is likely to be accentuated by the end of the Cold War, which has reduced incentives to cooperate on economic issues for the sake of political solidarity.[40]

The mixture to be expected of multilateral cooperation and tough interstate bargaining is exemplified by recent patterns in international trade. During the 1980s the GATT dispute-settlement procedure was more actively employed than ever in the past; and it frequently led to the settlement of trade issues.[41] Furthermore, the Uruguay Round of GATT will subject many service sectors and agriculture to multilateral regulation to which they have not been subject previously and should thus lead to substantial liberalization of world trade. However, bilateralism appears to have grown during the 1980s with the negotiation of formal bilateral agreements by the United States as well as the maintenance of so-called voluntary export restraints and the use of bilateral agreements to resolve issues on which major countries such as the United States have taken aggressive unilateral action. Between 10 and 20 percent of OECD imports are subject to nontariff measures; in some sectors such as textiles the figures approach 50 percent. In December 1993 the Uruguay Round GATT negotiations were brought to a successful conclusion after having continued for almost three years beyond their original deadline of December 1990. But we simultaneously observe increases in globalization and in mercantilist policy.[42] Yet I expect that the OECD democracies will continue to have sufficient interest in securing the benefits of the international division of labor such that full-scale economic warfare, much less military conflict, will remain unlikely.

Under these conditions of complex interdependence, and even outside of the institutions of the EC, the meaning of sovereignty changes. Sovereignty no longer enables states to exert effective supremacy over what occurs within their territories: Decisions are made by firms on a global basis, and other states' policies have major impacts within one's own boundaries. Reversing this process would be catastrophic for investment, economic growth, and electoral success. What sovereignty does confer on states under conditions of complex interdependence is legal authority that can either be exercised to the detriment of other states' interests or be bargained away in return for influence over others' policies and therefore greater gains from exchange. Rather than connoting the exercise of supremacy within a given territory, sovereignty provides the state with a legal grip on an aspect of a transnational process, whether involving multinational investment, the world's ecology, or the movement of migrants, drug dealers, and terrorists. *Sovereignty is less a territorially defined barrier than a bargaining resource for a politics characterized by complex transnational networks.* Although this shift in the function of sovereignty is a result of interdependence, it does not necessarily reduce discord, since there are more bargaining issues between states that are linked by multiple channels of contact than between those with barriers between them. Such discord takes place within a context from which military threats are excluded as a policy option, but distributional bargaining is tough and continuous.

I suggest, therefore, that within the OECD area the principle and practice of sovereignty are being modified quite dramatically in response to changes in international interdependence and the character of international institutions. In the European Community the relevant changes in international institutions have a juridical dimension; indeed, one implication of European Community law is that bargaining away sovereignty to the EC may be effectively irreversible, since the EC takes over the authority formerly reserved to states. In other parts of the OECD area, states accept limits on their formerly sovereign authority as a result of agreeing to multilateral regimes with less organizational or legal authority than the EC; and sovereignty may therefore be easier to recapture, albeit at a cost, in the future. In the aspiring democracies of Eastern Europe, some of my colleagues have recently observed a pattern of "anticipatory adaptation," by which one of these countries unilaterally adopts "norms associated with membership in an [international] organization prior to its actually being accorded full status in that organization."[43] We can understand the pattern of often conflictual cooperation among the economically advanced democracies as one of "cooperation under anarchy" if we are very careful about what anarchy means, but it may be more useful to see it as a question of institutional change.[44] The institution of sovereign statehood, which was well adapted for the Westphalian system, is being modified, although not superseded, in response to the interests of participants in a rapidly internationalizing political economy.

Zones of peace and conflict: a partially Hobbesian world

Unfortunately, the institutionalist solution to Hobbes's dilemma is difficult to implement both domestically and internationally. Although constitutional democracy was remarkably successful in Western Europe and North America, it requires demanding conditions to be realized. These conditions are not met in much of the world and are unlikely to be met during the next several decades. Many countries of the former Soviet Union, much of the Middle East and Asia, and almost all of Africa do not have good prospects of becoming constitutional democracies in this generation. They have not built up social capital in the form of practices of cooperation, norms of participation, and institutions of civil society.[45] Nor do many of them have characteristics that seem correlated with the recent "third wave" of democratization, such as broad-based economic development, the prevalence of Christianity, proximity to democratic regions, and previous experience with attempts at democratization.[46] It is indeed remarkable how much democratization has taken place since the mid-1970s, and in some parts of Latin America, Eastern Europe, and Asia democracy seems to have quite a good chance of taking root. However, in many countries democratization has been shallow. Indeed, it is quite possible that the "third wave" is already beginning to recede.

Enthusiasm for a new world order might lead some to believe that even if democratization does not spread spontaneously, powerful democratic states will act to ensure democracy worldwide. In this view, collective security will be instituted not merely against aggression but against autocracy. Democracy will be achieved not from the bottom up but from the top down. This scenario seems to me to overlook issues of incentives for the powerful states and the basis of policies in interests. Democracies may act to stop starvation or extreme abuses of human rights, as in Somalia, but they are unlikely to sacrifice significant welfare for the sake of democracy, particularly when people realize how hard it is to create democracy and how ineffective intervention often is in doing so. Reintegration of China into the world economy after 1989, Western acceptance of coups in Algeria and Peru, and weak support for Yeltsin in Russia all suggest the naïveté of the view that powerful democracies will institutionalize democracy on a global basis.

What seems more likely is that domestic and international political institutions will remain highly varied in form, strength, and function in different parts of the world. The OECD area, or much of it, will remain characterized by complex interdependence. Nationalism may be strengthened in some countries but will not threaten the status of the OECD area as a zone of peace in which pluralistic conflict management is successfully institutionalized. International regimes will continue to provide networks of rules for the management of both interstate and transnational relationships, although increased economic competition is likely to both limit the growth of these regimes and provide grounds for sharp disagreements about how their rules should be applied. The domestic institutional basis for these regimes will be provided by the maintenance of pluralist, constitutional democracies that will not fight each other, whose governments are not monolithic, and between which there is sufficient confidence that agreements can be made.[47] As argued in the previous section, sovereignty is likely, in these areas, to serve less as a justification of centralized territorial control and a barrier to intervention and more as a bargaining tool for influence over transnational networks. It will be bargained away in somewhat different ways within different contexts involving security, economic issues, arrangements for political authority, and cultural linkages among countries.[48]

In other parts of the world complex interdependence will not necessarily prevail. Some of these areas may be moving towards a situation in which force is not employed and in which the domestic conditions for democracy are emerging: this seems to be true in much of East Asia and Latin America. In others relatively stable patterns of authoritarian rule may emerge or persist. For much of the developing world, therefore, some shift toward sovereignty as a bargaining resource in transnational networks will be observable. For instance, the developing countries were able to use their ability to withhold consent to the Montreal Protocol on depletion of the ozone layer to secure a small fund to facilitate the transition to production of less harmful substitutes for chlorofluorocarbons (CFCs).[49]

In much of the former Soviet Union and in parts of Africa, the Middle East, and Asia, however, neither domestic institutions nor prospects of economic gain are likely to provide sufficient incentives for international cooperation. In these zones of conflict, military conflict will be common. The loyalties of populations of states may be divided, as in Bosnia, along ethnic or national lines, and no state may command legitimacy. Secessionist movements may prompt intervention from abroad, as in Georgia. Governments of neighboring countries may regard shifts of power in nearby states as threatening to them and be prompted therefore to intervene to prevent these changes. New balances of power and alliances, offensive as well as defensive, may emerge in a classic and often bloody search for power and order. Since traditional security risks – involving fears of cross-border attacks, civil wars, and intervention – will remain paramount, sovereignty will remain highly territorial and the evolution toward sovereignty as a bargaining resource in transnational relations that is taking place in the OECD area will be retarded. Intervention and chaos may even ensue.[50]

We do not know precisely which regions, much less countries, will be characterized by endemic strife. On the basis of past conflict or ethnic division, the Middle East, much of Africa, the southern tier of the former Soviet Union, and parts of South Asia would seem to be in the greatest danger. In Chapter 6 of *Whose World Order? Uneven Globalization and the End of the Cold War*, Vladislav Zubok is relatively optimistic about the prospects that Russia will not disintegrate despite the stressful transition that it is now experiencing, and Gowher Rizvi, in Chapter 4 of the same book, emphasizes the coherence provided to the multiethnic Indian state by its democratic institutions. To suggest that Hobbesian conflict is likely to occur in certain areas of the world is not to make a deterministic argument that all countries in those geographical regions are doomed to internal collapse and external war. Nor is this to forecast a *bifurcation* of the world: there will be a range of patterns, from highly institutionalized patterns of complex interdependence (as in Western Europe) to the conflict-ridden exercise of force. The point of referring to zones of peace and zones of conflict, however, is to emphasize that in much of the world, order cannot be taken for granted (see also Chapter I of *Whose World Order? Uneven Globalization and the End of the Cold War*).

Responses to conflict: is the United States bound to lead?

Threats to the rich democracies from the zones of conflict may include terrorism, unwanted migration, the proliferation of nuclear weapons, and ecological damage. The United States and other rich countries will attempt to deter or prevent such threats to their vital economic, military, or ecological interests. They will seek to isolate conflict, reduce refugee flows, keep nuclear weapons from being used, make nuclear power plants safer or shut them down, and limit wars so that large wars do not occur. Preventive diplomacy is likely to take new forms. Relations between the North and South (both increasingly differentiated) will also be affected to some extent by feelings of injustice that some Northerners have toward the blatant inequalities of contemporary world politics.[51] However, with the Cold War ended, Northerners will demand better government in the South in return for aid: as one participant commented at a meeting in 1993, "We don't want to write more checks for Mobutu."

Some proponents of a new world order have suggested that intervention will become much more extensive, that unified action by the major powers under the aegis of the United Nations will enable these states, working within this international institution, to subordinate the sovereignty of smaller states to their rule. As Inis L. Claude and Martin Wight both pointed out early, the UN's founders in 1945 believed that the successful working of the United Nations would depend on great-power unanimity.[52] And consistent with their realist premises, the United Nations has been effective in peace enforcement only when the permanent members of the Security Council have been united.[53]

But sovereignty is not likely to be so easily superseded by joint action. Conflicts of interest among the permanent members of the Security Council will appear, as occurred with respect to Bosnia in spring 1993. Indeed, since the costs of intervention are specific to the intervenor but the benefits are diffuse, endemic free-rider problems will develop. These conflicts of interest are likely to be accentuated by one aspect of globalization: intense international economic competition. Insofar as policing the world draws attention and material resources away from commercial technological innovation, governments are likely to be increasingly wary of it. The combination of globalization and the end of the Cold War will, therefore, reduce the incentives for major powers to maintain order in the zones of conflict. We will observe more frequently the "after you, Alphonse," routine that was evident in Bosnia – with the United States urging more vigorous use of force on the Europeans and the Europeans suggesting that the United States first send ground troops that would be exposed to retaliation themselves.

In one sense the United States remains, in Joseph Nye's felicitous phrase, "bound to lead": as the Iraq and Bosnian crises made clear, only the United States has the combination of economic and military capabilities and political prestige and self-confidence to take decisive action in such situations.[54] As the Gulf War showed, the United States no longer has the material capabilities to lead unilaterally without the financial and political support of others. Hence, it has to persuade rather than dominate; and it can only persuade when, as in the Gulf but not in Bosnia, it is willing to make a major commitment itself, putting its soldiers as well as its economy and its political prestige at risk. Yet the end of the Cold War means that the United States is no longer bound to lead in the sense of clearly having to do so in order to pursue its own self-interests. On few issues outside its borders – indeed, only on those involving either influence over major centers of manufacturing and technological power, especially Western Europe and Japan, or access to oil resources, as in the Middle East – are US interests sufficiently involved that such a commitment would make sense. On other issues, US leadership will tend to be hortatory; and hortatory leadership in world politics is hardly very effective.

The general point is that the *incentives* for major countries to intervene on a global scale are unlikely to be sufficient to support effective UN action on a consistent basis. Powerful democratic countries from the zone of peace will be reluctant to intervene, except where this can be done at low cost. The great powers will indeed seek to forestall threats to their security or power, as continued intervention in Iraq shows: threat control may replace both traditional balance of power and collective security as the major principle of security. Yet maintaining peace among contentious peoples will be elusive, even if not as utopian as instituting democracy worldwide. Western reluctance to get militarily involved in Bosnia, Armenia, Georgia, or other areas of civil strife in the former Soviet Union make this point clear. The great powers are unlikely to attempt to supersede sovereignty except in highly exceptional cases such as that of Saddam Hussein's Iraq. And even if this great-power condominium were feasible over the long term, the Hobbesian paradox would still bedevil attempts to solve the problem of international political order in a broadly acceptable way through concentration of power.[55]

Under these conditions, sovereignty in the zones of conflict may retain its traditional role, moderating the effects of anarchy by conferring supreme authority over delimited territories and populations and, as in sixteenth- and seventeenth-century Europe, erecting barriers to intervention and universalization of strife. Bosnia will be divided not on the basis of the legitimacy accorded to pre-civil war provincial borders by the great powers, or in line with ethnic equity, but on the basis of the balance of military forces. The horrors of civil war will come to an end not in a meaningful new federalism but in a redivision of the area into sovereign states with unequal economic and military resources and political power. The role of outside powers will not be to dictate new lines of division, much less to invent new federal institutional arrangements, but, through credible threats of force, to limit the ability of the winners to impose their will when the human costs are too high. In 1993 the political will existed to save Sarajevo but not to preserve (or rather, restore) Bosnia. In view of the conflictual conditions prevailing in areas such as Bosnia, traditional sovereign statehood may be an appropriate international institution. At any rate, the subordination of sovereignty to great-power rule is both unacceptable to politically mobilized populations and to the great powers themselves; and the concept of sovereignty as a bargaining resource in complex interdependence is premature when the conditions for complex interdependence – most notably, the political irrelevance of military force – do not exist.

Conclusion

Globalization and the end of the Cold War have created a new situation in world politics. In some ways, the new world is more like traditional world politics than was the world from 1945 to the mid-1980s: political alignments will become more fragmented and fluid, and economic competition will not be muted by alliance cooperation. In other respects, however, the new world will be very different from the world before World War II. Globalization seems irreversible with all its implications for the permeability of borders and the transformation of sovereignty among the economically advanced democracies; and international institutions have become central to the political and military as well as the economic policies of the major states.[56]

Yet Hobbes's dilemma cannot be ignored. Without well-developed constitutional institutions, the alternatives in many countries lie between anarchy and predation, neither of which is attractive. The extensive patterns of agreement characteristic of complex interdependence depend on pluralist democratic institutions. Less ambitious forms of world order, relatively peaceful but not necessarily so cooperative, depend on stable domestic institutions, although whether they depend on democracy is not yet entirely clear. At any rate, predatory authoritarian states are likely to become involved in international conflict, and intensely divided states are particularly prone to do so. The latter are likely targets for intervention by the former. It seems unlikely not only that democracy will sweep the world but also that all states will be governed by stable institutions, even authoritarian ones. Hence, "world order" does not seem to be impending: a global security community is unlikely soon to come into existence.

Seeking to follow the Hobbesian prescription of centralized authoritarian states in an anarchic world would be disastrous: this "solution" has been shown to be deficient. Indeed, the failure of Hobbes's solution is mirrored in the misleading neorealist reification of the dichotomy between anarchy and hierarchy, as found in the work of Kenneth N. Waltz.[57] The characterization of domestic politics as hierarchic and international relations as anarchic constitutes an oversimplification that obscures crucial issues of institutional structure and choice, just as Hobbes falsely posed the issue as one of anarchy versus Leviathan. Even the Westphalian system included a degree of institutionalization in the form of a conception of sovereignty linked to reciprocity. In the short run, absent institutionalization, people may face Hobbes's dilemma; but over time, institutions help them escape it. And the growth of such institutions, international as well as domestic, has rendered obsolete the more rigid forms of realism.

The key problem of world order now is to seek to devise institutional arrangements that are consistent both with key features of international relations and the new shape of domestic politics in key countries. It will be very difficult to construct such institutions. They must be built not only by governments but by international civil society under conditions of globalization. They must be constructed not by a single hegemonic power but by several countries whose interests conflict in multiple ways. Nevertheless, among advanced democracies appropriate institutions could facilitate political and economic exchange by reducing transaction costs, providing information, and making commitments credible. The resulting benefits will accrue not only to governments but to transnational corporations and professional societies, and to some workers as well, in both developing and developed countries. But adjustment costs will be high, hence there will be losers in the short run; there may also be long-run losers, since globalization will continue to put downward pressure on wages for those workers in developed countries who can be replaced by workers in poorer parts of the world or who compete in national labor markets with such workers. Hence, domestic institutions that provide retraining, that spread the costs of adjustment, and perhaps that redistribute income on a continuing basis to globally disadvantaged groups will be essential corollaries to maintaining and strengthening international institutions in an age of globalization.

Ideal institutions will never exist, but prospective gains from international agreement will continue to provide incentives for the creation of approximations to them. Hence, among the advanced democracies I expect the strengthening of international institutions over time in response to globalization, although conflicts of interest and problems of credibility will lead to reversals from time to time and will make successful institution-building difficult. The vicissitudes of the European Monetary Union (EMU) illustrate how poorly designed schemes (in this case, violating the economic principle that open capital markets, fixed exchange rates, and independent monetary and fiscal policies are incompatible with one another) can contribute to institutional crisis or temporary stagnation.

In any event, effective international institutions are inconsistent with rigid maintenance of traditional conceptions of sovereignty. Instead, they will rest on the willingness of states to give up their legal freedom of action in return for more certainty about their environments as a result of having some control over other states' actions. Thus, insofar as globalization leads to stronger international institutions with more authority and clearer rules, it implies modification of the theory or practice of sovereignty. In the zone of peace, characterized by complex interdependence, sovereignty will become more a resource to be traded off in exchange for partial authority over others' policies than a set of barriers to intervention.

The relationship between globalization and institutional change does not only work in one direction. Globalization is fundamentally a social process, not one that is technologically predetermined. Like all other social processes, it requires the underpinning of appropriate social institutions. If the sovereignty-modifying institutions essential for continued globalization do not emerge, globalization itself can slow down or even go into reverse. If the effects of global interdependence become uncertain and unmanageable, leading to high levels of domestic and international strife, governments could (at substantial costs and in varying ways in different parts of the world) cope with it through regionalization or perhaps even (in the case of the United States if no other country) through unilateral action. Globalization and international institutionalization are mutually contingent.

However, the fragmentation of political authority in much of the world, most notably within the territory of the former Soviet Union, means that in the zones of conflict, wars, international and civil, will remain common. Nation-building was a bloody 300-year process in the West and is likely to continue to be conflict-laden in the future.[58] As Robert Putnam has shown, the sources of social capital for effective civil society are often centuries old. Investments in democratic institutions, building both on interests and on previous patterns of reciprocity, can make a difference; but we should be aware that the chances for successful democracy depend to a considerable extent on previous economic, social, and political conditions.

In the zones of conflict, the traditional functions of sovereignty – to clarify boundaries, institutionalize practices of reciprocity, and limit intervention – will probably be more salient than its use as a resource in bargaining over issues involving transnational networks. Global institutions, designed to deal with the zones of conflict, will only incrementally be able to alter traditional conceptions of sovereignty, since the danger that sovereignty was invented to deal with – chronic, ideologically justified intervention – will remain prominent. Those who try to manage these institutions should recognize the limitations on international action. International institutional strategies may be crucially important at the margin, at critical moments, but the fundamental problems involve domestic institutional development, an incremental, difficult process. The United Nations should seek to act on the margin to reduce conflict and violence but should be wary about excessive ambition and institutional overload. The most fundamental problems of state-building will not be solved by international organizations.

Nevertheless, the institutionalist perspective on international relations theory remains relevant in the zones of conflict. Institutional "solutions" applicable to the zone of peace cannot simply be transferred to the zones of conflict; to escape Hobbes's dilemma, institutional change is essential. The relevant institutional strategy is likely to be modest, incremental, and long-term in nature, but crisis managers should not lose sight of the necessity to build institutions if the crisis-creating conditions of this part of the world are eventually to be superseded. In the long run, norms and values need to be modified, with shifts in the conception of sovereignty reflecting changes in domestic as well as international and transnational politics. Such processes – whether referred to as social learning or otherwise – are important to study although beyond the scope of this chapter.

Social scientists viewing the new world order should be humble on two dimensions. Our failure to foresee the end of the Cold War should make us diffident about our ability to predict the future. And the weakness of our knowledge of the conditions for constitutional democracy and for peace should make us reluctant to propose radical new plans for global democratization or peacekeeping. Nevertheless, we can go beyond the Hobbesian solution to Hobbes's dilemma of anarchy and order: We can focus on how institutions embodying the proper incentives can create order without predation within societies, and how even much weaker international institutions can moderate violence and facilitate cooperation in international relations. Strong institutions cannot be suddenly created: Both constitutional democracy and a reciprocity-laden conception of sovereignty emerged over a period of centuries. Nevertheless, it is imperative to avoid the magnitude of violence and dysfunction that occurred in the West. We should encourage the creation and maintenance of institutions, domestic and international, that provide incentives for the moderation of conflict, coherent decision-making to provide collective goods, and the promotion of economic growth. It is in such lasting institutions that our hopes for the future lie.

Notes

1 I am grateful for comments on earlier versions of this paper to Stanley Hoffmann, Nannerl O. Keohane, and Jack Levy; to my fellow contributors to *Whose World Order? Uneven Globalization and the End of the Cold War*, who met near Copenhagen on May 14–16, 1993, especially to Michael Zürn and the editors; and to participants at a seminar of the Olin Institute at the Center for International Affairs, Harvard University, March 1, 1993, especially to Tom Berger, Tom

Christensen, Barbara Farnum, Yuen Khong, Lisa Martin, Celeste Wallander, and Richard Weitz. An earlier version of this chapter appeared as a working paper (May 1993) of the Center for International Affairs, Harvard University.

2 Joanne Gowa, "Bipolarity, Multipolarity and Free Trade," *American Political Science Review* 83 no. 4 (December 1989): 1245–1256.

3 U.S. House, Special Committee on Post-War Economic Policy and Planning, *Hearings* (Washington, DC: GPO, 1945), p. 1082. Cited in Gabriel Kolko, *The Politics of War: The World and United States Foreign Policy, 1943–1945* (New York: Vintage Books of Random House, 1968), p. 254.

4 Kenneth N. Waltz, *Theory of International Politics* (Reading, Mass.: Addison Wesley, 1979).

5 Thucydides, *The Peloponnesian War*, Book 3, paras. 81–82.

6 On the "realist trap," see Robert O. Keohane, "Theory of World Politics: Structural Realism and Beyond," in Keohane, *International Institutions and State Power: Essays in International Relations Theory* (Boulder: Westview Press, 1989), pp. 35–73, especially pp. 65–66.

7 Hans-Henrik Holm and Georg Sørensen, "A New World Order: The Withering Away of Anarchy and the Triumph of Individualism? Consequences for IR-Theory," *Cooperation and Conflict* 28, no. 3 (1993): 265–301.

8 For this definition, see Robert O. Keohane, *International Institutions and State Power*, pp. 3–7 and Chap. 7.

9 Robert O. Keohane and Joseph S. Nye, Jr., *Power and Interdependence: World Politics in Transition* (Boston: Little, Brown, 1977 and 1989).

10 In terms of the paradigms discussed by Holm and Sørensen in "A New World Order," this chapter could be considered to be "pluralist" but sympathetic to realism's emphasis on the significance of conflicts of interest and interstate power competition in world politics.

11 Thomas Hobbes, *Leviathan* (Paris, 1651), Book 1, Chap. 13.

12 Martin Wight, *International Theory: The Three Traditions* (New York: Holmes & Meier, 1992), p. 35.

13 *Leviathan*, Part 2, Chap. 17.

14 *Leviathan*, Part I, Chap. 13.

15 John M. Herz, *International Politics in the Atomic Age* (New York: Columbia University Press, 1959).

16 Evan Luard, *War in International Society* (New Haven: Yale University Press, 1987), p. 247, says that perhaps 40 percent of the rural and town population of Germany may have died, although this estimate may be too high. On battle deaths, see Charles Tilly, *Coercion, Capital and European States, AD* 990–1990 (Oxford: Basil Blackwell, 1990), p. 165.

17 Sovereign statehood in my view has helped shape states' conceptions of self-interest. For instance, great-power intervention in Africa during the Cold War was focused on helping the great power's clients gain power within unified states, rather than on promoting fragmentation. The one major attempt to change boundaries by war – Somalia's invasion of Ethiopia in the late 1970s – led to withdrawal of US support for Somalian military actions and a resounding defeat. For an astute analysis, see Robert H. Jackson and Carl G. Rosberg, "Why Africa's Weak States Persist: The Empirical and the Juridical in Statehood," *World Politics* 35, no. 1 (October 1982): 1–24.

18 Adam Smith, *An Inquiry into the Nature and Causes of the Wealth of Nations* (1776), especially Volume 1, Book 1, Chaps. 1, 3, 4, and Book 4. Edited by Edwin Cannan (Chicago: University of Chicago Press, 1976), p. 8.

19 Oliver Williamson, *The Economic Institutions of Capitalism* (New York: Free Press, 1985).

20 The same point applies for all authoritarian states: somehow, the state must be

able to make credible commitments not to exploit members of society whose activities create wealth. Stable property rights require constitutional government, although not necessarily democracy. Hence the desire for economic growth provides a set of incentives for constitutionalism, as can be observed in Korea and Taiwan and perhaps in the future will emerge in China. But these incentives are not necessarily decisive; other favorable conditions have to apply before constitutionalism can be effectively instituted.

21 See Margaret Levi, *Of Rule and Revenue* (Berkeley: University of California Press, 1988), especially Chap. 1.

22 Douglass C. North and Robert Paul Thomas, *The Rise of the Western World* (Cambridge: Cambridge University Press, 1973), pp. 2–3.

23 Charles P. Kindleberger, *A Financial History of Western Europe* (London: George Allen & Unwin, 1984); Douglass C. North and Barry R. Weingast, "Constitutions and Commitment: The Evolution of Institutions Governing Public Choice in Seventeenth-Century England," *Journal of Economic History* 49, no. 4 (December 1989): 803–832.

24 F. H. Hinsley, *Sovereignty*, 2nd ed. (Cambridge: Cambridge University Press, 1986), p. 1.

25 Bernard Bailyn, *The Ideological Origins of the American Revolution* (Cambridge: Belknap Press of Harvard University Press, 1967), pp. 201–229.

26 Madison to Jefferson, October 24, 1787. J. P. Boyd, ed., *The Papers of Thomas Jefferson* (Princeton: Princeton University Press, 1955), pp. 278–279.

27 Hans J. Morgenthau, *Politics Among Nations*, 4th ed. (New York: Knopf, 1967), p. 305.

28 Stephen D. Krasner, "Westphalia and All That," draft chapter (October 1992) for Judith Goldstein and Robert O. Keohane, eds, *Ideas and Foreign Policy: Beliefs, Institutions and Political Change* (Ithaca, NY: Cornell University Press, forthcoming).

29 Wight, *International Theory*, pp. 2–3.

30 Hedley Bull, *The Anarchical Society* (New York: Columbia University Press, 1977), pp. 34–37. Martin Wight makes this connection between sovereignty and reciprocity explicit by saying that "reciprocity was inherent in the Western conception of sovereignty." *Systems of States* (Leicester: Leicester University Press, 1977), p. 135.

31 One difficulty with realist characterizations of anarchy is that they conflate three different meanings of the term: (1) lack of common government; (2) insignificance of institutions; and (3) chaos, or Hobbes's "war of all against all." Only the first meaning can be shown to be true in general of international relations. For a good discussion of anarchy in international relations, see Helen V. Milner, "The Assumption of Anarchy in International Relations Theory: A Critique," *Review of International Studies* 17, no. 1 (January 1991): 67–86.

32 Robert O. Keohane, *After Hegemony: Cooperation and Discord in the World Political Economy* (Princeton: Princeton University Press, 1984); Stephen D. Krasner, ed., *International Regimes* (Ithaca, NY: Cornell University Press, 1982). Note that a demand for international regimes does not create its own supply; hence a functional theory does not imply, incorrectly, that efficient institutions always emerge or that we live in the (institutionally) best of all possible worlds.

33 Alexander Wendt, "Anarchy Is What States Make of It," *International Organization* 46, no. 2 (Spring 1992): 414–415.

34 Georg Sørensen, "The Limits of Neorealism: Western Europe After the Cold War," paper presented at the Nordic International Studies Association (NISA) Inaugural Conference, Oslo, August 18–19, 1993, p. 9.

35 Wendt, "Anarchy Is What States Make of It," p. 423.

36 Peter J. Katzenstein, *Small States in World Markets* (Ithaca, NY: Cornell

University Press, 1984); Peter Gourevitch, *Politics in Hard Times* (Ithaca, NY: Cornell University Press, 1986); Helen V. Milner, *Resisting Protectionism* (Princeton: Princeton University Press, 1988); Ronald Rogowski, *Commerce and Coalitions* (Princeton: Princeton University Press, 1989); Jeffry A. Frieden, "National Economic Policies in a World of Global Finance," *International Organization* 45, no. 4 (Autumn 1991): 425–452; Andrew Moravcsik, "Liberalism and International Relations Theory," working paper, no. 92–6, Center for International Affairs, Harvard University, October 1992.

37 See Inis L. Claude, *Power and International Relations* (New York: Random House, 1962).

38 For Waltz a sovereign state "decides for itself how it will cope with its internal and external problems." That is, sovereignty is the equivalent of self-help, which derives from anarchy. Waltz, *Theory of International Politics*, p. 96. A brilliant critique of Waltz's failure to incorporate a historical dimension in his theory is by John Gerard Ruggie, "Continuity and Transformation in the World Polity: Toward a Neorealist Synthesis," *World Politics* 35 (January 1983): 261–285. For Ruggie's chapter, other commentaries, and a reply by Waltz, see Robert O. Keohane, ed., *Neorealism and Its Critics* (New York: Columbia University Press, 1986).

39 For general discussions see Robert O. Keohane and Stanley Hoffmann, *The New European Community: Decisionmaking and Institutional Change* (Boulder: Westview Press, 1991); and Alberta M. Sbragia, ed., *Europolitics: Institutions and Policymaking in the "New" European Community* (Washington, DC: Brookings, 1992). On the European Court of Justice and neofunctional theory, see Anne-Marie Burley and Walter Mattli, "Europe Before the Court: A Political Theory of Legal Integration," *International Organization* 47, no. 1 (Winter 1993): 41–76. It is not clear that the Maastricht Treaty, even if ratified, will fundamentally alter practices relating to sovereignty in the EC. On Maastricht, see Wayne Sandholtz, "Choosing Union: Monetary Politics and Maastricht," *International Organization* 47, no. 1 (Winter 1993): 1–40.

40 For a general argument about the "security externalities" of agreements to open borders to free trade, see Joanne Gowa, "Bipolarity, Multipolarity and Free Trade," *American Political Science Review* 83, no. 4 (December 1989): 1245–1256.

41 Robert E. Hudec, Daniel L. M. Kennedy, and Mark Sgarabossa, "A Statistical Profile of GATT Dispute Settlement Cases: 1948–1990," unpublished manuscript, University of Minnesota Law School, 1992.

42 See Helge Hveem, "Hegemonic Rivalry and Antagonistic Interdependence: Bilateralism and the Management of International Trade," paper presented at the First Pan-European Conference in International Studies, Heidelberg, September 16–20, 1992. His figures come from the UNCTAD database on trade control measures. On p. 16 Hveem quotes Robert Gilpin about the "complementary development" of globalization and mercantilism, citing "The Transformation of the International Political Economy," *Jean Monnet Chair Papers* (The European Policy Unit at the European University Institute, Firenze).

43 Stephan Haggard, Marc A. Levy, Andrew Moravcsik, and Kalypso Nicolaides, "Integrating the Two Halves of Europe: Theories of Interests, Bargaining and Institutions," in Robert O. Keohane, Joseph S. Nye, and Stanley Hoffmann, eds, *After the Cold War: International Institutions and State Strategies in Europe, 1989–1991* (Cambridge, Mass: Harvard University Press, 1993), p. 182.

44 Kenneth A. Oye, ed., *Cooperation Under Anarchy* (Princeton: Princeton University Press, 1986).

45 Robert D. Putnam, with Robert Leonardi and Rafaella Nanetti, *Making Democracy Work: Civic Traditions in Modern Italy* (Princeton: Princeton University Press, 1993).

46　See Samuel P. Huntington, *The Third Wave: Democratization in the Late Twentieth Century* (Norman: Oklahoma University Press, 1991), especially Chap. 2 (pp. 31–108).

47　Democratic pluralism in necessary for the multiple channels of contact between societies characteristic of complex interdependence. With respect to restraints on the use of force, it seems clear from the large literature on democracy and war that democracies have rarely, if ever (depending on one's definition), fought one another, although they vigorously fight nondemocracies. However, nondemocracies have often been at peace with one another, so democracy is certainly not necessary to peace. Furthermore, until recently democracies have been relatively few and either scattered or allied against a common enemy (or both); so the empirical evidence for the causal impact of mutual democracy is weak. Among the OECD countries peace seems ensured by a combination of mutual economic and political interests, lack of territorial conflict, and mutual democracy. On theoretical grounds, however, no one has yet succeeded in showing that mutual democracy is sufficient: to do so, one would have to develop and test a convincing theory of why democracies should not fight one another. For some of this literature, see Michael Doyle, "Kant, Liberal Legacies and Foreign Affairs," *Philosophy and Public Affairs* 12 (1983): 205–235 and 323–353 (two-part article); Zeev Maos and Nasrin Abdolali, "Regime Types and International Conflict," *Journal of Conflict Resolution* 33 (1989): 3–35; and Georg Sørensen, "Kant and Processes of Democratization: Consequences for Neorealist Thought," *Journal of Peace Research* 29 (1992): 397–414. My thinking on this issue has been affected by a stimulating talk given at the Harvard Center for International Affairs by Professor Joanne Gowa of Princeton University on May 6, 1993, and by a just-completed PhD dissertation at Harvard University by John Owen on sources of "democratic peace."

48　My characterization of emerging patterns of world politics has much in common with the stimulating discussion of "plurilateralism" offered by Philip G. Cerny in "Plurilateralism: Structural Differentiation and Functional Conflict in the Post-Cold War World Order," *Millenium: Journal of International Studies* 22 (Spring 1993): 27–52.

49　Edward A. Parson, "Protecting the Ozone Layer," in Peter M. Haas, Robert O. Keohane, and Marc A. Levy, eds, *Institutions for the Earth: Sources of Effective International Environmental Protection* (Cambridge Mass.: MIT Press, 1993), pp. 49–50.

50　For a similar argument, contrasting a liberal core and a realist periphery, see James M. Goldgeier and Michael McFaul, "A Tale of Two Worlds: Core and Periphery in the Post Cold War Era," *International Organization* 46, no. 1 (Spring 1992): 467–492.

51　For an argument that humanitarian concerns played a key role in the provision of foreign aid, see David Halloran Lumsdaine, *Moral Vision in International Politics: The Foreign Aid Regime, 1949–1989* (Princeton: Princeton University Press, 1993).

52　Wight points out the Hobbesian premises of the charter – in the event of a lack of unanimity "the social contract will be dissolved." He sardonically remarks that "it is perhaps difficult to find the United Nations intellectually appetizing, but one of its few thrills is in seeing how the penetrating vision of a great political philosopher has this kind of prophetic quality." Martin Wight, *International Theory*, pp. 35–36. Inis L. Claude, *Power and International Relations* (New York: Random House, 1962).

53　The exception is the UN operation in Korea, which was made possible by a Soviet boycott of the Security Council and which permitted the council to approve UN action without Soviet consent. Certain peacekeeping operations of the 1950s and 1960s were also somewhat successful despite great power disagreement.

54 Joseph S. Nye, Jr., *Bound to Lead: The Changing Nature of American Power* (New York: Basic Books, 1990).
55 The Hobbesian paradox implies that if the Security Council became effective, it would be expected to act in the interests of its dominant members and thus to become oppressive.
56 On international institutions, see Keohane, Nye, and Hoffmann, *After the Cold War*.
57 Waltz, *Theory of International Politics*, Chap. 5.
58 Classic accounts include Barrington Moore, Jr, *Social Origins of Dictatorship and Democracy* (Boston: Beacon Press, 1966); Theda Skocpol, *States and Social Revolution: A Comparative Analysis of France, Russia and China* (Cambridge: Cambridge University Press, 1979); Charles Tilly, ed., *The Formation of National States in Western Europe* (Princeton: Princeton University Press, 1975).

5 Risk, threat, and security institutions[1]

Celeste A. Wallander and
Robert O. Keohane

(1999)

The post-Cold War world presents challenges for both policy and theory in international relations. One important challenge to international relations theory is the anomaly of NATO's continuity after the Cold War. Inspired by the Soviet threat, created under American leadership, designed to bolster the security of its members against the Soviet Union by aggregating defence capabilities, NATO ought to be either collapsing or withering away: dying with a bang or a whimper. Indeed, since the end of the Cold War theorists working in the realist tradition have clearly and forcefully predicted NATO's demise, if not in "days" then in "years."[2]

This prediction turned out to be wrong. More than nine years after the Berlin Wall was dismantled and seven years after the Soviet Union collapsed, NATO not only continues to exist but is growing and taking on new tasks. It is an obvious magnet for states of Central and Eastern Europe; it plays a central role in the former Yugoslavia; and it clearly remains the primary instrument of American security policy in Europe. Reports of NATO's death were exaggerated: like other established international institutions, it remains valuable because of the uncertainty that would result if it disappeared.[3]

What went wrong with realist theory and right with NATO? In this chapter, we develop a typology of security institutions and propositions on their form, function, persistence, and change. We use contractual theories of institutions to suggest answers to a general question which the response of NATO to the end of the Cold War illustrates: what happens to alliances when their precipitating threats disappear? Our framework and propositions complement the more in-depth analyses of the effects and dynamics of a variety of security institutions developed by the authors in Chapters 2–10 of *Imperfect Unions: Security Institutions over Time and Space*.

The core of our analysis is based on recognition that security institutions, like any institutions, vary both in their levels of institutionalization and in their forms. Major wars, and long struggles such as the Cold War, generate alliances, which are institutionalized security coalitions designed to aggregate capabilities and coordinate strategies to cope with perceived threats. When threats disappear, the original *raison d'être* of alliances would appear to have vanished and we might expect the institutions to be discarded. But when threats disappear, other security problems remain. Hence, efforts may be made to maintain the institutionalized security coalitions, but to transform their functions to cope with the more diffuse set of security problems we characterize as risks, and thus to transform alliances into security management institutions. Such institutional transitions have been difficult to effect. After the Napoleonic Wars and this century's two World Wars, attempts were made to transform alliances or alignments into security management institutions; and only in the earliest case, that of the Concert of Europe, did this transformation work. Yet in the contemporary case of NATO, it appears that an alliance is being transformed into a security management institution. We seek to understand, through conceptual and historical analysis, what the conditions are for such a successful transformation to occur. In doing so, we both broaden institutional theory beyond its roots in political economy and deepen its explanatory power by advancing institutional hypotheses on change.

To help us understand the transformation of security institutions, we construct a new typology of security coalitions, based on three dimensions: the degree to which they are institutionalized, whether they are organized exclusively or inclusively, and whether they are designed to cope with threats or risks. We use this typology to generate two key propositions. The first proposition is a standard institutional hypothesis: highly institutionalized alliances are more likely to persist, despite changes in the environment, than non-institutionalized alignments. Our second proposition, more novel, builds on the other two dimensions of our typology. Alliances are exclusive security institutions, designed principally to deal with threats from non-members. Some alliances, however, also have to cope with risks of conflicts among members, and therefore develop an "inclusive" aspect, oriented toward risk-management. Our key hypothesis is that these more complex alliances are more likely to be able to adapt to the ending of threats by elaborating and developing those practices designed to cope with risks rather than threats. In our terminology, the rules and practices of "hybrid" institutions will be more "portable" than the rules and practices of single-purpose alliances focused only on threat.

We explain our typology in the first section of this chapter, by elaborating our distinctions between threat and risk and exclusivity versus inclusivity; and by discussing what we mean by institutionalization. In the second section we set out our hypotheses, which we illustrate with reference to previous situations in which threats disappeared, and with reference to NATO. However, we do not pretend to test our hypotheses in this chapter. A number of the authors of other chapters in *Imperfect Unions* use our typology, or some of our hypotheses, to structure their empirical investigations. The evidence is mixed and far from comprehensive; but our concepts and arguments seem relevant to change in security institutions, and to NATO in particular.

The final section of this chapter argues for the reframing of the problem of NATO enlargement – from one of alliance expansion to institutional change. We argue that NATO is changing from an alliance to a security management institution; that this transformation should be encouraged because it encourages stability in Europe; and that it implies the continued expansion of NATO to include all countries in the region that can reliably be counted on to support its principles and follow its rules. Eventually, NATO as a security management institution could even include a democratic Russia. Refocusing the issue as one of institutional change rather than mere expansion sheds new light both on the criticisms of NATO expansion and on the conditions that should be fulfilled for such expansion to continue.

A typology of security institutions

Some commonly understood rules are intrinsic to all diplomatic interchange, so in that sense, all of international politics is institutionalized. But the institutionalization of security coalitions (as of other practices in international relations) varies greatly, from minimal to substantial. As we will see, it matters for a security coalition how institutionalized its practices are.

Institutionalization can be measured along three dimensions: commonality, specificity, and differentiation.[4]

1. Commonality refers to the degree to which expectations about appropriate behavior are shared by participants.
2. Specificity refers to the degree to which specific and enduring rules exist, governing the practices of officials, obligations of states, and legitimate procedures for changing collective policy. Greater specificity is reflected in more detailed and demanding primary rules, specifying what members must do; and secondary rules, indicating how rules can be changed or recognized as binding, that are clear, more comprehensive, and that provide for rule-change and recognition that preclude vetoes by individual members.[5] For example, the European Union now is more institutionalized in this sense than its predecessor, the European Economic Community, was in the 1970s; and NATO, although less institutionalized than the European Union, is more institutionalized than it was in the 1950s.
3. Functional differentiation refers to the extent to which the institution assigns different roles to different members. As Kenneth Waltz has argued, one mark of an "anarchic" international system is that it is composed of "like units," performing similar functions in so far as their differing capabilities permit them to do so.[6] Conversely, a mark

of an institution is that it organizes and legitimizes a division of responsibility, with different participants performing different functions.

Threats and risks

The security strategies with which we are concerned in this chapter involve measures to protect the territorial integrity of states from the adverse use of military force; efforts to guard state autonomy against the political effects of potential use; and policies designed to prevent the emergence of situations that could lead to the use of force against one's territory or vital interests.[7] Where a state's leaders regard it as facing a positive probability that another state will either launch an attack or seek to threaten military force for political reasons, it faces a *threat*. Threats pertain when there are actors that have the capabilities to harm the security of others and that are perceived by their potential targets as having intentions to do so. When no such threat exists, either because states do not have the intention or the capability to harm the security of others, states may nevertheless face a security *risk*.[8]

To illustrate the distinction, consider the classic security dilemma as discussed by John Herz and Robert Jervis. Herz and Jervis explained that when states with purely defensive or status quo intentions adopt policies to provide for their own security, they can unintentionally lead other states to take countermeasures that lead toward a spiral of mutual fear and antagonism.[9] Although intentional threat is absent, states may still face serious security problems.

In modern informational terms, the essence of the security dilemma lies in uncertainty and private information. As realists have long recognized, the key problem for policy-makers is the difficulty of distinguishing revisionist states with exploitative preferences from status quo states with defensive intentions. It may be possible for security dilemmas to be avoided or ameliorated if status quo states can provide credible information to distinguish themselves from revisionists eager to exploit the unwary.[10]

Another way to understand the distinction between threats and risks is to build on an analytical distinction between collaboration and coordination first drawn by Arthur Stein and referred to in the Introduction. While collaboration problems, such as Prisoners' Dilemma, entail threats because they involve the potential for cheating and exploitation, coordination (or bargaining) problems do not entail threats. The problem in coordination situations is that the players will be unable to come to an agreement because of competitive incentives, but if they can manage to agree both are satisfied with the outcome and would not exploit the other. Lisa Martin has further elaborated the distinction and discusses assurance problems, which are akin to coordination problems in that they do not involve the threat of exploitation and cheating but instead entail the risk that states will fail to achieve or maintain mutually beneficial cooperation because of fear, mistrust, and uncertainty.[11]

Thus, security arrangements may be designed not only to cope with security threats, as are classic alliances, but also with security risks. Because the means to deal with these different security problems vary, we would expect institutional forms to vary as well. Institutions meant to cope with security threats will have rules, norms, and procedures to enable the members to identify threats and retaliate effectively against them. Institutions meant to cope with security risks will have rules, norms, and procedures to enable the members to provide and obtain information and to manage disputes in order to avoid generating security dilemmas. This distinction is the first building-block in our typology.

Inclusivity and exclusivity

Another dimension along which security coalitions can vary is their inclusivity or exclusivity. Coalitions can be designed to involve all states that could pose threats or risks, or they can deliberately exclude some of them. Collective security arrangements are inclusive, since they are designed to deal with threats among members; alliances are exclusive because they deter and defend against external threats.[12]

Although in principle states are free to choose either inclusive or exclusive strategies to cope with both threats and risks, exclusive strategies seem better suited to coping with threats, while inclusive strategies appear to be better able to cope with and manage risks.[13] Threats to national security posed by states with aggressive intentions are best met by aggregating capabilities and sending strong and credible signals of resolve, as in classic balancing alliances. Collective security arrangements are often vulnerable and ineffective because aggressive states may be able to exploit their symmetrically framed rules and processes, which present opportunities for obfuscation, delay, or vetoing action.[14] On the other hand, the problems posed for national security by risks and the security dilemma tend to be exacerbated by exclusive coalitions, because the institutions associated with such coalitions do not provide for transparency and information exchange between those states that are most likely to come into armed conflict with one another. Indeed, close coordination within alliances, along with distant relationships between them, may exacerbate suspicions associated with the security dilemma.

Combining the dimensions

Our distinctions between threats and risks, and inclusive versus exclusive institutions, yield the fourfold typology of Figure 5.1.[15] For reasons sketched above, the most successful arrangements will be found in the lower-left and upper-right sections of the diagram: exclusive arrangements will be associated with threats (alliances and alignments) and inclusive coalitions will be associated with situations of risk (security management).

Figure 5.2 directs attention to the two most important and successful types of security coalitions: (i) inclusive coalitions designed to deal with risk, and (ii) exclusive coalitions designed to cope with threat – the upper right and lower left section of Figure 5.1, respectively. Let us first consider inclusive coalitions.

Diplomatic conferences called to discuss specific issues, such as the Geneva Conference of 1954 on Korea and Indochina, are inclusive and only minimally institutionalized. The Geneva Conference included China, the Soviet Union, Britain, France, and (reluctantly) the United States, as well as the Vietminh. It developed rules, but they were not highly elaborated; the expectations of participants were not closely aligned, and the institution did not prescribe functionally differentiated roles.

We use the term "security management institution" to denote an inclusive, risk-oriented arrangement with highly institutionalized practices. The Concert of Europe in the nineteenth century and the Organization for Security and Cooperation in Europe today provide clear examples of security management institutions.[16] The League of Nations and United Nations were designed in part as collective security institutions (inclusive, seeking to cope with threats), but they also served as security management institutions, seeking to deal with risks – as exemplified by United Nations efforts at peaceful settlement of disputes under Chapter 6 of the Charter.

Alignments and alliances, unlike diplomatic conferences and security management institutions, are directed against specific threats and are exclusive in membership form. We make a clear distinction between alliances – which we

Participation Criteria:			
inclusive		collective security	**security management institutions and diplomatic conferences**
exclusive		**alliances and alignments**	out-of-area coalitions
		threat	risk
		Situation facing states	

Figure 5.1 Variation in security coalitions

Participation Criteria and Focus of the Arrangement:	inclusive/ risk	diplomatic conferences	security management institutions
	exclusive/ threat	alignments	alliances
		minimally	highly

How institutionalized are the coalitions?

Figure 5.2 Institutional variation in security arrangements

define as exclusive security institutions oriented towards threat – and alignments. Alignments are minimally institutionalized: examples include the 1967 Arab coalition against Israel and the coalition supporting UN action against Iraq during the Gulf War in 1990–1, which included both Syria and the United States.[17] In its earliest years, before being institutionalized, NATO was an alignment. Alliances, in contrast, are institutionalized security coalitions directed against specific threats. Alliances have rules, norms, and procedures to enable the members to identify threats and retaliate effectively against them. Expectations about actions in the event of future contingencies are shared among members; rules of behavior are specific; and different roles are assigned to different participants. NATO, of course, is a model alliance, highly institutionalized.[18]

The key points are that we expect successful security coalitions to develop institutionalized rules and practices (as both NATO and UN peacekeeping have done); and that these rules and practices will broadly reflect the functions performed by the institutions. Institutions meant to cope with security threats will have rules, norms, and procedures to enable the members to identify threats and retaliate effectively against them. Institutions meant to cope with security risks will have rules, norms, and procedures to enable the members to provide and obtain information and to manage disputes in order to avoid generating security dilemmas.

Our categories are ideal types. Institutionalization is always a matter of degree and mapping actual security institutions into Figure 5.2 would yield a continuum in the horizontal dimension. The vertical dimension would also be a continuum: alliances, as we will see in the case of NATO, may seek to manage the risks of conflict among members as well as to amass resources and coordinate members' actions against external threat. That is, alliances may function in part as security management institutions.[19] Nevertheless our typology makes useful distinctions which are helpful in explaining change in security coalitions and institutions, now and in the past. In particular, it highlights the important risk–threat distinction, which is often overlooked; and it emphasizes the importance of institutionalization for the actual operation of security coalitions.[20]

Institutional hypotheses on change and adaptation

Institutional theory in international relations has addressed itself principally to two questions: (i) what explains variation in degree of institutionalization and institutional form? and (ii) what are the principal effects of international institutions? An explanation for institutional change requires, in addition to these foundations, an integrated understanding of how changes in the environment create pressures for institutional change, and how character-istics of institutions themselves affect which changes actually take place. In this section, we will begin by focusing on exogenous changes, stemming from the environment; then discuss endogenous sources of change; and finally, illustrate our hypotheses by discussing institutional change after three major wars: the Napoleonic Wars, and the First and Second World Wars.

Uncertainty, problem durability, and issue density

Institutions arise, according to institutional theory, largely because of uncertainty, which generates a need for information. Uncertainty means not having information about other states' intentions and likely choices. Since choosing a strategy depends not merely on what a state wants but also on what it believes other states seek, uncertainty can be a very significant prob-lem in security relations.[21] Governments therefore find it worthwhile to invest in information that will enable them to design strategies that are appropriate to their environments. One way of investing in information is to create institu-tions that provide it. Institutions can serve as the informational and signalling mechanisms that enable states to get more information about the interests, preferences, intentions, and security strategies of other states. They reduce uncertainty by providing credible information.[22] Furthermore, successful institutions may regularize the behavior of states belonging to them, making it more predictable and decreasing uncertainty. Hence, if it is rational for states to invest in information, they may also invest in institutions that reduce uncertainty.

However, it is not only the information one receives, but the information one is able to provide to others that contributes to diplomatic success. This point has two distinct aspects. First, if one country influences the way others see the world – as the United States has during recent decades – it gains what Joseph S. Nye calls "soft power."[23] Much of US soft power is exercised through international institutions, ranging from the International Monetary Fund (IMF) to NATO. Second, within a given perceptual framework, being able to provide credible information to others is a source of influence.[24] Since uncertainty is high in world politics, the credibility of a state's own threats and promises becomes a factor in its ability to exercise influence over the behaviour of others. Hence, having a reputation for keeping commitments can be an asset.

Often theorists in the realist tradition argue that because institutions are costly to join (that is, they constrain state strategies) they will be avoided. However, this misses the point: it is precisely *because* actions are costly that they are credible and therefore can be valuable to self-interested states.[25] Institutions *enable* state strategies because it is costly to join and abide by them – thus, they are instruments for credible signalling. The question is whether the enabling benefits of joining a security institution are worth the costs and constraints. Institutionalist theory holds that to understand the demand for security institutions, we will need – as with other international institutions – to understand both how they provide information to states and how they affect credibility and reputation.

Uncertainty provides a generic reason for establishing security institutions. But institutions are costly to create, and do not arise automatically simply because they could be useful. We therefore need to ask what will affect the willingness of members (or potential members) to pay the costs of creating and sustaining the institutions. The key choice for potential members is between achieving cooperation on an *ad hoc* basis and investing in institutions. *Ad hoc* cooperation entails lower investment costs but forgoes the long-term benefits of having enduring rules and practices that facilitate future cooperation at low cost. Two variables should affect the willingness of potential members to make institution-specific investments: the durability of the problems and issue density.

The durability of the problems being faced is of obvious importance, since the longer challenges are expected to last, the more sensible it is to invest in institutions to deal with them. Thus variations in states' expectations of the durability of their security problems should help to explain variations in institutionalization. States will be more willing to pay for institutions when they expect the threat they face to be durable rather than transitory. For forty years after 1949, Western leaders expected what John F. Kennedy would call "a long twilight struggle" against the threat of Soviet communism. The establishment of NATO depended on its members' beliefs that the threats they faced were durable.

Issue density refers to "the number and importance of issues arising within a given policy space."[26] In dense policy spaces, issues are interdependent, and need to be dealt with in a coordinated way to avoid negative externalities from policies for one issue on other policies. In dense policy spaces, institutions may achieve "economies of scale." For example, the issue density in European security relations from 1946 to 1949, when NATO was created, was substantial: in addition to deterring a Soviet attack, the potential Western allies were faced with the problem of a weak and possibly revanchist divided Germany, the need ultimately to rearm Germany yet to control it, French distrust of German intentions, and devastated economies of the potential allies which virtually precluded substantial defence spending by individual states.[27] Issue density can be a function of domestic politics, high levels of economic and military interdependence, or close connections between internal politics and the external environment.

More generally, issue density means that interactions are likely to be repeated on related issues, providing the scope for strategies of reciprocity, which can sustain cooperation in iterated games.[28] Hence, issue density may increase states' confidence that their partners will not act opportunistically in such a way as to vitiate the investment in institutions.[29] Mutual confidence is likely to be reinforced by the institutionalization of these multiple relationships, for two reasons. First, past institutionalized practice will have reduced uncertainty and increased trust. Second, the existence of other valued institutions, which could be jeopardized by opportunism in one institution, will provide incentives not to behave opportunistically. We therefore expect cooperative responses to be more likely when institutionalized behavior has characterized the issue area in the past; and when related issue areas are highly institutionalized.

Problem durability and issue density both increase the number of issues that may be affected by sets of rules and practices that comprise institutions. When problems appear more durable and issue density higher, investments in institutions will have greater benefits, because they will pertain to more issues over a longer period of time. These benefits include providing information, increasing credibility, and reducing the costs of cooperation. We expect states to be most inclined to create institutions when problem durability and issue density create incentives to do so. And as long as densely clustered sets of problems exist, institutions that enable states to cope with them are likely to persist.

This framework, adapted from institutional theory, provides the basis for understanding the conditions that should be conducive to the institutionalization of security coalitions. In the next section we focus on endogenous sources of change: features of institutions that may facilitate a shift from institutions designed to cope with threats to institutions designed to cope with risks. We introduce two novel concepts – hybridization and portability – that help to explain variations in the adaptability and continuing significance of security institutions in general, and that throw light on the transformation of NATO into a security management institution.

Adaptation and hybridization

We have seen that security coalitions may be distinguished by their purposes as well as by their degree of institutionalization. In particular, they may be directed against a specific external threat or designed to deal with the more diffuse problem of risks. Alliances and alignments, which are designed to cope with threats, need effectively to aggregate the military capabilities of their members in order to pose credible deterrence threats or efficient instruments of defence. In contrast, security management institutions do not need to mount credible deterrents and effective defences against adversaries. They need to provide for transparency, consultation, and incentives for cooperative strategies among members.

The question we pose is the following: under what conditions do decreases in threat lead to the abandonment of existing alignments or alliances, or instead, to their evolution? Our first argument is that institutionalization matters: alliances are better candidates for adaptation than alignments. More highly institutionalized coalitions are more likely to persist, since the marginal costs of maintaining existing institutions are smaller than the average costs of new ones. The sunk costs of old institutions have already been paid: in economics, "bygones are bygones."[30] Hence, even if the old institution is not optimal for current purposes, it may be sensible to maintain it rather than to try to form a new one – especially if the costs of negotiating such an entity would be very high, or uncertainty about success is great.[31]

However, this inertial explanation is insufficient. When situations change – for example, from an international environment in which threats are the main security problem to one in which risks are the principal focus of attention – the continued relevance of institutions depends on how well they can adapt rules and procedures devised for one set of problems to the emerging issues of the day. A classic example of successful adaptation is the March of Dimes, which was founded to combat polio. After the Salk vaccine was developed, the March of Dimes was able to shift its orientation from polio to birth defects, because its organizational competence was in raising funds rather than being specific to polio. However, adaptability is by no means assured. In international relations, institutions that were built on principles contradictory to those of a new era may become worse than useless. After 1989, both the Warsaw Pact and CoCom – the institution devised by the United States and its allies to deny strategic materials to the Soviet bloc – disappeared.[32]

We use the word "portability" to describe the ease with which the rules and practices of one institution can be adapted to other situations. Institutional repertoires are often adjustable, at least within some range. Both portability and its limits are illustrated by the attempt by the United Nations to adapt its institutional arrangements for peacekeeping to the war in Bosnia. Sufficient similarity between traditional UN missions and the issues in Bosnia existed for the UN to be able to mount a Bosnian expedition and achieve some tactical successes by negotiating cease-fires as well as providing relief to the civilian population. But coercing belligerents was not part of the UN's peacekeeping repertoire, and the mission collapsed over its inability to perform that function, which was essential to achieving an enduring cease-fire.

We argue that institutions are more likely to adapt to new conditions when their rules and practices are portable. Institutions that combine a variety of functions are more likely than narrowly focused institutions to find that some of their rules and practices are more portable: the fact that they have a variety of rules and organizational repertoires means that some of those rules and repertoires are more likely to remain relevant after sudden environmental change occurs. Specifically, institutions that combine functions related to risk *and* threat are more likely than single-purpose institutions to have more rules and repertoires that are portable after threat declines. Paul Schroeder has argued that alliances can be "tools of management" as well as modes of aggregating power against threats.[33] We follow Schroeder's analysis in recognizing that alliances have in fact often contained measures to manage relations among members. We call institutions that combine risk-directed management functions with threat-directed power aggregation functions *hybrid institutions*. Hybrid security institutions deal both with security problems created by external threats or problems and those problem posed by risks, mistrust, and misunderstandings among members. The classic conceptualization of alliances as arrangements to aggregate power does not allow for these multiple purposes, and therefore fails to capture the reality of contemporary alliances. For instance, the highly institutionalized bilateral alliance between the United States and Japan has developed a rich set of common expectations and specific rules and a clear functional division of labour, both to guard against external threats and, increasingly, to deal with the risk that tensions on economic issues between the two countries would disrupt their security partnership.[34] On the other hand, alignments such as that of the Axis powers during the Second World War, or even the Grand Alliance of Britain, the United States, and the Soviet Union, were not highly institutionalized and were dominated by the single purpose of winning the war. The point is that security arrangements differ with respect to degree of hybridization, because some focus only on threats while others encompass issues of risk as well. We put forward the hypothesis – although we do not prove it – that hybrid institutions are generally more adaptable than non-hybrid arrangements.

The concept of portability helps us understand why member states attempt to use existing NATO practices, procedures, and rules to deal with new security problems and to overcome new obstacles to security cooperation among the allies. It also suggests that having discovered over time that some such procedures are portable, members will become more willing to invest in them in the future. We see this pattern in the reliance of NATO members on NATO infrastructure and procedures to develop, deploy, and operate multinational peace enforcement forces in Bosnia, even though those procedures and that infrastructure were created to deter and defend against the Soviet threat – quite a different matter. This development is also apparent in the resources NATO has invested in Partnership for Peace.

We turn now to a comparative analysis of alliance adaptation, illustrating the historical relevance of our concepts, and our argument, for the attempted transformations of 1815, 1919, and 1945. In the final section we will return to the case of NATO.

Institutional adaptation when threats decline: three cases

Our argument holds that the functions performed by alignments or alliances will become less valuable to members when threats are transformed into risks, but the functions that could be performed by security management institutions will become potentially more valuable. States will therefore have incentives, when threats disappear but risks persist, to seek to transform alignments or alliances into security management institutions. In this section we briefly examine one alliance and two alignments that successfully dealt with threats to their members: the Quadruple Alliance formed during the Napoleonic Wars and renewed in 1815; the Anglo-French alignment of the First World War (1914–18), joined by the United States in 1917; and the Grand Alliance (in our terms, an alignment) of Great Britain, the Soviet Union, and the United States of 1941–5. Each alignment or alliance was followed by attempts to establish a security institution to deal with post-war risks, but these institutions varied in members' commitment, durability, and effectiveness. Our claim is that successful transformation of alignments or alliances into security management institutions requires three conditions: (i) a change in the security environment to one of risks rather than threats; (ii) the previous construction of a genuine alliance – an institution – rather than merely an alignment; and (iii) that the previous alliance be a hybrid, possessing some rules and practices that were designed to mediate disputes and prevent the emergence of security dilemmas among them.

Napoleon and the Concert of Europe

The Concert of Europe, which was established by the victorious allies of the Napoleonic Wars along with the restored monarchy of France, is generally recognized as a case of successful security cooperation. It is commonly explained as the result of the recognition by four European great powers, Great Britain, Austria–Hungary, Prussia, and Russia, that their previous competitive behaviour had allowed France under Napoleon to conquer most of Europe and nearly destroy it in the process. In 1815, these powers did not perceive a threat from any of them, including a France with legitimate monarchical rule re-established; but they worried about the risks inherent in great power rivalry. They recognized that they had substantial long-term common interests in a stable Europe resistant to revolution – that "problem durability" was high. They also believed that many issues would arise on which there might be incentives for one state or another to seek unilateral advantage, but that such self-serving activities could lead once again to war. Hence "issue density" was high as well. Recognizing their common interests, these great powers were able to develop a system based on consultation, norms of reciprocity, and rules of behaviour which precluded unilateral advantage and supported mutual restraint.[35] As Louise Richardson shows in Chapter 2 of *Imperfect Unions: Security Institutions over Time and Space*, this system of rules and norms (by any definition, a security institution) had a significant impact on the security relations of the great powers in the first half of the nineteenth century, and contributed to an unprecedented period of peace among them.

Our argument attributes the formation of the Concert of Europe not only to problem durability, issue density, and the common values and interests of its members, but to the previous anti-Napoleonic alliance having been a hybrid institution. The earliest anti-French coalitions were usually *ad hoc* commitments which states could and did easily escape. Faced with the threat of the French armies poised to attack, erstwhile allies defected at the crucial hour, thus contributing to Napoleon's military success. Indeed, until 1812, the European great powers were defeated as much by their own perfidy as by French military power. Over time, however, as the futility of such behaviour became apparent to European leaders, they sought to develop more precise commitments and greater coordination in their diplomatic and military campaigns against France. As Schroeder shows, after 1812 they did a better job of managing and containing the temptation to exploit others and seek deals with France. High-level policy-makers met in virtually continuous session, and self-consciously followed rules that minimized attempts at exploiting situations for unilateral advantage. The anti-Napoleon alliances were not solely directed against the external threat; they were designed to keep an eye on allies and reduce the potential for defection or mitigate its effects.[36] That is, the post-1812 alliances were, to a significant extent, hybrid security institutions. In our framework, therefore, it is not surprising that the post-1812 alliance's basic practices served as something of a precedent when far-sighted leaders such as Metternich and Castlereagh sought to create a mechanism for managing their rivalries and uncertainties.

The First World War and Versailles

The end of the First World War brought an end to severe threats to the security of the victorious Western allies, but left risks, including Bolshevism, revival of Germany, and the spread of nationalism in the former Ottoman and Habsburg empires. The League of Nations was designed to meet these risks. However, the condition for success in developing a security management institution – the existence of a previous hybrid alliance institution – was not present in 1919.

The Entente Cordiale between Great Britain and France, which provided the core of the victorious coalition of the First World War, was a very loose association between two traditional rivals. When war broke out in 1914, "vital questions of strategic deployment and military coordination remained unresolved . . . The stage was set for a war of attrition between the allies as each struggled for military authority and strategic control on their common front."[37] For over three years, this struggle divided the political and military leaders of each country, as well as pitting the governments against one another. The British and French governments both sought to impose more burdens on their partners and gain more benefits for themselves, while the military and political leaders of each country contested with each other for authority over strategy and tactics. Only in November 1917 was a Supreme

War Council established, at the insistence of British Prime Minister Lloyd George, and with the mandate to prepare war plans, subject to the approval of the governments involved; and only due to the shock of the German offensive of March 1918, and the uncoordinated British–French reaction to it, was General Ferdinand Foch made generalissimo for the western front. Even then, Foch did not have the right to issue orders to subordinate commanders, but only to have "strategic direction" of operations. Effective unity of command eluded the allies, due to the differences among the governments concerned, and sometimes within governments, "about the objectives for which they were fighting and the means they needed to deploy to achieve them."[38] And the bureaucracy set up to service the Supreme War Council could not overcome fundamental differences of allied interests.[39]

Ad hoc bargaining on the basis of resources available and power positions characterized decision-making on security issues, not adherence to institutionalized rules, norms, and practices.[40] Indeed, those agreements that were made between Britain and France were subject to opportunistic reneging when circumstances changed, as indicated by the fate of the Sykes–Picot agreement on the Middle East, which Britain overturned in 1918, to the dismay of its French ally.[41] On 3 October, Lloyd George told the War Cabinet that "Britain had won the war in the Middle East and there was no reason why France should profit from it."[42]

The lack of institutionalization in the Entente meant that the architects of the post-war system, centered around the League of Nations, had to build their institutions from scratch. The sad story of the League, beginning with the defection of the United States and the weakness of Britain and France, is familiar. The Versailles Treaty, in which the League was embedded, failed to become legitimate, even to the victors' publics. Germany was not reintegrated into a mutually beneficial international order, unlike the treatment of France in 1815. The victors of 1918 failed to build effective post-war security institutions.

Had the allies formed an institutionalized alliance – an effective tool of management as well as a means of aggregating power – the history of the League might well have been different. The US Senate might have been more willing to join; practices of promoting cooperation among allies might have spilt over into Anglo–American–French cooperation after 1919. It is also possible, however, that the centrifugal forces of interest and parochialism would have torn even such a League apart. All we can say with confidence is that failure to make the League of Nations into an effective security management institution is consistent with our argument, since a non-institutionalized alignment was not transformed into a security management institution.

The Second World War, the Grand Alliance, and the Cold War

During the Second World War, the Soviet Union, United Kingdom, and United States were linked by the Grand Alliance, which was closer, in our terms, to an alignment than to an alliance. Due to logistical necessity it became more institutionalized than the Entente of the First World War, but its institutionalization was limited by conflicts of interests and intense mutual suspicion. The Grand Alliance was a stark response to the demands of national survival. The previous two decades had provided little basis for amicable relations between the Anglo–American countries and the Soviet Union, and good reason for suspicion. However, after the German attack on the Soviet Union in June and the Japanese attack on Pearl Harbor in December 1941, the fates of all three countries became bound together. Survival of the Soviet Union became crucial for British security. Prime Minister Churchill said that "if Hitler invaded Hell I would make at least a favourable reference to the Devil in the House of Commons."[43] Although not codified in a single trilateral treaty (indeed, only the Soviet Union and United Kingdom concluded an official treaty), this alignment was based on a series of meetings and commitments in 1941 and 1942.[44]

The cornerstone of the alignment was an agreement that despite the Anglo–American war against Japan in the Pacific, defeat of Germany was the unquestionable priority. This agreement implied an Anglo–American commitment to a "second front" in Europe. It also generated massive Western logistical aid to the Soviet Union, including shipments of thousands of aircraft and tanks and hundreds of thousands of trucks.[45] Cooperation in the field of intelligence was also extensive.[46] However, although the United States and Britain mounted joint military operations in North Africa and the Normandy landings, no such joint command developed with the Soviet Union. The fact that the war was fought on separate eastern and western fronts limited joint military operations between the Soviet Union and its allies to such enterprises as the use by American and British aircraft of Soviet bases for bombing operations in Hungary and joint naval operations in the north.

While adapting their separate practices to win the war, the three countries failed utterly to agree upon norms, rules, or procedures for coping with their suspicions about one another, particularly (though not exclusively) between the Soviet Union on one side and the Anglo–American countries on the other. Most important, the allies never developed an institutional solution to the conundrum of Eastern and Central Europe: how both to ensure the independence of the small countries of the region and to reassure the Soviets about their own security. The recent history of German invasion, the intense hostility between the Soviet Union and the West since the Bolshevik Revolution, and the territorial ambitions of Stalin rendered such a solution elusive, despite efforts at the wartime conferences at Teheran (1943), Yalta (1945), and Potsdam (1945).[47]

The absence of a highly institutionalized wartime alliance surely made post-war cooperation between Russia and America more difficult than it would otherwise have been. But even had such an alliance existed, the fundamental rivalry between the Soviet Union and the West would probably have prevented extensive cooperation. By 1947 the security environment was one of threats rather than risks. Our argument is that both an absence of threat from one's former partners and a previous history of institutionalized cooperation are necessary for threat-oriented alliances to be transformed into security management institutions. Neither condition for successful transformation was present after the Second World War, and it is therefore not surprising that, despite the provisions of Chapters 6 and 7 of its Charter, the United Nations did not become an effective security management institution in the aftermath of the Second World War.

The transformation of NATO

The question of NATO's future has emerged as one of the most important and difficult issues of post-Cold War European security. The North Atlantic Treaty Organization was established in 1949. In the well-known turn of phrase of its first secretary-general Lord Ismay, it was created "to keep the Russians out, the Americans in, and the Germans down." Its sixteen member states are Belgium, Canada, Denmark, France, Germany (since 1955), Greece (since 1952), Iceland, Italy, Luxembourg, the Netherlands, Norway, Portugal, Spain (since 1982), Turkey (since 1952), the United Kingdom, and the United States. It is a political and military collective defence arrangement: article 4 of the treaty provides for consultations among the allies whenever any members believe their territorial integrity, political independence, or security is threatened, while article 5 provides directly for military cooperation by stipulating that an armed attack against one or more of the members in Europe or North America is considered an attack against them all.

At its beginning, the North Atlantic Treaty was the foundation for an *alignment*, in our terms, between the United States and Western Europe. "NATO I"[48] was essentially a unilateral security guarantee by the United States, reassuring Western Europe about American support against a Soviet threat, and reassuring the countries that had recently fought Germany against a revival of the German threat. Without much in the way of institutionalization, there was not much "organization" to NATO.

This changed after the outbreak of the Korean War in June 1950. The United States deployed troops in Europe, and NATO established a supreme command under the initial leadership of General Dwight D. Eisenhower. Over the years, NATO developed extensive structures for multilateral cooperation among its members, from the summit-level North Atlantic Council to committees for many aspects of defence planning and integration.

A major cause of the institutionalization of NATO after 1951 was heightened threat: the Korean War shocked American and European leaders into a reassessment of the Soviet threat and of the necessary form of a military presence in Europe for deterrence and defence. The result was a decision by the Truman administration to commit ground forces to Europe, contradicting previous assurances by Secretary of State Dean Acheson in hearings on the treaty that the United States would not expect to station substantial numbers of troops in Europe on a permanent basis. After a "great debate" lasting from

January through March 1951, the US Senate voted 69–21 on 4 April to approve sending troops to Europe.[49] The second major cause of NATO's institutionalization was the need to cope with a large set of intra-alliance problems generated by the need to make the alliance effective by including West Germany in its military structure and by "locking in" US participation and thus reassuring its European partners. The rejection of the European Defence Community (EDC) by the French National Assembly in 1954 led directly to innovations that made NATO a hybrid institution, combining extensive security management functions with power aggregation. At London in the early fall of that year, six continental European countries plus Britain, Canada, and the United States agreed on a complex bargain involving German membership in NATO, resting on three mutually reinforcing commitments: (i) a US nuclear guarantee and promise to maintain troops in Europe; (ii) a British promise to keep troops on the continent; and (iii) a commitment by Germany to rearm in a way that was politically acceptable to its allies.[50] This bargain meant that to succeed as an alliance, NATO also had to be an effective security management institution – that is, it had to manage "the German question." NATO therefore developed a security management repertoire as well as an alliance repertoire, a hybrid combination that served it well when security management functions became most in demand after 1989.

The functions of NATO II centred on security cooperation among its members, integration of Germany and the United States in European defence (although for different purposes), and maintaining a substantial defence capability to deter possible Soviet military attack. Consequently, its structures emphasized intra-alliance consultation, provisions to make American military deployments sustainable given the vagaries of domestic politics, and impressive military capabilities. NATO developed rules, procedures, and processes which were meant not only to mount a credible deterrent and defence against the Soviet Union, but to bind Germany in such a way that it could no longer threaten the countries of Western Europe, which were now its partners in NATO. A major aspect of Western European security management therefore entailed creating mechanisms for intra-alliance transparency and rules meant to reinforce the democratic character of NATO member governments.

NATO was thus mixed in institutional form because its purposes were mixed. Sometimes the institutional features which served one target served the other: the deployment of allied forces on German territory both enhanced the credibility of NATO's military threat against the Soviet Union, and severely constrained any potential independent German military options. Sometimes, however, NATO's purposes brought alliance members into tension with one another or generated domestic dissension, as in the cases of the decision to permit German rearmament in order to create sufficiently capable conventional forces in the 1950s, and of the decision to enhance the credibility of NATO's nuclear deterrent in the 1970s by deploying Pershing II and cruise missiles.[52] Indeed, coalitions with mixed objectives may be generally prone to such crises.[51]

As the European context began to change in 1989, NATO acquired incentives to shed structures that had become dysfunctional and to create structures to deal with the new requirements of the changing security environment. Militarily, NATO needed to reduce its huge forces directed against the Soviet Union, which had become a major liability in pursuing security cooperation. The alliance has sought to develop smaller forces with greater flexibility and adaptability, including a Rapid Reaction Force, more truly multinational military formations, and the creation of Combined Joint Task Forces designed to make NATO's joint military assets usable for wider operations by NATO nations or by the WEU. Even before the creation of the UN-approved Implementation Force (IFOR) and Stabilization Force (SFOR), NATO played an important role in the UN operations, beginning with the April 1993 enforcement of air-exclusion zones over Bosnia. NATO operations in Bosnia since 1995, sanctioned by the United Nations, were facilitated by these organizational changes, which enabled NATO as an institution, rather than merely its members as independent states, to respond to UN calls for peacekeeping and peace enforcement.

NATO has also adapted politically to an environment in which threat is not the main security problem. Its London Declaration of July 1990 and the new Strategic Concept adopted at the Rome Summit in November 1991 declared that the countries of the former Warsaw Pact were not adversaries but rather partners for Western security, and reduced the alliance's dependence on nuclear weapons. Also at the Rome summit, NATO created the North Atlantic Cooperation Council (NACC) as a political organization, and invited all the members of the former Warsaw Pact to join. This action served two functions: it brought countries in, and extended the function of NATO to consultations, information exchange, and transparency.[53]

These decisions reflected the beliefs of European élites and decision-makers that the problem of security in Europe is different from that of the Cold War. For example, the threat of deliberate aggression by either Russia or Germany is held by leaders in either country to be very low, and German and Russian officials and politicians told one of the authors repeatedly that the new problem of security in Europe was now one of "risks" or "challenges" rather than "threats" and that this entailed fundamentally different problem with fundamentally different requirements. In particular, it requires policies and instruments to increase stability and transparency; in general, it requires integration rather than deterrence.[54]

Yet NACC did not directly address the fundamental question, which was the relationship between the membership and purpose of NATO after the Cold War. While the functions of NATO could be expanded and adapted to the new environment, and its activities coordinated with non-alliance members, there remained the fundamental problem: whether NATO itself should expand. Partly as a way to move towards enlargement and partly as a way to deflect political attention from the issue at the time, the alliance created the Partnership for Peace (PfP) program in 1994, and by 1996 twenty-six states including Russia had joined. The stated purpose of PfP was to improve cooperation between NATO members and prospective members, although membership in PfP did not imply eventual NATO membership. Its activities focus on transparency in defence planning and budgets; democratic control of military forces; training and readiness for UN and OSCE operations; and military coordination and training with NATO for peacekeeping, humanitarian, and search and rescue missions.

Despite the institutional innovations of NACC and PfP, the issue of NATO enlargement would not go away. NACC and PfP turned out not to be substitutes for the enlargement of NATO, whose members agreed in May 1997 to admit Hungary, Poland and the Czech Republic to membership, and which left the door open for additional accessions later.

The NATO that is expanding, however, is not the old NATO – an alliance focused on threats from the Soviet Union. NATO is in the process of changing from an alliance to a security management institution. As US Secretary of State Madeleine Albright recently wrote, "NATO does not need an enemy. It has enduring purposes."[55] NATO III remains an organization, but it is designed less as an alliance, and more as a security management institution. For example, the NATO–Russia agreement of May 1997 which paved the way for Russia's reluctant acquiescence to enlargement committed NATO to the position that it has "no plans, no reason, and no intention" to forward deploy conventional military forces or nuclear forces on the territory of any new member states. This commitment thus eliminates one of the core defining features of NATO's Cold War military alliance practices and reduces its effective capability for collective defence.

The nature of the environment in Europe – risks rather than threats – goes quite far towards explaining NATO's transformation. Equally critical, however, are the continued commitments of its major member states to NATO institutions. Supporting these commitments are NATO's legitimacy as a mechanism for Western security and the deep, wide networks of officials and politicians in the NATO countries who are committed to the alliance and familiar with one another. Other potential rivals, such as the Western European Union (WEU) or the Organization for Security and Cooperation in Europe (OSCE), do not have such resources at their disposal. US commitment to NATO is vastly greater than its commitment to OSCE; and, of course, it is not a member of WEU.

More tentatively, we suggest that the hybrid nature of NATO's institutions is also important. NATO developed explicit practices to control security dilemmas among its members through its experience with Germany. These practices are portable and can be transferred at relatively low cost to new situations. Proposals for extending membership to new members or for merely extending cooperation of the alliance with non-members (i.e. Partnership for Peace) aim at the further development and institutionalization of practices meant to create transparency and cooperation among NATO members during the Cold War.[56] Because NATO has already developed rules, procedures, and structures for security management among states, it is more efficient to rely upon them than to create new institutions from scratch. NATO has been able to become the leading security management institution in Europe, we suggest, not only because it was a successful alliance, but also because it was a successful hybrid security institution.[57]

Our argument has policy implications. If NATO is indeed becoming a security management institution, the implication of our argument in the first section is that it should become inclusive rather than remaining exclusive. Responding to risks rather than threats, it should include the other countries of Europe, especially those where security problems and instabilities lie. NATO's expansion could thus foreshadow, not the enlargement of a threat-oriented military alliance, but the transformation of an alliance into a security management institution.

Conclusions

NATO is changing from an exclusive alliance focused on threats to an inclusive security management institution concerned chiefly with risks. The contemporary debate in the United States on NATO expansion seems to miss this point. Some opponents have worried about alienating Russia, while others have criticized the alleged dilution of NATO's military capabilities as a result of the May 1997 consultation agreements with Russia. Both seem to assume that NATO will remain a military alliance, although one set of critics laments expansion of such an alliance (allegedly threatening Russia) and the other side attacks what they see as weakening of article 5 guarantees and measures to give Russia a voice in NATO decision-making.

If NATO is becoming a security management institution, the debate looks very different. NATO's military functions will decline as threats diminish; and it should gradually expand to encompass all democratic European states that are committed to maintaining peaceful, friendly relations on the basis of the territorial status quo. Those who want to encourage a peaceful transition to democracy in Russia should endorse, not oppose, this sort of transformation.

Clearly such an institutional transformation would be difficult, and could only take place over a substantial period of time. It may be quite some time before Russia becomes a stable democracy that could be a worthy partner in NATO. In the meantime, it might be necessary to restructure NATO decision-making so that it could act effectively even with twenty or twenty-five members: as in the European Union, this might require some form of qualified majority voting. In any case, NATO's expansion has to be carried out with the clear understanding that the point is not to expand the geographical scope of an exclusive military alliance – there should be no prospect of applying article 5 to Russian borders to its south or east – but to create an inclusive security management institution, limited to Europe.

For the moment, what is most important is to avoid confusion, leading statesmen or policy-influential élites in Russia, Western Europe, or the United

States to believe that NATO remains an exclusive alliance focused on threats. Policies based on such a premiss will be inappropriate and self-defeating.

If the transformation of NATO is as successful as we hope, NATO will be only the second security institution – along with the Concert of Europe – to endure for a significant period of time with high levels of commitments from its members. History should therefore make us only cautiously optimistic. But NATO is differentiated by extensive institutionalization and an extraordinarily high level of commitment on the part of its members, compared both to these past alignments or alliances, and to other contemporary organizations, such as OSCE and WEU.

Having been a successful alliance, NATO is building on the practices and networks constructed in response to threat, as resources for its adaptation to the role of international security institution. Like the March of Dimes, it resists the logic that expects institutional collapse as a result of functional success. Its prospects for transformation into an inclusive security management institution seem bright, as long as policy-makers recognize that the expansion of NATO must be accompanied by its reorientation toward problems of risk rather than threat.

Notes

1 This research was supported by the Weatherhead Center for International Affairs of Harvard University (WCFIA); the National Council for Soviet and East European Research; and the German Marshall Fund of the United States. They are not responsible for the contents or findings of this study. We thank Lois Kaznicki for her excellent research assistance. For their insights, ideas, and critiques, we especially thank members of the WCFIA Study Group on Alliances and members of the Arbeitsstelle Transatlantische Außen- und Sicherheitspolitik of the Freie Universistät, Berlin, with whom we have had many productive meetings on these issues. We also express our gratitude to participants at a panel on alliance theory at the 1995 ISA conference in Chicago and to participants at an Olin Institute National Security Group seminar at the Center for International Affairs. We are grateful to Robert Art, Peter Barschdorff, Marc Busch, John Duffield, Christopher Gelpi, Hein Goemans, Peter Gourevitch, Iain Johnston, Mark Kramer, David Lake, Jeff Legro, Lisa Martin, Andrew Moravcsik, James Morrow, Joseph S. Nye, Jr, Robert Paarlberg, Dan Reiter, Louise Richardson, Stephen Walt, and Reinhard Wolf for written comments on various versions of this paper. Special thanks go to our colleague, Helga Haftendorn, who offered astute and comprehensive comments on several drafts over several years.
2 Mearsheimer (1990); Waltz (1993).
3 This statement paraphrases a sentence in Keohane and Nye (1993: 19).
4 This discussion builds on, and modifies, Keohane (1989: 4–5).
5 Hart (1961).
6 Waltz (1979).
7 Security can be defined much more broadly, even to the point where it becomes identical with preservation of any value, as in "economic security" and "environmental security." Since definitions are not matters of right or wrong, the fact that we have defined security in a relatively limited way does not imply that we reject such definitions; but such a broadening of the concept is not necessary for our

purposes. See Walt (1991), Art (1994), and Wolfers (1962) for relatively narrow definitions of security. For a good discussion of the boundaries of the concept of security and the limitations of such a restrictive definition, see Haftendorn (1991).

8 Daase (1992: 70–2 and 74–5); Wallander (1999: Ch. 3).
9 Herz (1951); Jervis (1978).
10 Wolfers (1962); Fearon (1994); Powell (1996).
11 Stein (1990); Martin (1992b).
12 Wolfers (1962: 183).
13 Wallander (1999: Ch. 2).
14 Betts (1992).
15 We are indebted to Hein Goemans for suggesting the terms "inclusive" and "exclusive," which clarified distinctions we had earlier tried to make, and to Carsten Tams for developing the exclusive/risk category and term "out-of-area" (see Ch. 3 of *Imperfect Unions: Security Institutions over Time and Space*).
16 On OSCE, see ch. 7, *Imperfect Unions: Security Institutions over Time and Space*, by Ingo Peters.
17 On the 1967 coalition, see Walt (1987: 101). The Syria–United States example was suggested by James Morrow in a seminar at Harvard University, 28 Feb. 1995.
18 Ch. 5 by Tuschhoff shows how NATO was institutionalized in all three ways.
19 Schroeder (1976, 1994a).
20 The emphasis on threats in the realist literature has led to an emphasis on exclusive security coalitions, and realism's underemphasis of the significance of institutionalization has contributed to its lack of interest in institutional variation, which is seen as either unimportant or merely a function of underlying power relations.
21 Jervis (1976).
22 Keohane (1984); Milgrom *et al.* (1990); Shepsle (1986).
23 Nye (1990).
24 Schelling (1960).
25 Powell (1990); Martin (1992a); Fearon (1994).
26 Keohane (1982: 339–40).
27 Osgood (1962: 72–4, 96–8); Hanrieder (1989: 40–1); Kugler (1993: 41–50); Duffield (1995: 39–40).
28 Axelrod (1984); Martin (1995: 77).
29 On opportunism, see Williamson (1985).
30 For this argument, see Keohane (1984: 100–3). Stinchcombe (1968: 120–1) has a good discussion of sunk costs. The phrase, "in economics, bygones are bygones," was the first part of a *bonmot* of Charles Kindleberger, the second half of which was, "while in politics, they're working capital."
31 For this inertial institutional argument, see McCalla (1996).
32 CoCom stands for Coordinating Committee for Export Controls. On CoCom's demise and institutional successor, the Wassenaar Accord, see Wallander (1999: Ch. 7).
33 Schroeder (1976).
34 On the US–Japanese security dialogue, which in our terms sought further to institutionalize the relationship by establishing firmer common expectations, see Nye (1995).
35 Jervis (1986).
36 Schroeder (1994b: Chs 10–12).
37 Philpott (1996: 1).
38 French (1995: 226).
39 Ibid. 288. See also Cruttwell (1936: 36), who claims that the function of the Supreme War Council "in the crucial days before the March [1918] disaster was little more than that of a military debating society."

40 For eight months, from March to Nov. 1918, technical cooperation among ministers of operational agencies, unmediated by foreign offices, characterized the Allied Maritime Transport Council, established to coordinate shipping requirements for the allies. However, even the secretary of the AMTC, and author of its history, admitted that "a power of decision vested in a single authority, the British Government, which could compel observation of a programme it considered reasonable, whether agreed or not, by a refusal to allot British ships except on specified conditions." Whether such an interministerial arrangement would have continued to operate after the United States also had shipping available to allocate is unclear. See Salter (1921: 242).
41 M.L. Dockrill and J.D. Goold (1981: 131–50).
42 French (1995: 262), citing War Cabinet minutes.
43 Quoted in Feis (1967: 7).
44 Nadeau (1990); Feis (1967); Edmonds (1991: Chs 9–11).
45 Ulam (1974: 329–30).
46 Bradley F. Smith (1996).
47 Gormly (1990). For detailed discussion on specific Soviet demands of the allies at the war-time conferences, see Ulam (1974: 350–7, 367–77, 388–94).
48 Helga Haftendorn distinguishes different stages in NATO's development as NATO I, NATO II, and NATO III. Haftendorn (1997).
49 P. Williams (1985: 87–91).
50 Kugler (1993); Schwartz (1991).
51 Risse-Kappen (1988).
52 Richardson (1996).
53 Wallander (1999: Ch. 6).
54 Wallander (1999: Ch. 3).
55 *Economist* (15 Feb. 1997), 22.
56 Some arguments on whether NATO should expand its membership and functions focus on these issues. See Asmus *et al.* (1993); Brzezinski (1995); Glaser (1993); Holbrooke (1995); Brown (1995).
57 For this insight we are indebted to Tim Snyder of the Olin Institution, Center for International Affairs, Harvard University, in a comment at a meeting there on security institutions, 17–19 Mar. 1997. Whether NATO will continue to transform itself successfully remains to be seen, and is beyond the scope of this paper. For a comparison of NATO with OSCE, see Wallander (1999: Ch. 6).

References

Art, Robert J. 1994. A defensible defense: America's grand strategy after the Cold War. *International Security*, **15**: 5–53.
Asmus, Ronald D., Richard L. Kugler, and F. Stephen Larrabee. 1993. Building a new NATO. *Foreign Affairs*, **72**: 28–40.
Axelrod, Robert. 1984. *The Evolution of Cooperation*. New York: Basic Books.
Betts, Richard K. 1992. Systems for peace or causes of war? Collective security, arms control, and the new Europe. *International Security*, **17**: 5–44.
Brown, Michael E. 1995. The flawed logic of NATO expansion. *Survival*, **37**: 34–52.
Brzezinski, Zbigniew. 1995. A plan for Europe. *Foreign Affairs*, **74**: 26–42.
Cruttwell, Charles Robert Mowbray Fraser. 1936. *The role of British strategy in the Great War*. London: The University Press.
Daase, Christopher. 1992. Bedrohung, Verwundbarkeit und Risiko in der 'Neuren Weltordnung': Zum Paradigmenwechsel in der Sicherheitspolitik. In *Sicherheits-*

politik in den 90er Jahren: Politische under ethische Positionsbestimmungen für die Bunderswehr, Bernard Moltmann (ed.), 68–83. Frankfurt am Main: Haagen und Herchen.

Dockrill, Michael L. and J. Douglas Goold. 1981. *Peace without promise: Britain and the peace conferences, 1919–23.* Hamden, CT: Archon Books.

Duffield, John S. 1995. *Power rules: the evolution of NATO's conventional force posture.* Stanford: Stanford University Press.

Edmonds, Robin. 1991. *The Big Three: Churchill, Roosevelt, and Stalin in peace and war.* New York: W.W. Norton.

Fearon, James D. 1994. Domestic political audiences and the escalation of international disputes. *American Political Science Review,* **88**: 577–92.

Feis, Herbert. 1967. *Churchill, Roosevelt, Stalin: the war they waged and the peace they sought.* Princeton: Princeton University Press.

French, David. 1995. *The strategy of the Lloyd George coalition, 1916–1918.* Oxford: Clarendon Press.

Glaser, Charles L. 1993. Why NATO is still best: future security arrangements for Europe. *International Security,* **18**: 5–50.

Gormly, James L. 1990. *From Potsdam to the Cold War: Big Three diplomacy, 1945–47.* Wilmington: Scholarly Resources.

Haftendorn, Helga. 1991. The security puzzle: theory-building and discipline-building in international security. *International Security,* **35**: 1–15.

Haftendorn, Helga. 1996. *NATO and the nuclear revolution: a crisis of credibility, 1966–67.* Oxford: Clarendon Press.

Hanrieder, Wolfram. 1989. *Germany, America, Europe: forty years of German foreign policy.* New Haven, CT: Yale University Press.

Hart, H.L.A. 1961. *The concept of law.* Oxford: Clarendon Press.

Herz, John H. 1951. *Political realism and political idealism.* Chicago: University of Chicago Press.

Holbrooke, Richard. 1995. America: a European power. *Foreign Affairs,* **74**: 38–52.

Jervis, Robert. 1976. *Perception and misperception in international politics.* Princeton: Princeton University Press.

Jervis, Robert. 1978. Cooperation under the security dilemma. *World Politics,* **30**: 167–214.

Jervis, Robert. 1986. From balance to concert: a study of international security cooperation. In *Cooperation under anarchy,* Kenneth A. Oye (ed.), 58–79. Princeton: Princeton University Press.

Keohane, Robert O. 1982. The demand for international regimes. *International Organization,* **36**: 325–355.

Keohane, Robert O. 1984. *After Hegemony: Cooperation and Discord in the World Political Economy.* Princeton: Princeton University Press.

Keohane, Robert O. 1989. *International institutions and state power: essays in international relations theory.* Boulder: Westview.

Keohane, Robert O. and Joseph S. Nye, 1993. Introduction: the End of the Cold War in Europe. In Keohane, Nye and Hoffmann, 1993: 1–19.

Keohane, Robert O., Joseph S. Nye, and Stanley Hoffmann, 1993. *After the Cold War: international institutions and state strategies in Europe, 1989–91.* Cambridge, MA: Harvard University Press.

Keohane, Robert O. and Elinor Ostrom (eds). 1995. *Local commons and global interdependence: heterogeneity and cooperation in two domains.* London: Sage Publishers.

Knorr, Klaus (ed.). 1976. *Historical problems of national security.* Lawrence, Kansas: University of Kansas Press.

Kugler, Richard L. 1993. *Commitment to purpose: how alliance partnership won the Cold War.* Santa Monica, CA: Rand.

McCalla, Robert B. 1996. NATO's persistence after the Cold War. *International Organization,* **50**: 445–476.

Martin, Lisa L. 1992a. *Coercive cooperation: explaining multilateral economic sanctions.* Princeton, NJ: Princeton University Press.

Martin, Lisa L. 1992b. Interests, power and multilateralism. *International Organization,* **46**: 765–792.

Martin, Lisa L. 1995. Heterogeneity, linkage and commons problems. In Keohane and Ostrom (eds), 1995: 71–91.

Mearsheimer, John J. 1990. Back to the future: instability in Europe after the Cold War. *International Security,* **15**: 5–57.

Milgrom, Paul R., Douglass C. North and Barry R. Weingast. 1990. The role of institutions in the revival of trade: the law merchant, private judges, and the champagne fairs. *Economics and Politics,* **2**: 1–23.

Nadeau, Remi. 1990. *Stalin, Churchill, and Roosevelt divide Europe.* New York: Praeger.

Nye, Joseph S., Jr. 1990. *Bound to Lead: The Changing Nature of American Power.* New York: Basic Books.

Nye, Joseph S. 1995. East Asian security: the case for deep engagement. *Foreign Affairs,* **74** (July–August): 90–102.

Osgood, Robert E. 1962. *NATO: The Entangling Alliance.* Chicago: University of Chicago Press.

Philpott, William James. 1996. *Anglo–French relations and strategy on the western front, 1914–18.* London: Macmillan.

Powell, Robert, 1990. *Nuclear deterrence theory: the search for credibility.* Cambridge: Cambridge University Press.

Powell, Robert, 1996. Uncertainty, shifting power and appeasement. *American Political Science Review,* **90:4** (December): 749–764.

Richardson, Louise. 1996. *When allies differ: Anglo–American relations during the Suez and Falklands crises.* New York: St. Martin's Press.

Risse-Kappen, Thomas. 1988. *The zero option: INF, West Germany, and arms control.* Boulder: Westview.

Salter, J.A. 1921. *Allied shipping control: an experiment in international administration.* Oxford: Clarendon Press.

Schelling, Thomas C. 1960. *The strategy of conflict.* Cambridge: Harvard University Press.

Schroeder, Paul. 1976. Alliances, 1815–1945: weapons of power and tools of management. In Knorr (ed.) 1976.

Schroeder, Paul. 1994. *The transformation of European politics.* New York: Oxford University Press.

Schwartz, Thomas Alan. 1991. *America's Germany: John J. McCloy and the Federal Republic of Germany.* Cambridge, MA: Harvard University Press.

Shepsle, Kenneth A. 1986. Institutional equilibrium and equilibrium institutions. In *Political science: the science of politics,* Herbert Weisberg (ed.). New York: Agathon Press, Inc.

Smith, Bradley F. 1996. *How the allies traded intelligence, 1941–1945.* Lawrence: University of Kansas Press.

Stein, Arthur A. 1990. *Why nations cooperate: circumstance and choice in international relations*. Ithaca: Cornell University Press.

Stinchcombe, Arthur. 1968. *Constructing social theories*. New York: Harcourt, Brace and World.

Ulam, Adam B. 1974. *Expansion and coexistence: Soviet foreign policy 1917–73*, second edition. Fort Worth: Holt, Rinehart, and Winston.

Wallander, Celeste A. 1999. *Mortal Friends, Best Enemies: German–Russian Cooperation after the Cold War*. Ithaca: Cornell University Press.

Walt, Stephen M. 1987. *The origins of alliances*. Ithaca: Cornell University Press.

Walt, Stephen M. 1991. The renaissance of security studies. *International Studies Quarterly*, **35**: 211–240.

Waltz, Kenneth N. 1979. *Theory of international politics*. Reading, MA: Addison-Wesley.

Waltz, Kenneth N. 1993. The emerging structure of international politics. *International Security*, **18**: 44–79.

Williams, Phil. 1985. *The Senate and US Troops in Europe*. New York: St. Martin's.

Williamson, Oliver. 1985. *The economic institutions of capitalism*. New York: Free Press.

Wolfers, Arnold. 1962. *Discord and collaboration: essays on international politics*. Baltimore: Johns Hopkins University Press.

Part II
Law

6 International relations and international law: two optics[1]

Robert O. Keohane
(1996)

> The surprising thing about international law is that nations ever obey its strictures or carry out its mandates.[2]

> Public international law appears to be quite a well articulated and complete legal order even though it is difficult to locate the authoritative origin or substantive voice of the system in any particular area. Each doctrine seems to free ride somewhat on this overall systemic image. . . . Thus the variety of references among these discursive areas always shrewdly locate the moment of authority and the application in practice elsewhere – perhaps behind us in process or before us in the institutions of dispute resolution.[3]

These quotations from international lawyers encapsulate some of the puzzlement that faces a political scientist trying to understand the political underpinnings of international law. Governments make a very large number of legal agreements, and, on the whole, their compliance with these agreements seems quite high.[4] Yet what this level of compliance implies about the causal impact of commitments remains a mystery.

If states' respect for international law is surprising or puzzling to eminent professors of the subject, it is probably more so to many political scientists. Traditionally, political scientists have styled themselves as "realistic" rather than "idealistic." They are utilitarians of one form or another. According to this view, elite states seek to maintain position, wealth, and power in an uncertain world by acquiring, retaining, and wielding power – resources that enable them to achieve multiple purposes. States use the rules of international law as instruments to attain their interests. International law can thus be interpreted through such an "instrumentalist optic." In political science, work on international regimes – the rules guiding cooperative practices in international relations – has focused on many issues familiar to international lawyers, using a more or less nuanced version of this optic. Indeed, one eminent international lawyer – conversant with and sympathetic to political scientists' work on regimes – has characterized such work on regimes as "reinventing international law in rational-choice language."[5] That is to say, political scientists have "discovered" what to lawyers seems obvious: rules structure politics. However, as Professor Slaughter herself was generous enough to observe, political scientists have attempted more rigorously to explain phenomena with which international lawyers regularly deal. The result has been a greater convergence of research agendas than we observed two decades ago. In Professor Slaughter's words, "regime theorists" and international lawyers agree that "legal rules and decision-making procedures can be used to structure international politics,"[6] and the functions they ascribe to international regimes are remarkably similar.

Therefore, research in both law and political science has recently focused on the effects of rules in international affairs. However, there remain great differences in how observers interpret what they see. The "instrumentalist optic" puts little weight on a major theme of students of international law, namely the impact that shared norms, and the processes by which those norms are interpreted, have on state policies. Hence the "instrumentalist optic" is challenged by a "normative" one.[7] Contrasting these two optics helps to identify a key issue: how important is persuasion on the basis of norms in contemporary world politics?

I recognize that some authors, notably Friedrich Kratochwil, have viewed this causal way of looking at the problem as questionable.[8] Such an analysis indeed separates causal explanation from the function of moral judgment to which norms are fundamental.[9] By doing so, however, it hardly denies that such judgments are made. And the causal issue is surely central to the debate about the role of rules, even though causal inferences, especially in complex situations such as these, are always flawed. Not to confront the causal impact of rules is to evade the central issue of the role of international regimes and international law in world politics. Hence, I regard the distinction between my two optics as revolving around the problem of causality.

Both optics suffer from poorly articulated causal mechanisms or pathways. That is, it is often unclear how predicted results follow from the theory's assumptions. After discussing each optic, I will seek to sketch three concepts which seem intrinsic to the causal pathways on which both optics rely – interests, reputation, and international institutions. The role of norms could be better understood if we can construct a synthesis of the two optics that is more explicit about the role of these concepts in linking norms to actions. This chapter will attempt to integrate the best elements of the two optics into a more coherent and convincing image of how rules are used by states and how they affect state behavior.

The "instrumentalist optic"

The "instrumentalist optic" focuses on interests and argues that rules and norms will matter only if they affect the calculations of interests by agents. International institutions exist because they perform valuable functions for states. They can make a difference, but only when their rules create specific opportunities and impose constraints which affect state interests. A crude version of instrumentalism discounts the observation that states often conform to rules. In this view, states only accede to rules that they favor, and comply because such conformity is convenient. According to this optic, when their interests diverge from the rules, the latter will be modified, reinterpreted, or broken to suit the convenience of powerful states. Loopholes and exceptions may be found. States will attempt to "free-ride." Even if a state benefits from other states' compliance with rules, it may benefit more if others continue to comply while it pursues its short-term self-interest. The more compelling the interest to a state in behaving contrary to the rule, the more modification, reinterpretation, and breach there will be. Compliance will be explained more by interests and power than by legitimacy.

Subtler instrumentalist arguments recognize that rules, as part of the environment faced by a state, exert an impact on state behavior. They do so, in this view, not because the norms they reflect persuade people that they should behave differently. Rather, they alter incentives, not merely for states conceived of as units, but for interest groups, organizations, members of professional associations, and individual policymakers within governments.

This optic is by no means exclusively the province of political scientists. The revised Restatement of American Foreign Relations Law emphasizes state interests: "international law generally is largely observed because violations directly affect the interests of states, which are alert to deter, prevent, or respond to violations."[10] Another compliance-inducing interest is the desire to maintain a pattern of beneficial cooperation. A state "may decide to forgo the short-term advantages derived from violating rules because it has an overriding interest in maintaining the overall system."[11]

Law professors, however, tend to extend their analysis beyond interests. From their standpoint, a significant drawback of relying on interests is that the impact of law itself in such a conceptualization is small. Abram and Antonia Chayes view the instrumental approach as too passive. "In our view, what is left out of this institutionalist account is the active role of the regime in modifying preferences, generating new options, persuading the parties to move toward increasing compliance with regime norms, and guiding the evolution of the normative structure in the direction of the overall objectives of the regime."[12]

For many political scientists, interest-based propositions are more congenial. However, even those who are attracted to instrumentalism and its functional logic should recognize that it handles poorly that which makes politics interesting; that is, the unanticipated consequences of human action.

Instrumentalism, especially its most powerful tool, game theory, does quite well as long as we can assume that actors can anticipate the conditions of future strategic choice. However, instrumentalism cannot deal very well with situations in which choices today affect what people will believe tomorrow when the interests can be reinterpreted.

Instrumentalist arguments are too often taken as obvious, not requiring testing. State "interests" may be inferred from their behavior, which is then "explained" by the very same interests. When states violate rules, they must have had interests in doing so; when they refrain from reneging, their interests determined that as well. Like Viola in the first act of *Twelfth Night*, such an argument is "fortified against all denial."[13] We do not yet have a well-specified or empirically tested instrumentalist theory of compliance with international commitments.

International law and the "normative optic"

International lawyers often argue that the legitimacy of norms and rules has causal effect. Phillip Trimble declares that international law is a form of "rhetoric," whose persuasiveness is largely a function of its legitimacy. Legitimacy, in turn, is related to the process by which it is created, its consistency with accepted general norms, and its perceived fairness or specificity.[14] Legitimacy, says Thomas M. Franck, exerts a "compliance pull," which competes with the pull exerted by interests in reneging. Rules that are determinate and coherent – important components of legitimacy – are associated with greater compliance than those that are not, at least in part because their clarity makes it possible "to dismiss bogus, self-serving interpretations."[15] Officials may routinely keep many commitments because they have respect for law.[16] "Because of the requirements of law or of some prior agreement, nations modify their conduct in significant respect and in substantial degrees."[17]

Several international lawyers emphasize that the normative power of treaty rules, whether one calls it "legitimacy" or something else, is "derive[d] from a complicated dialogic process of interpretation and application, extending over time."[18] In this view, law operates through the activities of "interpretive communities," which operate largely through international institutions. The International Monetary Fund, the Standing Consultative Commission in the SALT agreements, the International Labor Organization, and the International Whaling Commission constitute examples of institutions within which challenges and defenses of state behavior, relative to rules, take place. Interpretive communities, in this view, constrain subjective interpretations, promote habitual compliance, and impose reputational costs on violators of norms, as interpreted by these communities.[19]

According to this "normative optic," norms have causal impact. The impact of interests and power is by no means denied, but such explanations are not sufficient. Norms and rules do not operate mechanically; they are always subject to contestation, interpretation, and reinterpretation. But the norms and rules themselves set the terms of the interpretive discourse. They exert a profound impact on how people think about state roles and obligations, and therefore on state behavior. This "normative optic" shows respect for the discourse that takes place when commitments are contested. It is also consistent with the attention that policymakers pay to norms and ideas about what makes norms legitimate. How else can one account for the enormous amount of argument over rule interpretation? The assumption on which this activity relies is that states are obliged to follow rules to which they have consented.

When one looks for strong motivations for governments to take the discourse seriously, however, the arguments become vague. The "central proposition" of *The New Sovereignty* is that "the interpretation, elaboration, application, and ultimately, enforcement of international rules is accomplished through a process of (mostly verbal) interchange among the interested parties."[20] But why should such verbal interchange exert such an impact? Compliance is said to preserve "connection to the real world" and prevent "isolation,"[21] but it is not clear that noncompliance leads to isolation. Much of this discourse can be explained as facilitating the solution of problems of coordination or assurance, through generally understood and precise language, by specifying focal points, and by linking issues together through the use of precedent. However, the literature promoting the normative optic says little about the boundaries of effectiveness of such discourse; it is not always effective. What conditions facilitate or inhibit its operation? In the end, the claim that discourse leads to compliance rests largely on a reputational argument. In this view, an important motive of state leaders is to maintain their reputation, which exerts a substantial pull toward compliance. "In an interdependent and interconnected world, a reputation for reliability matters."[22] But as Heymann and Kratochwil have perceptively argued, reputation is a tricky concept, and may provide a weak basis for confidence in the impact of rules, unless the conditions under which such confidence is justified are carefully specific.[23] I will discuss reputation, and its implications for the two optics, below.

Empirically, it is hard to validate causal arguments about the impact of norms or discourse. It is often pointed out that norms can exist even if human behavior sometimes contradicts them.[24] This is a fair point, but as I have noted, it begs the causal questions in which I am most interested. "Legitimacy" is difficult to measure independent from the compliance that it is supposed to explain. For instance, Franck describes a rule's compliance "pull power" as "its index of legitimacy."[25] Yet legitimacy is said to explain "compliance pull," making the argument circular. Phillip Trimble admits that his claim that compliance may depend on legitimacy "may be difficult to prove empirically."[26]

In addition, there are some serious methodological issues not fully addressed by writers in this tradition. Assume arguendo that the crude instrumentalists were right: states only comply with rules that are in their material interests to obey or that are enforced by the threats of powerful states. We could then assume in this hypothetical illustration that norms carry little weight. Now let us make some other assumptions about the particular situation that we observe.

1. Agents are quite good at assessing their interests and anticipating the actions of others.
2. A few powerful states made most of the rules and seek to enforce them, and
3. Coordination and assurance situations – in which everyone has an interest in following the rules provided that others do so as well – are common.

Under these conditions, we would expect to see many international legal agreements, and a high level of compliance, even if norms played no role whatsoever. We would only be observing a "selection effect;" that is, agreements that were neither self-enforcing nor enforceable by the powerful states' threats, would normally not be made in the first place. Observing that states follow international law most of the time does not, therefore, yield a valid causal inference. Certainly legal rules provide "focal points" for coordinating state behavior.[27] Do they also exert a significant causal impact on the behavior of states? Or more properly, under what conditions do they exert such an impact? The normative optic presents us with intriguing observations that seem anomalous for the mainstream political science view. However, when we seek to establish causality, we are left with an incomplete argument and empirical ambiguity.

Evaluation

Both of these optics seem necessary, yet neither is sufficient. It is as if each observer only has one eye, and is wearing blinders. What each one sees emerges with great clarity, but it is not the whole picture, and neither viewer has any depth perception. It can hardly be disputed that some states follow the instrumentalist optic some of the time. Most of the time the policies of all states are affected by their material interests, as perceived by their elites; and the relative power capabilities of states are relevant to the degree to which they can achieve their purposes. The literature on international institutions has demonstrated, over the last twenty years, that states do modify their behavior in light of rules, although the extent to which they do so is contested.

What is at issue, however, is not the relevance of the instrumentalist optic, but its sufficiency. Is persuasion on the basis of norms also important in world politics? Are interests redefined in light of principled beliefs, rather than only instrumentally in terms of power, wealth, and position? At this point, my rhetorical dichotomy between the instrumentalist and normative optics begins to break down. Instrumental arguments play a key role in the claims of analysts who attribute persuasive weight to rules. In particular, as discussed above, concern for reputation – a classically instrumentalist concept – plays a major role in arguments about why states obey rules. We will now have to move from outlining the differences between the two optics, to analyzing how the normative optic depends on, but goes beyond, the instrumental one. The fundamental question can be stated simply: do discourse and persuasion matter, or are calculations of interest and power all that really count?

To answer this question, we need somehow to trace out the causal pathways on which these two optics rely and to generate testable propositions from them. Although not attempted in the present chapter, researchers should eventually test these hypotheses against evidence chosen to minimize bias, rather than merely to illustrate arguments. My approach here is to focus on three concepts that seem essential to any coherent account of how rules relate to state action: interests, reputation, and institutions. They are nodes on causal pathways; one could not make a coherent argument about the impact of rules without passing through these nodes. Both optics recognize the role of interests and reputation. The normative optic, and the most persuasive versions of instrumentalism, also acknowledge the role of institutions – discounted only by crude self-styled "realists," to their peril.

The optics' causal pathways and their common nodes

The persuasiveness of either optic relies on a narrative account that traces a causal pathway from its favored explanatory variables to compliance. Such a pathway has to pass through the elites within countries, and in both optics, these elites are viewed as making calculations about the consequences of their actions. That is, they are rational in the limited sense that they seek to relate means to ends in such a way as to achieve their ends most reliably. These rational elites do not have full information, either about alternatives or about their consequences. On the contrary, they operate under considerable uncertainty.[28] Making decisions under uncertainty, they need to calculate interests and assess the reputations of others, within the context of institutional procedures and rules.

Interests

Both optics focus on the "interests" of policy elites. For instrumentalists, these interests are usually taken to be power, wealth, and position (position in the international system with regard to states and offices for individuals). The basic instrumentalist heuristic is to attribute observed behavior to the rational pursuit of self-interest. The ideal instrumentalist "explanation" identifies a causal pathway linking behavior to underlying interests. Other causal processes, such as those involving misinformation or cognitive failure, may be appealed to. However, they usually gain their heuristic force from the failure of rational-interest explanations to provide a compelling account of the behavior in question.

An implication sometimes drawn from instrumentalist argument is that more demanding international rules are likely to be more vulnerable than rules requiring less extensive cooperation. For instance, George Downs and Stephen Rocke calculate how vulnerable different tariff reductions would be in GATT based on various assumptions about transparency and the required time for retaliation. They assume that states, being instrumentalists, will break rules when it is advantageous to do so. They wish to understand what level of cooperation can be sustained by reciprocity-based strategies.[29] They fail to consider the possibility that demanding rules, involving liberalization of tariffs, would alter participants' conceptions of their interests. Yet it is the fixity or plasticity of interests that is precisely at issue in many contemporary international relations debates. International institutions may affect states' formulations of their own interests. If interests become "endogenous" in this sense, institutions with demanding rules could be less, rather than more, vulnerable to reneging, as the increasing authority of the European Union would appear to suggest.

International lawyers also discuss interests, but they are inclined to point out, along with many political scientists, that "the concept of self-interest is itself problematic."[30] Whose self? Which interest? High-level governmental actors play multiple roles, ranging from tough negotiator with foreign governments to official sworn to uphold the law. It is not obvious which role will define the individual's view on a given issue. Even if the role is clear, there are likely to be competing interests. For instance, the President may need to choose between the immediate benefits of reneging on a commitment and the uncertain, longer-term costs of doing so. Over time, as the examples of trade politics and the European Union illustrate, policies will alter the structure of the political economy – including existing firms and groups and their own preferences. Hence, policies may alter the interests of states.[31] Often, as historical institutionalists have argued, these changes are not anticipated by the agents who initiated the policy change.

Furthermore, constructivist lawyers and political scientists have made a strong case that the roles that representatives of states assume, and even their conceptions of self-interest, depend significantly on the rules and practices of international institutions.[32] Consequently, how actors' interests are constructed remains an open question. The instrumentalist optic has interests more sharply in focus than the normative optic: it is clearer what those interests are, and that the arguments being made are not circular. But the fact that institutions can structure interests means that interests are not the instrumentalists' trump cards after all.

Reputation

Both optics recognize that policymakers are concerned about their reputations. Hence, their immediate interests are not necessarily controlling. They may be concerned about what Robert Axelrod has called "the shadow of the future" – that is, the effects of their present actions on others' future behavior.[33] To many international lawyers, reputation is a bulwark for the maintenance of commitments: "Considerations of 'honor,' 'prestige,' 'leadership,' 'influence,' 'reputation,' which figure prominently in governmental decisions, often weigh in favor of observing law."[34] However, it may be desirable to have a reputation not only for keeping agreements, but for vigorously pursuing one's interests, helping one's friends, and punishing one's enemies.[35] Clearly, these reputational incentives may be in conflict; and the latter incentives do not necessarily counsel compliance with commitments. Reputations come in many forms. Our joint optic must take into account the potential value of a reputation for keeping agreements; but it must also consider the less savory forms of reputation.

As Philip Heymann observed, reneging on commitments has consequences for reputation only when a limiting set of conditions is met. "[A]ny violation must be known; it must be known by a party whose reactions to the violation are important to the violator; and the expected costs of violation to the violator must exceed the benefits of giving in to the conflicting temptation."[36] Furthermore, for the expected costs of reneging to be substantial, some party other than the violator must have both the ability and the incentive to react to the violation. Unfortunately for those who rely on reputation, these conditions are often not met in the world of politics.

There is a second problem with reputation as a guarantor of compliance. Governments may value reputations for toughness or even for being willing to bully weaker states, more than they value reputations for compliance with commitments. United States intervention in the Caribbean helped it maintain a reputation for toughness, whether against pro-communist rulers or detested dictators, while foregoing an opportunity to forge a reputation for fidelity with commitments. Reneging on its financial commitments to the United Nation seems to have conferred additional leverage on the United States, rather than reducing its influence as a result of a weakened reputation.

A third difficulty with reliance on reputation is that strong governments are sometimes monopolists in the sense that they can compel others to interact with them.[37] For example, once the United States became a great power, and particularly after it became hegemonic in the West, other countries could not avoid dealing with it. The United States was "the only game in town," and even if its reputation suffered, other governments had little choice as to with whom to transact.

Finally, even if governments are concerned about their reputations for compliance with agreements, they may be able to devise strategies, or legal arguments, to veil their noncompliance. If concealing noncompliance is impossible, they may still seek to differentiate the situations in which they failed to comply, from ongoing relationships on which they want to continue to make agreements.

A dramatic instance of such differentiation occurred at the peace conference at Ghent in 1814 between the United States and Great Britain. Britain, which had been allied with various Indian tribes, sought a definite and permanent boundary between the United States and Indian territories, a request that the United States negotiators refused on the grounds that the population of the United States must have room to expand. The American negotiators worked to differentiate this aim (which entailed frequent breaking of commitments) from reneging on boundary agreements with European countries.

> If this be a spirit of aggrandizement, the undersigned are prepared to admit, in that sense, its existence; but they must deny that it affords the slightest proof of an intention not to respect the boundaries between them and European nations, or of a desire to encroach upon the territories of Great Britain. . . . They will not suppose that [Great Britain] will avow, as the basis of their policy towards the United States, the system of arresting their natural growth within their own territories, for the sake of preserving a perpetual desert for savages.[38]

In other words, reneging on commitments to "savages" was not to affect the United States reputation for keeping commitments to "civilized" powers.

Before discussing the third "node" in our decision-making process – institutions – let us assess briefly the two nodes analyzed above. Interests are indeed important. However, actors can redefine their own interests, in light of policies followed by others and the practices of international institutions. Hence, interests are neither fixed nor firm; they are not a solid platform on which to build a theory of rational self-interest. Both optics see reputation as important, but reputations can be instrumental for a variety of purposes, depending on the context. The normative optic seems to make reputation both more one-dimensional than it is, and larger than life – like a cardboard cutout figure in the normative telescope. Concerns about reputation sometimes lead to the fulfillment of commitments, but they do not always do so. Thinking creatively about institutions could derive clues to a better understanding of both interests and reputation, and how norms could affect state decisions through their effects on interests and reputation.

Institutions

Lawyers and political scientists both recognize that institutions matter. In modern states, calculations about the consequences of different courses of action, in response to changes in the external world, depend on the authority of legislatures, executives, and courts, and on the rules that govern the access to power of nongovernmental actors. International lawyers have had a lot to say about the role of domestic governments, domestic courts, and the European Court of Justice, in the implementation and interpretation of law.[39]

Sophisticated instrumentalists recognize that the rational, self-interested actions of the political actors they study are contingent on institutions. Agenda-setting and delegation have become important topics in political science.[40] Two of the most important functions of institutions are to provide information to participants and to link issues to one another in the context of a larger set of valued activities.[41] By looking more closely at the role of information, we can see how a coherent instrumentalism is dependent on beliefs and, therefore, on norms.[42] Indeed, we could understand the mutual relationship between beliefs and interests in a more sophisticated way by sketching missing links that involve institutions and reputation. There are three components.

First, we could begin with the instrumentalist premise that institutions depend on interests. But as game theory shows, behavior also depends on the information one has. In Prisoners' Dilemma and Assurance games, strategy is contingent upon expectations about others' behavior. Indeed, the major lesson of modern game theory is how behavior is sensitive to different information conditions. Since world politics involves strategic interaction, any good theory of world politics needs to treat information as a variable.

Second, it follows that interests as interpreted by actors (even when the motivational base is entirely material self-interest) depend on information as well as on underlying payoffs. Therefore, interests depend on reputations.

Finally, reputations depend on institutions. States cultivate reputations because of what good reputations will enable them to achieve. In the normative optic, their purpose is to realize their principles; in the instrumentalist one, to achieve self-interested objectives. Institutions that lengthen the shadow of the future or link otherwise separate issues together may create incentives to cooperate now for the sake of promoting cooperation by others later.[43] Hence institutions matter even if they cannot enforce rules from above because they affect reputations which are useful to cultivate. But concern about reputation is not a magic elixir that aligns self-interests with benign norms such as promise-keeping.

Thinking clearly about reputation and institutions helps us to see how the insights of the instrumentalist and normative optics may jointly contribute to our understanding of international regimes and international law. Interests shape institutions, which affect beliefs, including reputations, which in turn affect interests. In particular, institutions can affect what kind of reputation it is most useful for governments to acquire. Institutions that states strongly value can promote cooperation by linking normatively prescribed behavior, such as fulfilling commitments, to the continued receipt of material or normative benefits from the institutions.

The benefits of fulfilling one's own commitments may be material, such as the rewards of most-favored nation treatment in the World Trade Organization. They may also be instrumental to other self-interested objectives. For instance, not being a notable violator of GATT or WTO rules is important if a state seeks to bring cases against other states that arguably are breaking or bending the rules. Blocking a consensus in the European Union on issues of importance to others may be costly to the success of one's own initiatives. Conversely, reneging on commitments to the United Nations, as the withholding of United States dues has shown, may carry few costs, and may even enhance the reneger's leverage in institutional bargaining.

The benefits of fulfilling commitments may also be normative. The reward may be acceptance as a "member in good standing" of the international trading community, or even the knowledge that one is helping to uphold valued institutions. But it is hardly of great normative value to have a reputation for supporting institutions that one despises. There are few rewards for blindly acquiescing in attempts by a majority in the United Nations to create law that is inconsistent both with one's principles and interests.

Within the context of valued institutions, instrumental and normative incentives work in tandem with each other, not at cross-purposes. In instrumentalist language, what is essential to an institution for it to function well is that it helps to align these various types of incentives in ways that support the mission of the institution. In normative language, well-functioning institutions are those that facilitate persuasion and cooperation on the basis of widely held values. In practice, these two descriptions may amount to the same thing.

Conclusion

The two optics that I have constructed here are stylizations, perhaps even stereotypes. Few experienced or perceptive observers of international relations would exclusively adopt one or the other. I share the aspirations of many commentators to find a productive synthesis between them. Let me briefly review the keys to my proposed synthesis. Interests are changeable, responding to changes in descriptive information, causal beliefs, and principled beliefs. Hence, norms matter for interests. So do beliefs about others' beliefs; that is, reputation. Concern for reputation can be a means of reconciling instrumentalist prescriptions with normative ones. However, this reconciliation only takes place reliably within the context of highly valued institutions, which align material and extra-material incentives. Institutions are especially important for the way in which they can alter beliefs, can sometimes influence what we want or do, and can always affect how others will behave if they have any impact at all.

If I am right, much depends in world politics not only on material interests and on normative views but on how institutions are designed. Institutions need to be consistent with both broad patterns of power and interests. But they also need to create interests and incentives to develop reputations which support the institutions. Institutions also need to be consistent with the basic normative commitments of their members, so that having a reputation for supporting the institution has intrinsic, as well as instrumental, value.

My analysis, if true, has implications for our work as citizens, advocates, and policy advisors.

Since institutions tend to persist, democratic governments should be alert to ensure that their principles and rules reflect the values of democratic societies, while being sufficiently flexible to adapt to the changing demands of international society. We need to align our interests with the norms we value, as we adjust these practices to the demands of others. Such alignments of interests with values require institutions. Showing the necessity for such institutions, and helping to craft them, constitute intellectual and policy challenges for international lawyers and political scientists. Designing effective international institutions is a worthy vocation that international lawyers and political scientists can embrace together, with enthusiasm and a sense of purpose.

Notes

1 Originally given as a Sherrill Lecture at Yale University Law School on February 22, 1996.
2 Thomas M. Franck, "Legitimacy in the International System," **82** *Am. J. Int'l. L.* 705 (1988).
3 David Kennedy, *International Legal Structures*, p. 293 (1987).
4 Louis Henkin, *How Nations Behave: Law and Foreign Policy* (2nd ed. 1979).
5 Anne-Marie Slaughter Burley, "International Law and International Relations Theory: A Dual Agenda," **87** *Am J. Int'l.* L. 205, 220 (1993)
6 Idem. at 221.
7 My discussion of instrumentalist and normative optics parallels my analysis of "rationalistic" and "reflective" approaches to international relations some years ago. Robert O. Keohane, "International Institutions: Two Approaches," **32** *Int'l Stud.* Q. 379 (1988), reprinted in Robert O. Keohane, *International Institutions and State Power* p. 158 (1989). Here I am focusing less on abstract arguments, and more on attempts to understand the impact of norms on specific patterns of state behavior. Work on international law during the past few years has done quite a bit to bridge the gap between the abstraction of reflectivist theorizing, on the one hand, and observed state behavior, on the other.
8 *See* Friedrich V. Kratochwil, *Rules, Norms and Decisions: On the Conditions of Practical and Legal Reasoning in International Relations and Domestic Affairs* (1989).
9 *See* idem. at 100.
10 *In* Louis Henkin *et al.*, *International Law: Cases and Materials* 1007 (1987) [hereinafter *ILC*].
11 Phillip R. Trimble, "International Law: World Order and Critical Legal Studies," **42** *Stan. L. Rev.* 811, 833 (1990).
12 Abram Chayes and Antonia Handler Chayes. *The New Sovereignty: Compliance with International Regulatory Agreements*, p. 229 (1995).
13 William Shakespeare, *Twelfth Night*, act 1, sc. 5.
14 *See* Trimble, *supra* note 10, at 839–40.

15 Franck, *supra* note 1, at 738.
16 *See* Thomas M. Franck, *The Power of Legitimacy Among Nations* (1990); Trimble, *supra* note 10.
17 *ILC*, *supra* note 9 at 9; *see also* Louis Henkin, *How Nations Behave: Law and Foreign Policy*, p. 42 (2nd ed. 1979).
18 Chayes and Chayes, *supra* note 11, at 134.
19 *See* Ian Johnstone, "Treaty Interpretation: The Authority of Interpretive Communities," **12** *Mich. J. Int'l L.* 371 (1991), excerpted in Anthony D'Amato, *International Law Anthology*, pp. 121–24 (1994).
20 Chayes and Chayes, *supra* note 11, at 118.
21 Idem. at 27.
22 Idem. at 230.
23 *See* Philip B. Heymann, "The Problem of Coordination: Bargaining and Rules," **86** *Harv. L. Rev.* 797 (1973); Kratochwil, *supra* note 7.
24 *See* idem.
25 Franck, *supra* note 1, at 712.
26 Trimble, *supra* note 10, at 842.
27 Geoffrey Garrett and Barry Weingast, "Ideas, Interests, and Institutions: Constructing the European Community's Common Market," in *Ideas and Foreign Policy* p. 173 (Judith Goldstein and Robert O. Keohane eds, 1993).
28 Charles E. Lindblom, *The Intelligence of Democracy* (1965).
29 *See* George Downs and Stephen A. Rocke, *Optimal Imperfection*, Ch. 4 (1995).
30 Trimble, *supra* note 10, at 842 n. 115.
31 Ronald Rogowski, *Commerce and Coalitions* (1989).
32 Kratochwil, *supra* note 7; Alexander Wendt, "Anarchy Is What States Make of It: The Social Construction of Power Politics," **46** *Int'l Org.* 39 (1992).
33 Robert Axelrod, *The Evolution of Cooperation* (1984).
34 Henkin, *supra* note 16, at 52, *cited with approval in* Johnstone, *supra* note 18, at 390.
35 Thomas Schelling, *The Strategy of Conflict* (1980); *see also* David Kreps and Robert Wilson, "Reputation and Imperfect Information," **27** *J. Econ. Theory* 253 (1982).
36 Heymann, *supra* note 22, at 822–23.
37 *But see* Robert Keohane, *After Hegemony: Cooperation and Discord in the World Political Economy*, pp. 129–30 (1984). In this previous work, I relied on an analogy between reputation and the credit ratings of borrowers, as discussed by Walter Bagehot. Unfortunately, this analogy is fallacious. Lenders have many borrowers to lend to. If one borrower's reputation suffers, creditors can lend to others at only a slight cost, representing the reduction in interest rates resulting from a decline in demand.
38 **9** *American State Papers*, p. 407 (2nd. ed., T.B. Wait and Sons, 1817).
39 Benedetto Conforti, *International, Law and the Role of Domestic Legal Systems* (1993); Burley, *supra* note 4; Anne-Marie Burley and Walter Mattli, "Europe Before the Court: A Political Theory of Legal Integration," **47** *Int'l Org.* 41 (1993).
40 Andrew Moravcsik, *Why the European Community Strengthens the State: Domestic Politics and International Cooperation* (Center for European Studies Working Paper Series No. 52, 1994); J. Mark Ramsayer and Frances McCall Rosenbluth, *Japan's Political Marketplace* (1993); Kenneth Shepsle and Barry Weingast, "The Institutional Foundations of Committee Power," **81** *Am. Pol. Sci. Rev.* 85 (1987); Lisa L. Martin, *Democratic Commitments: Legislatures and International Cooperation* (Oct. 1995) (unpublished manuscript, on file with Harvard University Center for International Affairs).
41 *See* Keohane, *supra* note 36, at 244–45; Lisa L. Martin, "Interests, Power and Multilateralism," **46** *Int'l Org.* 765 (1992).

42 *Cf.* David Kreps, "Corporate Culture and Economic Theory," in *Perspectives on Positive Political Economy*, p. 90 (James E. Alt and Kenneth A. Shepsle eds, 1990) (analyzing the proposition in the area of corporate culture); Paul Milgrom *et al.*, "The Role of the Institutions in the Revival of Trade: The Law Merchant, Private Judges, and the Champagne Fairs," 2 *Econ. and Pol.* 1 (1990).
43 Axelrod, *supra* note 32; Lisa L. Martin, "Heterogeneity, Linkage, and Commons Problems," in *Local Commons and Global Interdependence: Heterogeneity and Cooperation in Two Domains*, p. 71 (Robert O. Keohane and Elinor Ostrom eds, 1995).

7   The concept of legalization

Kenneth W. Abbott, Robert O. Keohane,
Andrew Moravcsik, Anne-Marie Slaughter,
and Duncan Snidal

(2000)

We understand legalization as a particular form of institutionalization characterized by three components: obligation, precision, and delegation. In this article, we introduce these three characteristics, explore their variability and the range of institutional forms produced by combining them, and explicate the elements of legalization in greater detail.

The elements of legalization

"Legalization" refers to a particular set of characteristics that institutions may (or may not) possess. These characteristics are defined along three dimensions: obligation, precision, and delegation. *Obligation* means that states or other actors are bound by a rule or commitment or by a set of rules or commitments. Specifically, it means that they are *legally* bound by a rule or commitment in the sense that their behavior thereunder is subject to scrutiny under the general rules, procedures, and discourse of international law, and often of domestic law as well. *Precision* means that rules unambiguously define the conduct they require, authorize, or proscribe. *Delegation* means that third parties have been granted authority to implement, interpret, and apply the rules; to resolve disputes; and (possibly) to make further rules.

Each of these dimensions is a matter of degree and gradation, not a rigid dichotomy, and each can vary independently. Consequently, the concept of legalization encompasses a multidimensional continuum, ranging from the "ideal type" of legalization, where all three properties are maximized; to "hard" legalization, where all three (or at least obligation and delegation) are high; through multiple forms of partial or "soft" legalization involving different combinations of attributes; and finally to the complete absence of legalization, another ideal type. None of these dimensions – far less the full spectrum of legalization – can be fully operationalized. We do, however, consider in the section entitled "The Dimensions of Legalization" a number of techniques by which actors manipulate the elements of legalization; we also suggest several corresponding indicators of the strength or weakness of legal arrangements.

Statutes or regulations in highly developed national legal systems are generally taken as prototypical of hard legalization. For example, a congressional statute setting a cap on emissions of a particular pollutant is (subject to any special exceptions) legally binding on US residents (obligation), unambiguous in its requirements (precision), and subject to judicial interpretation and application as well as administrative elaboration and enforcement (delegation). But even domestic enactments vary widely in their degree of legalization, both across states – witness the vague "proclamations" and restrictions on judicial review imposed by authoritarian regimes – and across issue areas within states – compare US tax law to "political questions" under the Constitution. Moreover, the degree of obligation, precision, or delegation in formal institutions can be obscured in practice by political pressure, informal norms, and other factors. International legalization exhibits similar variation; on the whole, however, international institutions are less highly legalized than institutions in democratic rule-of-law states.

Note that we have defined legalization in terms of key characteristics of rules and procedures, not in terms of effects. For instance, although our definition includes delegation of legal authority (to domestic courts or agencies as well as equivalent international bodies), it does not include the degree to which rules are actually implemented domestically or to which states comply with them. To do so would be to conflate delegation with effective action by the agent and would make it impossible to inquire whether legalization increases rule implementation or compliance. Nor does our definition extend to the substantive content of rules or their degree of stringency. We regard substantive content and legalization as distinct characteristics. A conference declaration or other international document that is explicitly not legally binding could have exactly the same substantive content as a binding treaty, or even a domestic statute, but they would be very different instruments in terms of legalization.

Our conception of legalization creates common ground for political scientists and lawyers by moving away from a narrow view of law as requiring enforcement by a coercive sovereign. This criterion has underlain much international relations thinking on the topic. Since virtually no international institution passes this standard, it has led to a widespread disregard of the importance of international law. But theoretical work in international relations has increasingly shifted attention away from the need for centralized enforcement toward other institutionalized ways of promoting cooperation.[1] In addition, the forms of legalization we observe at the turn of the millennium are flourishing in the absence of centralized coercion.

Any definition is ultimately arbitrary at the margins. Yet definitions should strive to meet certain criteria. They should be broadly consistent with ordinary language, but more precise. To achieve precision, definitions should turn on a coherent set of identifiable attributes. These should be sufficiently few that situations can be readily characterized within a small number of categories, and sufficiently important that changes in their values will influence the processes being studied. Defining legalization in terms of obligation, precision, and delegation provides us with identifiable dimensions of variation whose effects on international behavior can be empirically explored.

Our concept of legalization is a working definition, intended to facilitate research. Empiricist in origin, it is tailored to the phenomena we observe in international relations. We are not proposing a definitive definition or seeking to resolve age-old debates regarding the nature of law or whether international law is "really" law. Highly legalized arrangements under our conception will typically fall within the standard international lawyer's definition of international law. But many international commitments that to a lawyer entail binding legal obligations lack significant levels of precision or delegation and are thus partial or soft under our definition.

We acknowledge a particular debt to H.L.A. Hart's *The Concept of Law*.[2] Hart defined a legal system as the conjunction of primary and secondary rules. Primary rules are rules of obligation bearing directly on individuals or entities requiring them "to do or abstain from certain actions." Secondary rules, by contrast, are "rules about rules" – that is, rules that do not "impose obligations," but instead "confer powers" to create, extinguish, modify, and apply primary rules.[3] Again, we do not seek to define "law" or to equate our conception of legalization with a definition of a legal system. Yet Hart's concepts of primary and secondary rules are useful in helping to pinpoint the distinctive characteristics of the phenomena we observe in international relations. The attributes of obligation and precision refer to international rules that regulate behavior; these closely resemble Hart's primary rules of obligation. But when we define obligation as an attribute that incorporates general rules, procedures, and discourse of international law, we are referring to features of the international system analogous to Hart's three main types of secondary rules: recognition, change, and adjudication. And the criterion of delegation necessarily implicates all three of these categories.[4]

The variability of legalization

A central feature of our conception of legalization is the variability of each of its three dimensions, and therefore of the overall legalization of international norms, agreements, and regimes. This feature is illustrated in Figure 7.1. In Figure 7.1 each element of the definition appears as a continuum, ranging from the weakest form (the absence of legal obligation, precision, or delegation, except as provided by the background operation of the international legal system) at the left to the strongest or "hardest" form at the right.[5] Figure 7.1 also highlights the independence of these dimensions from each other: conceptually, at least, the authors of a legal instrument can combine any level of obligation, precision, and delegation to produce an institution exactly suited to their specific needs. (In practice, as we shall explain, certain combinations are employed more frequently than others.)

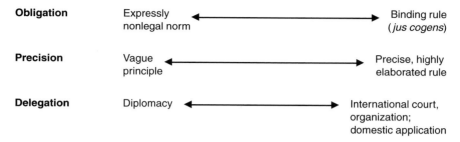

Obligation	Expressly nonlegal norm	←——————————→ Binding rule (*jus cogens*)
Precision	Vague principle	←——————————→ Precise, highly elaborated rule
Delegation	Diplomacy	←——————————→ International court, organization; domestic application

Figure 7.1 The dimensions of legalization

It would be inappropriate to equate the right-hand end points of these dimensions with "law" and the left-hand end points with "politics," for politics continues (albeit in different forms) even where there is law. Nor should one equate the left-hand end points with the absence of norms or institutions; as the designations in Figure 7.1 suggest, both norms (such as ethical principles and rules of practice) and institutions (such as diplomacy and balance of power) can exist beyond these dimensions. Figure 7.1 simply represents the components of legal institutions.

Using the format of Figure 7.1, one can plot where a particular arrangement falls on the three dimensions of legalization. For example, the Agreement on Trade-Related Aspects of Intellectual Property (TRIPs), administered by the World Trade Organization (WTO), is strong on all three elements. The 1963 Treaty Banning Nuclear Weapons Tests in the Atmosphere, in Outer Space, and Under Water is legally binding and quite precise, but it delegates almost no legal authority. And the 1975 Final Act of the Helsinki Conference on Security and Cooperation in Europe was explicitly not legally binding and delegated little authority, though it was moderately precise.

The format of Figure 7.1 can also be used to depict variations in the degree of legalization between portions of an international instrument (John King Gamble, Jr. has made a similar internal analysis of the UN Convention on the Law of the Sea[6]) and within a given instrument or regime over time. The Universal Declaration of Human Rights, for example, was only minimally legalized (it was explicitly aspirational, not overly precise, and weakly institutionalized), but the human rights regime has evolved into harder forms over time. The International Covenant on Civil and Political Rights imposes binding legal obligations, spells out concepts only adumbrated in the declaration, and creates (modest) implementing institutions.[7]

Table 7.1 further illustrates the remarkable variety of international legalization. Here, for concise presentation, we characterize obligation, precision, and delegation as either high or low. The eight possible combinations of these values are shown in Table 7.1; rows are arranged roughly in order of decreasing legalization, with legal obligation, a peculiarly important

Table 7.1 Forms of international legalization

Type	Obligation	Precision	Delegation	Examples
Ideal type:				
Hard law				
I	High	High	High	EC; WTO–TRIPs; European human rights convention; International Criminal Court
II	High	Low	High	EEC Antitrust, Art. 85–6; WTO–national treatment
III	High	High	Low	US–Soviet arms control treaties; Montreal Protocol
IV	Low	High	High (moderate)	UN Committee on Sustainable Development (Agenda 21)
V	High	Low	Low	Vienna Ozone Convention; European Framework Convention on National Minorities
VI	Low	Low	High (moderate)	UN specialized agencies; World Bank; OSCE High Commissioner on National Minorities
VII	Low	High	Low	Helsinki Final Act; Nonbinding Forest; Principles; technical standards
VIII	Low	Low	Low	Group of 7; spheres of influence; balance of power
Ideal type: Anarchy				

facet of legalization, weighted most heavily, delegation next, and precision given the least weight. A binary characterization sacrifices the continuous nature of the dimensions of legalization as shown in Figure 7.1 and makes it difficult to depict intermediate forms. Yet the table usefully demonstrates the range of institutional possibilities encompassed by the concept of legalization, provides a valuable shorthand for frequently used clusters of elements, and highlights the tradeoffs involved in weakening (or strengthening) particular elements.

Row I on this table corresponds to situations near the ideal type of full legalization, as in highly developed domestic legal systems. Much of European Community (EC) law belongs here. In addition, the WTO administers a remarkably detailed set of legally binding international agreements; it also operates a dispute settlement mechanism, including an appellate tribunal with significant – if still not fully proven – authority to interpret and apply those agreements in the course of resolving particular disputes.

Rows II–III represent situations in which the character of law remains quite hard, with high legal obligation and one of the other two elements coded as "high." Because the combination of relatively imprecise rules and strong delegation is a common and effective institutional response to uncertainty, even in domestic legal systems (the Sherman Antitrust Act in the United States is a prime example), many regimes in row II should be considered virtually equal in terms of legalization to those in row I. Like the Sherman Act, for example, the original European Economic Community (EEC) rules of competition law (Articles 85 and 86 of the Treaty of Rome) were for the most part quite imprecise. Over time, however, the exercise of interpretive authority by the European courts and the promulgation of regulations by the Commission and Council produced a rich body of law. The 1987 Montreal Protocol on Substances that Deplete the Ozone Layer (row III), in contrast, created a quite precise and elaborate set of legally binding rules but did not delegate any significant degree of authority for implementing them. Because third-party interpretation and application of rules is so central to legal institutions, we consider this arrangement less highly legalized than those previously discussed.

As we move further down the table, the difficulties of dichotomizing and ordering our three dimensions become more apparent. For example, it is not instructive to say that arrangements in row IV are necessarily more legalized than those in row V; this judgment requires a more detailed specification of the forms of obligation, precision, and delegation used in each case. In some settings a strong legal obligation (such as the original Vienna Ozone Convention, row V) might be more legalized than a weaker obligation (such as Agenda 21, row IV), even if the latter were more precise and entailed stronger delegation. Furthermore, the relative significance of delegation vis-à-vis other dimensions becomes less clear at lower levels, since truly "high" delegation, including judicial or quasi-judicial authority, almost never exists together with low levels of legal obligation. The kinds of delegation typically seen in rows IV and VI are administrative or operational in nature (we describe this as "moderate" delegation in Table 7.1). Thus one might reasonably regard a precise but nonobligatory agreement (such as the Helsinki Final Act, row VII) as more highly legalized than an imprecise and nonobligatory agreement accompanied by modest administrative delegation (such as the High Commissioners on National Minorities of the Organization for Security and Cooperation in Europe, row VI).[8] The general point is that Table 7.1 should be read indicatively, not as a strict ordering.

The middle rows of Table 7.1 suggest a wide range of "soft" or intermediate forms of legalization. Here norms may exist, but they are difficult to apply as law in a strict sense. The 1985 Vienna Convention for the Protection of the Ozone Layer (row V), for example, imposed binding treaty obligations, but

most of its substantive commitments were expressed in general, even hortatory language and were not connected to an institutional framework with
independent authority. Agenda 21, adopted at the 1992 Rio Conference on
Environment and Development (row IV), spells out highly elaborated norms
on numerous issues but was clearly intended not to be legally binding and is
implemented by relatively weak UN agencies. Arrangements like these are
often used in settings where norms are contested and concerns for sovereign
autonomy are strong, making higher levels of obligation, precision, or
delegation unacceptable.

Rows VI and VII include situations where rules are not legally obligatory,
but where states either accept precise normative formulations or delegate
authority for implementing broad principles. States often delegate discretionary authority where judgments that combine concern for professional standards with implicit political criteria are required, as with the International
Monetary Fund (IMF), the World Bank, and the other international organizations in row VI. Arrangements such as those in row VII are sometimes
used to administer coordination standards, which actors have incentives to
follow provided they expect others to do so, as well as in areas where legally
obligatory actions would be politically infeasible.

Example of rule systems entailing the very low levels of legalization in row
VIII include "balances of power" and "spheres of influence." These are not
legal institutions in any real sense. The balance of power was characterized by
rules of practice[9] and by arrangements for diplomacy, as in the Concert of
Europe. Spheres of influence during the Cold War were imprecise, obligations
were partly expressed in treaties but largely tacit, and little institutional
framework existed to oversee them.

Finally, at the bottom of the table, we approach the ideal type of anarchy
prominent in international relations theory. "Anarchy" is an easily misunder-
stood term of art, since even situations taken as extreme forms of international anarchy are in fact structured by rules – most notably rules defining
national sovereignty – with legal or pre-legal characteristics. Hedley Bull
writes of "the anarchical society" as characterized by institutions like sovereignty and international law as well as diplomacy and the balance of power.[10]
Even conceptually, moreover, there is a wide gap between the weakest forms
of legalization and the complete absence of norms and institutions.

Given the range of possibilities, we do not take the position that greater
legalization, or any particular form of legalization, is inherently superior.[11]
As Kenneth Abbott and Duncan Snidal argue in "Hard and Soft Law
in International Governance", institutional arrangements in the middle or
lower reaches of Table 7.1 may best accommodate the diverse interests of
concerned actors. A concrete example is the argument made by Judith Goldstein and Lisa Martin in their article "Legalization, Trade Liberalization, and
Domestic Politics: A Cautionary Note": more highly legalized trade rules can
be problematic for liberal trade policy. (Both articles appear in *International
Organization* **54–3**, Summer 2000.)

On a related set of issues – whether international legalization is increasing, or likely to increase, over time – we take no position. The comparative statics approach that informs this chapter is not suitable for analyzing such dynamic phenomena. Yet the issues are important and intriguing. We undoubtedly witness increasing legalization in many issue areas. The ozone depletion regime, for example, began in 1985 with a binding but otherwise weakly legalized convention (row V). It was augmented two years later by the more precise and highly elaborated Montreal Protocol (row III). Since then, through practice and subsequent revisions, the regime has developed a "system for implementation review," with a noncompliance procedure that still falls short of third-party dispute resolution but appears to have had some impact on behavior.[12] In other issue areas, like the whaling regime described by John K. Setear, the level of legalization appears to remain largely constant over time, even as the substance of the regime changes.[13] And in still others, legalization seems to decline, as in the move from fixed to floating exchange rates. Exploration of legal dynamics would be the logical next step in the research program to which this chapter seeks to contribute.

In the remainder of this article we turn to a more detailed explication of the three dimensions of legalization. We summarize the discussion in each section with a table listing several indicators of stronger or weaker legalization along the relevant dimension, with delegation subdivided into judicial and legislative/administrative components.

The dimensions of legalization

Obligation

Legal rules and commitments impose a particular type of binding obligation on states and other subjects (such as international organizations). Legal obligations are different in kind from obligations resulting from coercion, comity, or morality alone. As discussed earlier, legal obligations bring into play the established norms, procedures, and forms of discourse of the international legal system.[14]

The fundamental international legal principle of *pacta sunt servanda* means that the rules and commitments contained in legalized international agreements are regarded as obligatory, subject to various defenses or exceptions, and not to be disregarded as preferences change. They must be performed in good faith regardless of inconsistent provisions of domestic law. International law also provides principles for the interpretation of agreements and a variety of technical rules on such matters as formation, reservation, and amendments. Breach of a legal obligation is understood to create "legal responsibility," which does not require a showing of intent on the part of specific state organs.

The international legal system also contains accepted procedures and remedies for breaches of legal commitments. Only states injured by a breach have standing to complain; and the complaining state or its citizens must exhaust any domestic remedies within the breaching state before making an international claim. States may then pursue their claims diplomatically or through any formal dispute procedure they have accepted. International law also prescribes certain defenses, which include consent, self-defense, and necessity, as well as the broad doctrine called *rebus sic stantibus*: an agreement may lose its binding character if important conditions change materially. These doctrines automatically inject a degree of flexibility into legal commitments; by defining particular exceptions, though, they reinforce legal obligations in other circumstances.

When breach leads to injury, legal responsibility entails an obligation to make reparation, preferably through restitution. If this is not possible, the alternative in the event of material harm is a monetary indemnity; in the event of psychological harm, "satisfaction" in the form of an apology. Since achieving such remedies is often problematic, international law authorizes self-help measures, including reprisals, reciprocal measures (such as the withdrawal of equivalent concessions in the WTO), and retorsions (such as suspending foreign aid). Self-help is limited, though, by the doctrine of proportionality and other legal conditions, including restrictions on the unilateral use of force.

Finally, establishing a commitment as a legal rule invokes a particular form of discourse. Although actors may disagree about the interpretation or applicability of a set of rules, discussion of issues purely in terms of interests or power is no longer legitimate. Legalization of rules implies a discourse primarily in terms of the text, purpose, and history of the rules, their interpretation, admissible exceptions, applicability to classes of situations, and particular facts. The rhetoric of law is highly developed, and the community of legal experts – whose members normally participate in legal rule-making and dispute settlement – is highly socialized to apply it. Thus the possibilities and limits of this discourse are normally part and parcel of legalized commitments.

Commitments can vary widely along the continuum of obligation, as summarized in Table 7.2. An example of a hard legal rule is Article 24 of the Vienna Convention on Diplomatic Relations, which reads in its entirety: "The archives and documents of the mission shall be inviolable at any time

Table 7.2 Indicators of obligation

High
Unconditional obligation; language and other indicia of intent to be legally bound
Political treaty: implicit conditions on obligation
National reservations on specific obligations; contingent obligations and escape clauses
Hortatory obligations
Norms adopted without law-making authority; recommendations and guidelines
Explicit negation of intent to be legally bound
Low

and wherever they may be." As a whole, this treaty reflects the intent of the parties to create legally binding obligations governed by international law. It uses the language of obligation; calls for the traditional legal formalities of signature, ratification, and entry into force; requires that the agreement and national ratification documents be registered with the UN; is styled a "Convention;" and states its relationship to preexisting rules of customary international law.[15] Article 24 itself imposes an unconditional obligation in formal, even "legalistic" terms.

At the other end of the spectrum are instruments that explicitly negate any intent to create legal obligations. The best-known example is the 1975 Helsinki Final Act. By specifying that this accord could not be registered with the UN, the parties signified that it was not an "agreement . . . governed by international law." Other instruments are even more explicit: witness the 1992 "Non-Legally Binding Authoritative Statement of Principles for a Global Consensus" on sustainable management of forests. Many working agreements among national government agencies are explicitly nonbinding.[16] Instruments framed as "recommendations" or "guidelines" – like the OECD Guidelines on Multinational Enterprises – are normally intended not to create legally binding obligations.[17]

These contrasting legal forms have distinctive implications. Under legally binding agreements like the Vienna Convention, states may assert legal claims (under *pacta sunt servanda*, state responsibility and other doctrines of international law), engage in legal discourse, invoke legal procedures, and resort to legal remedies. Under nonbinding instruments like the Forest Principles states may do none of these things, although they may make normative claims, engage in normative discourse, and resort to political remedies. Further theorizing and empirical investigation are needed to determine whether these distinctions – at least in the absence of strong delegation – lead to substantial differences in practice. The care with which states frame agreements, however, suggests a belief that they do.

Actors utilize many techniques to vary legal obligation between these two extremes, often creating surprising contrasts between form and substance. On the one hand, it is widely accepted that states expect some formally binding "political treaties" not to be observed if interests or circumstances change.[18] More frequently, provisions of legally binding agreements are worded to circumscribe their obligatory force. One common softening device is the contingent obligation: the 1994 Framework Convention on Climate Change, for example, requires parties to take various actions to limit greenhouse gas emissions, but only after considering "their specific national and regional development priorities, objectives, and circumstances."

Another widely used device is the escape clause.[19] The European Convention for the Protection of Human Rights and Fundamental Freedoms, for example, authorizes states to interfere with certain civil rights in the interest of national security and the prevention of disorder "when necessary in a democratic society," and more broadly during war "or other public emergency threatening the life of the nation."[20] Most arms control agreements include the following clause, repeated verbatim from the Limited Test Ban Treaty: "Each party shall in exercising its national sovereignty have the right to withdraw from [this agreement], if it decides that extraordinary events, related to the subject matter of [this agreement], have jeopardized the supreme interests of its country."[21] Many instruments, from the Outer Space Treaty to the Convention on the Settlement of Investment Disputes, simply allow for withdrawal after a specified notice period.

Other formally binding commitments are hortatory, creating at best weak legal obligations. Article IV of the IMF Articles of Agreement, for example, requires parties only to "endeavor" to adopt specified domestic economic policies and to "seek to promote" economic stability, "with due regard to [their] circumstances." The International Covenant on Economic, Social, and Cultural Rights requires parties only "to take steps . . . with a view to achieving progressively the full realization of the rights recognized in the . . . Covenant."[22]

On the other hand, a large number of instruments state seemingly unconditional obligations even though the institutions or procedures through which they were created have no direct law-creating authority! Many UN General Assembly declarations, for example, enunciate legal norms, though the assembly has no formal legislative power.[23] Instruments like the 1992 Rio Declaration on Environment and Development and the 1995 Beijing Declaration on Women's Rights are approved at UN conferences with no agreed law-making power.[24]

Instruments like these should not be troublesome in legal terms, since they do not conform to the established "rules of recognition" of international law. In fact, though, they are highly problematic. Over time, even nonbinding declarations can shape the practices of states and other actors and their expectations of appropriate conduct, leading to the emergence of customary law or the adoption of harder agreements. Soft commitments may also implicate the legal principle of good faith compliance, weakening objections to subsequent developments. In many issue areas the legal implications of soft instruments are hotly contested. Supporters argue for immediate and universal legal effect under traditional doctrines (for example, that an instrument codifies existing customary law or interprets an organizational charter) and innovative ones (for example, that an instrument reflects an international "consensus" or "instant custom"). As acts of international governance, then, soft normative instruments have a finely wrought ambiguity.[25]

Precision

A precise rule specifies clearly and unambiguously what is expected of a state or other actor (in terms of both the intended objective and the means of achieving it) in a particular set of circumstances. In other words, precision narrows the scope for reasonable interpretation.[26] In Thomas Franck's terms, such rules are "determinate."[27] For a set of rules, precision implies not just that each rule in the set is unambiguous, but that the rules are related to one another in a noncontradictory way, creating a framework within which case-by-case interpretation can be coherently carried out.[28] Precise sets of rules are often, though by no means always, highly elaborated or dense, detailing conditions of application, spelling out required or proscribed behavior in numerous situations, and so on.

Precision is an important characteristic in many theories of law. It is essential to a rationalist view of law as a coordinating device, as in James D. Morrow's account of the laws of war.[29] It is also important to positivist visions of law as rules to be applied, whether through a centralized agency or through reciprocity.[30] Franck argues that precision increases the legitimacy of rules and thus their normative "compliance pull." Lon L. Fuller, like other liberals, emphasizes the social and moral virtues of certainty and predictability for individual actors.[31] In each case, clarity is essential to the force of law.

In highly developed legal systems, normative directives are often formulated as relatively precise "rules" ("do not drive faster than 50 miles per hour"), but many important directives are also formulated as relatively general "standards" ("do not drive recklessly").[32] The more "rule-like" a normative prescription, the more a community decides *ex ante* which categories of behavior are unacceptable; such decisions are typically made by legislative bodies. The more "standard-like" a prescription, the more a community makes this determination *ex post*, in relation to specific sets of facts; such decisions are usually entrusted to courts. Standards allow courts to take into account equitable factors relating to particular actors or situations, albeit at the sacrifice of some *ex ante* clarity.[33] Domestic legal systems are able to use standards like "due care" or the Sherman Act's prohibition on "conspiracies in restraint of trade" because they include well-established courts and agencies able to interpret and apply them (high delegation), developing increasingly precise bodies of precedent.

In some international regimes, the institutional context is sufficiently thick to make similar approaches feasible. In framing the EEC's common competition policy, for example, the drafters of the Treaty of Rome utilized both rules and standards.[34] Where they could identify disfavored conduct in advance, they specified it for reasons of clarity and notice: Article 85, for example, prohibits agreements between firms "that . . . fix purchase or selling prices." Because they could not anticipate all problematic conduct, though, the drafters also authorized the European Court to apply a general standard, prohibiting "agreements . . . which have as their object or effect the . . . distortion of competition within the common market."

In most areas of international relations, judicial, quasi-judicial, and administrative authorities are less highly developed and infrequently used. In this thin institutional context, imprecise norms are, in practice, most often interpreted and applied by the very actors whose conduct they are intended to govern. In addition, since most international norms are created through the direct consent or practice of states, there is no centralized legislature to overturn inappropriate, self-serving interpretations. Thus, precision and elaboration are especially significant hallmarks of legalization at the international level.

Much of international law is in fact quite precise, and precision and elaboration appear to be increasing dramatically, as exemplified by the WTO trade agreements, environmental agreements like the Montreal (ozone) and Kyoto (climate change) Protocols, and the arms control treaties produced during the Strategic Arms Limitation Talks (SALT) and subsequent negotiations. Indeed, many modern treaties are explicitly designed to increase determinacy and narrow issues of interpretation through the "codification" and "progressive development" of customary law. Leading examples include the Vienna Conventions on the Law of Treaties and on Diplomatic Relations, and important aspects of the UN Convention on the Law of the Sea. Even many nonbinding instruments, like the Rio Declaration on Environment and Development and Agenda 21, are remarkably precise and dense, presumably because proponents believe that these characteristics enhance their normative and political value.

Still, many treaty commitments are vague and general, in the ways suggested by Table 7.3.[35] The North American Free Trade Agreement side agreement on labor, for example, requires the parties to "provide for high labor standards." Article VI of the Treaty on the Non-Proliferation of Nuclear Weapons calls on the parties "to pursue negotiations in good faith on effective measures relating to cessation of the nuclear arms race . . . and to nuclear disarmament." Commercial treaties typically require states to create "favorable conditions" for investment and avoid "unreasonable" regulations. Numerous agreements call on states to "negotiate" or "consult," without specifying particular procedures. All these provisions create broad areas of discretion for the affected actors; indeed, many provisions are so general that one cannot meaningfully assess compliance, casting doubt on their legal force.[36] As Abbott and Snidal emphasize in their article,[37] such imprecision is not generally the result of a failure of legal draftsmanship, but a deliberate choice given the circumstances of domestic and international politics.

Imprecision is not synonymous with state discretion, however, when it occurs within a delegation of authority and therefore grants to an

Table 7.3 Indicators of precision

High
   Determinate rules: only narrow issues of interpretation
   Substantial but limited issues of interpretation
   Broad areas of discretion
   "Standards": only meaningful with reference to specific situations
   Impossible to determine whether conduct complies
Low

---

international body wider authority to determine its meaning. The charters of international organizations provide important examples. In these instruments, generality frequently produces a broader delegation of authority, although member states almost always retain many levers of influence. A recent example makes the point clearly. At the 1998 Rome conference that approved a charter for an international criminal court, the United States sought to avoid any broad delegation of authority. Its proposal accordingly emphasized the need for "clear, precise, and specific definitions of each offense" within the jurisdiction of the court.[38]

Delegation

The third dimension of legalization is the extent to which states and other actors delegate authority to designated third parties – including courts, arbitrators, and administrative organizations – to implement agreements. The characteristic forms of legal delegation are third-party dispute settlement mechanisms authorized to interpret rules and apply them to particular facts (and therefore in effect to make new rules, at least interstitially) under established doctrines of international law. Dispute settlement mechanisms are most highly legalized when the parties agree to binding third-party decisions on the basis of clear and generally applicable rules; they are least legalized when the process involves political bargaining between parties who can accept or reject proposals without legal justification.[39]

In practice, as reflected in Table 7.4, dispute-settlement mechanisms cover an extremely broad range: from no delegation (as in traditional political decision-making); through institutionalized forms of bargaining, including mechanisms to facilitate agreement, such as mediation (available within the WTO) and conciliation (an option under the Law of the Sea Convention); nonbinding arbitration (essentially the mechanism of the old GATT); binding arbitration (as in the US–Iran Claims Tribunal); and finally to actual adjudication (exemplified by the European Court of Justice and Court of Human Rights, and the international criminal tribunals for Rwanda and the former Yugoslavia).

Another significant variable – the extent to which individuals and private groups can initiate a legal proceeding – is explored by Robert O. Keohane, Andrew Moravcsik, and Anne-Marie Slaughter in "Legalized Dispute Resolution" (*International Organization*, **54–3**, Summer 2000). Private actors can influence governmental behavior even in settings where access is limited to states (such as the WTO and the International Court of Justice). Increasingly, though, private actors are being granted access to legalized dispute settlement mechanisms, either indirectly (through national courts, as in the EC, or a supranational body like the European Commission on Human Rights) or directly (as will shortly be the case for the European Court of Human Rights). As Keohane, Moravcsik, and Slaughter argue, private access appears to increase the expansiveness of legal institutions.

Table 7.4 Indicators of delegation

a. Dispute resolution
High
Courts: binding third-party decisions; general jurisdiction; direct private access; can interpret and supplement rules; domestic courts have jurisdiction
Courts: jurisdiction, access or normative authority limited or consensual
Binding arbitration
Nonbinding arbitration
Conciliation, mediation
Institutionalized bargaining
Pure political bargaining
Low
b. Rule making and implementation
High
Binding regulations; centralized enforcement
Binding regulations with consent or opt-out
Binding internal policies; legitimation of decentralized enforcement
Coordination standards
Draft conventions; monitoring and publicity
Recommendations; confidential monitoring
Normative statements
Forum for negotiations
Low

As one moves up the delegation continuum, the actions of decision-makers are increasingly governed, and legitimated, by rules. (Willingness to delegate often depends on the extent to which these rules are thought capable of constraining the delegated authority.) Thus, this form of legal delegation typically achieves the union of primary and secondary rules that Hart deemed necessary for the establishment of a legal system. Delegation to third-party adjudicators is virtually certain to be accompanied by the adoption of rules of adjudication. The adjudicative body may then find it necessary to identify or develop rules of recognition and change, as it sorts out conflicts between rules or reviews the validity of rules that are the subject of dispute.

Delegation of legal authority is not confined to dispute resolution. As Table 7.4 indicates, a range of institutions – from simple consultative arrangements to full-fledged international bureaucracies – helps to elaborate imprecise legal norms, implement agreed rules, and facilitate enforcement.

Like domestic administrative agencies, international organizations are often authorized to elaborate agreed norms (though almost always in softer ways than their domestic counterparts), especially where it is infeasible to draft precise rules in advance and where special expertise is required. The EU Commission drafts extensive regulations, though they usually become binding only with the assent of member states. Specialized agencies like the International Civil Aviation Organization and the Codex Alimentarius

Commission promulgate technical rules – often framed as recommendations – in coordination situations. In cases like these, the grant of rule-making authority typically contains (in Hart's terms) the rule of recognition; the governing bodies or secretariats of international organizations may subsequently develop rules of change. At lower levels of delegation, bodies like the International Labor Organization and the World Intellectual Property Organization draft proposed international conventions and promulgate a variety of nonbinding rules, some for use by private actors. International organizations also support interstate negotiations.

Many operational activities serve to implement legal norms.[40] Virtually all international organizations gather and disseminate information relevant to implementation; many also generate new information. Most engage in educational activities, such as the WTO's training programs for developing country officials. Agencies like the World Health Organization, the World Bank, and the UN Environment Program have much more extensive operations. These activities implement (and thus give meaning to) the norms and goals enunciated in the agencies' charters and other agreements they administer. Although most international organizations are highly constrained by member states, the imprecision of their governing instruments frequently leaves them considerable discretion, exercised implicitly as well as through formal interpretations and operating policies. The World Bank, for example, has issued detailed policies on matters such as environmental impact assessment and treatment of indigenous peoples; these become legally binding when incorporated in loan agreements.[41] The World Bank's innovative Inspection Panel supervises compliance, often as the result of private complaints.[42]

In Austinian approaches, centralized enforcement is the sine qua non of law. Yet even domestically, many areas of law are not closely tied to enforcement; so too, much international legalization is significant in spite of a lack of centralized enforcement. And international law can draw on some centralized powers of enforcement. The UN Security Council, for example, imposed programs of inspection, weapons destruction, and compensation on Iraq for violations of international law; it also created ad hoc tribunals for Rwanda and the former Yugoslavia that have convicted national officials of genocide, crimes against humanity, and other international crimes. As in domestic legal systems, moreover, some international agencies can enforce norms through their power to confer or deny benefits: international financial institutions have the greatest leverage, but other organizations can deny technical assistance or rights of participation to violators. (These actions presuppose powers akin to rule interpretation and adjudication.) Further, international organizations from the Security Council to the WTO legitimate (and constrain) decentralized sanctioning by states. Many also monitor state behavior and disseminate information on rule observance, creating implicit sanctions for states that wish to be seen as trustworthy members of an international community.

Legalized delegation, especially in its harder forms, introduces new actors and new forms of politics into interstate relations. As other articles in *International Organization*, **54–3**, Summer 2000 discuss, actors with delegated legal authority have their own interests, the pursuit of which may be more or less successfully constrained by conditions on the grant of authority and concomitant surveillance by member states. Transnational coalitions of nonstate actors also pursue their interests through influence or direct participation at the supranational level, often producing greater divergence from member state concerns. Deciding disputes, adapting or developing new rules, implementing agreed norms, and responding to rule violations all engender their own type of politics, which helps to restructure traditional interstate politics.

Conclusion

Highly legalized institutions are those in which rules are obligatory on parties through links to the established rules and principles of international law, in which rules are precise (or can be made precise through the exercise of delegated authority), and in which authority to interpret and apply the rules has been delegated to third parties acting under the constraint of rules. There is, however, no bright line dividing legalized from nonlegalized institutions. Instead, there is an identifiable continuum from hard law through varied forms of soft law, each with its individual mix of characteristics, to situations of negligible legalization.

This continuum presupposes that legalized institutions are to some degree differentiated from other types of international institutions, a differentiation that may have methodological, procedural, cultural, and informational dimensions.[43] Although mediators may, for example, be free to broker a bargain based on the "naked preferences" of the parties,[44] legal processes involve a discourse framed in terms of reason, interpretation, technical knowledge, and argument, often followed by deliberation and judgment by impartial parties. Different actors have access to the process, and they are constrained to make arguments different from those they would make in a nonlegal context. Legal decisions, too, must be based on reasons applicable to all similarly situated litigants, not merely the parties to the immediate dispute.

On the whole, however, our conception of legalization reflects a general theme of *International Organization*, **54–3**, Summer 2000: the rejection of a rigid dichotomy between "legalization" and "world politics." Law and politics are intertwined at all levels of legalization. One result of this interrelationship, reflected in many of the articles in this volume, is considerable difficulty in identifying the causal effects of legalization. Compliance with rules occurs for many reasons other than their legal status. Concern about reciprocity, reputation, and damage to valuable state institutions, as well as other normative and material considerations, all play a role. Yet it is reasonable to assume that most of the time, legal and political considerations combine to influence behavior.

At one extreme, even "pure" political bargaining is shaped by rules of sovereignty and other background legal norms. At the other extreme, even international adjudication takes place in the "shadow of politics": interested parties help shape the agenda and initiate the proceedings; judges are typically alert to the political implications of possible decisions, seeking to anticipate the reactions of political authorities. Between these extremes, where most international legalization lies, actors combine and invoke varying degrees of obligation, precision, and delegation to create subtle blends of politics and law. In all these settings, to paraphrase Clausewitz, "law is a continuation of political intercourse, with the addition of other means."

Notes

1 See the debate between the "managerial" perspective that emphasizes centralization but not enforcement, Chayes and Chayes 1995, and the "compliance" perspective that emphasizes enforcement but sees it as decentralized, Downs, Rocke, and Barsoom 1996.
2 Hart 1961.
3 Hart 1961, 79.
4 Hart, of course, observed that in form, though not in substance, international law resembled a primitive legal system consisting only of primary rules. We sidestep that debate, noting only that the characteristics we observe in international legalization leave us comfortable in applying Hart's terms by analogy. We also observe that the international legal framework has evolved considerably in the decades since Hart wrote. Franck reviews these changes and argues that international law has developed a general rule of recognition tied to membership in the international community. Franck 1990, 183–207.
5 On the "obligation" dimension, *jus cogens* refers to an international legal rule – generally one of customary law, though perhaps one codified in treaty form – that creates an especially strong legal obligation, such that it cannot be overridden even by explicit agreement among states.
6 Gamble 1985.
7 The declaration has also contributed to the evolution of customary international law, which can be applied by national courts as well as international organs, and has been incorporated into a number of national constitutions.
8 Interestingly, however, while the formal mandate of the OSCE High Commissioner on National Minorities related solely to conflict prevention and did not entail authority to implement legal (or nonlegal) norms, in practice the High Commissioner has actively promoted respect for both hard and soft legal norms. Ratner 2000.
9 Kaplan 1957.
10 Bull 1977.
11 Compare Goldstein, Kahler, Keohane, and Slaughter, *International Organization*, **54–3** (Summer 2000): 385–399.
12 Victor, Raustalia, and Skolnikoff 1998, especially Chap. 4.
13 Setear 1999.
14 In linking obligation to the broader legal system, we are positing the existence of international law as itself imposing a body of accepted and thereby legitimized obligations on states. If the ultimate foundation of a legal system is its acceptance as such by its subjects, through a Kelsenian *Grundnorm* or an ultimate rule of

recognition, then we are positing the existence of that acceptance by states with regard to the existing international legal system. The degree of obligation that we seek to measure refers instead to acceptance by subject states of a particular rule as a legal rule or not, that is, as binding or not binding as a matter of international law.

15 Under accepted legal principles, many of which are codified in the Vienna Convention on the Law of Treaties, the intent of the parties to an agreement determines whether that instrument creates obligations that are legally binding, not merely personal or political in effect, and that are governed by international law, rather than the law of some nation. Intent is sometimes explicitly stated; otherwise it must be discerned from the overall context of an agreement, its negotiating history, the nature of its commitments, and its form. As a practical matter, however, legalization is the default position: significant agreements between states are assumed to be legally binding and governed by international law unless the parties indicate otherwise. US practice on this score is summarized in the State Department's *Foreign Relations Manual*, pt. 181.

16 Zaring 1998.

17 Although precise obligations are generally an attribute of hard legalization, these instruments use precise language to avoid legally binding character.

18 See Baxter 1980; and Schachter 1977.

19 In addition to the explicit escape clauses considered here, states are often able to escape from the strictures of particular provisions by filing reservations, declarations, and other unilateral conditions after an agreement has been negotiated.

20 These avenues of escape are quite precisely drafted and are supervised by the European Commission and Court of Human Rights, limiting the ability of states to evade their substantive obligations.

21 In contrast to the European Convention on Human Rights, this withdrawal clause is self-judging, increasing its softening effect. Nonetheless, the clause was originally inserted to impose some constraints on what might otherwise have been seen as an unconditional right to withdraw.

22 Some agreements authorize particular conduct rather than requiring or prohibiting it. Such provisions are usually couched as rights, using the word *may*. Gamble 1985.

23 See Chinkin 1989; and Gruchalla-Wesierski 1984.

24 This discussion also applies to instruments adopted by organizations with lawmaking competency but outside prescribed procedures. A significant example is the European Social Charter, adopted by all members of the EC Council except the United Kingdom. These states bypassed a unanimity requirement to avoid a UK veto, adopting a softer instrument to guide subsequent legislative action.

25 Palmer 1992.

26 A precise rule is not necessarily more constraining than a more general one. Its actual impact on behavior depends on many factors, including subjective interpretation by the subjects of the rule. Thus, a rule saying "drive slowly" might yield slower driving than a rule prescribing a speed limit of 55 miles per hour if the drivers in question would normally drive 50 miles per hour and understand "slowly" to mean 10 miles per hour slower than normal. (We are indebted to Fred Schauer for both the general point and the example.) In addition, precision can be used to define limits, exceptions, and loopholes that reduce the impact of a rule. Nevertheless, for most rules requiring or prohibiting particular conduct – and in the absence of precise delegation – generality is likely to provide an opportunity for deliberate self-interested interpretation, reducing the impact, or at least the potential for enforceable impact, on behavior.

27 Franck 1990.

28 Franck labels this collective property "coherence." We use the singular notion of precision to capture both the precision of a rule in isolation and its precision within a rule system.

29 Morrow 1997 and 1998.

30 Simma and Paulus 1999.

31 Fuller 1964.

32 The standard regime definition encompasses three levels of precision: "principles," "norms," and "rules." Krasner 1983. This formulation reflects the fact that societies typically translate broad normative values into increasingly concrete formulations that decision-makers can apply in specific situations.

33 Kennedy 1976.

34 Similarly, agreements administered by the WTO can, with similar legitimacy and effectiveness, specify detailed rules on the valuation of imports for customs purposes and rely on broad standards like "national treatment."

35 Operationalizing the relative precision of different formulations is difficult, except in a gross sense. Gamble, for example, purports to apply a four-point scale of "concreteness" but does not characterize these points. Gamble 1985.

36 The State Department's *Foreign Relations Manual* states that undertaking couched in vague or very general terms with no criteria for performance frequently reflect an intent not to be legally bound.

37 Abbott and Snidal, *International Organization*, **54–3** (Summer 2000): 421–456.

38 US Releases Proposal on Elements of Crimes at the Rome Conference on the Establishment of an International Criminal Court, statement by James P. Rubin, US State Department spokesperson, 22 June 1998, <secretary.state.gov/www/briefings/statements/1998/ps980622b.html>, accessed 16 February 1999.

39 Law remains relevant even here. The UN Charter makes peaceful resolution of disputes a legal obligation, and general international law requires good faith in the conduct of negotiations. In addition, resolution of disputes by agreement can contribute to the growth of customary international law.

40 Abbott and Snidal 1998.

41 Boisson de Chazournes 1998.

42 Shihata 1994.

43 Schauer and Wise 1997.

44 Sunstein 1986.

The references for this chapter have been combined with those for Chapter 8 and appear at the end of that chapter.

8 Legalized dispute resolution: interstate and transnational

*Robert O. Keohane, Andrew Moravcsik,
and Anne-Marie Slaughter*

(2000)

International courts and tribunals are flourishing. Depending on how these bodies are defined, they now number between seventeen and forty.[1] In recent years we have witnessed the proliferation of new bodies and a strengthening of those that already exist. "When future international legal scholars look back at . . . the end of the twentieth century," one analyst has written, "they probably will refer to the enormous expansion of the international judiciary as the single most important development of the post-Cold War age."[2]

These courts and tribunals represent a key dimension of legalization. Instead of resolving disputes through institutionalized bargaining, states choose to delegate the task to third-party tribunals charged with applying general legal principles. Not all of these tribunals are created alike, however. In particular, we distinguish between two ideal types of international dispute resolution: interstate and transnational. Our central argument is that the formal legal differences between interstate and transnational dispute resolution have significant implications for the politics of dispute settlement and therefore for the effects of legalization in world politics.

Interstate dispute resolution is consistent with the view that public international law comprises a set of rules and practices governing *interstate* relationships. Legal resolution of disputes, in this model, takes place between states conceived of as unitary actors. States are the subjects of international law, which means that they control access to dispute resolution tribunals or courts. They typically designate the adjudicators of such tribunals. States also implement, or fail to implement, the decisions of international tribunals or courts. Thus in interstate dispute resolution, states act as gatekeepers both to the international legal process and from that process back to the domestic level.

In transnational dispute resolution, by contrast, access to courts and tribunals and the subsequent enforcement of their decisions are legally insulated from the will of individual national governments. These tribunals are therefore more open to individuals and groups in civil society. In the pure ideal type, states lose their gatekeeping capacities; in practice, these capacities are attenuated. This loss of state control, whether voluntarily or unwittingly surrendered, creates a range of opportunities for courts and their constituencies to set the agenda.

Before proceeding to our argument, it is helpful to locate our analysis in a broader context (see ch. 7 on "legalization"). Legalization is a form of institutionalization distinguished by obligation, precision, and delegation. Our analysis applies primarily when obligation is high.[3] Precision, on the other hand, is not a defining characteristic of the situations we examine. We examine the decisions of bodies that interpret and apply rules, regardless of their precision. Indeed, such bodies may have greater latitude when precision is low than when it is high.[4] Our focus is a third dimension of legalization: delegation of authority to courts and tribunals designed to resolve international disputes through the application of general legal principles.[5]

Three dimensions of delegation are crucial to our argument: independence, access, and embeddedness. As we explain in the first section, independence specifies the extent to which formal legal arrangements ensure that adjudication can be rendered impartially with respect to concrete state interests. Access refers to the ease with which parties other than states can influence the tribunal's agenda. Embeddedness denotes the extent to which dispute resolution decisions can be implemented without governments having to take actions to do so. We define low independence, access, and embeddedness as the ideal type of interstate dispute resolution and high independence, access, and embeddedness as the ideal type of transnational dispute resolution. Although admittedly a simplification, this conceptualization helps us to understand why the behavior and impact of different tribunals, such as the International Court of Justice (ICJ) and the European Court of Justice (ECJ), have been so different.

In the second section we seek to connect international politics, international law, and domestic politics. Clearly the power and preferences of states influence the behavior both of governments and of dispute resolution tribunals: international law operates in the shadow of power. Yet within that political context, we contend that institutions for selecting judges, controlling access to dispute resolution, and legally enforcing the judgments of international courts and tribunals have a major impact on state behavior. The formal qualities of legal institutions empower or disempower domestic political actors other than national governments. Compared to interstate dispute resolution, transnational dispute resolution tends to generate more litigation, jurisprudence more autonomous of national interests, and an additional source of pressure for compliance. In the third section we argue that interstate and transnational dispute resolution generate divergent longer-term dynamics. Transnational dispute resolution seems to have an inherently more expansionary character; it provides more opportunities to assert and establish new legal norms, often in unintended ways.

This article should be viewed as exploratory rather than an attempt to be definitive. Throughout, we use ideal types to illuminate a complex subject, review suggestive though not conclusive evidence, and highlight opportunities for future research. We offer our own conjectures at various points as to useful starting points for that research but do not purport to test definitive conclusions.

A typology of dispute resolution

Much dispute resolution in world politics is highly institutionalized. Established, enduring rules apply to entire classes of circumstances and cannot easily be ignored or modified when they become inconvenient to one participant or another in a specific case. In this article we focus on institutions in which dispute resolution has been delegated to a third-party tribunal charged with applying designated legal rules and principles. This act of delegation means that disputes must be framed as "cases" between two or more parties, at least one of which, the defendant, will be a state or an individual acting on behalf of a state. (Usually, states are the defendants, so we refer to defendants as "states." However, individuals may also be prosecuted by international tribunals, as in the proposed International Criminal Court and various war crimes tribunals.[6]) The identity of the plaintiff depends on the design of the dispute resolution mechanism. Plaintiffs can be other states or private parties – individuals or nongovernmental organizations (NGOs) – specifically designated to monitor and enforce the obligatory rules of the regime.

We turn now to our three explanatory variables: independence, access, and embeddedness. We do not deny that the patterns of delegation we observe may ultimately have their origins in the power and interests of major states, as certain strands of liberal and realist theory claim. Nevertheless, our analysis here takes these sources of delegation as given and emphasizes how formal legal institutions empower groups and individuals other than national governments.[7]

Independence: who controls adjudication?

The variable *independence* measures the extent to which adjudicators for an international authority charged with dispute resolution are able to deliberate and reach legal judgments independently of national governments. In other words, it assesses the extent to which adjudication is rendered impartially with respect to concrete state interests in a specific case. The traditional international model of dispute resolution in law and politics places pure control by states at one end of a continuum. Disputes are resolved by the agents of the interested parties themselves. Each side offers its own interpretation of the rules and their applicability to the case at issue; disagreements are resolved through institutionalized interstate bargaining. There are no permanent rules of procedure or legal precedent, although in legalized dispute resolution, decisions must be consistent with international law. Institutional rules may also influence the outcome by determining the conditions – interpretive standards, voting requirements, selection – under which authoritative decisions are made.[8] Even where legal procedures are established, individual governments may have the right to veto judgments, as in the UN Security Council and the old General Agreement on Tariffs and Trade (GATT).

Movement along the continuum away from this traditional interstate mode of dispute resolution measures the nature and tightness of the political constraints imposed on adjudicators. The extent to which members of an international tribunal are independent reflects the extent to which they can free themselves from at least three categories of institutional constraint: selection and tenure, legal discretion, and control over material and human resources.

The most important criterion is independent selection and tenure. The spectrum runs from direct representatives of unconstrained national governments to a more impartial and autonomous process of naming judges. Judges may be selected from the ranks of loyal politicians, leading members of the bar, and justice ministries; or they may be drawn from a cadre of specialized experts in a particular area of international law. Their tenure may be long or short. After serving as adjudicators, they may be dependent on national governments for their subsequent careers or may belong to an independent professional group, such as legal academics. The less partisan their background, the longer their tenure; and the more independent their future, the greater the independence of adjudicators.

Selection and tenure rules vary widely. Many international institutions maintain tight national control on dispute resolution through selection and tenure rules.[9] Some institutions – including the UN, the International Monetary Fund, NATO, and the bilateral Soviet–US arrangements established by the Strategic Arms Limitation Treaty (SALT) – establish no authoritative third-party adjudicators whatsoever. The regime creates instead a set of decision-making rules and procedures, a forum for interstate bargaining, within which subsequent disputes are resolved by national representatives serving at the will of their governments. In other institutions, however, such as the EU, governments can name representatives, but those representatives are assured long tenure and may enjoy subsequent prestige in the legal world independent of their service to individual states. In first-round dispute resolution in GATT and the World Trade Organization (WTO), groups of states select a stable of experts who are then selected on a case-by-case basis by the parties and the secretariat, whereas in ad hoc international arbitration, the selection is generally controlled by the disputants and the tribunal is constituted for a single case.

In still other situations – particularly in authoritarian countries – judges may be vulnerable to retaliation when they return home after completing their tenure; even in liberal democracies, future professional advancement may be manipulated by the government.[10] The legal basis of some international dispute resolution mechanisms such as the European Court of Human Rights (ECHR), requires oversight by semi-independent supranational bodies. The spectrum of legal independence as measured by selection and tenure rules is shown in Table 8.1.

Legal discretion, the second criterion for judicial independence, refers to the breadth of the mandate granted to the dispute resolution body. Some legalized dispute resolution bodies must adhere closely to treaty texts; but the ECJ, as Karen Alter describes it, has asserted the supremacy of European Community (EC) law without explicit grounding in the treaty text or the intent of national governments. More generally, institutions for adjudication arise, as Abbott and Snidal argue, under conditions of complexity and uncertainty, which render interstate contracts necessarily incomplete. (Both articles appear in *International Organization*, **54–3**, Summer 2000.) Adjudication is thus more than the act of applying precise standards and norms to a series of concrete cases within a precise mandate; it involves interpreting norms and resolving conflicts between competing norms in the context of particular cases. When seeking to overturn all but the most flagrantly illegal state actions, litigants and courts must inevitably appeal to particular interpretations of such ambiguities. Other things being equal, the wider the range of considerations the body can legitimately consider and the greater the uncertainty concerning the proper interpretation or norm in a given case, the more potential legal independence it possesses. Where regimes have clear norms, single goals, and narrow scope – as in, say, some purely technical tasks – we expect to see limited legal discretion. Where legal norms are valid across a wide area – as in the jurisprudence of the ECJ, which is connected to the broad, open-ended EC – there is more scope to promulgate general principles within the context of specific cases.[11] Similarly, greater legal independence exists where cross-cutting interpretations are plausible, such as over the scope of legitimate exceptions to norms like free trade, nonintervention, and individual rights. For instance, GATT and WTO dispute resolution bodies, or human rights courts, are increasingly being called upon to designate the margin of appreciation granted to national governments in pursuing legitimate state purposes other than free trade or human rights protection.

Table 8.1 The independence continuum: selection and tenure

Level of independence	Selection method and tenure	International court or tribunal
Low	Direct representatives, perhaps with single-country veto	UN Security Council
Moderate	Disputants control ad hoc selection of third-party judges	PCA
	Groups of states control selection of third-party judges	ICJ, GATT, WTO
High	Individual governments appoint judges with long tenure	ECJ
	Groups of states select judges with long tenure	ECHR, IACHR

The third criterion for judicial independence, *financial and human resources*, refers to the ability of judges to process their caseloads promptly and effectively.[12] Such resources are necessary for processing large numbers of complaints and rendering consistent, high-quality decisions. They can also permit a court or tribunal to develop a factual record independent of the state litigants before them and to publicize their decisions. This is of particular importance for human rights courts, which seek to disseminate information and mobilize political support on behalf of those who would otherwise lack direct domestic access to effective political representation.[13] Many human rights tribunals are attached to commissions capable of conducting independent inquiries. The commissions of the Inter-American and UN systems, for example, have been active in pursuing this strategy, often conducting independent, on-site investigations.[14] Indeed, inquiries by the Inter-American Commission need not be restricted to the details of a specific case, though a prior petition is required. In general, the greater the financial and human resources available to courts and the stronger the commissions attached to them, the greater their legal independence.

In sum, the greater the freedom of a dispute resolution body from the control of individual member states over selection and tenure, legal discretion, information, and financial and human resources, the greater its legal independence.

Access: who has standing?

Access, like independence, is a variable. From a legal perspective, access measures the range of social and political actors who have legal standing to submit a dispute to be resolved; from a political perspective, access measures the range of those who can set the agenda. Access is particularly important with respect to courts and other dispute-resolution bodies because, in contrast to executives and legislatures, they are "passive" organs of government unable to initiate action by unilaterally seizing a dispute. Access is measured along a continuum between two extremes. At one extreme, if no social or political actors can submit disputes, dispute-resolution institutions are unable to act; at the other, anyone with a legitimate grievance directed at government policy can easily and inexpensively submit a complaint. In-between are situations in which individuals can bring their complaints only by acting through governments, convincing governments to "espouse" their claim as a state claim against another government, or by engaging in a costly procedure. This continuum of access can be viewed as measuring the "political transaction costs" to individuals and groups in society of submitting their complaint to an international dispute-resolution body. The more restrictive the conditions for bringing a claim to the attention of a dispute-resolution body, the more costly it is for actors to do so.

Near the higher-cost, restrictive end, summarized in Table 8.2, fall purely interstate tribunals, such as the GATT and WTO panels, the Permanent

Table 8.2 The access continuum: who has standing?

Level of access	Who has standing	International court or tribunal
Low	Both states must agree	PCA
Moderate	Only a single state can file suit	ICJ
	Single state files suit, influenced by social actors	WTO, GATT
High	Access through national courts	ECJ
	Direct individual (and sometimes group) access if domestic remedies have been exhausted	ECHR, IACHR

Court of Arbitration, and the ICJ, in which only member states may file suit against one another. Although this limitation constrains access to any dispute-resolution body by granting one or more governments a formal veto, it does not permit governments to act without constraint. Individuals and groups may still wield influence, but they must do so by domestic means. Procedures that are formally similar in this sense may nonetheless generate quite different implications for access, depending on principal-agent relationships in domestic politics. Whereas individuals and groups may have the domestic political power to ensure an ongoing if indirect role in both the decision to initiate proceedings and the resulting argumentation, state-controlled systems are likely to be more restrictive than direct litigation by individuals and groups.

In state-controlled systems, the individual or group must typically lobby a specialized government bureaucracy, secure a majority in some relevant domestic decisionmaking body, or catch the attention of the head of government. State officials are often cautious about instigating such proceedings against another state, since they must weigh a wide range of cross-cutting concerns, including the diplomatic costs of negotiating an arrangement with the foreign government in question. Such indirect arrangements for bringing a case are costly, prohibiting government action to serve extremely narrow or secondary interest groups.

In other cases, state action under such arrangements can be considered prohibitively expensive because of the government's role as a veto player. The most obvious circumstance is one in which individuals and groups seek to file suit challenging the actions of their home state. (This is generally the type of litigation before most human rights and many regional economic integration bodies – which do not restrict access to states.) Although, in theory, an individual or group could secure access to international adjudication by mustering a large enough domestic bloc to override the outright hostility of the state, this rarely occurs in practice.

Within these constraints, GATT/WTO panels and the ICJ differ in their roles toward domestic individuals and groups. In the GATT and now the

WTO, governments nominally control access to the legal process, yet in practice injured industries are closely involved in both the initiation and the conduct of the litigation by their governments, at least in the United States. A firm or industry group, typically represented by an experienced Washington law firm, will lobby the US Trade Representative to bring a claim against another country allegedly engaging in GATT violations. The industry lawyers may then participate quite closely in the preparation of the suit and wait in the halls for debriefing after the actual proceeding. In the ICJ, by contrast, individual access is more costly. The ICJ hears cases in which individuals may have a direct interest (such as the families of soldiers sent to fight in another country in what is allegedly an illegal act of interstate aggression). However, these individuals usually have little influence over a national government decision to initiate interstate litigation or over the resulting conduct of the proceedings. As in the WTO, finally, individuals are unable to file suit against their own government before the ICJ. Because the ICJ tends to handle cases concerning "public goods" provision across national jurisdictions, such as boundary disputes and issues concerning aggression, the groups influenced by ICJ decisions tend to be diffuse and unorganized, except through the intermediation of national governments.

Near the permissive end of the spectrum is the ECJ. Individuals may ultimately be directly represented before the international tribunal, though the decision to bring the case before it remains in the hands of a domestic judicial body. Under Article 177 of the Treaty of Rome, national courts may independently refer a case before them to the ECJ if the case raises questions of European law that the national court does not feel competent to resolve on its own. The ECJ answers the specific question(s) presented and sends the case back to the national court for disposition of the merits of the dispute. Litigants themselves can suggest such a referral to the national court, but the decision to refer lies ultimately within the national court's discretion. Whether the interests involved are narrow and specific – as in the landmark *Cassis de Dijon* case over the importation of French specialty liquors into Germany – or broad, the cost of securing such a referral is the same. As Karen Alter shows in her article referenced above, different national courts have sharply different records of referral, but over time national courts as a body have become increasingly willing to refer cases to the ECJ. These referrals may involve litigation among private parties rather than simply against a public authority.[15]

Also near the low-cost end of the access spectrum lie formal human rights enforcement systems, including the ECHR, the IACHR, the African Convention on Human and People's Rights, and the UN's International Covenant on Civil and Political Rights. Since the end of World War II we have witnessed a proliferation of international tribunals to which individuals have direct access, though subject to varying restrictions. Even in the ECHR, a relatively successful system, individual access broadened slowly over time. Under the "old ECHR" – the one that existed prior to very recent reforms – individuals could bring cases themselves only if the government being sued had previously accepted an optional clause in the convention recognizing individual petition; otherwise only states could file petitions. This clause was initially accepted by only a few countries and not by all until the 1980s. NGOs and other third parties were excluded; anonymous petitions were not permitted. Any complaint to the system had, moreover, to be reviewed by the European Human Rights Commission before being passed on to the court – assuming that the government had accepted compulsory jurisdiction. Only if the commission decided in favor of referring the case would it finally be heard before the ECHR.

Although this process only rarely constituted an outright barrier to a suit, it could be time consuming. Recent reforms have abolished this intermediate step. The new ECHR, by contrast, gives individuals direct access to the court without any domestic or international intermediary.[16] Even so, however, it continues to require that any individual or group exhaust all national remedies before appealing to the system, typically meaning that litigants must first sue in a lower national tribunal and appeal the resulting judgment up the chain of administrative tribunals and domestic courts. The path to international dispute resolution is thus long, costly, and uncertain, even in this permissive environment; the process can take six to eight years and requires substantial legal expertise.

The Inter-American, UN, and nascent African systems of formal human rights enforcement are in some ways more permissive. As in the new ECHR, individual petition is mandatory. Under the IACHR, other actors have standing to bring suit on behalf of individuals and groups whose rights may be being violated. Indeed, the individuals and groups need not even consent to the suit, and anonymous petitions are permitted. The IACHR Commission has also adopted a very broad and permissive interpretation of what it means to exhaust domestic remedies.[17] Under the African Charter on Human and People's Rights, individuals and states may submit complaints, which will be heard if a majority on a commission so decide. The commission will soon be able to send cases on to the future African Court of Human and People's Rights only if the state against which a claim is being brought has accepted an optional clause. As under the ECHR, domestic remedies must be exhausted. The UN requires individual petitions to trigger a process, though NGOs may be involved in the process. Whereas in the ECHR context, the commission took a relatively permissive attitude toward references to the court, this was not so in the Americas. For many years, the IACHR Commission declined to refer cases to the court – to the point where the court admonished the commission for failing to fulfill its "social duty to consider the advisability of coming to the Court."[18]

Among world courts and tribunals, the Central American Court of Justice, established in 1991 as the principal judicial organ of the Central American Integration System, offers the easiest access. Any state, supranational body, or natural or legal person can bring suit against a state party to assure domestic enforcement of regime norms. In addition, domestic courts can request advisory opinions in a preliminary reference procedure similar to the EC's Article 177.

Legal embeddedness: who controls formal implementation?

There is no monopoly on the legitimate use of force in world politics – no world state, police, or army. Therefore, even if authority to render judgments is delegated to an independent international tribunal, implementation of these judgments depends on international or domestic action by the executives, legislatures, and/or judiciaries of states. Implementation and compliance in international disputes are problematic to a far greater degree than they are in well-functioning, domestic rule-of-law systems. The political significance of delegating authority over dispute resolution therefore depends in part on the degree of control exercised by individual governments over the legal promulgation and implementation of judgments. State control is affected by formal legal arrangements along a continuum that we refer to as embeddedness.

The spectrum of domestic embeddedness, summarized in Table 8.3, runs from strong control over promulgation and implementation of judgments by individual national governments to very weak control. At one extreme, that of strong control, lie systems in which individual litigants can veto the promulgation of a judgment *ex post*. In the old GATT system, the decisions of dispute-resolution panels had to be affirmed by consensus, affording individual litigants an *ex post* veto. Under the less tightly controlled WTO, by contrast, disputes among member governments are resolved through quasi-judicial panels whose judgments are binding unless *reversed* by unanimous vote of the Dispute Settlement Body, which consists of one representative from each WTO member state.

Table 8.3 The embeddedness continuum: who enforces the law?

Level of embeddedness	Who enforces	International court or tribunal
Low	Individual governments can veto implementation of legal judgment	GATT
Moderate	No veto, but no domestic legal enforcement; most human rights systems	WTO, ICJ
High	International norms enforced by domestic courts	EC, incorporated human rights norms under ECHR, national systems in which treaties are self-executing or given direct effect

Most international legal systems fall into the same category as the WTO system; namely, states are bound by international law to comply with judgments of international courts or tribunals, but no domestic legal mechanism assures legal implementation. If national executives and legislatures fail to take action because of domestic political opposition or simply inertia, states simply incur a further international legal obligation to repair the damage. In other words, if an international tribunal rules that state *A* has illegally intervened in state *B*'s internal affairs and orders state *A* to pay damages, but the legislature of state *A* refuses to appropriate the funds, state *B* has no recourse at international law except to seek additional damages. Alternatively, if state *A* signs a treaty obligating it to change its domestic law to reduce the level of certain pollutants it is emitting, and the executive branch is unsuccessful in passing legislation to do so, state *A* is liable to its treaty partners at international law but cannot be compelled to take the action it agreed to take in the treaty.

This is not to say that individuals and groups have no impact on compliance. Interstate bargaining takes place in the shadow of normative sanctions stemming from the international legal obligation itself. Even if governments do not ultimately comply, a negative legal judgment may increase the salience of an issue and undermine the legitimacy of the national position in the eyes of domestic constituents. And it is difficult for recalcitrant governments to get the offending international law changed. Multilateral revision is rendered almost impossible by the requirement of unanimous consent in nearly all international organizations.[19]

At the other end of the spectrum, where the control of individual governments is most constrained by the embeddedness of international norms, lie systems in which autonomous national courts can enforce international judgments against their own governments. The most striking example of this mode of enforcement is the EC legal system. Domestic courts in every member state recognize that EC law is superior to national law (supremacy) and that it grants individuals rights on the basis of which they can litigate (direct effect). When the ECJ issues advisory opinions to national courts under the Article 177 procedure described in detail in Karen Alter's article referenced above, national courts tend to respect them, even when they clash with the precedent set by higher national courts. These provisions are nowhere stated explicitly in the Treaty of Rome but have been successfully "constitutionalized" by the ECJ over the past four decades.[20] The European Free Trade Association (EFTA) court system established in 1994 permits such referrals as well, though, unlike the Treaty of Rome, it neither legally obliges domestic courts to refer nor legally binds the domestic court to apply the result. Domestic courts do nonetheless appear to enforce EFTA court decisions.[21]

International legal norms may also be embedded in domestic legal systems through legal incorporation or constitutional recognition. Although the direct link between domestic and international courts found in the EC is unique among international organizations, in some situations the national government has incorporated or transposed the international document into domestic law subject to the oversight of an autonomous domestic legal system. Many governments have, for example, incorporated the European Convention into domestic law, permitting individuals to enforce its provisions before domestic courts. Despite the lack of a direct link, there is evidence that domestic courts tend to follow the jurisprudence of the ECHR in interpreting the Convention.[22] Even without explicit statutory recognition, some legal systems – such as that of the Netherlands – generally recognize international treaty obligations as equal to or supreme over constitutional provisions. In the United States, the president and federal courts have sometimes invoked international treaty obligations as "self-executing" or "directly applicable" and therefore both binding on the US government and domestic actors and enforceable in domestic courts – though Congress has increasingly sought to employ its control over ratification to limit this practice explicitly.[23]

Two ideal types: interstate and transnational dispute resolution

The three characteristics of international dispute resolution – independence, access, and embeddedness – are closely linked. This is evident from an examination of the extent to which different international legal systems are independent, embedded, and provide access. The characteristics of the major courts in the world today are summarized in Table 8.4, which reveals a loose correlation across categories. Systems with higher values on one dimension have a greater probability of having higher values in the other dimensions. This finding suggests that very high values on one dimension cannot fully compensate for low values on another. Strong support for independence, access, or embeddedness without strong support for the others undermines the effectiveness of a system.

Combining these three dimensions creates two ideal-types. In one ideal-type – interstate dispute resolution – adjudicators, agenda, and enforcement are all subject to veto by individual national governments. Individual states decide who judges, what they judge, and how the judgment is enforced. At the other end of the spectrum, adjudicators, agenda, and enforcement are all substantially independent of individual and collective pressure from national governments. We refer to this ideal type as transnational dispute resolution.[24] In this institutional arrangement, of which the EU and ECHR are the most striking examples, judges are insulated from national governments, societal individuals and groups control the agenda, and the results are implemented by an independent national judiciary. In the remainder of this article we discuss the implications of variation along the continuum from interstate to transnational dispute resolution for the nature of, compliance with, and evolution of international jurisprudence.

In discussing this continuum, however, let us not lose sight of the fact that *values on the three dimensions move from high to low at different rates*. Table 8.4 reveals that high levels of independence and access appear to be more

Table 8.4 Legal characteristics of international courts and tribunals

International court or tribunals	Legal characteristics		
	Independence	*Access*	*Embeddedness*
ECJ	High	High	High[f]
ECHR, since 1999	High	High	Low to high[c]
ECHR, before 1999	Moderate to high[a]	Low to high[b]	Low to high[c]
IACHR	Moderate to high[a]	High	Moderate
WTO panels	Moderate	Low to moderate[d]	Moderate
ICJ	Moderate	Low to moderate[d]	Moderate
GATT panels	Moderate	Low to moderate[d]	Low
PCA	Low to moderate	Low[e]	Moderate
UN Security Council	Low	Low to moderate[g]	Low

Source: Sands *et al.* 1999.

[a] Depends on whether government recognizes optional clauses for compulsory jurisdiction of the court.
[b] Depends on whether government accepts optional clause for individual petition.
[c] Depends on whether domestic law incorporates or otherwise recognized the treaty.
[d] Depends on mobilization and domestic access rules for interest groups concerned.
[e] Both parties must consent. Recent rule changes have begun to recognize nonstate actors.
[f] Embeddedness is not a formal attribute of the regime but the result of the successful assertion of legal sovereignty.
[g] Permanent members of the Security Council can veto; nonmembers cannot.

common than high levels of embeddedness, and, though the relationship is weaker, a high level of independence appears to be slightly more common than a high level of access. In other words, between those tribunals that score high or low on all three dimensions, there is a significant intermediate range comprising tribunals with high scores on independence and/or access but not on the others.[25] Among those international legal institutions that score high on independence and access but are not deeply embedded in domestic legal systems are some international human rights institutions. Among those institutions that score high on independence but not on access or embeddedness are GATT/WTO multilateral trade institutions and the ICJ.

The politics of litigation and compliance: from interstate to judicial politics

Declaring a process "legalized" does not abolish politics. Decisions about the degree of authority of a particular tribunal, and access to it, are themselves sites of political struggle. The sharpest struggles are likely to arise *ex ante* in the bargaining over a tribunal's establishment; but other opportunities for political intervention may emerge during the life of a tribunal, perhaps as a result of its own constitutional provisions. Form matters, however. The characteristic politics of litigation and compliance are very different under transnational dispute resolution than under interstate dispute resolution. In this section we explicate these differences and propose some tentative conjectures linking our three explanatory variables to the politics of dispute resolution.

The interstate and transnational politics of judicial independence

What are the politics of judicial independence? As legal systems move from interstate dispute resolution toward the more independent judicial selection processes of transnational dispute resolution, we expect to observe greater judicial autonomy – defined as the willingness and ability to decide disputes against national governments. Other things being equal, the fewer opportunities national governments have to influence the selection of judges, the available information, the support or financing of the court, and the precise legal terms on which the court can decide, the weaker is their likely influence over the decisions of an international tribunal.

Political interference is common in some domestic political systems. The secretary general of the Arab Lawyers Union has described routine "intervention with the judiciary through higher decisions" and by appointment of military and special courts in much of the Arab world.[26] Judges in Central and South America have been subjected to threats and assassinations. Even in domestic systems with strong courts, political selection of judges can affect decisions. And in the United States, where federal judges serve for life, the openly politicized nature of Supreme Court appointments is said to induce many aspiring lower federal judges to alter their decisions in anticipation of possible confirmation hearings before the Senate. The Italian and German Constitutional Courts are even more overtly politically balanced.[27] Perhaps the most infamous example of interference with the composition of a sitting court is President Franklin D. Roosevelt's effort in 1937 to "pack" the Supreme Court with additional justices of his choice. Instead, "a switch in time saved nine," as key justices suddenly changed their tune and found delegation to the plethora of new administrative agencies constitutional. In the context of de facto single-party rule in Japan, Mark Ramseyer and Frances Rosenbluth have documented the significant impact of decisions on the career trajectory of domestic judges, permitting the inference that selection processes affected judicial decisions.[28]

Evidence of government efforts to influence an international tribunal's direction through judicial selection is anecdotal. Rarely is the attempt at influence as crude as the case in September 1984, when a Swedish member of the Iran–US Tribunal was assaulted by two younger and stronger Iranian judges.[29] Influence is typically more subtle. It was widely rumored, for instance, that the German government sought to rein in the ECJ by appointing a much less activist judge in the 1980s than previous German candidates, but hard evidence is virtually impossible to find. One leading ECJ judge, a long-time skeptic of the notion that the ECJ could be politicized in this way, nevertheless noted in the mid-1990s that "Things have changed. It is now 8–7 for us [that is, the supranationalists]."[30]

Restrictions on the financial resources available to tribunals may limit their independence. Such limitations have hampered efforts to transform the African Convention on Human and People's Rights into a system as effective as those found in Europe and, recently, the Americas.[31] Similarly, it has been argued that the members of the UN Security Council authorized the creation of the International Criminal Tribunal for the Former Yugoslavia to satisfy public opinion but tried to deny it sufficient resources to do its work.[32] If this strategy failed, it may have been in part because resources were ultimately provided from private sources such as foundations and wealthy individuals.[33] On the other hand, a striking difference between the ECJ and ECHR, as well as bodies such as the UN Human Rights Committee, is the relative distribution of resources, without which even an active court cannot process its caseload and make itself heard to a wider audience. Other drags include excessively cumbersome procedural rules, often designed to frustrate all but the most persistent individual litigants, and limits on judicial capacities, such as a court's autonomous ability to find the facts in a particular case rather than having to depend solely on the representations of litigants. Where one of the litigants is a government, the court is likely to find itself unable to challenge the government's version of events without the independent ability to call witnesses or even conduct inspections.[34]

Such potential restrictions on autonomy – along with the threat of noncompliance or treaty revision – may increase judicial solicitude for state interests. We shall return to this question in our later discussion of long-term dynamism. Broadly, however, this discussion suggests the following conjecture: the more formally independent a court, the more likely are judicial decisions to challenge national policies.

The interstate and transnational politics of access

What are the political implications of movement from low access (interstate dispute resolution) to high access (transnational dispute resolution)? Our central contention is that we are likely to observe, broadly speaking, a different politics of access as we move toward transnational dispute resolution – where individuals, groups, and courts can appeal or refer cases to international tribunals. As the actors involved become more diverse, the likelihood that cases will be referred increases, as does the likelihood that such cases will challenge national governments – in particular, the national government of the plaintiff. The link between formal access and real political power is not obvious. States might still manipulate access to judicial process regarding both interstate and transnational litigation by establishing stringent procedural rules, bringing political pressure to bear on potential or actual litigants, or simply carving out self-serving exceptions to the agreed jurisdictional scheme. Consider the evidence.

Access to classic arbitral tribunals, such as those constituted under the Permanent Court of Arbitration, requires the consent of both states. With regard to access, the Permanent Court of Arbitration is as close as we come to a pure system of interstate dispute resolution. Slightly more constraining arrangements are found in classic interstate litigation before the Permanent Court of International Justice in the 1920s and 1930s, the ICJ since 1945, and the short-lived Central American Court of Justice. In these systems, a single state decides when and how to sue, even if it is suing on behalf of an injured citizen or group of citizens. The state formally "espouses" the claim of its national(s), at which point the individual's rights terminate (unless entitled to compensation as a domestic legal or constitutional matter), as does any control over or even say in the litigation strategy. The government is thus free to prosecute the claim vigorously or not at all, or to engage in settlement negotiations for a sum far less than the individual litigant(s) might have found acceptable. Such negotiations can resemble institutionalized interstate bargaining more than a classic legal process in which the plaintiff decides whether to continue the legal struggle or to settle the case.

Under interstate dispute resolution, political calculations inevitably enter into the decision to sue. For instance, in 1996 the United States adopted the Helms-Burton legislation, which punishes firms for doing business with Cuba. Although the EU claimed that this legislation violated WTO rules and threatened to take the case to the WTO, in the end it failed to do so: an agreement was reached essentially on US terms. The forms of legalization do not, therefore, guarantee that authoritative decisions will be honored by third parties. Hence, even among formally highly legalized processes, the degree of operational authority of the third-party decision makers may vary considerably. More systematic evidence comes from the EU, where governments tend to be reluctant to sue one another, preferring instead to bring their complaints to the EU Commission. The Commission, in turn, was initially – and to an extent, remains – reluctant to sue member states, due to its fear of retaliation and need to establish its own political legitimacy.[35]

Although in interstate dispute resolution states decide when and whether to sue other states, they cannot necessarily control whether they are sued. If they are sued, whether any resulting judgments can be enforced depends both on their acceptance of compulsory jurisdiction and, where the costs of complying with a judgment are high, on their willingness to obey an adverse ruling. US relations with the ICJ provide an example. After pushing for the creation of the ICJ as part of the UN Charter, the United States promptly accepted the compulsory jurisdiction of the ICJ by Senate resolution.[36] The same resolution, however, included the Connally reservation, providing that US acceptance "shall not apply to . . . disputes with regard to matters which are essentially within the domestic jurisdiction of the United States as determined by the United States."[37] In other words, the Senate insisted that the United States remain judge in its own case as to whether disputes were sufficiently "international" to go to the court.

To be sure, the Connally reservation has always been controversial in the United States, and the State Department has resisted invoking it when the United States has been called before the ICJ. Yet control of access does not stop there. In 1984, when the ICJ appeared to take Nicaragua's complaints against the United States seriously, the United States revoked its agreement to the ICJ's compulsory jurisdiction. The United States deposited with the secretariat of the UN a notification purporting to exclude, with immediate effect, from its acceptance of the court's compulsory jurisdiction "disputes with any Central American state" for two years.[38] It litigated the first round of the case, arguing that its revocation of jurisdiction was effective, but then simply failed to appear in the second round after the court ruled that it did indeed have jurisdiction.[39]

This sort of flagrant defiance is rarely necessary. The de facto system is one in which most states, like the United States, reserve the right to bring specific cases to the ICJ or to be sued in specific cases as the result of an ad hoc agreement with other parties to a dispute of specific provisions in a bilateral or multilateral treaty. This system ensures direct control over access to the ICJ by either requiring all the parties to a dispute to agree both to third-party intervention and to choose the ICJ as the third party, or by allowing two or more states to craft a specific submission to the court's jurisdiction in a limited category of disputes arising from the specific subject matter of a treaty.[40] In the ICJ, procedural provisions govern time limits requiring a state to accept a tribunal's jurisdiction before a particular suit arises, time limits for filing the suit itself, the reciprocal nature of the opposing parties' acceptance of jurisdiction, and rules governing intervention by a third state whose interests may be directly affected by disposition of an ongoing suit.[41] Such procedural provisions are key weapons in the litigator's arsenal, with the result that many interstate cases, like suits between individuals, stalemate for years in procedural maneuvering. Some such provisions are promulgated by tribunals themselves, but the majority are bargained out *ex ante* among states contemplating submission to third-party dispute resolution.

More informally, potential defendants may exert political pressure on plaintiff states not to sue or to drop a suit once it has begun. When confronted by an unfavorable GATT panel judgment (in favor of Mexico) concerning US legislation to protect dolphins from tuna fishing, the United States exercised its extra-institutional power to induce Mexico to drop the case before the judgment could be enforced. Another more subtle example concerns the US – Nicaraguan dispute referred to earlier. Although the United States refused to participate in proceedings on the merits of the case, the ICJ ruled on 27 June 1986 that the United States' mining of Nicaraguan harbors violated provisions of customary international law, which were similar to, and should be interpreted in light of, the UN Charter.[42] The United States refused to comply with the decision, and on 27 October 1986 it vetoed a Security Council resolution, which received eleven affirmative votes, calling for it to comply with the ICJ ruling.[43] Nicaragua asked for more than $2 billion in damages, but with the electoral defeat of the Sandinistas, it requested postponement of further proceedings. In 1990 the United States asked the Nicaraguan government of President Violeta Barrios de Chamorro to abandon its claim; it was reported that the Bush administration told Nicaragua that future US aid would depend on such abandonment.[44]

The preceding discussion of access suggests two conjectures:

1. The broader and less costly the access to an international court or tribunal, the greater the number of cases it will receive.
2. The broader and less expensive the access to an international court or tribunal, the more likely that complaints challenge the domestic practices of national governments – particularly the home government of the complainant.

We cannot thoroughly evaluate these conjectures here, but a preliminary analysis suggests their plausibility. Consider, for example, the size of an international tribunal's docket. Broadly speaking, the greater the formal access, the greater the caseload we should expect to observe. Courts cannot work without cases. They are quite literally out of business and without even a toehold to begin building their reputations and developing constituencies that will give them voice and at least a measure of independent power. Thus, for instance, if the access rules of the ECJ only gave states and the Commission the right to sue, the ECJ would – like the ICJ – probably have adjudicated relatively few cases and would play a role on the margins of European politics. The vast majority of significant cases in the history of the EU have been brought under Article 177 by individuals who request (or hope) that national courts will send them to the ECJ for adjudication. Another highly developed example is found in international human rights courts. The optional clause of the ECHR, Article 10, permitting individuals to bring complaints, has been the source of nearly all complaints before the Commission and the ECJ. Interstate complaints have been few in number, less than fifteen (all but a few involving state interest in co-nationals in other countries), compared with thousands of individual complaints.[45] The IACHR functions in a similar manner.

The comparative data summarized in Table 8.5 further support this conjecture. The average caseload of six prominent international courts varies as predicted, with legal systems granting low access generating the fewest number of average cases, those granting high access generating the highest number of cases, and those granting moderate access in between. The difference between categories is roughly an order of magnitude or more. While we should be cautious about imputing causality before more extensive controlled studies are performed, the data suggest the existence of a strong relationship.

Case study evidence supports the conjecture that transnational dispute-resolution systems with high levels of access tend to result in cases being brought in national courts against the *home* government. This is the standard

Table 8.5 Access rules and dockets of international courts and tribunals

Level of access	International court or tribunal	Average annual number of cases since founding
Low	PCA	0.3
Medium	ICJ	1.7
	GATT	4.4
	WTO	30.5
High	Old ECHR	23.9
	ECJ	100.1

Source: Sands *et al.* 1999, 4, 24, 72, 125, 200.

method by which cases reach the ECJ. For example, the *Cassis de Dijon* case – a classic ECJ decision in 1979 establishing the principle of mutual recognition of national regulations – concerned the right to export a French liquor to Germany, yet a German importer, not the French producer, sued the German government, charging that domestic regulations on liquor purity were creating unjustified barriers to interstate trade.[46]

The interstate and transnational politics of embeddedness

Even if cases are brought before tribunals and these tribunals render judgments against states, the extent to which judgments are legally enforceable may differ. We have seen that most international legal systems create a legal obligation for governments to comply but leave enforcement to interstate bargaining. Only a few legal systems empower individuals and groups to seek enforcement of their provisions in domestic courts. However, in our ideal type of transnational dispute resolution, international commitments are embedded in domestic legal systems, meaning that governments, particularly national executives, no longer need to take positive action to ensure enforcement of international judgments. Instead, enforcement occurs directly through domestic courts and executive agents who are responsive to judicial decisions. The politics of embedded systems of dispute resolution are very different from the politics of systems that are not embedded in domestic politics.

Under interstate dispute resolution, external pressure for compliance stems ultimately from the power and interests of national governments of participating states, which back demands with threats of reciprocal denial or punishment. Reciprocity and retaliation are often effective means of enforcement, at least for powerful states whose interests are engaged. As Judith Goldstein and Lisa Martin point out in their article, governments have made little use of the escape clause in GATT, arguably because doing so would have required providing compensation at the expense of other industrial sectors. That is, reciprocity on the international level implies that gains from reneging on a given arrangement will have to be balanced by losses to some other sector; and the political protests from that sector are likely to be shrill. Using the concept of "compliance constituencies" articulated by Miles Kahler, it is important to recognize that even if international law is not embedded in domestic legal processes, past agreements, linked to reciprocity, may create strong political pressures for compliance. If domestic "compliance constituencies" are the key to enforcement, we should expect to see more domestic pressure for compliance in trade regimes, where concentrated, mobilized constituencies like exporters and importers tend to press for compliance with tariff liberalization. Goldstein and Martin find evidence for such pressures for compliance. (Both articles appear in *International Organization*, **54–3**, Summer 2000.)

Yet despite the real successes, in some circumstances, of interstate dispute resolution, it clearly has political limitations, especially where compliance constituencies are weak. Under interstate dispute resolution, pressures for compliance have to operate through governments. The limitations of such practices are clear under arbitration, and notably with respect to the ICJ. In the case involving mining of Nicaragua's harbors, the United States did not obey the ICJ's judgment. Admittedly, the Reagan administration did not simply ignore the ICJ judgment with respect to the mining of Nicaragua's harbors, but felt obliged to withdraw its recognition of the ICJ's jurisdiction – a controversial act with significant domestic political costs for a Republican president facing a Democratic Congress. Nevertheless, in the end the United States pursued a policy contrary to the ICJ's decision. Even in trade regimes, political pressure sometimes leads to politically bargained settlements, as in the case of the US Helms–Burton legislation. And a number of countries have imposed unilateral limits on the ICJ's jurisdiction.

More broadly, reciprocity does not work well when interdependence and power are highly asymmetric. Under these circumstances, reciprocal denials of policy concessions may have much more severe consequences for the more dependent party. Furthermore, powerful governments may threaten weaker targets not only with reciprocal denial of policy concessions but also with further retaliation in linked areas. The United States has, for example, used unilateral threats of sanctions under Section 301 and with respect to anti-dumping and countervailing duty status. It has also threatened numerous governments with economic and military sanctions in an effort to compel compliance with international human rights norms. Overall, interstate dispute resolution presents many opportunities for powerful states to set the agenda for a legal process, to introduce political bargaining into decision making, and to thwart implementation of adverse legal decisions.

The politics of transnational dispute resolution are quite different. By linking direct access for domestic actors to domestic legal enforcement, transnational dispute resolution opens up an additional source of political pressure for compliance, namely favorable judgments in domestic courts. This creates a new set of political imperatives. It gives international tribunals additional means to pressure or influence domestic government institutions in ways that enhance the likelihood of compliance with their judgments. It pits a recalcitrant government not simply against other governments but also against legally legitimate domestic opposition; an executive determined to violate international law must override his or her own legal system. Moreover, it thereby permits international tribunals to develop a constituency of litigants who can later pressure government institutions to comply with the international tribunal's decision.[47] Consider the language of the ECJ in its landmark 1963 decision announcing that selected provisions of the Treaty of Rome would be directly effective as rules governing individuals in national law: "The Community constitutes a new legal order ... for the benefit of which the states have limited their sovereign rights ... and the subjects of which comprise not only Member States but also their nationals. Independently of the legislation of the Member States, Community law therefore imposes obligations on individuals but is also intended to confer on them rights which become part of their legal heritage."[48] The primary individuals and groups the ECJ had in mind were importers and exporters, many of whom came to understand that they had a direct interest in helping the court hold governments to their word on scheduled tariff reductions. Individuals and groups also have incentives to bring cases in other substantive contexts, including human rights and environmental law.[49]

The politics of compliance under transnational dispute resolution tends to give courts more leverage than they enjoy under interstate dispute resolution. The result is an environment in which judicial politics (the interplay of interests, ideas, and values among judges) and intrajudicial politics (the politics of competition or cooperation among courts) are increasingly important. Judicial politics are subject to a wide range of constraints that may or may not intersect with state interests – for example, the exigencies of legal reasoning, which Thomas Franck has distilled as the legitimacy-based demands of consistency, coherence, and adherence,[50] not to mention simple logic; the texts and case law available to shape a particular decision; and the political preferences and judicial ideology of individual judges.[51] More broadly, however, the relationships between international and national courts are central to the politics of transnational dispute resolution. In the words of Joseph Weiler, "The relationship between the European Court and national courts is the most crucial element for a successful functioning of the European legal order."[52]

Transnational dispute resolution does not sweep aside traditional interstate politics, but the power of national governments has to be filtered through norms of judicial professionalism, public opinion supporting particular conceptions of the rule of law, and an enduring tension between calculations of short- and long-term interests. Individuals and groups can zero in on international court decisions as focal points around which to mobilize, creating a further intersection between transnational litigation and democratic politics.

This discussion of the politics of interstate and transnational dispute resolution suggests that the following two conjectures deserve more intensive study.

1. Other things being equal, the more firmly embedded an international commitment is in domestic law, the more likely is compliance with judgments to enforce it.
2. Liberal democracies are particularly respectful of the rule of law and most open to individual access to judicial systems; hence attempts to embed international law in domestic legal systems should be most effective among such regimes. In relations involving nondemocracies, we should observe near total reliance on interstate dispute resolution. Even among liberal democracies, the trust placed in transnational dispute resolution may vary with the political independence of the domestic judiciary.

Although embedding international commitments does not guarantee increased compliance, we find good reason to conclude that embeddedness probably tends to make compliance more likely in the absence of a strong political counteraction. However, as Goldstein and Martin argue in their article referenced above, by removing loopholes, legalization also takes away "safety valves" that can reduce political pressure for drastic changes in rules. As they argue with respect to the WTO, "moving too far in the direction of legalization could backfire, undermining the momentum toward liberalization that the weakly legalized procedures of GATT so effectively established." To be genuinely successful, international law needs to rest on a strong basis of collective political purpose and shared standards of legitimacy: where these conditions exist (as in the EU), embedding international law in domestic legal processes is more promising than when they are absent.

The interstate and transnational dynamics of legalization

We have considered the static politics of legalization. Yet institutions also change over time and develop distinctive dynamics. Rules are elaborated. The costs of veto, withdrawal, or exclusion from the "inner club" of an institution may increase if the benefits provided by institutionalized cooperation increase. Sunk costs create incentives to maintain existing practices rather than to begin new ones. Politicians' short time horizons can induce them to agree to institutional practices that they might not prefer in the long term, in order to gain advantages at the moment.[53]

What distinguishes legalized regimes is their potential for setting in motion a distinctive dynamic built on precedent, in which decisions on a small number of specific disputes create law that may govern by analogy a vast array of future practices. This may be true even when the first litigants in a given area do not gain satisfaction. Judges may adopt modes of reasoning that assure individual litigants that their arguments have been heard and responded to, even if they have not won the day in a particular case. Some legal scholars argue that this "casuistic" style helps urge litigants, whether states or individuals, to fight another day.[54]

Although both interstate and transnational dispute resolution have the potential to generate such a legal evolution, we maintain that transnational dispute resolution increases the potential for such dynamics of precedent. The greater independence of judges, wider access of litigants, and greater potential for legal compliance insulates judges, thereby allowing them to develop legal precedent over time without triggering noncompliance, withdrawal, or reform by national governments. We next consider in more detail the specific reasons why.

The dynamics of interstate third-party dispute resolution

In interstate legal systems, the potential for self-generating spillover depends on how states perform their gatekeeping roles. As we will show, where states open the gates, the results of interstate dispute resolution may to some degree resemble the results of transnational dispute resolution. However, in the two major international judicial or quasi-judicial tribunals – the Permanent Court of Arbitration and the ICJ – states have been relatively reluctant to bring cases. The great majority of arbitration cases brought before the Permanent Court of Arbitration were heard in the court's early years, shortly after the first case in 1902. The court has seen little use recently – the Iran Claims Tribunal being an isolated if notable exception.

States have been reluctant to submit to the ICJ's jurisdiction when the stakes are large.[55] Hence the ICJ has been constrained in developing a large and binding jurisprudence. Even so, it has triggered overt and effective national opposition. Before the United States revoked compulsory jurisdiction in advance of the Nicaragua case, France had previously revoked its acceptance of the ICJ's compulsory jurisdiction in response to suits brought against it by Australia and New Zealand concerning its nuclear testing in the South Pacific in the 1960s.[56] Since the USSR and China had never accepted compulsory jurisdiction, Great Britain stood alone by late 1985 as the only permanent member of the UN Security Council willing to expose itself to the risk of being brought before the ICJ on an open-ended basis. What has emerged in the ICJ is essentially a system of discretionary submission to its jurisdiction, allowing states to control access case by case. In 1945 75 percent of all states that had ratified the Statute of the Permanent Court of International Justice also accepted the ICJ's compulsory jurisdiction; as of 1995 only 31 percent of states party to statute accept compulsory jurisdiction.[57] As measured by the level of legal obligation, legalization in the ICJ has moved *backwards* over the last half-century.

Still, it is fair to note that use of the ICJ did increase substantially between the 1960s and 1990s, reaching an all-time high of nineteen cases on the docket in 1999.[58] Although this increase does not equal the exponential growth of economic and human rights jurisprudence in this period, it marks a significant shift. In part this reflects pockets of success that have resulted in expansion of both the law in a particular area and the resort to it. The ICJ has consistently had a fairly steady stream of cases concerning international boundary disputes. In these cases the litigants have typically already resorted to military conflict that has resulted in stalemate or determined that such conflict would be too costly. They thus agree to go to court. The ICJ, in turn, has profited from this willingness by developing an extensive body of case law that countries and their lawyers can use to assess the strength of the case on both sides and be assured of a resolution based on generally accepted legal principles.[59]

Another factor in the expansion of the ICJ's caseload over the past two decades may have been the court's willingness to find against the United States in the Nicaragua case, thereby enhancing its legitimacy with developing countries.[60] At the same time, it has received a number of very high profile cases that seem likely to have been filed in the hope of publicizing a particular political dispute as much as securing an actual resolution. Examples include the suit brought by the United States against Iran over the 1979 taking of diplomatic hostages, Iran's suit against the United States for the destruction of oil platforms in the Persian Gulf, two suits brought by Libya against the United States and Great Britain arising out of the Lockerbie air disaster, and Bosnia's suit against Yugoslavia for the promotion of genocide. Although such cases are vigorously litigated by teams of distinguished international lawyers on both sides, the likelihood of compliance by the losing state seems dubious.

The ambiguous, even paradoxical consequences of the Nicaragua case suggest that the interaction between dispute resolution mechanisms and substantive agreement over time is complex. Not only does the nature of substantive agreement influence the probable development of legal systems over time, as we have seen, but the nature of legalization may influence the nature of substantive cooperation. In some cases legalization may even lead to more contention and conflict over the nature of the rules. This is an area where more research would be welcome.

The dynamics of transnational dispute resolution

The key to the dynamics of transnational dispute resolution is access. Transnational dispute resolution removes the ability of states to perform gatekeeping functions, both in limiting access to tribunals and in blocking implementation of their decisions. Its incentives for domestic actors to mobilize, and to increase the legitimacy of their claims, gives it a capacity for endogenous expansion. As we will see with respect to GATT and the WTO, even a formally interstate process may display similar expansionary tendencies, but continued expansion under interstate dispute resolution depends on continuing decisions by states to keep access to the dispute settlement process open. Switching to a set of formal rules nearer the ideal type of transnational dispute resolution makes it much harder for states to constrain tribunals and can give such tribunals both incentives and instruments to expand their authority by expanding their caseload. Indeed, tribunals can sometimes continue to strengthen their authority even when opposed by powerful states – particularly when the institutional status quo is favorable to tribunals and no coalition of dissatisfied states is capable of overturning the status quo.[61]

The pool of potential individual litigants is several orders of magnitude larger than that of state litigants. Independent courts have every incentive to recruit from that pool. Cases breed cases. A steady flow of cases, in turn, allows a court to become an actor on the legal and political stage, raising its profile in the elementary sense that other potential litigants become aware of its existence and in the deeper sense that its interpretation and application of a particular legal rule must be reckoned with as a part of what the law means in practice. Litigants who are likely to benefit from that interpretation will have an incentive to bring additional cases to clarify and enforce it. Further, the interpretation or application is itself likely to raise additional questions that can only be answered through subsequent cases. Finally, a court gains political capital from a growing caseload by demonstrably performing a needed function.

Transnational tribunals have the means at their disposal to target individual litigants in various ways. The most important advantage they have is the nature of the body of law they administer. Transnational litigation, whether deliberately established by states (as in the case of the ECHR) or adapted and expanded by a supranational tribunal itself (as in the case of the ECJ), only makes sense when interstate rules have dimensions that make them directly applicable to individual activity. Thus, in announcing the direct effect doctrine in *Van Gend and Loos*, the ECJ was careful to specify that only those portions of the Treaty of Rome that were formulated as clear and specific prohibitions on or mandates of member states' conduct could be regarded as directly applicable.[62] Human rights law is by definition applicable to individuals in relations with state authorities, although actual applicability will also depend on the clarity and specificity of individual human rights prohibitions and guarantees.

In this way, a transnational tribunal can present itself in its decisions as a protector of individual rights and benefits against the state, where the state itself has consented to these rights and benefits and the tribunal is simply holding it to its word. This is the clear thrust of the passage from *Van Gend and Loos* quoted earlier, in which the ECJ announced that "Community law . . . imposes obligations on individuals but is also intended to confer on them rights that become part of their legal heritage." The ECHR, for its part, has developed the "doctrine of effectiveness," which requires that the provisions of the European Human Rights Convention be interpreted and applied so as to make its safeguards "practical and effective" rather than "theoretical or illusory"[63] Indeed, one of its judges has described the ECHR in a dissenting opinion as the "last resort protector of oppressed individuals."[64] Such rhetoric is backed up by a willingness to find for the individual against the state.[65]

Ready access to a tribunal can create a virtuous circle: a steady stream of cases results in a stream of decisions that serve to raise the profile of the court and hence to attract more cases. When the ECJ rules, the decision is implemented not by national governments – the recalcitrant defendants – but by national courts. Any subsequent domestic opposition is rendered far more difficult. In sum, transnational third-party dispute resolution has led to a de facto alliance between certain national courts, certain types of individual litigants, and the ECJ. This alliance has been the mechanism by which the supremacy and direct effect of EC law, as well as thousands of specific substantive questions, have been established as cornerstones of the European legal order.[66]

The significance of the alliance between domestic and supranational courts lies in part in the fact that it was an unintended consequence of European integration. There is no doubt it was unforeseen by the member states; Article 177 was an incidental provision suggested by a low-level German customs official in the Treaty of Rome negotiations. However welcome the functional benefits of ECJ jurisprudence may subsequently have been – and the fact that in recent years member states have deliberately strengthened the enforcement power of the ECJ while limiting its jurisdiction suggests that they were – the founding members of the EC intended to create something much closer to a classical interstate dispute-resolution system. Individual member states often opposed the efforts of the ECJ to transform the institutions set forth in the treaty into a functioning transnational dispute-resolution system. Nothing similar exists in the annals of interstate dispute-resolution bodies.

The assertion of the importance of the ECJ in this process – in particular, the assertion of the supremacy of European law and its direct effect in domestic legal systems – was not automatic. International tribunals with transnational jurisdiction deliberately exploit this link to deepen domestic enforcement. The role of the ECJ in encouraging the cooperation of national courts has been amply documented.[67] A new generation of scholarship has focused much more on the motives driving the national courts to ally themselves with the ECJ, noting substantial variation in the willingness both of different courts within the same country and of courts in different countries to send references to the ECJ and to abide by the resulting judgments. What is most striking about these findings is the extent to which specific national courts acted independently not only of other national courts but also of the executive and legislative branches of their respective governments.[68] A German lower financial court, for example, insisted on following an ECJ judgment in the face of strong opposition from a higher financial court as well as from the German government.[69] The French Court of Cassation accepted the supremacy of EC law, following the dictate of the ECJ, even in the face of threats from the French legislature to strip its jurisdiction amid age-old charges of "*gouvernment par juges.*"[70] British courts overturned the sacrosanct doctrine of parliamentary sovereignty and issued an injunction blocking the effect of a British law pending judicial review at the European level.[71]

The motives of these national courts are multiple. They include a desire for "empowerment,"[72] competition with other courts for relative prestige and power,[73] a particular view of the law that could be achieved by following EC precedents over national precedents,[74] recognition of the greater expertise of the ECJ in European law,[75] and the desire to advantage or at least not to disadvantage a particular constituency of litigants.[76] Similar dynamics of intracourt competition may be observed in relations between national courts and the ECHR.[77] National courts appear to have been more willing to challenge the perceived interests of other domestic authorities once the first steps had been taken by other national courts. Weiler has documented the cross-citation of foreign supreme court decisions by national supreme courts accepting the supremacy of EC law for the first time. He notes that though they may have been reluctant to restrict national autonomy in a way that would disadvantage their states relative to other states, they are more willing to impose such restrictions when they are "satisfied that they are part of a trend." An alternative explanation of this trend might be ideational; courts feel such a step is more legitimate.[78]

The incentives for expansion of a transnational docket also assume a certain familiarity and comfort with litigation as a means of dispute resolution among the potential pool of litigants. Litigants in countries with a tradition of "public interest litigation," for instance, whereby NGOs use the courts to vindicate the rights of particular minorities or otherwise disadvantaged social groups, may readily see a transnational tribunal as another weapon in their arsenal.[79] More fundamentally, litigants in any country must perceive some use in resorting to the courts at all, suggesting a correlation between the most successful transnational tribunals and those presiding over countries with at least a minimum tradition of the rule of law. Alternatively, litigants in counries with a once-functioning legal system that has been corrupted or otherwise damaged may be quicker to resort to an international tribunal as a substitute or corrective for ineffective or blatantly politicized domestic adjudication.[80]

Yet even within the EU legal system, the most studied of all transnational litigation processes, we still know "surprisingly little about the behavior and organization of litigators of EC law, and nothing from a comparative perspective [across EU countries]."[81] Even within apparently dynamic and expansive jurisdictions, the process is not unidirectional, varying considerably across different national courts, different issue-areas in the same court, and across countries.[82] Direct institutional links between individual litigants and an international tribunal create an internal logic of legalization that can become a powerful catalyst for growth, yet more research is required to explain precisely how this decisively important evolution unfolds.

The evolution of the ECHR has been less purely legal. In the ECHR system, as we have seen, litigants have been encouraged over time by the publicity accorded ECHR judgments and the growing willingness of national legislatures and administrative entities, as well as courts, to comply, rather than by a direct legal link on the model of Article 177 of the Treaty of Rome. The clauses in the European Human Rights Convention allowing individuals to bring cases before the Commission (Article 10) and recognizing the compulsory jurisdiction of the ECHR (Article 25) were initially optional among the members of the Council of Europe. It was three decades until individual access and recognition of the court's jurisdiction became universal. These practices were then codified in Protocol 11 to the convention, signed in 1994, whereby all parties recognized the compulsory jurisdiction of the permanent ECHR and permit individuals direct access to it in all cases. Signature of the new protocol was made a condition of admission for any new members, a simultaneous recognition of the greatly enhanced effectiveness of transnational over interstate litigation. In many cases new democracies strongly committed to a successful political transition enthusiastically embraced the clauses.[83] In other cases such willingness may have reflected the relative weakness of the candidate states relative to the members of the largely West European club they were seeking to join.

Beyond formalism: the dynamics of GATT and the WTO

The contrast between the two ideal types of dispute resolution we have constructed – interstate and transnational – illuminates the impact of judicial independence, differential rules of access, and variations in the domestic embeddedness of an international dispute-resolution process. The ICJ fits the interstate dispute-resolution pattern quite well; the ECJ approximates the ideal type of transnational dispute resolution. The form that legalization takes seems to matter.

Form, however, is not everything. Politics is affected by form but not determined by it. This is most evident when we seek to explain more fine-grained variations in the middle of the spectrum between the two ideal types. The evolution of the GATT, and recently the WTO, illustrates how politics can alter the effects of form. Formally, as we pointed out earlier, GATT is closer to the ideal type of interstate dispute resolution than to transnational dispute resolution. The independence of tribunals is coded as moderate for both GATT and WTO. On the embeddedness criterion, GATT was low and WTO, with its mandatory procedures, is moderate (see Table 8.4). Most important, however, are access rules: in both the old GATT and the ITO (since 1 January 1995), states have the exclusive right to bring cases before tribunals. In formal terms, therefore, states are the gatekeepers to the GATT/WTO process.

We noted in the first section, however, that the relationships between actors in civil society and representatives of the state are very different in GATT/WTO than in the ICJ. In the GATT/WTO proceedings the principal actors from civil society are firms or industry groups, which are typically wealthy enough to afford extensive litigation and often have substantial political constituencies. Industry groups and firms have been quick to complain about allegedly unfair and discriminatory actions by their competitors abroad, and governments have often been willing to take up their complaints. Indeed, it has often been convenient for governments to do so, since the best defense against others' complaints in a system governed by reciprocity is often the threat or reality of bringing one's own case against their discriminatory measures. In a "tit-for-tat" game, it is useful to have an army of well-documented complaints "up one's sleeve" to deter others from filing complaints or as retaliatory responses to such complaints. Consequently, although states retain formal gatekeeping authority in the GATT/WTO system, they often have incentives to open the gates, letting actors in civil society set much of the agenda.

The result of this political situation is that the evolution of the GATT dispute-settlement procedure looks quite different from that of the ICJ: indeed, it seems intermediate between the ideal types of interstate and transnational dispute resolution. Dispute-resolution activity levels have increased substantially over time, as the process has become more legalized. Adjudication in the GATT of the 1950s produced vague decisions, which were nevertheless relatively effective, arguably because GATT was a "club" of like-minded trade officials.[84] Membership changes and the emergence of the EC in the 1960s led to decay in the dispute resolution mechanism, which only began to reverse in the 1970s. Diplomatic, nonlegalized attempts to resolve disputes, however, were severely criticized, leading to the appointment of a professional legal staff and the gradual legalization of the process. With legalization came better-argued decisions and the creation of a body of precedent.

Throughout this period, the formal procedures remained entirely voluntary: defendants could veto any step in the process. This "procedural flimsiness," as Robert E. Hudec refers to it, is often taken as a major weakness of GATT; but Hudec has shown that it did not prevent GATT from being quite effective. By the late 1980s, 80 percent of GATT cases were disposed of effectively – not as a result of legal embeddedness but of political decisions by states. This is a reasonably high level of compliance, though not as high as attained by the EC and ECHR. The WTO was built on the success of GATT, particularly in recent years, rather than being a response to failure.[85]

We infer from the GATT/WTO experience that although the formal arrangements we have emphasized are important, their dynamic effects depend on the broader political context. Our ideal-type argument should not be reified into a legalistic, single-factor explanation of the dynamics of dispute resolution. Even if states control gates, they can under some conditions be induced to open them, or even to encourage actors from civil society to enter the dispute resolution arena. The real dynamics of dispute resolution typically lie in some interaction between law and politics, rather than in the operation of either law or politics alone.

The foregoing discussion of dynamics suggests that the following three conjectures deserve detailed empirical evaluation:

1. Compared with interstate dispute resolution, transnational dispute resolution offers greater potential for the widening and deepening of dispute resolution over time, for unintended consequences, and for progressive restrictions on the behavior of national governments.

2. Judges in transnational dispute-resolution systems are more likely than those in interstate dispute-resolution systems to exploit the potential for independence, access, and embeddedness to centralize political authority in international institutions, particularly dispute-resolution bodies themselves.
3. Whereas very large political differences between ideal-typical systems are well explained by formal institutional characteristics of international legal regimes, more fine-grained differences reflect differences in the ability of domestic political groups to exploit those institutional characteristics.

Conclusion

We have constructed two ideal types of legalized dispute resolution, inter-state and transnational, which vary along the dimensions of independence, access, and embeddedness. When we examine international courts, we find that the distinction between the two ideal types appears to be associated with variation in the size of dockets and levels of compliance with decisions. The differences between the ICJ and the ECJ are dramatic along both dimensions. The causal connections between outcomes and cor-respondence with one ideal type or the other will require more research and analysis to sort out; but the differences between the ICJ and ECJ patterns cannot be denied. Their dynamics also vary greatly: the ECJ has expanded its caseload and its authority in a way that is unparalleled in the ICJ.

The GATT/WTO mechanisms do not reflect our ideal types so faithfully. States remain formal legal gatekeepers in these systems but have often refrained from tightly limiting access to dispute resolution procedures. As a result, the caseload of the GATT processes, and the effectiveness of their decisions, increased even without high formal levels of access or embedded-ness. Hence, GATT and the WTO remind us that legal form does not neces-sarily determine political process. It is the interaction of law and politics, not the action of either alone, that generates decisions and determines their effectiveness.

What transnational dispute resolution does is to insulate dispute resolution to some extent from the day-to-day political demands of states. The more we move toward transnational dispute resolution, the harder it is to trace individual judicial decisions and states' responses to them back to any simple, short-term matrix of state or social preferences, power capabilities, and cross-issues. Political constraints, of course, continue to exist, but they are less closely binding than under interstate dispute resolution. Legalization imposes real constraints on state behavior; the closer we are to transnational third-party dispute resolution, the greater those constraints are likely to be. Transnational dispute-resolution systems help to mobilize and represent particular groups that benefit from regime norms. This increases the costs of reversal to national governments and domestic constituents, which can in turn make an important contribution to the enforcement and extension of international norms. For this reason, transnational dispute resolution systems have become an important source of increased legalization and a factor in both interstate and intrastate politics.

Notes

1 Romano 1999, 723–28. By the strictest definition, there are currently seventeen permanent, independent international courts. If we include some bodies that are not courts, but instead quasi-judicial tribunals, panels, and commissions charged with similar functions, the total rises to over forty. If we include historical examples and bodies negotiated but not yet in operation, the total rises again to nearly one hundred.
2 Ibid., 709.
3 See ch. 7 above, Table 7.1 (p. 136), types I–III and IV.
4 Hence we do not exclude types II and V (Table 7.1 of ch. 7, above) from our purview.
5 See ch. 7, above.
6 We do not discuss the interesting case of international criminal law here. See Bass 1998.
7 This central focus on variation in the political representation of social groups, rather than interstate strategic interaction, is the central tenet of theories of international law that rest on liberal international relations theory. Slaughter 1995a. Our approach is thus closely linked in this way to republican liberal studies of the democratic peace, the role of independent executives and central banks in structuring international economic policy coordination, and the credibility of commitments by democratic states more generally. See Keohane and Nye 1977; Moravcsik 1997; Doyle 1983a,b; and Goldstein 1996.
8 Helfer and Slaughter 1997.
9 Even less independent are ad hoc and arbitral tribunals designed by specific countries for specific purposes. The Organization for Security and Cooperation in Europe, for example, provides experts, arbiters, and conciliators for ad hoc dispute resolution. Here we consider only permanent judicial courts. See Romano 1999, 711–13.
10 For a domestic case of judicial manipulation, see Ramseyer and Rosenbluth 1997.
11 Weiler 1994.
12 Helfer and Slaughter 1997.
13 Keck and Sikkink 1998.
14 Farer 1998.
15 It therefore remains unclear, on balance, whether the EC or the ECHR provides more ready access. Whereas the EC system under Article 177 allows only domestic courts, not individuals, to refer cases, the EC does not require, as does the ECHR and all other human rights courts, that domestic remedies be exhausted.
16 In response to the widespread success of the individual petition mechanism in Europe, the growth of the number of states party to the convention, and an increasing backlog of cases, the Council of Europe had sought to improve upon the existing judicial review machinery. After months of arduous negotiation, a majority of states signed Protocol 11, which, once ratified, will abolish the European Commission on Human Rights and create a permanent European Court of Human Rights. For a discussion of both systems, see Moravcsik 2000.

17 Sands, Mackenzie, and Shany 1999, 233–45.
18 Advisory Opinion OC-5/85, 5 Inter-American Ct. of H.R. (ser.A) (1985), 145, cited in Henkin *et al.* 1999, 525.
19 The EC, with qualified majority voting, is an exception. But here the unique power of proposal in the legislative process that generates most EC economic regulations is held by the Commission, which is unlikely to propose such a rollback of EC powers. Tsebelis 1994.
20 Weiler 1991.
21 Sands, Mackenzie, and Shany 1999, 148.
22 Drzemczewski 1983.
23 Although customary international law is generally viewed as self-executing in the United States, and therefore can be applied by courts as domestic law, most international treaties do not create private rights of action. US courts, moreover, have been hesitant to enforce customary international law against a superseding act of the federal government. See Henkin 1996; and Jackson 1992.
24 We use the term "transnational" to capture the individual to individual or individual to state nature of many of the cases in this type of dispute resolution. However, many of the tribunals in this category, such as the ECJ and the ECHR, can equally be described as "supranational" in the sense that they sit "above" the nation-state and have direct power over individuals and groups within the state. One of the authors has previously used the label "supranational" to describe these tribunals (Helfer and Slaughter 1997); no significance should be attached to the shift in terminology here.
25 Not surprisingly, domestic legal embeddedness is less common than widespread domestic access, since the former is a prerequisite for the latter.
26 Eissa 1998.
27 Weiler 1998. Selection of a judge of an identifiable political stripe does not always guarantee corresponding decisions, however. Once on the bench, judges are subject to a specific set of professional norms and duties and develop their personal conception of the role they have been asked to fill in ways that can yield surprises. A paradigmatic case is President Eisenhower's appointment of Justice William Brennan, who gave little sign of the strong liberal standard-bearer he would become.
28 Ramseyer and Rosenbluth 1997.
29 Feldman 1986, 1004.
30 Lecture by Federico Mancini, Public Representation: A Democratic Deficit? Conference at Harvard University, Center for European Studies, 29–31 January 1993.
31 Welch 1992.
32 Forsythe 1994.
33 See Bass 1998; and Bassiouni 1998.
34 Helfer and Slaughter 1997.
35 See Alter 1998b; Stein 1981; and Dashwood and White 1989.
36 S. Res. 196, 79th Cong., 2d sess., 92 *Cong. Rec.* 10706 (1946).
37 Ibid.
38 Briggs 1985, 377.
39 Schwebel 1996.
40 Rosenne 1995.
41 Ibid.
42 ICJ, *Military and Paramilitary Activities in and Against Nicaragua.* (Nicaragua v. United States of America.) Merits, Judgment. ICJ Reports 1986, 97–99.
43 See *New York Times*, 29 October 1986, A3.
44 See *New York Times*, 30 September 1990.
45 Moravcsik 1995.

46 Case 120/78, *Rewe-Zentrale AG v. Bundesmonopolverwaltung fur Branntwein* (Cassis de Dijon), 1978.
47 Helfer and Slaughter 1997.
48 Case 26/62, *N. V. Algemene Transp. and Expeditie Onderneming Van Gend and Loos v. Nederslandse administratie der belastingen*, 1963 E.C.R. 1, 12.
49 This dynamic is not limited to Europe. David Wirth explains it succinctly in his analysis of compulsory third-party dispute resolution as a mechanism for enforcing international environmental law. Wirth 1994.
50 Franck 1990.
51 Mattli and Slaughter 1995.
52 Weiler 1998, 22. The ECHR has experienced considerable variation in its effectiveness, which does not seem on its face to be well explained by embeddedness. With respect to the ECHR, we believe that more research is needed to evaluate explanations that rely on embeddedness.
53 See Keohane and Hoffmann 1991; Alter 1998a; and Pollack 1997.
54 See White 1990; Glendon 1991; and Sunstein 1996.
55 Chayes 1965.
56 Rosenne 1995, 270 n. 17. See also *Nuclear Tests (Australia v. France)*, 1974 I.C.J. 253 (20 December); and *Nuclear Tests (New Zealand v. France)*, 1974 I.C.J. 457 (20 December).
57 Schwebel 1996.
58 Ibid.
59 See, for example, Charney 1994.
60 Schwebel 1996.
61 See Alter 1998a; and Alter, *International Organization*, **54–3** (Summer 2000): 401–419.
62 Case 26/62, *N. V. Algemene Transp. and Expeditie Onderneming Van Gend and Loos v. Nederslandse administratie der belastingen.* 1963 E.C.R. 1, 12.
63 Bernhardt 1994.
64 *Cossey v. United Kingdom*, 184 E.C.H.R., ser. A (1990).
65 Helfer and Slaughter 1997.
66 See Burley and Mattli 1993; and Weiler 1991 and 1999.
67 See Stein 1981; Weiler 1991; and Burley and Mattli 1993.
68 This conclusion is not uncontroversial. Some political scientists argue that these national courts were in fact following the wishes of their respective governments, notwithstanding their governments' expressed opposition before the ECJ. The claim is that all EC member states agreed to economic integration as being in their best interests in 1959. They understood, however, that they needed a mechanism to bind one another to the obligations undertaken in the original treaty. They thus established a court to hold each state to its respective word. See Garrett 1992; Garrett and Weingast 1993; and Garrett, Kelemen, and Schulz 1998. On this view, intrajudicial politics within the EU were either anticipated by the founding states or were epiphenomenal. For a debate on precisely this point, see Garrett 1995; and Mattli and Slaughter 1995.
69 Alter 1996b.
70 See Alter 1996b; and Plötner 1998.
71 Craig 1998.
72 See Weiler 1991; and Burley and Mattli 1993.
73 Alter 1996b, and 1998a,b.
74 Mattli and Slaughter 1998b.
75 Craig 1998.
76 Plötner 1998.
77 Jarmul 1996.
78 See Weiler 1994; and Finnemore and Sikkink 1998.

79 See Harlow and Rawlings 1992; and Alter and Vargas 2000.
80 See Helfer and Slaughter 1997; and Stone Sweet 1999.
81 Stone Sweet 1998, 330. See also Harlow 1992.
82 Golub 1996.
83 Moravcsik 2000.
84 This paragraph and the subsequent one rely on Hudec 1999, especially 6–17.
85 The annual number of cases before the WTO has risen to almost twice the number
    during the last years of GATT; but Hudec argues that this change is accounted for
    by the new or intensified obligations of the Uruguay Round, rather than being
    attributable to changes in the embeddedness of the dispute resolution mechanism.
    Hudec 1999, 21. Hudec acknowledges, however, that he is arguing against the
    conventional wisdom.

References

Abbott, Kenneth W. and Duncan Snidal. 1998. Why States Use Formal International
Organizations, *Journal of Conflict Resolution*, **42** (1), 3–32.

Alter, Karen J. 1996. The Making of a Rule of Law: The European Court and the
National Judiciaries, PhD dissertation, Massachusetts Institute of Technology.

Alter, Karen J. 1998a. Explaining National Court Acceptance of European Court
Jurisprudence: A Critical Evaluation of Theories of Legal Integration. In *The
European Court and National Court – Doctrine and Jurisprudence: Legal Change in
Its Social Context*, Anne-Marie Slaughter, Alec Stone Sweet and J.H.H. Weiler
(eds), Oxford: Hart Publishing, 227–52.

Alter, Karen J. 1998b. Who Are the Masters of the Treaty? European Governments and the European Court of Justice, *International Organization*, **52** (1),
121–47.

Alter, Karen J. and Jeannette Vargas. 2000. Explaining Variation in the Use of
European State Litigation Strategies: EC Law and UK Gender Equality Policy,
Comparative Political Studies, **33** (4), 316–46.

Bass, Gary Jonathan. 1998. Judging War: The Politics of International War Crimes
Tribunals, PhD dissertation, Harvard University.

Bassiouni, M. Cherif (compiler). 1998. *The State of the International Criminal Court:
A Documentary History*, New York: Transnational Publishers.

Baxter, R.R. 1980. International Law in Her Infinite Variety, *International and
Comparative Law Quarterly*, **29**, 549–66.

Bernhardt, Rudolf. 1994. Human Rights and Judicial Review: The European Court of
Human Rights. In *Human Rights and Judicial Review: A Comparative Perspective*,
David M. Beatty (ed.), Dordrecht: Martinus Nijhoff, 297–319.

Boisson de Chazournes, Laurence. 1998. Policy Guidance and Compliance Issues in
Financial Activities: The World Bank Operational Standards (paper prepared for
meeting of the American Society of International Law Project on Compliance with
Soft Law, 8–10 October, Baltimore, Md).

Briggs, Herbert W. 1985. Nicaragua v. United States: Jurisdiction and Admissibility,
American Journal of International Law, **79**, 373–78.

Bull, Hedley. 1977. *The Anarchical Society: A Study of Order in World Politics*, New
York: Columbia University Press.

Burley, Anne-Marie and Walter Mattli. 1993. Europe Before the Court: A Political
Theory of Legal Integration, *International Organization*, **47** (1), 41–76.

Charney, Jonathan I. 1994. Progress in Maritime Boundary Delimitation Law, *American Journal of International Law*, **88** (2), 227–56.

Chayes, Abram. 1965. A Common Lawyer Looks at International Law, *Harvard Law Review*, **78** (7), 1396–1413.

Chayes, Abram. 1995. *The New Sovereignty: Compliance with International Regulatory Agreements*, Cambridge, Mass.: Harvard University Press.

Chinkin, C.M. 1989. The Challenge of Soft Law: Development and Change in International Law, *International and Comparative Law Quarterly*, **38**, 850–66.

Craig, P.P. 1998. Report on the United Kingdom: Constitutional Doctrine Within the United Kingdom; The Impact of the EC. In *The European Court and National Courts – Doctrine and Jurisprudence: Legal Change in Its Social Context*, Anne-Marie Slaughter, Alec Stone Sweet and J.H.H. Weiler (eds), Oxford: Hart Publishing, 195–224.

Dashwood, Alan and Robin White. 1989. Enforcement Actions Under Articles 169 and 170 EEC, *European Law Review*, **14** (6), 388–413.

Downs, George W., David M. Rockie and Peter N. Barsoom. 1996. Is the Good News About Compliance Good News About Cooperation?, *International Organization*, **50** (3), 379–406.

Doyle, Michael W. 1983a. Kant, Liberal Theories and Foreign Affairs (Part 1), *Philosophy and Public Affairs*, **12** (4), 205–35.

Doyle, Michael W. 1983b. Kant, Liberal Theories and Foreign Affairs (Part 2), *Philosophy and Public Affairs*, **12** (4), 323–53.

Drzemczewski, Andrew Z. 1983. *European Human Rights Convention in Domestic Law: A Comparative Study*, Oxford: Oxford University.

Eissa, Farouk Abu. 1998. Promotion of the Rule of Law in the Arab Region, *American Bar Association World Under Law Reporter*, **5** (2), 5.

Farer, Tom J. (ed.). 1998. The Rise of the Inter-American Human Rights Regime: No Longer a Unicorn, Not Yet an Ox. *The Inter-American System of Human Rights*, David Harris and Stephen Livingstone (eds), Oxford: Clarendon, 31–64.

Feldman, Mark B. 1986. Ted L. Stein on the Iran–US Claims Tribunal – Scholarship Par Excellence, *Washington Law Review*, **61** (3), 997–1005.

Forsythe, David. 1994. Politics and the International Tribunal for the Former Yugoslavia, *Criminal Law Forum*, **5**, 401–22.

Franck, Thomas M. 1990. *Power of Legitimacy Among Nations*, New York: Oxford University Press.

Fuller, Lon L. 1964. *The Morality of Law*, New Haven, Conn.: Yale University Press.

Gamble, John King, Jr. 1985. The 1982 United Nations Convention on the Law of the Sea as Soft Law, *Houston Journal of International Law*, **8**, 37–47.

Garrett, Geoffrey. 1992. International Cooperation and International Choice: The European Community's Internal Market, *International Organization*, **46** (2), 533–60.

Garrett, Geoffrey. 1995. The Politics of Legal Integration in the European Union, *International Organization*, **49** (1), 171–81.

Garrett, Geoffrey and Barry Weingast. 1993. Ideas, Interests and Institutions: Constructing the EC's Internal Market. In *Ideas and Foreign Policy: Beliefs, Institutions and Political Change*, Judith Goldstein and Robert O. Keohane (eds), Ithica, NY: Cornell University Press.

Garrett, Geoffrey, R. Daniel Kelemen and Heiner Schulz. 1998. The European Court of Justice, National Governments and Legal Integration in the European Union, *International Organization*, **52** (1), 149–76.

Glendon, Mary Ann. 1991. *Rights Talk: The Impoverishment of Political Discourse*, New York: Free Press.

Goldstein, Judith. 1996. International Law and Domestic Institutions: Reconciling North American 'Unfair' Trade Laws, *International Organization*, **50** (4), 541–64.

Golub, Jonathan. 1996. The Politics of Judicial Discretion: Rethinking the Interaction Between National Courts and the European Court of Justice, *West European Politics*, **19** (2), 360–85.

Gruchalla-Wesierski, Tadeusz. 1984. A Framework for Understanding Soft Law, *McGill Law Journal*, **30**, 37–88.

Harlow, Carol. 1992. Toward a Theory of Access for the European Court of Justice, *Yearbook of European Law*, **12**, 213–48.

Harlow, Carol and Richard Rawlings. 1992. *Pressure Through Law*, New York: Routledge.

Hart, H.L.A. 1961. *The Concept of Law*, Oxford: Clarendon Press.

Helfer, Laurence and Anne-Marie Slaughter. 1997. Toward a Theory of Effective Supranational Adjudication, *Yale Law Journal*, **107** (2), 273–391.

Henkin, Louis. 1996. *Foreign Affairs and the United States Constitution* (2nd Edition), Oxford: Oxford University Press.

Hudec, Robert E. 1999. The New WTO Dispute Settlement Procedure, *Minnesota Journal of Global Trade*, **8** (1), 1–53.

Jackson, John H. 1992. The Status of International Treaties in Domestic Legal Systems: A Policy Analysis, *American Journal of International Law*, **86** (2), 310–29.

Jarmul, Holly Dawn. 1996. Effects of Decisions of Regional Human Rights Tribunals on National Courts. In *International Law Decisions in National Courts*, Thomas M. Franck and Gregory H. Fox (eds), Irvington-on-Hudson, NY: Transnational Publishers, 247–84.

Kaplan, Morton A. 1957. *System and Process in International Politics*, New York: Wiley.

Keck, Margaret E. and Kathryn Sikkink. 1998. *Activists Beyond Borders: Advocacy Networks in International Politics*, Ithaca, NY: Cornell University Press.

Kennedy, Duncan. 1976. Forum and Substance in Private Law Adjudication, *Harvard Law Review*, **89**, 1685–1778.

Keohane, Robert O. and Joseph S. Nye, Jr. 1977. *Power and Interdependence: World Politics in Transition*, Boston: Little, Brown.

Keohane, Robert O. and Stanley Hoffmann (eds). 1991. *The New European Community: Decision-Making and Institutional Change*, Boulder, Colo.: Westview Press.

Krasner, Stephen D. (ed.). 1983. *International Regimes*, Ithaca, NY: Cornell University Press.

Mattli, Walter and Anne-Marie Slaughter. 1995. Law and Politics in the European Union: A Reply to Garrett, *International Organization*, **49** (1), 183–90.

Mattli, Walter and Anne-Marie Slaughter. 1998. Revisiting the European Court of Justice, *International Organization*, **52** (1), 177–209.

Moravcsik, Andrew. 1995. Explaining International Human Rights Regimes: Liberal Theory and Western Europe, *European Journal of International Relations*, **1** (2), 157–89.

Moravcsik, Andrew. 1997. Taking Preferences Seriously: A Liberal Theory of International Politics, *International Organization*, **51** (4), 513–53.

Moravcsik, Andrew. 2000. The Origin of International Human Rights Regimes:

Democratic Delegation in Postwar Europe, *International Organization*, **54** (2), 217–52.

Morrow, James D. 1997. The Laws of War as an International Institution (paper presented at 'Program on International Politics, Economics and Security', February, University of Chicago).

Morrow, James D. 1998. The Institutional Features of the Prisoner of War Treaties (paper presented at the 'Conference on Rational International Institutions', April, University of Chicago).

Palmer, Geoffrey. 1992. New Ways to Make International Environmental Law, *American Journal of International Law*, **86**, 259–83.

Plötner, Jens. 1998. Report on France: The Reception of the Direct Effect and Supremacy by the French Supreme Courts. In *The European Court and National Courts – Doctrine and Jurisprudence: Legal Change in Its Social Context*, Anne-Marie Slaughter, Alec Stone Sweet and J.H.H. Weiler (eds), Oxford: Hart Publishing, 41–75.

Pollack, Mark. 1997. Delegation, Agency and Agenda Setting in the European Community, *International Organization*, **51** (1), 99–134.

Ramseyer, J. Mark and Frances McCall Rosenbluth. 1997. *Japan's Political Marketplace*, Cambridge, Mass.: Harvard University Press.

Ratner, Steven. 2000. Does International Law Matter in Preventing Ethnic Conflict?, *New York University Journal of International Law and Politics*, **32**, 591–698.

Romano, Cesare. 1999. The Proliferation of International Judicial Bodies: The Pieces of the Puzzle, *New York University Journal of International Law and Politics*, **31** (4), 709–51.

Rosenne, Shabtai. 1995. *The World Court: What It Is and How It Works* (5th Edition), Dordrecht: Martinus Nijhoff.

Sands, Philipe, Ruth Mackenzie and Yuval Shany (eds). 1999. *Manual on International Courts and Tribunals*, London: Butterworths.

Schachter, Oscar. 1977. The Twilight Existance of Nonbinding International Agreements, *American Journal of International Law*, **71**, 296–304.

Schwebel, Stephen M. 1996. The Performance and Prospects of the International Court of Justice. In *Perspectives of Air Law, Space Law and International Business Law for the Next Century*, Karl-Heinz Bockstiegel (ed.), Köln: Carl Heymanns Verlag, 291–98.

Setear, John K. 1999. Whaling and Legalization (unpublished manuscript), University of Virginia, Charlottesville, Virginia.

Shihata, Ibrahim F. 1994. *The World Bank Inspection Panel*, New York: Oxford University Press for The World Bank.

Simma, Bruno and Andreas L. Paulus. 1999. The Responsibility of Individuals for Human Rights Abuses in Internal Conflicts: A Positivist View, *American Journal of International Law*, **93**, 302–16.

Slaughter, Anne-Marie. 1995. International Law in a World of Liberal States, *European Journal of International Law*, **6**, 503–38.

Stein, Eric. 1981. Lawyers, Judges and the Making of a Transnational Constitution, *American Journal of International Law*, **75**, 1–27.

Stone Sweet, Alec. 1998. Constitutional Dialogues in the European Community. In *The European Court and National Courts – Doctrine and Jurisprudence: Legal Change in Its Social Context*, Anne-Marie Slaughter, Alec Stone Sweet and J.H.H. Weiler (eds), Oxford: Hart Publishing, 305–30.

Stone Sweet, Alec. 1999. Judicialization and the Construction of Governance, *Comparative Political Studies*, **32** (2), 147–84.

Sunstein, Cass R. 1986. Legal Interference with Private Preferences, *Univeristy of Chicago Law Review*, **53**, 1129–74.

Sunstein, Cass R. 1996. *Legal Reasoning and Political Conflict*, New York: Oxford University Press.

Tsebelis, George. 1994. The Power of the European Parliament as a Conditional Agenda-Setter, *American Political Science Review*, **88** (1), 128–42.

Victor, David G., Kal Raustalia and Eugene B. Skolnikov. 1998. *The Implementation and Effectiveness of International Environmental Commitments: Theory and Practice*, Cambridge, Mass.: MIT Press.

Weiler, J.H.H. 1991. The Transformation of Europe, *Yale Law Journal*, **100**, 2403–83.

Weiler, J.H.H. 1994. A Quiet Revolution: The European Court of Justice and Its Interlocutors, *Comparative Political Studies*, **26** (4), 510–34.

Weiler, J.H.H. 1998. Epilogue – The European Courts of Justice: Beyond Doctrine or the Legitimacy Crisis of European Constitutionalism. In *The European Court and National Courts – Doctrine and Jurisprudence: Legal Change in Its Social Context*, Anne-Marie Slaughter, Alec Stone Sweet and J.H.H. Weiler (eds), Oxford: Hart Publishing, 365–91.

Weiler, J.H.H. 1999. *The Constitution of Europe: Do the New Clothes Have an Emperor? And Other Essays on European Integration*, Cambridge: Cambridge University Press.

Welch, Claude E., Jr. 1992. The African Commission on Human and People's Rights: A Five-Year Report and Assessment, *Human Rights Quarterly*, **14**, 43–57.

White, James Boyd. 1990. *Justice as Translation: An Essay in Cultural and Legal Criticism*, Chicago: University of Chicago Press.

Wirth, David A. 1994. Re-examining Decision-Making Processes in International Environmental Law, *Iowa Law Review*, **79**, 769–802.

Zaring, David. 1998. International Law by Other Means: The Twilight Existence of International Financial Regulatory Organizations, *Texas International Law Journal*, **33**, 218–330.

Part III

Globalism, liberalism, and governance

9 Governance in a globalizing world

Robert O. Keohane and
Joseph S. Nye Jr.
(2000)

Globalization became a buzzword in the 1990s, as "interdependence" did in the 1970s. Sometimes, it seems to refer to anything that the author thinks is new or trendy. But globalization, as this book shows, refers to real changes of fundamental importance. These changes have profound implications for politics as well as for economics, military activities, and the environment. In this chapter we ask three fundamental questions. One, how are patterns of globalization evolving in the first part of the twenty-first century? Two, how does this affect governance, previously closely associated with the nation-state? Three, how might globalism itself be governed?

Globalization will affect governance processes and be affected by them. Frequent financial crises of the magnitude of the crisis of 1997–99 could lead to popular movements to limit interdependence and to a reversal of economic globalization. Chaotic uncertainty is too high a price for most people to pay for somewhat higher average levels of prosperity. Unless some aspects of globalization can be effectively governed, it may not be sustainable in its current form. Complete laissez-faire was not a viable option during earlier periods of globalization and is not likely to be viable now. The question is not – will globalization be governed? – but rather, *how* will globalization be governed?

Defining globalism

Globalism is a state of the world involving networks of interdependence at multicontinental distances.[1] These networks can be linked through flows and influences of capital and goods, information and ideas, people and force, as well as environmentally and biologically relevant substances (such as acid rain or pathogens). Globalization and deglobalization refer to the increase or decline of globalism. In comparison with interdependence, globalism has two special characteristics:[2]

1.   Globalism refers to networks of connections (multiple relationships), not simply to single linkages. We would refer to economic or military

interdependence between the United States and Japan but not to globalism between the United States and Japan. US–Japanese interdependence is part of contemporary globalism but by itself is not globalism.

2. For a network of relationships to be considered "global," it must include multicontinental distances, not simply regional networks. Distance is of course a continuous variable, ranging from adjacency (for instance, between the United States and Canada) to opposite sides of the globe (for instance, Britain and Australia). Any sharp distinction between "long-distance" and "regional" interdependence is therefore arbitrary, and there is no point in deciding whether intermediate relationships – say, between Japan and India or between Egypt and South Africa – would qualify. Yet "globalism" would be an odd word for proximate regional relationships. Globalization refers to the shrinkage of distance but on a large scale. It can be contrasted with localization, nationalization, or regionalization.

Some examples may help. Islam's quite rapid diffusion from Arabia across Asia to what is now Indonesia was a clear instance of globalization; but the initial movement of Hinduism across the Indian subcontinent was not, according to our definition. Ties among the countries of the Asia-Pacific Economic Cooperation Forum (APEC) qualify as multicontinental interdependence, because these countries include the Americas as well as Asia and Australia; but the Association of Southeast Asian Nations (ASEAN) is regional.

Globalism does not imply universality. At the turn of the millennium, a quarter of the American population used the World Wide Web compared with one hundredth of 1 percent of the population of South Asia. Most people in the world today do not have telephones; hundreds of millions of people live as peasants in remote villages with only slight connections to world markets or the global flow of ideas. Indeed, globalization is accompanied by increasing gaps, in many respects, between the rich and the poor. It does not imply homogenization or equity.[3] An integrated world market would mean free flows of goods, people, and capital, and convergence in interest rates. That is far from the facts. While world trade grew twice as fast and foreign direct investment three times as fast as world output in the second half of the twentieth century, Britain and France are only slightly more open to trade (ratio of trade to output) today than in 1913, and Japan is less so. By some measures, capital markets were more integrated at the beginning of the century, and labor is less mobile than in the second half of the nineteenth century when 60 million people left Europe for new worlds.[4] In social terms, contacts among people with different religious beliefs and other deeply held values have often led to conflict.[5] Two symbols express these conflicts: the notion of the United States as the Great Satan, held by Islamic fundamentalism in Iran; and student protestors' erection in Tiananmen Square in China, in 1989, of a replica of the Statue of Liberty. Clearly, in social as well as economic terms, homogenization does not follow necessarily from globalization.

The dimensions of globalism

Interdependence and globalism are both multidimensional phenomena. All too often, they are defined in strictly economic terms, as if the world economy defined globalism. But other forms of globalism are equally important. The oldest form of globalization is environmental: climate change has affected the ebb and flow of human populations for millions of years. Migration is a long-standing global phenomenon. The human species began to leave its place of origin, Africa, about 1.25 million years ago and reached the Americas sometime between 30,000 and 13,000 years ago. One of the most important forms of globalization is biological. The first smallpox epidemic is recorded in Egypt in 1350 BC. It reached China in 49 AD, Europe after 700; the Americas in 1520, and Australia in 1789.[6] The plague or Black Death originated in Asia, but its spread killed a quarter to a third of the population of Europe between 1346 and 1352. When Europeans journeyed to the New World in the fifteenth and sixteenth centuries they carried pathogens that destroyed up to 95 percent of the indigenous population.[7] Today, human impact on global climate change could affect the lives of people everywhere. However, not all effects of environmental globalism are adverse. For instance, nutrition and cuisine in the Old World benefited from the importation of such New World crops as the potato, corn, and the tomato.[8]

Military globalization dates at least from the time of Alexander the Great's expeditions of 2,300 years ago, which resulted in an empire that stretched across three continents from Athens through Egypt to the Indus. Hardest to pin down, but in some ways the most pervasive form of globalism, is the flow of information and ideas. Indeed, Alexander's conquests were arguably most important for introducing Western thought and society, in the form of Hellenism, to the eastern world.[9] Four great religions of the world – Buddhism, Judaism, Christianity, and Islam – have spread across great distances over the past two millennia; and in this age of the Internet other religions such as Hinduism, formerly more circumscribed geographically, are doing so as well.[10]

Analytically, we can differentiate dimensions according to the types of flows and perceptual connections that occur in spatially extensive networks:

- Economic globalism involves long-distance flows of goods, services, and capital, and the information and perceptions that accompany market exchange. It also involves the organization of the processes that are linked to these flows: for example, the organization of low-wage production in Asia for the US and European markets. Indeed, some economists define globalization in narrowly economic terms as "the transfer of technology and capital from high-wage to low-wage countries, and the resulting growth of labor-intensive Third World exports."[11] Economic flows, markets, and organization, as in multinational firms, all go together.

- Military globalism refers to long-distance networks of interdependence in which force, and the threat or promise of force, are employed. A good example of military globalism is the "balance of terror" between the United States and the Soviet Union during the cold war. Their strategic interdependence was acute and well recognized. Not only did it produce world-straddling alliances, but either side could have used intercontinental missiles to destroy the other within thirty minutes. It was distinctive not because it was totally new, but because the scale and speed of the potential conflict arising from interdependence were so enormous.

- Environmental globalism refers to the long distance transport of materials in the atmosphere or oceans or of biological substances such as pathogens or genetic materials that affect human health and well-being. Examples include the depletion of the stratospheric ozone layer as a result of ozone-depleting chemicals; human-induced global warming, insofar as it is occurring; the spread of the AIDs virus from central Africa around the world beginning at the end of the 1970s. As in the other forms of globalism, the transfer of information is important, both directly and through the movement of genetic material and indirectly as a result of inferences made on the basis of material flows. Some environmental globalism may be entirely natural – the earth has gone through periods of warming and cooling since before the human impact was significant – but much of the recent change has been induced by human activity.

- Social and cultural globalism involves movements of ideas, information, and images, and of people – who of course carry ideas and information with them. Examples include the movement of religions or the diffusion of scientific knowledge. An important facet of social globalism involves imitation of one society's practices and institutions by others: what some sociologists refer to as "isomorphism."[12] Often, however, social globalism has followed military and economic globalism. Ideas and information and people follow armies and economic flows, and in so doing, transform societies and markets. At its most profound level, social globalism affects the consciousness of individuals and their attitudes toward culture, politics, and personal identity. Indeed, social and cultural globalism interacts with other types of globalism, since military and environmental, as well as economic, activity convey information and generate ideas, which may then flow across geographical and political boundaries. In the current era, as the growth of the Internet reduces costs and globalizes communications, the flow of ideas is increasing.

One could imagine other dimensions. For example, political globalism could refer to that subset of social globalism that refers to ideas and information about power and governance. It could be measured by imitation effects (for example, in constitutional arrangements or the number of democratic states) or by the diffusion of government policies, or of international regimes. Legal globalism could refer to the spread of legal practices and institutions to a variety of issues, including world trade and the criminalization of war crimes by heads of state. Globalization occurs in other dimensions as well – for instance, in science, entertainment, fashion, and language.

One obvious problem with considering all these aspects of globalism to be dimensions on a par with those we have listed is that when categories proliferate, they cease to be useful. To avoid such proliferation, therefore, we treat these dimensions of globalism as subsets of social and cultural globalism. Political globalism seems less a separate type than an aspect of any of our four dimensions. Almost all forms of globalization have political implications. For example, the World Trade Organization (WTO), Non-Proliferation Treaty (NPT), Montreal Convention, and United Nations Educational, Scientific, and Cultural Organization (UNESCO) are responses to economic, military, environmental, and social globalization.

In the aftermath of Kosovo and East Timor, ideas about human rights and humanitarian interventions versus classical state sovereignty formulations were a central feature of the 1999 UN General Assembly. UN Secretary General Kofi Annan argued that in a global era, "The collective interest is the national interest," and South African President Thabo Mbeki stated that "the process of globalization necessarily redefines the concept and practice of national sovereignty." President Abdelaziz Bouteflika of Algeria, the head of the Organization of African Unity, replied that he did not deny the right of northern public opinion to denounce breaches of human rights, but "sovereignty is our final defense against the rules of an unequal world," and that "we [Africa] are not taking part in the decisionmaking process."[13] These were debates about the political implications of social and military globalization, rather than about political globalization as distinct from its social and military dimensions.

The division of globalism into separate dimensions is inevitably somewhat arbitrary. Nonetheless, it is useful for analysis, because changes in the various dimensions of globalization do not necessarily co-vary. One can sensibly say, for instance, that "economic globalization" took place between approximately 1850 and 1914, manifested in imperialism and in increasing trade and capital flows between politically independent countries; and that such globalization was largely reversed between 1914 and 1945. That is, economic globalism rose between 1850 and 1914 and fell between 1914 and 1945. However, military globalism rose to new heights during the two world wars, as did many aspects of social globalism. The worldwide influenza epidemic of 1918–19, which took 21 million lives, was propagated by the flows of soldiers around the world.[14] So did globalism decline or rise between 1914 and 1945?

It depends on the dimension of globalism one is referring to. Without an adjective, general statements about globalism are often meaningless or misleading.

Thick globalism: what's new?

When people speak colloquially about globalization, they typically refer to recent increases in globalism. Comments such as "globalization is fundamentally new" only make sense in this context but are nevertheless misleading. We prefer to speak of globalism as a phenomenon with ancient roots and of globalization as the process of increasing globalism, now or in the past.

The issue is not how old globalism is, but rather how "thin" or "thick" it is at any given time.[15] As an example of "thin globalization," the Silk Road provided an economic and cultural link between ancient Europe and Asia, but the route was plied by a small group of hardy traders, and the goods that were traded back and forth had a direct impact primarily on a small (and relatively elite) stratum of consumers along the road. In contrast, "thick" relations of globalization involve many relationships that are intensive as well as extensive: long-distance flows that are large and continuous, affecting the lives of many people. The operations of global financial markets today, for instance, affect people from Peoria to Penang. "Globalization" is *the process by which globalism becomes increasingly thick*.

Often, contemporary globalization is equated with Americanization, especially by non-Americans who resent American popular culture and the capitalism that accompanies it. In 1999, for example, some French farmers protecting "culinary sovereignty" attacked McDonald's restaurants.[16] Several dimensions of globalism are indeed dominated today by activities based in the United States, whether on Wall Street, in the Pentagon, in Cambridge, in Silicon Valley, or in Hollywood. If we think of the content of globalization being "uploaded" on the Internet, then "downloaded" elsewhere, more of this content is uploaded in the United States than anywhere else.[17] However, globalization long predates Hollywood and Bretton Woods. The spice trade and the intercontinental spread of Buddhism, Christianity, and Islam preceded by many centuries the discovery of America, much less the formation of the United States. In fact, the United States itself is a product of seventeenth- and eighteenth-century globalization. Japan's importation of German law a century ago, contemporary ties between Japan and Latin American countries with significant Japanese-origin populations, and the lending by European banks to emerging markets in East Asia also constitute examples of globalization not focused on the United States. Hence, globalism is not intrinsically American, even if its current phase is heavily influenced by what happens in the United States.

Globalism today is America-centric, in that most of the impetus for the information revolution comes from the United States, and a large part of the content of global information networks is created in the United States.

However, the ideas and information that enter global networks are down-loaded in the context of national politics and local cultures, which act as selective filters and modifiers of what arrives. Political institutions are often more resistant to transnational transmission than popular culture. Although the Chinese students in Tiananmen Square in 1989 built a replica of the Statue of Liberty, China has emphatically not adopted US political institu-tions. Nor is this new. In the nineteenth century, Meiji reformers in Japan were aware of Anglo-American ideas and institutions but deliberately turned to German models because they seemed more congenial.[18] For many coun-tries today Canadian constitutional practices, with their greater emphasis on duties, or German laws, restrictive of racially charged speech, are more con-genial than those of the United States.[19] The current wave of imitation of government reform started in Britain and New Zealand, not the United States.

The central position of the United States in global networks creates "soft power": the ability to get others to want what Americans want.[20] But the processes are in many respects reciprocal, rather than one way. Some US practices are very attractive to other countries – honest regulation of drugs, as in the Food and Drug Administration (FDA); transparent securities laws and practices, limiting self-dealing, monitored by the Securities and Exchange Commission (SEC). US-made standards are sometimes hard to avoid, as in the rules governing the Internet itself. But other US standards and practices – from pounds and feet (rather than the metric system) to capital punishment, the right to bear arms, and absolute protection of free speech – have encountered resistance or even incomprehension. Soft power is a reality, but it does not accrue to the United States in all areas of life, nor is the United States the only country to possess it.

Is there anything about globalism today that is fundamentally different? Every era builds on others. Historians can always find precursors in the past for phenomena of the present, but contemporary globalization goes "faster, cheaper and deeper."[21] The degree of thickening of globalism is giving rise to increased density of networks, increased "institutional velocity," and increased transnational participation.

Economists use the term "network effects" to refer to situations in which a product becomes more valuable once many other people also use it. This is why the Internet is causing such rapid change.[22] A knowledge-based economy generates "powerful spillover effects, often spreading like fire and triggering further innovation and setting off chain reactions of new inventions. . . . But goods – as opposed to knowledge – do not always spread like fire."[23] More-over, as interdependence and globalism have become thicker, the systemic relationships among different networks have become more important. There are more interconnections among the networks. As a result, "system effects" become more important.[24] Intensive economic interdependence affects social and environmental interdependence, and awareness of these connections in turn affects economic relationships. For instance, the expansion of trade can generate industrial activity in countries with low environmental standards, mobilizing environmental activists to carry their message to the newly industrializing but environmentally lax countries. The resulting activities may affect environmental interdependence (for instance, by reducing cross-boundary pollution) but may generate resentment in the newly industrializing country, affecting social and economic relations.

The extensivity of globalism means that the potential connections occur worldwide, sometimes with unpredictable results. Even if we thoroughly analyzed each individual strand of interdependence between two societies, we might well miss the synergistic effects of relationships between these linkages between societies.

Environmental globalism illustrates the point well. When scientists in the United States discovered chlorofluorocarbons (CFCs) in the 1920s, they and many others were delighted to have such efficient chemicals available for refrigeration (and other purposes) that were chemically inert, hence not subject to explosions and fires. Only in the 1970s was it suspected, and in the 1980s proved, that CFCs depleted the stratospheric ozone layer, which protects human beings against harmful ultraviolet rays. The environmental motto, "Everything is connected to everything else," warns us that there may be unanticipated effects of many human activities, from burning of carbon fuels (generating climate change) to genetically modifying crops grown for food.

Environmental globalism has political, economic, and social consequences. Discoveries of the ozone-depleting properties of CFCs (and other chemicals) led to this issue being put on international agendas, intranational, international, and transnational controversies about it, and eventually a series of international agreements, beginning at Montreal in 1987, regulating the production and sale of such substances. These agreements entailed trade sanctions against violators, thus affecting economic globalism. They also raised people's awareness of ecological dangers, contributing to much greater transnational transmission of ideas and information (social globalism) about ecological processes affecting human beings.

Another illustration of network interconnections is provided by the impact, worldwide, of the financial crisis that began in Thailand in July 1997. Unexpectedly, what appeared first as an isolated banking and currency crisis in a small "emerging market" country, had severe global effects. It generated financial panic elsewhere in Asia, particularly in Korea and Indonesia; prompted emergency meetings at the highest level of world finance and huge "bail-out" packages orchestrated by the International Monetary Fund; and led to a widespread loss of confidence in emerging markets and the efficacy of international financial institutions. Before that contagious loss of confidence was stemmed, Russia had defaulted on its debt (in August 1998), and a huge US-based hedge fund, Long-Term Capital Management, had to be rescued suddenly through a plan put together by the US Federal Reserve. Even after recovery had begun, Brazil required a huge IMF loan, coupled with devaluation, to avoid financial collapse in January 1999.

The relative magnitude of foreign investment in 1997 was not unprecedented. Capital markets were by some measures more integrated at the beginning than at the end of the twentieth century. The net outflow of capital from Britain in the four decades before 1914 averaged 5 percent of gross domestic product, compared with 2 to 3 percent for rich countries today.[25] The fact that the financial crisis of 1997 was global in scale also had precursors: "Black Monday" on Wall Street in 1929 and the collapse of Austria's Credit Anstalt bank in 1930 triggered a worldwide financial crisis and depression. (Once again, globalism is not new.) Financial linkages among major financial centers have always been subject to the spread of crisis, as withdrawals from banks in one locale precipitate withdrawals elsewhere, as failures of banks in one jurisdiction lead to failures even of distant creditors. Nevertheless, despite the greatly increased financial sophistication of this era compared with the interwar period, the crisis was almost totally unanticipated by most economists, governments, and international financial institutions. The World Bank had recently published a report entitled "The Asian Miracle" (1993), and investment flows to Asia rose rapidly to a new peak in 1996 and remained high until the crisis hit. In December 1998 Federal Reserve Board Chairman Alan Greenspan said, "I have learned more about how this new international financial system works in the last twelve months than in the previous twenty years."[26] Sheer magnitude, complexity, and speed distinguish contemporary globalization from earlier periods.[27]

There are also interconnections with military globalism. In the context of superpower bipolarity, the end of the cold war represented military deglobalization. Distant disputes became less relevant to the balance of power. But the rise of social globalization had the opposite effect. Humanitarian concerns interacting with global communications led to dramatization of some conflicts and military interventions in places like Somalia, Bosnia, and Kosovo. At the same time, other remote conflicts such as Southern Sudan, which proved less accessible, were largely ignored. At the tactical level, the asymmetry of global military power and the interconnections among networks raise new options for warfare. For example, in devising a strategy to stand up to the United States, some Chinese officers are proposing terrorism, drug trafficking, environmental degradation, and computer virus propagation. They argue that the more complicated the combination – for example, terrorism plus a media war plus a financial war – the better the results. "From that perspective, 'Unrestricted War' marries the Chinese classic *The Art of War* by Sun Tzu, with modern military technology and economic globalization."[28]

The general point is that the increasing thickness of globalism – the density of networks of interdependence – is not just a difference in degree from the past. Thickness means that different relationships of interdependence intersect more deeply at more different points. Hence, effects of events in one geographical area, on one dimension, can have profound effects in other geographical areas, on other dimensions. As in scientific theories of "chaos," and in weather systems, small events in one place can have catalytic effects, so that their consequences later and elsewhere are vast.[29] Such systems are very difficult to understand, and their effects are therefore often unpredictable. Furthermore, when these are human systems, human beings are often hard at work trying to outwit others, to gain an economic, social, or military advantage precisely by acting in an unpredictable way. As a result, we should expect that globalism will be accompanied by pervasive uncertainty. There will be a continual competition between increased complexity, and uncertainty, on the one hand; and efforts by governments, market participants, and others to comprehend and manage these increasingly complex interconnected systems, on the other.

Globalization and levels of governance

By governance, we mean the processes and institutions, both formal and informal, that guide and restrain the collective activities of a group. Government is the subset that acts with authority and creates formal obligations. Governance need not necessarily be conducted exclusively by governments and the international organizations to which they delegate authority. Private firms, associations of firms, nongovernmental organizations (NGOs), and associations of NGOs all engage in it, often in association with governmental bodies, to create governance; sometimes without governmental authority.

Contrary to some prophetic views, the nation-state is not about to be replaced as the primary instrument of domestic and global governance. There is an extensive literature on the effects of globalism on domestic governance, which in our view reaches more nuanced conclusions (summarized below). Instead, we believe that the nation-state is being supplemented by other actors – private and third sector – in a more complex geography. The nation-state is the most important actor on the stage of global politics, but it is not the only important actor. If one thinks of social and political space in terms of a nine-cell matrix, more governance activities will occur outside the box represented by national capitals of nation-states (Figure 9.1).

	Private	Governmental	Third sector
Supranational	TNCs	IGOs	NGOs
National	Firms	Central	Nonprofits
Subnational	Local	Local	Local

Figure 9.1 Governance activities

Not only is the geography of governance more complex, but so are its modalities at all three levels. Governance can be accomplished by law, norms, markets, and architecture. Taking a local example, one can slow traffic through a neighborhood by enforcing speed limits, posting "children at play" signs, charging for access, or building speed bumps in the roads. Consider an Internet world in which governance is shifting from law made by governments to architecture created by companies. "Effective regulation then shifts from lawmakers to code writers."[30] At the same time, private firms press governments for favorable legal regimes domestically and internationally, as do actors from the third sector. The result is not the obsolescence of the nation-state but its transformation and the creation of politics in new contested spaces.

Many writers in talking about the governance of globalism use what Hedley Bull referred to as the "domestic analogy."[31] It is commonplace for people to think of global governance as global government, because the domestic analogy is so familiar. Just as the nationalization of the American economy in the nineteenth century led to the nationalization of American government in the Progressive era, globalization of the world economy should lead to world government.[32] But the structure of federalism already existed in the United States, and it rested on a common language and political culture. (And even that did not prevent a bloody civil war in the middle of the century.)

Another example is the UN World Development Report, which portrays global governance in terms of strengthening UN institutions. It calls, for example, for a bicameral General Assembly, an investment trust that will redistribute the proceeds of taxes on global transactions, and a global central bank.[33] But it is state structures, and the loyalty of people to particular states, that enable states to create connections among themselves, handle issues of interdependence, and resist amalgamation, even if it might seem justified on purely functional grounds. Hence, world government during our lifetimes seems highly unlikely, at least in the absence of an overwhelming global threat that could only be dealt with in a unified way. In the absence of such a threat, it seems highly unlikely that peoples in some two hundred states will be willing to act on the domestic analogy for well into the new century. World government might or might not be desirable – we think it could have many adverse consequences – but in any event, it is hardly likely to be feasible.

Although we think world government is infeasible, we are not complacent about the effects of globalization without some coherent means of governance. Karl Polanyi made a powerful argument that the inability of polities to cope with the disruptive effects of nineteenth century globalization helped cause the great disturbances of the twentieth century – communism and fascism.[34] Along similar lines, Jeffrey Williamson has more recently documented how the "late nineteenth-century globalization backlash made a powerful contribution to interwar deglobalization."[35] Without regulation – or what was traditionally known as "protection" – personal insecurity for many individuals can become intolerable. As Polanyi, with his dramatic flair, put it, "To allow the market mechanism to be sole director of the fate of human beings and their natural environment ... would result in the demolition of society."[36]

If world government is unfeasible and laissez-faire a recipe for a backlash, we need to search for an intermediate solution: a set of practices for governance that improve coordination and create safety valves for political and social pressures, consistent with the maintenance of nation-states as the fundamental form of political organization. Such arrangements will, we argue, involve a heterogeneous array of agents – from the private sector and the third sector as well as from governments. And the governmental agents will not necessarily be operating on orders from the "top levels" of governments. The efficacy of these agents will depend on the networks in which they are embedded and their positions in those networks. And no hierarchy is likely to be acceptable or effective in governing networks.

One could refer very generally to the governance structures we envisage as "networked minimalism." Networked – because globalism is best characterized as networked, rather than as a set of hierarchies. Minimal – because governance at the global level will only be acceptable if it does not supersede national governance and if its intrusions into the autonomy of states and communities are clearly justified in terms of cooperative results.

To speak of "networked minimalism" is, of course, not to solve the problems of global governance but merely to point toward a generic response to them. In particular, such a phrase begs the question of accountability, which is crucial to democratic legitimacy.

Globalization and domestic governance

The literature on the effect of globalism on governance is extensive. The most persuasive work, it seems to us, converges on a number of general conclusions that suggest that nation-states will continue to be important; indeed, that the internal structures of states will be crucial in their ability to adapt to globalization and its effects on them.

First, it is important not to overstate the extent of the change in the near future. Global economic integration has a long way to go. From a strictly economic point of view, this can be considered "inefficiency." But from a political-economy perspective, it might be called a "useful inefficiency" that provides a buffer for domestic political differences while allowing openness to the global economy. With time and market integration, this useful inefficiency will be eroded. National political systems have strong effects that are not easily erased by technology. For example, John Helliwell's studies show that even in North America, national boundaries have a powerful effect on economic activity. Toronto trades ten times as much with Vancouver as it does with Seattle. Electronic commerce is burgeoning, but is still a small fraction of the total even in the United States. Geoffrey Garrett points out that despite talk of vanishing policy autonomy, "Globalization has not prompted a pervasive policy race to the neoliberal bottom among the OECD countries, nor have governments that have persisted with interventionist policies invariably been hamstrung by damaging capital flight."[37]

Second, although globalization may have powerful impacts on distributional politics and inequality, these impacts are not as clear with respect to contemporary globalization as they are, in retrospect, for the nineteenth century. Universal propositions about rising inequality and "the poor getting poorer" are too simple. First, one must distinguish between domestic and international inequality. In general, from the Heckscher-Ohlin theorem, we should expect increasing inequality in rich countries (capital and high-skill labor, the abundant factors, should benefit at the expense of unskilled labor), but we should expect, at least to some degree, increasing equality – at least as far as labor employed in the market sector is concerned – in developing countries. Reality may be more complicated than theory – and the nature of the political system and institutional weakness may be decisive in developing countries; but the point is, our baseline economic expectations should be different in rich and poor countries.

In economic terms, low-priced labor in poorer countries benefits from trade and migration; low-priced labor in richer ones suffers. This was certainly true in the late nineteenth century, given the magnitude of migration. Jeffrey Williamson concludes that "the forces of late nineteenth-century convergence included commodity price convergence and trade expansion, technological catch-up, and human-capital accumulation, but mass migration was clearly the central force."[38] In some relationships – such as that between Britain and the United States – the Heckscher–Ohlin effect was significant; but in others, it was not very important: "Heckscher and Ohlin may have gotten the sign right, but they were not very relevant when it came to magnitudes."[39]

Contemporary globalization is driven so much less by labor migration than in the nineteenth century that the contemporary implications of Williamson's argument are ambiguous. Globalization in the form of trade between rich and poor countries is likely to increase income inequality in rich countries, as Heckscher and Ohlin would have predicted.[40] However, in the nineteenth century, capital movements had the opposite effect, since they went largely to high-wage countries with unexploited natural resources.[41] The United States is a huge capital-importer now, despite being a high-wage country. So on an international basis, this form of globalization could be creating divergence rather than convergence. Migration, which generates convergence, is significant now but not nearly as important as it was in the nineteenth century.[42] And other potential causes of rising inequality exist in rich countries – technology and the changing composition of the labor force in particular. Common estimates are that trade may account for between 5 and 33 percent of the increase in wage gaps. We are not qualified to sort out these issues; but it is worth noting that such estimates in the analytical economic literature do not prevent "globalization," writ large, from bearing political blame for increasing income inequality. Even if skill-biased technological change is the primary cause of the increase in income inequality in rich countries during the past three decades, globalization is going to be politically contentious.[43]

Third, the impact of globalization on the state varies substantially by political-economic system.[44] One way of thinking about these issues is in terms of "production systems." In market systems, globalization leads to income inequality as market prices are bid up for skilled labor, and as the division of labor expands. In social democratic welfare states, transfer payments limit income inequality, but unemployment results.[45] In Japanese-style systems, globalization puts pressure on the lifetime employment system and other provisions for providing welfare through the corporation rather than the state. The overall point is that globalization interacts with domestic politics; it is neither true that globalization produces the same effects everywhere (much less destroys the welfare state, or destroys state power),[46] nor that globalization is irrelevant. Multiple feasible paths may be taken to deal with the effects of globalization, depending on history, structures, attitudes – the notion of a single "golden straitjacket" is not viable.

Does globalism weaken state institutions? The answers vary by the type of state and the type of function. It is true that market constraints on states are greater than three decades ago, but the effects vary greatly. France, Germany, and Sweden feel market pressures, but the core of their welfare state remains strong. Some less developed countries, however, feel market pressures but do not have strong safety nets or governmental institutions to begin with. Transnational mobility of capital and skilled labor undercut powers of taxation. Transnational communications and the Internet make it more difficult and costly for authoritarian police to control citizens. In some instances, differential development may stimulate ethnic tensions that can overwhelm the institutions of the state. And some less developed countries may have such weak institutions (for whatever historical and cultural reasons) that their leaders are unable to cope with the new challenges posed by globalization. For other developing countries, however, economic globalism has strengthened state institutions by creating a more robust economic base – witness the development of Singapore, Malaysia, or Korea. China is a special case. Linda Weiss argues that there is more of a transformation of state functions than a weakening of the state.[47] Our major conclusion about how globalism affects domestic governance is one of caution. Certainly, strong effects occur, but generalizations about the effect of globalism on the nation-state vary with the size, power, and domestic political culture of the states involved.

From the perspective of governance, what is striking about the last half of the twentieth century is the relative *effectiveness* of efforts by states to respond to globalization. The welfare state was a major step. Whether Polanyi's narrative about the inability of polities to cope with the disruptive effects of nineteenth-century globalization is correct or not, such views were widely held. After World War II, a compromise was struck in rich countries that John Ruggie has called "embedded liberalism."[48] The price of an open economy was a social safety net. Dani Rodrik has shown that openness and the welfare state are highly correlated. Coupled with the welfare state was the development of international regimes in areas such as finance and trade, designed to promote cooperation among states. The result in the last half of the twentieth century was a remarkable period in which economic growth was remarkably strong, despite periods of recession, and in which many economies became progressively more open to others' products and capital flows.

The big question is whether the coming era of economic globalization is different, because of changes in the degree of interdependence leading to fundamental transformations; or because of the information revolution.[49] In the view of Kenneth Waltz, the more things change, the more they remain the same. "Challenges at home and abroad test the mettle of states. Some states fail, and other states pass the tests nicely. In modern times, enough states always make it to keep the international system going as a system of states. The challenges vary; states endure."[50] In sharp contrast, some writers declare that as an externally sovereign actor, the state "will become a thing of the past."[51] And prophets of the Information Age argue that global cyberspace is replacing territorial space and making national governmental controls impossible.

When rapid, fundamental change is mixed with stability, it is hard to draw the balance easily. To say that states endure is to overlook the emergence of other significant actors and the constraints that they may impose on state autonomy. But to say that "everything is different" overlooks the fact that modern states are resilient and resourceful. While it is true that boundaries are becoming more porous, and some controls more problematic, the future of domestic governance is not so simple. The Internet was initially structured by hackers with a libertarian antigovernment culture, but commerce is rapidly changing the net. Commercial procedures for authentication of credentials are creating a framework that allows private regulation, and the presence of large commercial entities provides targets for an overlay of public regulation.[52]

As in the economic literature on globalism and the nation-state, the answer is unlikely to be that "everything is changed," or that nothing is. The question may be less one of erosion or maintenance of authority than of changes in how we think about space. While the messages of global electronic commerce cross borders freely, the processes by which they are produced often involve a reconfiguration of physical space. Saskia Sassen refers to a "relocation of politics" from national capitals to global cities constituting a "new economic geography of centrality, one that cuts across national boundaries and across the old North–South divide."[53]

Our expectation is that governance will remain centered in the nation-state. State power will remain crucially important, as will the distribution of power among states. Whether the United States remains dominant, or is successfully challenged by others, will fundamentally affect globalism and its governance. However, the image of "the state" may become increasingly misleading as agencies of states are linked in networks to private and third sector actors. Transgovernmental networks will become more important, as will transnational relations of all kinds.[54] Mixed coalitions will occur as parts of governments and NGOs may ally against other parts of governments allied with transnational corporations. Global networks will become more complex. Governance will require extensive networked cooperation, and hierarchical rules are likely to become less effective.

The governance of globalism: regimes, networks, norms

Global governance is not the same as world government, and the domestic analogy is not adequate. The world system of the twenty-first century is not merely a system of unitary states interacting with one another through diplomacy, public international law, and international organizations. In that model, states as agents interact, constituting an international system.[55] But this model's focus on the reified unitary state fails sufficiently to emphasize two other essential elements of the contemporary world system: *networks* among agents, and *norms* – standards of expected behavior – that are widely accepted among agents. We can think of this international system as the *skeleton* of the contemporary world system – essential to the functioning of the whole system – but not as a whole system. It therefore is a helpful simplified model with which we can begin to ask about global governance, although it by no means provides us with the basis for a comprehensive account.

Governments' responses to problems of governance

A worthwhile first cut is to see international regimes as a response to problems and opportunities faced by states. States devise international institutions to facilitate cooperation, which they seek to achieve their own purposes. Broadly speaking, this is a rational-functional account, in the sense that anticipation of effects explains action.[56] Interests within states are affected by the actions of other states and actors, and therefore a "demand for international regimes" develops.[57] That is, governments become willing to exchange some of their own legal freedom of action to have some influence on the actions of these other actors. Whether this involves "giving up sovereignty" is a legal issue that depends on the arrangement made. Besides purely domestic interests, transnational actors (corporations, NGOs) develop an interest in making transborder transactions more predictable and press for arrangements that do so. This functional explanation plausibly accounts for the existence of the hundreds of intergovernmental organizations and regimes that govern issues ranging from fur seals to world trade. It may also help to explain efforts to govern the international use of force stretching from the Hague peace treaties at the end of the nineteenth century through the League of Nations to the UN Charter and Security Council.

Only some of these governance patterns are global, and none of them corresponds to the image of "world government" promoted by world federalists in the past and derided by governments and academic experts alike during the past several decades. There are examples of formal global governance through multilateral institutions, in which states create international regimes and cede some power to intergovernmental organizations to govern specified issues. Such delegation to broadly defined institutions takes place for trade policy (in the World Trade Organization) and financial and development policy (notably, the International Monetary Fund [IMF] and the World Bank). More limited delegation is evident in environmental policy, for example, to institutions governing chemicals depleting the ozone layer or to fisheries outside the territorial zones of states. The global role of international institutions dedicated to protection of human rights is increasing – a trend that will be accentuated if the International Criminal Court becomes a reality. At the global level, what we find is not world government but the existence of regimes of norms, rules, and institutions that govern a surprisingly large number of issues in world politics. The islands of governance are more densely concentrated among developed states, but they often have global extension.

Importantly, governments' responses to increases in globalism need not take the form of initiating or supporting multilateral regimes on a global level. Indeed, three other responses are particularly evident:

- Unilateral. Some unilateral responses are isolationist and protectionist with the effect of diminishing globalism. Others' unilateral actions may increase global governance. Particularly interesting is the acceptance by states of the standards developed by others. This process ranges on a scale from voluntary to highly coercive. Unilateral acceptance of common standards can be highly voluntary – for example, when states and firms outside the United States learned how to conform to Y2K standards created (at greater cost) in the United States, or when they copy others' political arrangements to solve domestic problems that they have themselves identified. Adoption of common standards can be partially voluntary, as when states adopt generally accepted accounting principles, make their books more transparent, or establish regulatory agencies that imitate those of other countries.[58] In this case, the degree of voluntariness is limited by the fact that foreign investment or other benefits might be withheld by powerful external actors if such actions were not taken. Further toward the coercive end of the continuum are such phenomena as IMF conditionality, linked closely to acceptance of macroeconomic views that correspond to those of the "Washington consensus." Finally, powerful states may simply impose standards on the weak as Britain did with antislavery in the nineteenth century.[59]

- Where broad consensus is difficult or too costly, states may seek to construct bilateral or "minilateral" regimes with a few like-minded partners.[60] Hundreds of bilateral tax treaties exist. The Basle agreements on banking adequacy provide another example. One consequence of such a strategy may be to change the status quo point, therefore making non-participants worse off, and perhaps forcing them to join arrangements that are worse than the original status quo.[61]
- Regional. States may see themselves as better able to cope with global forces if they form regional groupings. Within a region, mutual recognition of one another's laws and policies may promote cooperation without extensive harmonization of laws. The recent strengthening of the European Union (EU) provides the principal example of such regionalism.

Our focus is on multilateral cooperation at the global level, although much that we say is relevant to "minilateral" or regional regimes. We believe that the patterns of multilateral cooperation that predominated in the second half of the twentieth century are changing and will have to change further if multilateral cooperation is to be successful in a rapidly globalizing world. To make this argument, however, we need first to describe two important sets of changes that are occurring – in the agents active on issues of international and transnational public policy and in the norms that are thought relevant to multilateral cooperation.

New agents in networks

The actors in world politics cannot simply be conceived of as states. Private firms, NGOs, and subunits of governments can all play independent or quasi-independent roles. These agents help to create or exacerbate the dilemmas of diffusion of power, transparency, and deadlock, afflicting international organizations. But they may also play a crucial role in governance. When they do, they operate as parts of networks.

Because the rapidly declining cost of communication is reducing the barriers to entry, other actors are becoming more involved in many governance arrangements that are not controlled by executives or legislatures of states. In other words, global governance involves both private sector and "third sector," or NGOs, actors as well as governments:

Transnational corporate networks   Transnational corporations respond to the absence of governance by providing their own governance forms. Airlines and computer firms form alliances with one another to gain competitive advantages. Other examples include commodity chains, producer driven or buyer driven.[62] Many crucial standard-setting exercises are private. In the chemical industry, "responsible care" standards, for example, are designed to head off national-level or international-level governance.[63] In cyberspace, commercially crafted codes have a powerful impact on issues such as privacy, property rights, and copyright law. Private rules about how an offer is accepted "may or may not be consistent with the contract rules of a particular jurisdiction. . . . Local governments lose control over the rules and the effective rule-maker shifts to cyber space."[64]

NGOs In the last decade of the twentieth century, the number of international NGOs grew from 6,000 to 26,000, ranging in size from the Worldwide Fund for Nature with 5 million members to tiny network organizations. They provide services, mobilize political action, and provide information and analysis. As a group, they provide more aid than the whole UN system. Besides providing services, others play lobbying and mobilization roles. About 1,500 NGOs signed an anti-WTO protest declaration that was circulated online in 1999, including groups from both rich and poor countries. Technically oriented groups offer sophisticated analysis and information that affected the verification system of the Chemical Weapons Treaty and the negotiations over global climate change.[65] In the eyes of some analysts, the real losers in this power shift are less obviously governments than intergovernmental institutions that lack political leverage over policymakers and whose public image tends to be faceless and technocratic.

The relations of the three sectors in governance should not be analyzed solely in isolation, much less in zero sum terms. State responses to the forces of globalism are supplemented by private and nongovernmental actors, some of which compete and some of which complement state actions. Transnational corporations may replace legislative functions of states. For example, when Nike and Mattel create codes of conduct governing their subcontractors in less developed countries, they may be imposing codes that would not have passed the legislatures of Honduras or India (and which those governments would have opposed at the WTO).

Similarly, companies may bypass the judicial branch of host governments because they regard them as slow or corrupt. More and more often commercial contracts are written with provisions for commercial arbitration to keep them out of national courts. The International Chamber of Commerce plays a large role. Some governments, however, are pleased when private rating agencies like Moody's or Standard and Poor's create ratings that lead foreign corporations to follow standards and procedures not necessarily in domestic law.

Some governments and parts of governments may also be pleased when NGOs influence agenda setting and press other governments for action. An important example is provided by the succession of UN-sponsored international conferences on women and issues, such as birth control, of particular interest to women. NGOs have taken the lead in promoting this agenda, but governments and the United Nations have also been active.[66] Or consider the effects of Transparency International in exposing corruption. In other instances, NGOs form coalitions with some governments against others: witness the landmine treaty in which Canada drew support against the United States. Some NGOs participate regularly in sessions of some intergovernmental organization such as the Organization for Economic Cooperation and Development or the World Bank. In some instances, such as human rights and refugees, they supply crucial information to governments as well as help provide services. Foundations play a similar role.

Trisectoral partnerships are also becoming more explicit.[67] Transnational corporations and NGOs sometimes work together and sometimes with IGOs to provide services. Citibank uses local NGOs to provide microfinance in Bangladesh. In 1998 Kofi Annan proposed a global compact in which corporations joined with the United Nations to support development and improved labor standards. The International Chamber of Commerce has offered its support. Other innovations include the World Commission on Dams, which consists of four commissioners from governments, four from private industry, and four from NGOs. And in the governance of Internet domain names, the US government helped create ICANN, an NGO that supplements but also works with private companies. The government turned to the NGO form because it feared that a formal IGO would be too slow and cumbersome in dealing with rapidly developing issues related to Internet domain names.

In short, areas of intergovernmental coordination exist in a competitive and cooperative relationship with private and third sector actors that provide some governance for several issues in global politics. Notably, in many of these arrangements the quasi-judicial capabilities and "soft legislative" capabilities, as exemplified in the development of soft law and norms, have moved ahead much faster than "hard legislative" or executive capabilities. The formal, obligatory rules of IGOs are established by states, but the IGOs themselves are becoming more important interpreters of their own rules, and often the operational rules go well beyond those that are formally obligatory. Meanwhile, the formal governance structures of IGOs remain quite weak and are often beset by deadlock.

Norms

Changes in agency are an important part of contemporary changes in governance of global issues. NGOs and private sector actors, operating in various competing networks, have become increasingly important. But there is something more. As constructivist theorists point out, changing ideas frame and channel interests. Convergence on knowledge, norms, and beliefs is a prelude to convergence on institutions and processes of governance.[68] Transnational communications, coupled with political democracy, promote the development of global norms as a backdrop against which the islands of governance stand out.

Changes in norms can be seen as part of the development of an incipient civil society. It is not entirely new. Nineteenth-century antislavery movements involved transnational ideas as well as domestic politics.[69] The spread of science is another early example. Examples in the twentieth century include the development of human rights ideology in the second half of the century. As Sassen points out, "Self determination is no longer enough to legitimate a state; respect for international human rights codes is also a factor."[70] Since the end of the cold war, the broad acceptance of liberal market forces is another example. In sharp contrast to the 1970s demands for a statist "new international economic order," when a newly created Group of 20 rich and poor countries met in 1999, the discussion was over details, not the desirability, of a neoliberal financial system.[71] Pressures on traditional territorial sovereignty in the security areas derive largely from human rights and humanitarian norms (at odds with traditional sovereignty norms), and they remain hotly contested. After Secretary General Annan's September 1999 speech to the General Assembly, the head of the Organization for African Unity expressed alarm that a right to humanitarian intervention threatened "our final defence against the rules of an unequal world," and in the United States a former official predicted "war, at least with the Republican Party."[72]

Soft power rests on the attractiveness of some actors, and their principles, to others. Soft power is therefore relative to norms: it is those actors who conform to widely admired norms that will gain influence as a result. It is hard to pinpoint specific changes in domestic law and practice that are directly affected by changes in norms. However, clearly, in areas such as human rights and the role of sovereignty, global norms are changing at a dramatic pace. Sovereignty is up for grabs in a way that has not been the case since the seventeenth century. The fact that it was criticized by Secretary General Annan – the leader of an intergovernmental organization whose Charter rests solidly on the Westphalian conception of sovereignty – reveals striking evidence of normative change.

Norms do not operate automatically but through the activities of agents in networks. Even binding international law does not meet with automatic and universal compliance. Even less automatic are the effects of soft law. China may have signed the International Convention on the Protection of Civil and Political Rights, hoping to avoid serious internal consequences, just as the Soviet Union signed onto "Basket Three" of the Helsinki Convention in 1975. Whether these norms will actually change policies, or undermine the legitimacy of regimes, depends on how agents operate: for instance, on the "boomerang effects" discussed by Margaret Keck and Kathryn Sikkink.[73]

To understand global governance for the twenty-first century, we will have to go well beyond understanding multilateral cooperation among states. We will have to understand how agents, in networks – including agents that are organizationally parts of governments as well as those who are not – interact in the context of rapidly changing norms. Governance is likely to be fragmented and heterogeneous. Whatever else it is, it is unlikely to be based on the domestic analogy.

Conclusions: globalism and governance

Globalization is strongly affecting domestic governance, but it is far from making the nation-state obsolete as some prophets claim. The existence of "useful inefficiencies" and the persistence of national political traditions and cultures means that the state will remain the basic institution of governance well into the century. But domestic polities will be under pressure from the erosion of economic inefficiency, tensions around the redistribution and inequality that accompany economic globalization, and the increasing roles of transnational and third sector actors. The compromise of embedded liberalism that created a social safety net in return for openness was successful in the second half of the twentieth century but is under new pressure. That compromise was the basis for Bretton Woods institutions that (along with other regimes) governed "issue islands" in world politics. This compromise worked to combine economic globalization with some domestic autonomy for democratic politics. Now, for reasons we have suggested, that system is under challenge. This does not mean that it must be discarded, but that new strategies will be necessary to resolve the dilemma of efficacy versus legitimacy that we have described.

Rulemaking and rule interpretation in global governance have become pluralized. Rules are no longer a matter simply for states or intergovernmental organizations. Private firms, NGOs, subunits of governments, and the transnational and transgovernmental networks that result, all play a role, typically with central state authorities and intergovernmental organizations. As a result, any emerging pattern of governance will have to be networked rather than hierarchical and must have minimal rather than highly ambitious objectives. "Networked minimalism" seeks to preserve national democratic processes and embedded liberal compromises while allowing the benefits of economic integration.

Networked minimalism is only a broad principle of governance – more a matter of what not to try (hierarchy and intrusiveness in domestic politics) than what to do. If multilateral cooperation is to continue, any networked arrangements will have to solve the classic governance problem of reaching legitimate decisions. The club model, based on decomposable sets of issues, reached decisions, but they are increasingly challenged. Somehow, the more diverse actors – more states, private sector actors, NGOs – that are now involved in global public policy will have to be brought into the system.[74] Cross-sectoral partnerships of government (and IGO), private, and third sector organization may provide part of a solution, but they still pose problems. More nuanced approaches to transparency and accountability of both international institutions and networks will be an important part of understanding global governance.

It is important not to think of legitimacy solely in terms of majoritarian voting procedures. Many parts of the American constitution (such as the Supreme Court) and political practice would fail that test. Democratic legitimacy has a number of sources, both normative and substantive. Legitimacy in international regimes will derive in part from delegation from elected national governments but also from effectiveness and transnational civil society. New modes of ensuring public participation, not relying entirely on elections, will have to be found. But insofar as major societies are democratic, legitimacy will depend on the popular views that international governance practices are consistent with democratic norms. Some from of transparency and accountability will be crucial. And since the legitimacy of global decisions will probably remain shaky for many decades, it will be crucial also to relax the pressure on multilateral institutions by preserving substantial space for separate domestic political processes – what in the language of the European Union is referred to as "subsidiarity." The practices of the WTO in allowing domestic politics to sometimes depart from international agreements without unraveling the whole system of norms are a useful example.

It is possible that the political base of intergovernmental organizations and international regimes will be too weak to sustain high levels of governance: that the need for international regimes will exceed the supply. Deadlock and frustration could result. But the results of such deadlock are not clear. They could lead to a move away from such institutions for governance, back to the state, limiting globalism, as occurred after 1914. But that is not likely. They could lead in other directions – toward the development of quasi-judicial processes internationally, "soft legislation," and effective governance of specific issue areas by transnational and trans-governmental networks. What is not likely is a mere repetition of the past or a return to a world of isolated nation-states. Globalism is here to stay. How it will be governed is the question.

Notes

1 Much of the material in this section is drawn from chapter 10 of Robert O. Keohane and Joseph S. Nye Jr., *Power and Interdependence*, 3rd ed. (Addison-Wesley, 2001).
2 Robert O. Keohane and Joseph S. Nye J., *Power and Interdependence: World Politics in Transition* (Little, Brown, 1977; Harper Collins, 2nd ed., 1989; Addison-Wesley, 3rd ed., 2001).
3 United Nations Development Program (UNDP), *Human Development Report* (Oxford University Press, 1999).
4 Keith Griffin, "Globalization and the Shape of Things to Come," in *Macalester International: Globalization and Economic Space*, vol. 7, Spring 1999, p. 3; and "One World?" *Economist*, October 18, 1997, pp. 79–80.
5 Samuel P. Huntington, *The Clash of Civilizations and the Remaking of World Order* (Simon and Schuster, 1996).
6 Nicolo Barquet and Pere Domingo, "Smallpox: The Triumph over the Most Terrible of the Ministers of Death," *Annals of Internal Medicine*, October 15, 1997, pp. 636–38.
7 Jared Diamond, *Guns, Germs and Steel: The Fates of Human Societies* (W.W.

Norton, 1998), pp. 202, 210; and William H. McNeill, *Plagues and Peoples* (London: Scientific Book Club, 1979), p. 168. See also Alfred W. Crosby, *Ecological Imperialism: The Biological Expansion of Europe, 900–1900* (Cambridge: Cambridge University Press, 1986).

8 Alfred Crosby, *The Columbian Exchange: Biological and Cultural Consequences of 1492* (Greenwood Press, 1972).

9 John P. McKay and others, *A History of Western Society*, 4th ed. (Houghton Mifflin, 1991), pp. 106–07.

10 Arjun Appuradai, *Modernity at Large* (University of Minnesota Press, 1996).

11 Paul Krugman, *The Return of Depression Economics* (Norton, 1999), p. 16.

12 John W. Meyer and others, "World Society and the Nation-State," *American Journal of Sociology*, vol. 103 (July 1997), pp. 144–81.

13 "U.N. Oratory: Pleas for Help, Pride in Democracy," *New York Times*, September 21, 1999, p. A12; "U.N. Chief Wants Faster Action to Avoid Slaughter in Civil Wars," *New York Times*, September 21, 1999, p. A12; and "General Assembly U.N. Chief Champions Security Council-Backed Humanitarian Intervention," *Financial Times* (London), September 21, 1999, p. 1.

14 Diamond, *Guns, Germs and Steel*, p. 202.

15 David Held and others, *Global Transformations: Politics, Economics and Culture* (Stanford University Press 1999), pp. 21–22.

16 "Fearful over the Future, Europe Seizes on Food," *New York Times*, August 29, 1999, sec. 4, p. 1.

17 Professor Anne-Marie Slaughter of Harvard University Law School used the expressions of "uploading" and "downloading" content, at John F. Kennedy School of Government Visions Project Conference on Globalization, Bretton Woods, N.H., 1999.

18 Richard Storry, *A History of Modern Japan* (Harmondsworth, UK: Penguin, 1960), pp. 115–16; and Hioaki Sato, "The Meiji Government's Remarkable Mission to Learn from Europe and Japan," *Japan Times*, October 14, 1999.

19 Frederick Schauer, "The Politics and Incentives of Legal Transplantation," paper presented at John F. Kennedy School of Government Visions Project Conference on Globalization, 1999.

20 Joseph S. Nye Jr. *Bound to Lead: The Changing Nature of American Power* (Basic Books, 1990), pp. 31–32.

21 Thomas Friedman, *The Lexus and the Olive Tree: Understanding Globalization* (Farrar Straus Giroux, 1999), pp. 7–8.

22 "A Semi-Integrated World," *Economist*, September 11, 1999, p. 42.

23 Joseph Stiglitz, "Weightless Concerns," *Financial Times* (London), February 3, 1999, op-ed page.

24 Robert Jervis, *System Effects: Complexity in Political and Social Life* (Princeton University Press, 1997).

25 "One World?" *Economist*, October 18, 1997, p. 80.

26 Greenspan quoted in Friedman, *The Lexus and the Olive Tree*, p. 368.

27 Held and others, *Global Transformations*, p. 235.

28 "China Ponders New Rules of 'Unrestricted War,'" *Washington Post*, August 8, 1999, p. 1.

29 M. Mitchell Waldrop, *Complexity: The Emerging Science at the Edge of Order and Chaos* (Touchstone Books, 1992).

30 Lawrence Lessig, *Code and Other Laws of Cyberspace* (Basic Books, 1999), pp. 88, 207.

31 Hedley Bull, *The Anarchical Society: A Study of Order in World Politics* (Columbia University Press, 1977), p. 46.

32 Michael J. Sandel, *Democracy's Discontents* (Harvard University Press, 1996). pp. 338 ff.

33 UNDP (United Nations Development Program), *Human Development Report 1999* (Oxford University Press, 1999).
34 Karl Polanyi, *The Great Transformation* (Rinehart, 1944).
35 Jeffrey G. Williamson, "Globalization and the Labor Market: Using History to Inform Policy," in Philippe Aghion and Jeffrey G. Williamson, eds, *Growth, Inequality and Globalization* (Cambridge University Press, 1998), p. 193.
36 Polanyi, *The Great Transformation*, p. 73.
37 Geoffrey Garrett, *Partisan Politics in the Global Economy* (Cambridge, UK: Cambridge University Press, 1998), p. 183.
38 Williamson, *Globalization and the Labor Market*, p. 168.
39 Ibid., p. 142.
40 Adrain Wood, *North–South Trade, Employment and Inequality* (Oxford: Clarendon Press, 1994).
41 Williamson, "Globalization and the Labor Market," p. 168.
42 George Borjas, *Heaven's Door: Immigration Policy and the American Economy* (Princeton University Press, 1999).
43 Dani Rodrik, *Has Globalization Gone Too Far?* (Washington: Institute for International Economics, 1997); and Robert Lawrence, *Single World, Divided Nations* (Brookings, 1996).
44 Robert O. Keohane and Helen V. Milner, *Internationalization and Domestic Politics* (Cambridge University Press, 1996); and Suzanne Berger and Ronald Dore, eds, *National Diversity and Global Capitalism* (Cornell University Press, 1996).
45 Amartya Sen, *Development as Freedom* (Knopf, 1999).
46 See Linda Weiss, *The Myth of the Powerless State* (Cornell University Press, 1998); Garrett, *Partisan Politics*; and Rodrik, *Has Globalization Gone Too Far?*
47 Weiss, *The Myth of the Powerless State.*
48 John G. Ruggie, "International Regimes, Transactions and Change: Embedded Liberalism in the Postwar Economic Order," in Stephen D. Krasner, ed., *International Regimes* (Cornell University Press, 1983).
49 Keohane and Nye, *Power and Interdependence*, 3rd ed., Chaps. 9, 10.
50 Kenneth N. Waltz, "Globalization and Governance," *PS, Political Science & Politics* (December 1999), p. 697.
51 Wolfgang Reinicke, "Global Public Policy," *Foreign Affairs* (November–December 1997), in Waltz, "Globalization and Governance," p. 697.
52 Lessig, *Code and Other Laws*, Chap. 4.
53 Saskia Sassen, *Cities in a World Economy*, 2nd ed. (Thousand Oaks: Pine Forge Press, 2000).
54 See Robert O. Keohane and Joseph S. Nye Jr., *Transnational Relations and World Politics* (Harvard University Press, 1972); and Anne-Marie Slaughter, "The Real New World Order," *Foreign Affairs* (September–October 1997), pp. 183–97.
55 Kenneth N. Waltz, *Theory of International Politics* (Addison-Wesley, 1979).
56 Robert O. Keohane, *After Hegemony: Cooperation and Discord in the World Political Economy* (Princeton University Press, 1984).
57 Robert O. Keohane, "The Demand for International Regimes," in Stephen D. Krasner, ed., *International Regimes* (Cornell University Press, 1983), pp. 141–71.
58 Meyer and others, "World Society and the Nation-State"; Martha Finnemore, *National Interests in International Society* (Cornell University Press, 1996); and Martha Finnemore, "Sovereign Default and Military Intervention," unpublished paper, 2000.
59 Chaim D. Kaufmann and Robert A. Pape, "Explaining Costly International Moral Action: Britain's Sixty-Year Campaign against the Atlantic Slave Trade," *International Organization* (Autumn 1999), pp. 631–68.

60 Miles Kahler, "Multilateralism with Small and Large Numbers," *International Organization* (Summer 1992), pp. 681–709.
61 Thomas Oatley and Robert Nabors, "Redistributive Cooperation: Market Failure, Wealth Transfers, and the Basle Accord," *International Organization* (Winter 1998), pp. 35–54.
62 Gary Gereffi and Miguel Korzeniewicz, eds., *Commodity Chains and Global Capitalism* (Greenwood Press, 1994).
63 Ronie Garcia-Johnson, *Exporting Environmentalism: US Multinational Chemical Corporations in Brazil and Mexico* (MIT Press, 2000).
64 Lessig, *Code and Other Laws of Cyberspace*, p. 197.
65 "After Seattle: The Nongovernmental Order," *Economist*, December 11, 1999, p. 21.
66 Margaret Keck and Kathryn Sikkink, *Activists beyond Borders: Advocacy Networks in International Politics* (Cornell University Press, 1998).
67 Wolfgang H. Reinicke, "The Other World Wide Web: Global Public Policy Networks," *Foreign Policy* (Winter 1999–2000), pp. 44–57.
68 Sheila Jasanoff, private note to authors, January 2000.
69 Keck and Sikkink, *Activists beyond Borders*, Kaufmann and Pape; "Explaining Costly International Moral Action."
70 Sassen, *Cities in a World Economy*, p. 96.
71 "Lively Debate at First G-20 Talks," *Financial Times*, December 17, 1999, p. 11.
72 "Head of OAU Opposes Call by Annan," *Financial Times*, September 21, 1999, p. 5; and "Kofi Annan Unsettles People as He Believes U.N. Should Do," *New York Times*, December 31, 1999, p. A1.
73 Keck and Sikkink, *Activists beyond Borders*, n. 70.
74 Wolfgang H. Reinicke, *Global Public Policy: Governing without Government* (Brookings, 1998).

10 The club model of multilateral cooperation and problems of democratic legitimacy

Robert O. Keohane and
Joseph S. Nye Jr.
(2001)

Multilateral cooperation was remarkably extensive, indeed unprecedented, in the latter half of the twentieth century. After World War II a compromise was struck in rich countries that John Ruggie has termed *embedded liberalism*.[1] Increasing economic openness became politically feasible in a democratic era through the development of the welfare state, and through a set of international regimes for finance and trade that accommodated the welfare state.

Until the end of the 1970s, what Fred Hirsch called "the missing legitimacy for a predominantly capitalist system in conditions of universal political participation" was provided by Keynesian policies that were tolerant of inflation. International regimes in this period "served the second-best objective of the liberal community, of maintaining an open international economy at whatever inflation rate [had] to be accepted to attain this."[2] Inflation eventually rose to the point where it caused political disaffection, and since the 1980s governments of the advanced capitalist economies have emphasized price stability. Legitimacy at the domestic level has apparently been maintained in these countries, judging from the lack of large-scale protests and the maintenance in power of governments – whether nominally of the Left or the Right – dedicated to preservation of a market system. Such legitimacy has different sources in different countries: in the United States, economic growth; in continental Europe, the preservation of a social safety net despite substantial unemployment; and in Japan, the maintenance of a still prosperous and orderly, if stagnant, political economy. In any event, the collapse of socialism in the Soviet Union, and the serious constraints on the expansion of the welfare state resulting from global competition, have reinforced the dominant position of liberal capitalism.[3]

Until recently, the international regimes for trade and money that made this system work were largely invisible to publics. We will characterize them as following a "club model" of institutions. As these institutions have become more important and their membership more diverse, they have become more controversial. The Seattle demonstrations against the World Trade Organization (WTO) in November 1999 and the Washington protests in

April 2000 against the International Monetary Fund (IMF) and World Bank are examples. The classic political issue of legitimacy, within the context of democratic norms, has been insistently raised. The club model has come under challenge.

In this essay we consider descriptive and normative aspects of legitimacy as it relates to international institutions, particularly to the WTO. First we describe the club model and how, in a stylized sense, it has operated for the past half-century on issues such as international trade. After distinguishing between adversary and unitary democracy, we consider the ways in which international organizations such as the WTO experience a "democratic deficit." Issues of transparency and participation are examined, but we emphasize the *insufficient politicization* of these organizations – their lack of effective politicians who link organizations to constituencies. Then a more detailed normative analysis of democratic legitimacy is offered. The legitimacy of institutions is affected on the "input" side – in particular, through procedures for accountability – and on the "output" side in terms of effectiveness. The chapter concludes with steps that the WTO and similar international organizations might take to enhance their legitimacy in a world infused by democratic norms.

The club model of multilateral cooperation

International institutions have facilitated cooperation by reducing the costs of making agreements, through established rules and practices, and by providing information, particularly about the extent to which governments were following these rules.[4] Beginning with the Bretton Woods conference of 1944, key regimes for governance operated like clubs. Cabinet ministers or the equivalent, working in the same issue-area, initially from a relatively small number of relatively rich countries, got together to make rules. Trade ministers dominated the General Agreement on Tariffs and Trade (GATT); finance ministers ran the IMF; defense and foreign ministers met at the headquarters of NATO (the North Atlantic Treaty Organization); central bankers convened at the Bank for International Settlements (BIS). They negotiated in secret, then reported their agreements to national legislatures and publics. Until recently, they were largely unchallenged.

Using Herbert Simon's terminology these traditional international regimes can be described as "decomposable hierarchies."[5] In the decomposable hierarchy model of international regimes – characteristic of the second half of the twentieth century, at least in formal terms – international regimes, with particular states as members, were established to govern "issue-areas," defined in terms of clusters of issues. In this respect they were hierarchic: governments collaborated to make binding rules. Some of these regimes were open to universal membership, others were selective or required meeting a set of standards imposed by the original participants. The regimes, thus defined by membership and issues, were "decomposable" from the rest of the system, in the sense that they operated without close links to other regimes in other issue-areas. Their members constructed rules – traditional international law or established but less obligatory practices known as "soft law" – to govern their relationships within the issue-area.

The club model was very convenient for officials negotiating agreements within issue-areas since in two ways it kept outsiders out. First, officials in other government bureaucracies and in international organizations in different issue-areas were excluded from the negotiations. Environmental, labor rights, and finance officials did not participate on a regular basis in WTO negotiations. In general, they did not object to their exclusion. After all, they were able to exclude outsiders from their own negotiations. Second, the public was confronted with a series of *faits accomplis*, making domestic politics easier to manage. It was difficult for outsiders to understand the actual positions taken in negotiations, how firmly they were held, and the bargaining dynamics that produced compromises; therefore, it was hard to hold negotiators accountable for their actions. From the standpoint of negotiators oriented toward reaching solutions, these were positive features of the negotiating situation. They could develop close working relationships with their colleagues from other countries, limiting the disruptive force of parochial concerns emanating from domestic politics. Keeping their internal deliberations confidential was in their collective interest. Under such conditions, as Michael Zürn comments, the opportunity for "strategic manipulation of information is wide open to decision-makers."[6]

Under the club model a lack of transparency to functional outsiders was a key to political efficacy. Protected by the lack of transparency, ministers could make package deals that were difficult to disaggregate or even sometimes to understand. For instance, after the US Congress deconstructed the trade agreements made during the Kennedy Round (1967), implementing unilateral modifications to bargains that had been reached, America's trade partners demanded modifications in internal US practices as a condition for the next trade round. The political response in the United States was a "fast-track" procedure, agreed to by Congress, that limited congressional power to pick apart agreements. In effect, Congress agreed to "tie itself to the mast" as it sailed past specific protectionist sirens.

Congress has voted many times for such procedures since its disastrous experience of unfettered participation in earlier years, culminating in the Smoot-Hawley tariff of 1930. It agreed to immunize international bargains from disaggregation in return for European, Japanese, and Canadian willingness to negotiate further reductions in trade barriers. Cooperation on international trade benefited, but the influence of labor unions and environmentalists was reduced by the practice. They have reacted strongly against it and the associated international institutions.

From the perspective of multilateral cooperation, the club model can be judged a great success. The world seems more peaceful, more prosperous, and even somewhat cleaner, at least on some environmental issues, than it would have been without such cooperation.[7] Admittedly, integration was often relatively shallow. The easier problems were tackled first. High rates of observed compliance with treaties do not necessarily indicate that noncompliance was a trivial problem.[8] Furthermore, the progress in institutional authority that did occur – as in the move from GATT to the WTO – was hardly the result of a sudden conversion of governments to the view that international law should prevail over national interests. As Robert Hudec has observed, the willingness of governments to negotiate the more precise rules and more authoritative procedures of the WTO stemmed from the US threat unilaterally to impose trade restrictions under Section 301 of its trade act:

> The change in position seems to have been a choice between two evils: between an almost certain legal meltdown if the United States were to carry out its new Section 301 instructions, and a very serious risk of legal failure, in the somewhat more distant future, if GATT adopted a dispute settlement procedure that was more demanding than governments could obey. In these circumstances, the fact that GATT governments chose the later option does not mean that they were confident it would work.[9]

The club model of cooperation, as illustrated in the Uruguay Round, had a political logic of its own. The governments of advanced capitalist countries understood that their electorates would hold them responsible for the results of trade negotiations. Liberalization would produce overall gains for the economy and for the electorates, but in the absence of compensation, protectionist interests "can be expected to resist, desperately and justifiably, their unhappy economic fate."[10] These groups, whose interests are more concentrated than those of consumers, could derail liberalizing trade measures unless they were "paid off" with rents from "voluntary" export restraints or subsidies of one type or another. In the United States each administration seeking liberalization bought off enough protectionist sectors (for example, textile manufacturers in the 1960s and 1970s) to pass liberalizing legislation.[11]

Negotiations in each trade round were tedious and fraught with anxiety for liberal trade forces. Yet they increased openness. Each round decreased the political weight of protectionist interests and increased the influence of their export-oriented opponents and of multinational firms allied with export interests.[12] As globalization progressed, the pro-liberal forces became more concentrated, since the largest firms in each country were highly multinational. The core political fact creating protectionism – that protectionist domestic producers were more concentrated than the far more numerous but less concentrated consumers – had been reversed. Exporters and multinationals were much more concentrated than the smaller and more scattered import-competing producers. Hence, liberalizers were playing a winning game in which each round of liberalization strengthened their own coalitions, and weakened their opponents', for the next round.

Armed with stronger mandates as a result of liberalizing domestic coalitions, the governments could negotiate with one another on the basis of reciprocity. Reciprocity took two complementary forms: specific reciprocity, since very precise deals were built into the agreements at the end of each trade round, and diffuse reciprocity, the belief that in the end everyone would benefit from liberalization, even if not all of the specific deals worked out as expected.[13] The result was a series of liberalizing trade agreements between the inauguration of GATT in 1948 and the completion of the Uruguay Round in 1994.

If the "club pattern" – under which small numbers of rich-country trade ministers controlled the agenda and made deals – were to continue in trade, so could this spiral of liberalization. However, in a dialectical fashion, the club arrangements are, we believe, being undercut by their success. Specifically, we can point to four reasons for the weakening of the old club system of trade politics.

First, increasing trade made publics more sensitive to further concessions. During the 1960s, 1970s, and 1980s, trade liberalization had been facilitated by the fact that substantial barriers to trade remained. Toronto still trades ten times as much with Vancouver as it does with Seattle, proportionate to the size of the latter two markets.[14] The barriers that produce this effect may be, in Richard Cooper's words, "political and psychological" more than natural in a geographical sense.[15] Yet from a political economy perspective, they created what could be termed a "useful inefficiency" that provided a buffer for domestic political differences while allowing openness to the global economy. Adjustment is an economic good but a political bad: it causes distress to many people, usually including potentially influential constituents of politicians. It is difficult to force adjustment quickly; hence barriers that reduce the pressure, or slow down the process, are often politically welcome. It has therefore been fortunate for politicians, although lamented by economists, that national borders matter so much for trade. The persistence of these barriers to both trade and capital movements, whether due to policy or psychology, helps to explain why national policy automony in fiscal and regulatory policy has not disappeared.[16]

With time and market integration, this useful inefficiency is being gradually eroded. Trade-to-GDP ratios are significantly higher than they were before the 1990s. Capital moves much more freely across borders than it did then. Sensitivity has increased during the last thirty years and can be expected to continue to do so. Increased sensitivity creates the potential for greater public pressure on policy.[17]

The second development that seems to have undercut the club system is that developing countries are demanding greater participation in policy-making. Their leaders are often ambivalent about the regimes, suspicious about the implications of rich-country leadership, and resentful of club rules, made by the rich, that they did not help to establish. Current hopes for a revival of serious negotiations on trade depend, in part, on developing countries' agreement to new rules. Many of these countries have been excluded from the club-like negotiations of the WTO. Early in 2000 India's commerce and industry minister complained that only about thirty countries were authorized to participate in the WTO's consultative process in Seattle at the end of November 1999. That process, he declared, "eliminated 100-plus countries from any participation at all, and some could not even enter the premises" where the negotiations were taking place.[18]

Governments of developing countries have their own agendas for trade negotiations, which are at odds both with the agendas of rich governments and with the agendas of rich-country nongovernmental organizations (NGOs). At the same time, the developing countries do not want to destroy the club; they want to join it and have more power within it. The challenge they pose is not to the legitimacy of the club concept per se but to its implementation. They are not pressing for the inclusion of environment ministers or nongovernmental actors. On the contrary, they have led the opposition to such changes. They are happy to have an intergovernmental club of trade ministers. The problem they pose is their number. As Harlan Cleveland once put it, how do you get everyone into the action and still get action? In principle, representative working groups with transparent processes might help to alleviate developing countries' concerns about legitimacy if such processes could be worked out.

Third, globalization has led to proliferation of nonstate agents, including business firms, business associations, labor unions, and NGOs; clamoring to make their voices heard, they have broadened the agenda of the WTO from trade policy.[19] During the 1990s, the number of international NGOs grew from 6,000 to 26,000, ranging in size from the Worldwide Fund for Nature with 5 million members to tiny network organizations.[20] The Seattle meetings of the WTO demonstrated the variety of such organizations and the intensity of members' feelings about the real or imagined links between trade and issues such as labor rights and environmental protection. Seen from a trade-specific transgovernmental perspective, the WTO is a club of trade ministers working with rules that have served well in that issue-area. But issue linkages ("trade and . . ." issues) are more problematic. Environment and labor ministers, for example, do not have a seat at the table. In other words, some relevant publics have no direct voice – only an indirect voice through national legislatures and executives.

The demonstrators at Seattle, incoherent and self-interested though they were, had a point. They wanted more direct access to the arena where their interests were being affected. In principle, this could be solved by linkages between the WTO and other international organizations, such as the UN Environment Program (UNEP) or the International Labor Organization (ILO). These organizations, however, do not have direct authority over trade policy, nor do they have as strong constituencies as does the WTO. Of course, there was not a single consistent NGO position at Seattle on these issues. Some NGO demonstrators wanted to weaken the World Trade Organization to protect sovereign regulation of the environment; others wanted to borrow the power of the organization to overcome sovereign regulation of labor conditions.

Nongovernmental organizations and their networks should not be viewed as a monolithic opposition to unitary states. On the contrary, different NGOs will participate in different transnational-transgovernmental coalitions with governmental officials, often pitted against other transnational–transgovernmental networks with different purposes.[21] Mixed or trisectoral coalitions are becoming more common in world politics. Agents will be connected to one another in networks and will work through competing and cooperating coalitions, but none of the components will be subordinate to another. Trade politics will be less dominated in the future by multilateral intergovernmental cooperation within a "decomposable" issue-area. The involvement of NGOs, the formation of transnational–transgovernmental networks, and linkages among issues are inherently connected.

This evolving pattern of transnational linkage politics intersects not only with the old club politics but also with the increasing assertiveness of governments of developing countries. At Seattle pressure from nongovernmental organizations, including politically influential US trade unions, led President Bill Clinton to demand that labor standards be incorporated in the WTO's trade agreements, and even to threaten sanctions to enforce them.[22] The reaction of India's commerce and industry minister was not only firm but scornful: "The threat of sanctions," said Murasoli Maran, "was the last straw. It was a nakedly protectionist act by a clique of developed countries behaving like a 'kangaroo court'."[23] Seattle made very clear the difficulties that a combination of heterogeneous state objectives, and activism by NGOs, can create for international trade negotiations.

The fourth force undermining the club system is the spread of democratic norms to more and more countries and attempts to implement them at the international level. There is more to the Seattle and Washington protests than the "protest envy" of young people whose parents demonstrated against the Vietnam War. Behind the protesters' annoyingly naïve characterizations of the WTO, IMF, and World Bank, and their frequent failure to understand even elementary economics, lies a deep concern with democratic procedures. When asked, students involved in these protests may concede ignorance on how the World Bank is organized or whether it has changed its policies to help the poor. Pressed on their economics, and on issues of fact, they come back to their normative base: global institutions are "undemocratic." Lori Wallach attributes half the success of the Seattle coalition to the notion that "the democracy deficit in the global economy is neither necessary nor acceptable." When it was pointed out that Mike Moore was appointed by democratically elected governments, she replied, "Between someone who actually got elected, and the director general of the WTO, there are so many miles that, in fact, he and his staff are accountable to no one."[24] This claim is debatable, but many social democrats in Europe claim that international institutions do not meet the procedural standards of democracy, particularly that of transparency.[25]

All of these pressures on international institutions are, ironically, reflections of their success. If international institutions were unimportant, as so-called "realists" claimed until recently, no one would care about their legitimacy.[26] But it is now recognized that the policies of the IMF, the World Bank, and the WTO make a difference. Hence they are judged not only on the results that these policies yield, but also on the procedures by which the policies are developed.

In the rest of this chapter, we focus on issues of democratic legitimacy raised by the pluralization of trade politics and the spread of democratic norms. These raise more novel questions of political theory than do the demands of governments of developing countries to have their voices heard within the club. In what sense does the club model of international regimes fail to meet democratic standards? Insofar as it does fail, what changes toward greater democracy would be feasible? And what trade-offs – for instance with liberalization and international cooperation in general – could be expected as democratization increased? Our interpretation of an actual political–economic problem – the endangered legitimacy of international political–economic institutions, including trade institutions such as the WTO – leads us to reconsider democratic theory as it may apply to issues of international governance.

Adversary democracy and unitary democracy in global institutions

In a book written right after the last great period of "creedal passion," Jane J. Mansbridge explored two types of democracy, which she called "adversary" and "unitary."[27] Adversary democracy assumes conflicting interests and employs established procedures to make decisions in the face of such conflicts. Unitary or direct democracy assumes that people have the same interests but may not know, individually, what is best to do. Face-to-face deliberation, as in the New England town meeting, is, in this view, the democratic way to reach decisions.[28] Mansbridge asks how both forms of democracy could be employed in a large country such as the United States. Admitting the decisionmaking advantages of adversary democracies, she asks her readers to appreciate the values of equal respect, or equal status, of unitary democracy. "The task confronting us," she says, "is to knit together these two fundamentally different kinds of democracy into a single institutional network that can allow us both to advance our common interests and to resolve our conflicting ones."[29]

Knitting these two forms together is a daunting task, and one that the United States certainly has not managed to accomplish in any coherent fashion. Indeed, participation in civil society in the United States, on a wide variety of dimensions, decreased during the second half of the twentieth century.[30] At the international level, with 6 billion people in the world, unitary or direct democracy appears a utopian dream. Nevertheless, adversary democracy does not have the inherently normative appeal that direct democracy often has.

One way to address the problems of democratic practices at the international level would be to apply an analogy between domestic and international politics.[31] International institutions would be viewed as if they were national institutions writ large. This perspective makes some sense for the European Union, which has extensive authority and elaborate institutions, including a parliament and a European Court of Justice. It is not surprising that Europeans have taken the lead in the debate on transparency, accountability, and the so-called democratic deficit, or that their chief target has been the European Union. Indeed, as Martin Wolf has commented, "if a country organized like the EU were to apply for membership, it would be rejected because it is not a democracy."[32] The mass resignation in March 1999 of the European Commission, under pressure from the European Parliament, is indicative of moves toward a European Union that may look more like a democratic federal state than it does now. Such an entity is unlikely to meet the standards of unitary democracy, although it may increasingly meet those of adversary democracy.

Direct democracy is more an impulse than an actual set of institutions. At an international level it would be utopian to suggest that anything like it is remotely feasible. However, its ideals should be kept in mind. They lie behind the protests against international institutions.

Transparency and participation in the WTO

Whether global regimes have a democratic deficit is more ambiguous than whether the European Union has one because the domestic analogy is less plausible for global regimes. Indeed, one could ask, "What's the fuss?" International institutions are weak relative to the governments of rich, powerful states. They operate formally according to democratic principles of delegation. And increasingly the WTO, in particular, conforms to the rule of law. We examine these three defenses of international institutions before taking a closer look at problems of transparency and participation in the WTO.

No international institution operating on a global scale has anything like the authority of the European Union, much less that of a state. Among international organizations, the WTO stands out as having quite authoritative and precise rules, and a relatively good record of eventual compliance with those rules by governments. So far, through diplomatic finesse and compromise the WTO has avoided outright refusals. The US Helms-Burton legislation, for instance, did not lead to a formal case at the WTO, precisely because both the United States and the EU feared that any decision by the WTO against the United States could lead to an anti-WTO backlash in this country. The WTO decisions on beef hormones and bananas strained EU support for the WTO, and the WTO decision on US export-tax benefits for corporations strained corporate support for the organization in the United States. The authoritative dispute settlement procedures of the WTO were, as Hudec has argued, a gamble. Despite successes so far, it remains unclear whether the WTO will have the ability to implement decisions that are strongly opposed by powerful states or the European Union.

The WTO-centered trade regime is strong compared with other international regimes. It compares favorably with the nonregime for exchange rates, with the fragmented international environmental regimes, and with the very weak regimes for international labor standards. The nominally central international organizations for environment and labor – the United Nations Environment Program and the International Labor Organization – are ineffective compared with the WTO. However, the reason for the WTO's relative strength is not that it has a powerful bureaucracy. On the contrary, the WTO has a weak bureaucracy that is kept on a short leash by its 135 member states. It has a secretariat of about 500 and a modest budget of $80 million. It decides by consensus, not by majority voting, and the autonomy of its management is much less than that of the IMF or the World Bank. The WTO must be highly responsive to the (mostly) elected governments of its member states.

The success of the WTO is not attributable to its organizational strength but to the fact that its dispute settlement procedures provide space for both diplomatic settlements and national democratic processes while still protecting the system of world trade. As in the case of Helms–Burton, diplomatic agreements can head off the appointment of a panel. After a panel ruling, the losing government typically appeals to the Appellate Body, which is certain to take into account political constraints and potential opposition when making its final decision. If pressures within a democracy cause a country to derogate from its agreements, the WTO does not have the authority (unlike the European Court of Justice) to enforce its rulings through national courts. What it can do is to authorize others to punish the noncompliant country and provide some measure of compensation. Instead of forcing its wishes on recalcitrant governments, the WTO serves the political function of a "circuit breaker" against a downward spiral of retaliation. Better for the lights to go out than for the house to burn down. Better to make concessions to the domestic politics of trade than to precipitate tit-for-tat retaliation, making everyone worse off. In a world of shallow integration, escape clauses and procedures are wise institutional arrangements. An overly legalistic WTO would be in danger of being both rigid and brittle.

The negotiations of the World Trade Organization meet democratic principles insofar as member governments are democratic. Negotiators are appointed by governments, and the final agreements must be ratified through domestic procedures. Representative government always relies on delegation. Rousseau and subsequent advocates of direct democracy have railed against representative government as keeping people "in chains," but no one has figured out how to make unitary democracy work at a scale larger than the city-state. Admittedly, even though international organizations are ultimately accountable to (mostly) democratically elected member governments, the international bureaucrats are more remote than national bureaucracies, and the chain of connection to elections is more indirect. But the chain of connections between elections and the actions of an under-secretary of the Treasury, an independent congressional commission, or a federal court is at least as indirect, and they are rarely accused, except by utopians, of being, for that reason, undemocratic.

The WTO also conforms better to the rule of law than did the GATT. Its Appellate Body set out detailed rules of procedure at the outset, and its opinions have included more rigorous legal analysis than was customary in GATT.[33] Compared with traditional diplomatic negotiations, the WTO's procedures are perfectly lucid. Democracy is not identical to the rule of law but certainly depends on it; in this regard also the WTO could be considered a democratic advance on its predecessors.

So what is the problem? From one democratic perspective, the WTO is almost the ideal design of an international institution. The international bureaucracy is weak; the organization is responsive to (mostly) elected governments. The escape clauses and dispute settlement procedures allow domestic political processes to prevail when severely challenged by international integration without at the same time destroying all rules and procedures. Thus the WTO contributes to the preservation of the embedded liberal bargain that has allowed the welfare state and increasing economic openness to co-exist.

The critics, however, have been emphasizing a different set of issues: direct participation and accountability. They see closed clubs indirectly linked to popular demands by long and opaque chains of delegation. Later in this paper we will address in more depth what we think *accountability* means and how it relates to legitimacy. Here we focus on three specific sets of issues: (1) a lack of transparency in the WTO process; (2) barriers to the participation of interested groups, who will clamor to be allowed in until institutional changes are made; and (3) the absence of politicians with ties both to the organization and to constituencies.

Transparency

Delegates to WTO bargaining sessions, though instructed and accountable to elected officials in democracies, often act in the privacy of the clubs built around their issues and related institutions. It is difficult independently to check their claims about how hard they bargained for particular advantages. Negotiators know how to "wink" – to signal when they are only going through the motions or wish to use a demand as a bargaining chip for something else. If outsiders cannot see the winks, they have a hard time judging how well they were represented in the process. Indeed, the opacity of the negotiations, taking place among club members behind closed doors, may facilitate intergovernmental bargaining.

WTO dispute settlement procedures have not been very transparent, although this is gradually changing. It was feared that transparency would lead governments to behave in more adversarial ways in order to appeal to domestic audiences. Lack of transparency and restrictions on participation adversely affect the public legitimacy of the WTO since, in accordance with democratic norms, "the public at large simply does not trust the honesty and legitimacy of secret proceedings."[34] It is therefore not surprising that even before the Seattle events, the United States was pressing to open panel and Appellate Body proceedings to the public, and for the right of private parties to submit briefs to panels and the Appellate Body.

US institutions that are deliberately insulated from elections – in particular, the Supreme Court and the Federal Reserve Board – routinely publish their deliberations or opinions, so that not only the results, but the reasoning and disagreements involved, can be publicly known. These institutions are held accountable through criticisms by professional networks, such as legal scholars writing in law journals and economists writing scholarly articles and offering opinions in the public media. Without transparency, these means of accountability would be eviscerated.

Transparency does not imply governance through elections, as the examples of the Supreme Court and the Federal Reserve Board show. Transparency does mean that the arguments and reasoning on trade rules, and the adjudication of those rules, are made public. Democratic societies demand this of institutions that allocate values profoundly affecting people's lives.

Participation

In representative democracies, participation is channeled and in many ways limited, but some opportunities are available to make one's views known. In the US Congress, for instance, hearings open to spokespeople from a variety of groups in part satisfy demands for participation. With respect to rulemaking in the WTO, only idealistic proponents of unitary democracy would demand that the public be allowed into the negotiating rooms where deals are being made. The consequences for trade liberalization of doing this would probably be grave. But allowing a certain number of observers and press at the Council meetings is a different matter. In addition, the WTO could consider the possibility of institutionalizing public hearings on trade policy – now limited to national forums. Particularly through the worldwide web, the WTO could reach out to individuals and groups around the globe to solicit their views. The perception that the WTO is an institution open to participation, rather than a closed bureaucracy, could be an asset to the organization in democratic societies.

In dispute settlement, a key demand is equal treatment. Under the current system, states are formally gatekeepers to the WTO process, but they often

have incentives to open the gates to powerful actors (such as firms and industry groups) within their societies. GATT, as Hudec has shown, became more
legalized and dealt with more cases, even before WTO came into effect.[35]
Trade lawyers not working for governments, or for powerful clients with
access to governments, claim that they are unfairly disadvantaged by not
being able to see what happens behind closed doors. On the other hand,
opening the adjudicatory process to nongovernmental organizations could
disadvantage governments of poor countries, which may lack the high-
powered legal resources to compete with well-funded environmental organizations and trade unions from rich countries. As is so often the case,
struggles over "fair procedures" reflect underlying struggles over substance –
"who gets what?" Charges of unaccountability and lack of democracy are
often used as instruments to pry open access or to cry "foul" when one has
lost on the merits.

Opening up the WTO's dispute settlement proceedings could have far-
reaching consequences. There are systematic differences between "international" and "transnational" modes of dispute resolution.[36] In international
dispute resolution, access to the adjudication process is limited to states,
whereas in transnational dispute resolution, nonstate parties can bring cases
and file briefs. International dispute resolution is epitomized by the International Court of Justice (ICJ); transnational dispute resolution, by the
European Court of Justice (ECJ). The major apparent consequence of differential access is that transnational dispute resolution is much more expansive
than international dispute resolution. The ECJ has become an authoritative
interpreter of EU law. Its opinions are regularly incorporated into the
decisions of national courts. This dynamic of expansion is fueled by a de
facto alliance between plaintiffs and their lawyers, on the one hand, and the
Court, on the other. Ready access to a tribunal creates cases – without which,
courts wither on the vine. When these cases are decided and the decisions
enforced, future plaintiffs are encouraged to bring more cases, and a spiral of
positive feedback ensues. By contrast, a much smaller proportion of ICJ
member states accepts its compulsory jurisdiction than did so in 1945,
undermining the authority of the ICJ.[37]

If the WTO became open to cases brought by nonstate actors, would it be
strengthened, as the ECJ has been? In the WTO, ambiguous formal rules
have to be interpreted by panels and the Appellate Body in order to make
them operational. The extent of this interpretation is such that, in effect, rules
are being made through the Dispute Settlement Mechanism rather than in
negotiations among governments.[38] When a similar process occurred in the
EU, the ECJ was able to draw on support from national courts that enforced
ECJ decisions. Since national courts were enforcing ECJ decisions, their own
governments could not rely on extralegal measures. Instead, they "were
forced to frame their response in terms that could persuade a legal audience,
and thus they became constrained by the legal rules of the game."[39] By
contrast, WTO rulings are not enforced by national courts but rely on

governments' political decisions to comply. The Appellate Body of the WTO does not have nearly as much elite or public support as the ECJ, which claims to speak for the idea of European union and the rule of law. Hence it would be much easier for a disgruntled government to raise a political challenge against the Appellate Body than for governments to challenge the authority of the ECJ.

Politicians and constituencies

The club model helps to overcome deadlock that accompanies the diffusion of power. Club-based intergovernmental organizations (IGOs) can move incrementally and gradually reinterpret their mandates insofar as their secretariats and leading states can build alliances with crucial private-sector and third-sector actors. But they cannot make large formal moves forward without a broad consensus about their proper purposes or without political institutions that can give them definitive guidance based on a wide expression of social views. As a result of the constraints and opportunities that they face, international organizations, like the WTO, tend to be dominated by small networks of professionals who can modify their informal rules and practices and sometimes develop a body of case law. Indeed, there is a danger of overreliance on judicial practices as a way to duck difficult political bargaining, with the effect of a hollowing out of institutions.

What is missing? The legitimating activity of broadly based politicians speaking directly to domestic publics. The absence of effective political leadership may have mattered less in the past when issues were less linked. Trade ministers' accountability to parliaments was sufficient to provide legitimacy. But with the linkage of issues, politicians are needed who can link specific organizations and policies with a broader range of public issues through electoral accountability. Someone has to take responsibility for making judgments about the relative importance of issues, and how to manage the trade-offs between them. And in a democratic society, politicians who take this responsibility have to be held accountable for their actions. Indeed, their very accountability is a source of credibility and strength, since policy pronouncements, for accountable officials, are potentially costly, rather than being mere "cheap talk."

If constituents have confidence in their elected officials, they are more likely to support policies endorsed by those officials, even if they do not understand the specifics of the policies. Politicians intermediate between organizations and constituencies in civil societies, strengthening the legitimacy of organizations in return for ensuring that constituencies have influence over the organizations' policies.

The lack of intermediating politicians is the most serious democratic deficit of international organizations in general and the WTO in particular. Lack of transparency and deficiencies of participation are relatively easy to fix, but without responsible politicians, "solving" these problems could create deadlock as more and more heterogeneous actors compete for publicity and over policy.

To enhance democratic accountability, the WTO would require a strong office of director-general – a move that would surely be resisted by many governments. But having an institutionally empowered director-general would not be sufficient. Somehow that director-general would have to become accountable to organized constituencies within the organization. In other words, the functional equivalent of political parties would be needed to perform the functions of interest aggregation and organization of debate that parties perform in democracies. Having done so, the director-general might have a fighting chance to compete with other political entrepreneurs for influence, and somehow to integrate a variety of concerns (trade liberalization, environmental protection, labor rights, protection for groups disadvantaged by liberalization) in a single policy matrix.

Merely to state the conditions is to suggest how utopian such a prospect is. The notion that functional equivalents of political parties will emerge, on a global basis, to represent constituencies with similar interests boggles the mind. Even in Europe, with all the successes of the European Union, there are no genuinely transnational political parties, only coalitions among generally like-minded parties in a weak European Parliament. The idea of a WTO parliament is likely to prove even more illusory, although inclusion of more parliamentarians in national delegations might help to sensitize trade officials to the need for public legitimacy. However, such modest measures will not correct the central legitimacy problem of the WTO: the absence of politicians to intermediate between policymakers and constituencies.

Conclusion

We have only managed to state the problem, not to provide a solution. The problem is how to increase transparency and accountability, while enhancing international cooperation and achieving some degree of policy integration. At a minimum, the goal is to reach agreements without subjecting all deals to deconstruction and unwinding. But social globalization, reflected in the explosion of NGOs, works against careful integration in the absence of collective identity. It will remain easier to pick packages apart than to put them together.

Democracy, legitimacy, and accountability

We turn now to some broader reflections on issues of legitimacy and accountability in international organizations. Democracy is government by officials who are accountable to the majority of the people in a jurisdiction, albeit with frequent provisions for supermajority voting and protections for individuals and minorities. For democracy to work well, "the people" have to regard themselves as a political community. Who are "we the people" when there is little sense of political identity or community, and the political world is organized largely around a system of unequal states? In a nondemocratic world in which international institutions merely facilitated interstate co-operation, such a question would be irrelevant. But in the contemporary world, democratic norms are increasingly applied to international institutions as a test of their legitimacy. If international institutions are to be legitimate, therefore, their practices and the results of their activities need to meet broadly democratic standards. But as noted earlier, the domestic analogy does not apply, since the world as a whole lacks a coherent public, a corresponding public space for discussion, and institutions linking the public, through elections, to governing organizations.

Democratic governments are judged both on the procedures they follow (inputs) and on the results they obtain (outputs). Despite having been, in several dimensions, quite an effective president, President Richard Nixon was forced to resign because he violated the law. Conversely, President Clinton's successes in managing the economy, and the high level of public appreciation of his performance in this realm, helped to rally support for him during the impeachment process in 1998. Both inputs and outputs affect legitimacy at the international level as well, and it is useful to consider them separately.

Inputs: procedures and accountability

On the input side, the key issue is one of accountability. In democracies, publics hold elites accountable for their actions through elections, which can result in removal from office. Accountability is by no means perfect: governing elites can sometimes manipulate publics, by controlling the agenda, through campaign spending, or otherwise. But the competition of elites provides some assurance that in the long run governments cannot defy the strongly felt will of a majority. "The democratic method," declared Joseph Schumpeter in 1942, "is that institutional arrangement for arriving at political decisions in which individuals acquire the power to decide by means of a competitive structure for the people's vote."[40]

International institutions lack the essential feature that makes democracy possible and that, in democracies, facilitates accountability: an acknowledged public operating within a political community in which there is a general consensus on what makes public decisions legitimate. What are the boundaries of the relevant electoral constituencies in which votes are held? If the moral claim for democracy rests on the worth and equality of individuals, then a basic rule is one person: one vote. One state: one vote is not democratic because a Maldive Islander would have 1,000 times the voting power of a citizen of China. On the other hand, a cosmopolitan view that treats the globe as one constituency implies the existence of a political community in which citizens of 198 states would be willing to be continually outvoted by a billion Chinese and a billion Indians. As Pippa Norris has shown, there is no evidence that national identities are changing in a manner that would make that feasible for a long time to come.[41] In the absence of such a community, the extension of domestic voting practices to the world scale would make little normative sense, even if it were feasible. Meaningful voting and associated democratic political activities occur within the boundaries of nation states that have democratic constitutions and processes. Minorities are willing to acquiesce to a majority in which they may not participate directly because they feel they participate in some larger community. Such a sense of community is clearly absent at the global level and creates severe normative as well as practical problems for the input side of global democracy.

However, as we have noted, accountability is not ensured through elections alone. Indeed, it is a multidimensional phenomenon. We can distinguish electoral accountability and nonelectoral accountability. At the interstate level, three types of mechanisms strengthen electoral accountability.[42] First, state control, through chains of delegation, can strengthen accountability. At the same time it can ensure that sufficient transparency exists so that members of the public can judge whether their government, operating within the international institution, is carrying out its mandate. It is not inherently any more undemocratic for the US president to delegate authority to the US trade representative to negotiate at the WTO than for the president to delegate authority to the attorney general to deal with organized crime. As long as the public knows what actions the delegated agent took, it can reward or punish the president and his party for its deeds. The key is transparency.

The second means of increasing the democratic accountability of international institutions is to strengthen mechanisms of domestic accountability. Indeed, many of the problems of aggregating interests and responding to different constituencies must be handled at the domestic level where democratic electoral procedures make sense. For instance, Denmark's parliament has developed procedures that give it much more information than is available to other parliaments in Europe about its government's actual policies within the European Union. The Danish government is therefore much more accountable, for better and worse, to its parliament for its actions within the European Union than are other member governments.[43] The third mechanism is to increase legislative control over policy at the supranational level, although this has been accomplished only through the European Parliament and, there, only in a rather halting and limited way.

Voting, delegation, and parliamentary action are not the only ways in which democratic governments are held accountable to publics. There are also important nonelectoral dimensions to accountability. Many democratic theorists would argue that elections, and the long shadows that elections cast, do not exhaust the voice that people should have on issues that affect their lives. Intensity of feeling also matters; and people should be able to exercise voice in the long intervals between elections, even if their representatives do not speak up on their behalf. The mechanisms of adversarial democracy stretch from polls to protests.

The boundaries for this nonelectoral type of input are less clearly defined than are those of electoral politics. A public space is an identifiable set of issues within a communicative environment in which people can speak to one another in comprehensible ways. The public is the group of people who communicate and agitate over their shared externalities in that space – sometimes at a local level and sometimes at transnational levels. In this sense of shared externalities and a degree of shared understanding, there may be some global publics even if there is no global community. NGOs contest and ally with each other and with parts of governments to set agendas and press for preferred actions by governments. The media play an important role as a target for NGO action and as a means to hold NGOs to some standards of accountability.

Another form of nonelectoral accountability is achieved through professional norms and transnational networks. As Arthur Applebaum has argued, professional ethical standards can be used to hold adversaries accountable.[44] Lawyers care about the opinion of the bar; academic economists about their standing in the eyes of some colleagues. Epistemic communities increasingly take the lead in raising the issues and constructing the domestic and transnational conversations necessary to create a public space.[45] They keep governing elites accountable in the same way in which networks of legal scholars or economists make the Supreme Court or the Federal Reserve accountable: through reasoned criticism and discussion rather than through elections.

Third, markets provide nonelectoral accountability. Obviously, people have unequal votes in markets depending upon the wealth they bring to the table. Thus competitive markets are not a form of pure democratic accountability. Nonetheless, corporations and governments that fail to perform well are held accountable through markets in ways that are often more rapid and effective than through electoral practices. Rating agencies help to consolidate and publicize a number of market judgments about firms. Governments that are closed and corrupt find it more difficult to attract capital and maintain the confidence of transnational investors. Firms whose goods are made in sweat shops may be held accountable to consumers through publicity and boycotts.

The problem of accountability for governance at the international level is not the complete absence of mechanisms for accountability. The problem is that the mechanisms are *disarticulated*. In a well-functioning domestic democracy, political inputs – popular activity, media attention, interest group lobbying, parties, elections, and formal legislation – are articulated together. There is a clear pathway by which laws can be created; and when laws are enacted, regular procedures and organizations exist to implement, amend, and change those laws. This is the procedural basis for democratic legitimacy. Internationally, however, the link between popular activity and policy is severely attenuated.

In a well-functioning domestic democracy, popular politics and the organization of interest groups lead through fairly well-defined pathways to legislation and to the implementation of such legislation. Since governing elites work hard to anticipate reactions to their actions, through such pathways, the effects of anticipated criticisms and electoral consequences can be even more important than ex post punishment. These connections are lacking at the international level. Intergovernmental organizations that make binding rules often lack the democratic legitimacy that comes from having transparent procedures, institutional arrangements that facilitate account-ability, and activities by politicians seeking reelection by appealing to publics. At the same time, the private and NGO sectors that agitate political issues internationally do not have any greater claim to democratic legitimacy. Despite their claims to represent civil society, they tend to be self-selected and often unrepresentative elites. The disjunction between international arrange-ments facilitating such public involvement and multilateral cooperation on binding decisions causes disputes over legitimacy and dangers of stalemate in intergovernmental institutions. This disjunction cannot be solved simply by adopting the domestic voting model at a global level. On the input side, mechanisms for accountability exist, but they are not joined into a coherent system with mutually reinforcing components.

Outputs: effectiveness

The legitimacy of governments is not determined solely by the procedures used on the input side. Substantive outputs also matter. Citizens are con-cerned about issues of security, welfare, and identity. When these substantive outputs are missing, procedural democracy on the input side is often not sufficient. Conversely, however, their past successes on the output side may give them some space for reform.

Effectiveness enhances legitimacy in both "macro" and "micro" ways. On the macro side, the overall accomplishments of an international regime in producing a collective good may be appreciated. The eradication of smallpox by the World Health Organization gave the WHO substantial legitimacy for being effective in dealing with global health problems, whereas its slowness in focusing on AIDs may have had the opposite effect. Critics of the IMF's performance in the world economic crisis of 1997–99 emphasize how much worse the crisis was because of the fund's misguided actions.[46] Defenders of the IMF, on the other hand, argue that its actions, while leading to pain at the time, account for the rapid recovery after 1998 in most of Asia. They seek to turn the crisis into a success for the IMF, enhancing its legitimacy.[47]

On the macro side, the legitimacy of the WTO rests on its fostering of trade liberalization. Since trade liberalization has been a fairly consistent policy of most rich-country governments during the past half-century and recently a policy of many developing countries as well, WTO's dedication to trade liberalization probably enhances its legitimacy. Trade liberalization is regarded as being a good thing. Hence, being "on the side of the angels" may have conferred some legitimacy on the WTO even in the absence of procedures ensuring transparency and participation.

At the micro level, the activities of international organizations build coalitions of individuals, firms, or groups that support them out of self-interest. For many international organizations, such coalitions are weak because the beneficiaries of the organization's actions are weak and fragmented or because the organizations are easy scapegoats for domestic politicians. Insofar as the World Bank seeks to help the poor, it ensures that it will have a weak political base, since neither powerful transnational capitalist interests, nor the governments of many developing countries, give priority to the interests of the poor in their own policies or lobbying. For the IMF, the micro-political problem is that its strong medicine usually is administered after the government of the country – through either political opportunism or incompetence – has made substantial policy blunders. Blaming the IMF is the obvious strategy for politicians seeking to avoid being held accountable for their own failed policies.

At the micro level, the WTO has one advantage over the World Bank and the IMF, since the WTO has a powerful constituency: multinational corporations that seek to expand their own exports and investments abroad. These firms, and related industry associations, have influential voices in policy councils at home and strong interests in continued liberalization. By and large, they have prevailed over labor unions that have advocated protectionism. Hence the WTO should have some coalitional support against more generalized, and symbolic, criticisms that focus on the input side – on accountability. If appealing changes can be made on the input side, the WTO may be able to recover more readily than international organizations that have less to show for their efforts.

Suggestions about legitimacy

There are vast differences in political context between domestic and international governance. Therefore, a more appropriate measure for judging democratic legitimacy is needed than the so-called democratic deficit based on the domestic analogy. The literature based on the European Union with its close links to the domestic analogy is not well suited to global institutions, for reasons given earlier. Nor will new theories based on the potential for direct voting in cyberdemocracy be sufficient. One can imagine technology making it possible for the votes of vast numbers of people to be collected easily in frequent plebiscites, but in the absence of community it is more difficult to envisage the effective processes of deliberation that would make such voting meaningful. With time such obstacles may be overcome and practices gradually develop, but even under the most optimistic assumptions, genuinely global public space is a long way off.

Another optimistic view is that transgovernmental relations, or "government networks," will help to solve problems of global governance. Transgovernmental networks (such as the Basle Committee of Central Bank Governors of rich countries or the International Organization of Securities Commissioners) act informally, aided by strong personal contacts among participants. They can often operate more quickly and effectively than formal bodies. However, they are not open to a broad range of participants, they are often secretive, and they are typically accountable to only a few relatively powerful elites. As Anne-Marie Slaughter has pointed out, "the informality, flexibility, and decentralization of networks mean that it is very difficult to establish precisely who is acting and when."[48] Hence, serious issues of accountability arise. Nevertheless, as she argues, the critics often miss several key points: legitimacy may derive from performance as well as process; governmental networks typically operate through persuasion rather than authoritative decision; and these networks may actually empower democratic politicians and their governments, by promoting cooperation among them, when the alternative could be leaving decisions to markets.

Another possibility is to supplement the work of the WTO with what Wolfgang Reinicke calls "trisectoral networks" of governments, multilateral organizations, and nongovernmental groups, both profit and nonprofit. For example, the World Commission on Dams consists of twelve members, four each from the public, private, and nonprofit sectors. It has been analyzing the effects of large dams and developing a set of standards for dams that it recommends to governments and the Bank.[49] One could imagine creating a similar group to work through some of the thorny issues of the club model and the trade regime. It is unlikely that states will turn over major decision-making activities, creating hard law, to transgovernmental and trisectoral networks, but what Sylvia Ostry calls "hybrid governance" involving such networks is likely to be an increasingly important part of the global policy process.[50] Insofar as it is effective, hybrid governance will be welcome as a supplement to other forms of governance. The legitimacy of government and trisectoral networks, however, will depend on whether they produce widely accepted outcomes and whether their processes appear sufficiently transparent and accountable to elites and publics in civil society.

As experiments continue with governance and trisectoral networks, it will be important to develop more modest normative principles and practices to enhance transparency and accountability – not only of IGOs but of corporations and NGOs that constitute global governance today. For example, increased transparency advances accountability, but transparency need not be instantaneous or complete. Consider the delayed release of Federal Reserve Board hearings or the details of Supreme Court deliberations. Similarly, accountability has many dimensions, only one of which is reporting up the chain of delegation to elected leaders. Markets aggregate the preferences (albeit unequally) of large numbers of people, and both governments and transnational corporations are accountable to them. Professional associations create and maintain transnational norms to which IGOs, NGOs, and government officials can be judged accountable. The practice, by nongovernmental organizations and the press, of "naming and shaming" of transnational corporations with valuable brand names also provides a sort of accountability. Similarly, Transparency International's naming and shaming of governments engaged in corrupt practices helps create accountability. While trisectoral cooperation and government networks can be productive, competition among sectors and among networks continues to be useful for transparency and accountability.

Greater cooperation with nongovernmental organizations might alleviate concerns about the World Trade Organization's accountability. For example, some NGOs might be given observer status at WTO Council meetings where rules are discussed. It would be problematic, however, to give NGOs the right to participate in trade bargaining sessions, since consummating deals often requires a certain degree of obfuscation of the trade-offs being made. The greater intensity of activity by groups threatened by losses, than by groups likely to reap gains, could foster deadlock.[51] A greater role for NGOs in the World Trade Organization has its own problems. For one thing, many developing countries would object to it, not only because of their devotion to the doctrine of sovereignty, but also because the preferences of NGOs (mostly from rich countries) are opposed to developing countries' interests. In addition, there is the problem of the lack of transparency and accountability of the nongovernmental organizations themselves. In principle, the World Trade Organization could set requirements of transparency of budgets and membership for NGOs that wish to participate, and as more of them develop in the South, the opposition of the developing countries may diminish.

The World Bank has been relatively successful in working with nongovernmental organizations. More than seventy NGO specialists (mostly from technically proficient organizations) work in the Bank's field offices. "From environmental policy to debt relief, NGOs are at the center of World Bank policy," the *Economist* noted. "The new World Bank is more transparent, but is also beholden to a new set of special interests."[52] Environmental NGOs have played effective roles at UN conferences. It was notable in April 2000 that Oxfam, an active NGO, did not participate in the demonstrations against the World Bank, declaring instead that it sought to continue to promote reform of the Bank rather than to agitate for its dissolution.

Whether involving – or co-opting – selected nongovernmental organizations would work for the World Trade Organization is an open question. Their democratic legitimacy is not established simply by their claims to be part of civil society. The legitimacy of favored NGOs could be called into question by co-optation, and excluded NGOs are likely to criticize those that are included for "selling out." Political battles among nongovernmental organizations will limit a co-optation strategy. Nonetheless, some form of NGO representation in the institutions involved in multilateral governance, and in particular the WTO, could help to maintain their legitimacy.

Conclusions: the WTO, legitimacy, and governance

The compromise of embedded liberalism created a social safety net in return for openness. Although successful in the second half of the twentieth century, it is under new pressure today. That compromise was the basis for Bretton Woods institutions that (along with other regimes) employed the club model to govern decomposable issue-areas in world politics. Now the club model is under challenge. Rulemaking and rule interpretation in global governance have become pluralized. Rules are no longer a matter for states or intergovernmental organizations alone. Private firms, NGOs, subunits of governments, and the resulting transnational and transgovernmental networks play a role as well. Any sustainable pattern of governance will have to institutionalize channels of contact between international organizations and constituencies within civil society. The international regimes, broadly conceived, must be political rather than technocratic. They must be linked to legitimate domestic institutions.

The club model, instead of being discarded entirely, requires modification. As a general precaution, it will be important not to put more weight on such institutions than they can bear. Rather than pursue strong institutions to foster deep integration at the global level, it is more appropriate to pursue an image of what we have elsewhere called "networked minimalism."[53] Multilateral institutions do not compete so much with domestic institutions as rely on them. They will only thrive when substantial space is preserved for domestic political processes – "subsidiarity" in the language of the European Union. By allowing domestic politics to sometimes depart from international agreements without unraveling the whole system of norms, the WTO provides a helpful model. Putting too much weight on international institutions before they are sufficiently legitimate to bear it is a recipe for deadlock, disruption, and failure.

In a world of active NGOs and strong democratic norms, more attention will have to be paid to issues of legitimacy. Some of these issues can be addressed at the level of the multilateral organization's own practices. But the prime components of democratic legitimacy will remain at the domestic level. Unless domestic processes are viewed as legitimate, the regimes that rest on those domestic processes will not be viewed as legitimate.

At the domestic or international levels, legitimacy should not be viewed solely in terms of majoritarian voting procedures. Many parts of the American constitution (such as the Supreme Court) and political practice would fail that test. Democratic legitimacy has a number of sources, both normative and substantive. Legitimacy in international regimes depends partly on effectiveness. Insofar as legitimacy depends on processes, accountability is central. Accountability need not take place exclusively through delegation from elected national governments with parliamentary oversight. Arrangements to ensure other forms of participation from civil society, ranging from protests to the involvement of NGOs in decisionmaking and dispute resolution, can enhance accountability. Markets and professional networks also play a role. Whatever form accountability takes, transparency will be crucial to ensure that accountability is meaningful.

In the absence of political institutions linking governance organizations with constituencies, the legitimacy of global institutions will probably remain shaky for many decades. Indeed, the political base of intergovernmental organizations and international regimes may be so weak that effective international cooperation on trade will decline or even collapse into deadlock. But the costs of deadlock would be high. If deadlock is to be avoided, international organizations such as the WTO will need to become more, rather than less, political. They must balance greater transparency and participation with opportunities for closer ties between public leadership and constituencies. A bewildering array of interests need to be aggregated in ways that are democratically acceptable. Devising effective and legitimate international institutions is indeed a crucial problem of political design for the twenty-first century.

Notes

1 John G. Ruggie, "International Regimes, Transactions and Change: Embedded Liberalism in the Postwar Economic Order," in Stephen D. Krasner, ed., *International Regimes* (Cornell University Press, 1983).
2 Fred Hirsch, "The Ideological Underlay of Inflation," in Fred Hirsch and John Goldthorpe, eds, *The Political Economy of Inflation* (London: Martin Robertson, 1978), pp. 284, 278.
3 For different views on the situation facing contemporary social democracy in western Europe, see Geoffrey Garrett, *Partisan Politics in the Global Economy* (Cambridge University Press, 1998); and Torben Iversen, *Contested Economic Institutions: The Politics of Macroeconomics and Wage Bargaining in Advanced Democracies* (Cambridge University Press, 1999).
4 Robert O. Keohane, *After Hegemony: Cooperation and Discord in the World Political Economy* (Princeton University, Press, 1984).
5 Herbert A. Simon, *The Sciences of the Artificial*, 3rd ed. (MIT Press, 1996), pp. 197–207.
6 Michael Zürn, "Democratic Governance beyond the Nation State: The EU and Other International Institutions," *European Journal of International Relations*, vol. 6, no. 2 (2000), pp. 183–222.
7 Peter M. Haas, Robert O. Keohane, and Marc Levy, eds., *Institutions for the Earth: Sources of Effective Environmental Protection* (MIT Press, 1993).
8 George W. Downs, David M. Rocke, and Peter N. Barsoom, "Is the Good News about Compliance Good News about Cooperation?" *International Organization*, vol. 50, no. 3 (1996), pp. 379–406.
9 Robert E. Hudec, "The New WTO Dispute Settlement Procedure: An Overview of the First Three Years," *Minnesota Journal of Global Trade, Inc.*, vol. 8, no. 1 (1999), p. 14.
10 Ronald Rogowski, *Commerce and Coalitions: How Trade Affects Domestic Political Alignments* (Princeton University Press, 1989), p. 172.

11 Vinod Aggarwal, *Liberal Protectionism: The International Politics of Organized Textile Trade* (University of California Press, 1985).

12 See Rogowski, *Commerce and Coalitions*; and Helen V. Milner, *Resisting Protectionism: Global Industries and the Politics of International Trade* (Princeton University Press, 1988).

13 Robert O. Keohane, "Reciprocity in International Relations," *International Organization*, vol. 40, no. 1 (1986), pp. 1–27.

14 John Helliwell, *How Much Do National Borders Matter?* (Brookings, 1998).

15 Richard N. Cooper, *The Economics of Interdependence: Economic Policy in the Atlantic Community* (McGraw-Hill, 1968), esp. Chap. 4 and p. 173.

16 See also, Geoffrey Garrett, *Partisan Politics in the Global Economy* (Cambridge University Press, 1998), p. 183.

17 Cooper pointed out in his classic study that increasing sensitivity not only increased the likelihood of imbalances in international payments, but would make such imbalances easier to deal with, since small policy changes would have larger effects. From an economic standpoint, therefore, increasing sensitivity could be a policy advantage. Nevertheless, from a political perspective, increasing sensitivity subjected policymakers to more pressures for accountability. See Cooper, *Economics of Interdependence*, p. 77.

18 Murasoli Maran, interviewed in the *Financial Times*, February 2, 2000, p. 5.

19 Wolfgang H. Reinicke, *Global Public Policy: Governing without Government* (Brookings, 1998).

20 *The Economist*, December 11, 1999, p. 21.

21 Robert O. Keohane and Joseph S. Nye Jr., *Transnational Relations and World Politics* (Harvard University Press, 1972).

22 *Financial Times*, December 2, 1999, p. 1.

23 *Financial Times*, February 2, 2000, p. 5.

24 "The FP Interview: Lori's War," *Foreign Policy*, no. 118 (Spring 2000), pp. 37, 47.

25 Zurn, "Democratic Governance." Zurn seeks to refute the arguments of social democrats such as Claus Offe that international and supranational institutions are undemocratic and therefore their further growth should be resisted.

26 John J. Mearsheimer, "The False Promise of International Institutions," *International Security*, vol. 19, no. 3 (1994–95), pp. 5–49. For responses, see *International Security*, vol. 20, no. 1 (1995).

27 Jane J. Mansbridge, *Beyond Adversary Democracy* (1980; University of Chicago Press, 1983). On "creedal passion," see Samuel P. Huntington, *American Politics: The Promise of Disharmony* (Cambridge, Mass.: Belknap Press, 1981).

28 Unitary democracy has a clear affinity with Jurgen Habermas's theory of communication, in which the persuasiveness of speech acts depends on the intersubjective ties between speaker and listener, as well as on the propositional content of the speech. See Jurgen Habermas, *Communication and the Evolution of Society*, translated by Thomas McCarthy (Beacon Press, 1979), chap. 1.

29 Mansbridge, *Beyond Adversary Democracy*, p. 7.

30 Robert D. Putnam, *Bowling Alone: The Collapse and Revival of American Community* (Simon and Schuster, 2000).

31 The term "domestic analogy" is used with a different meaning from ours by Hedley Bull, *The Anarchical Society: A Study of Order in World Politics* (Columbia University Press, 1977).

32 Martin Wolf, "Europe's Challenge," *Financial Times*, January 6, 1999, p. 12.

33 Hudec, "The New WTO Dispute Settlement Procedure," p. 28.

34 Ibid., p. 45.

35 Hudec, "The New WTO Dispute Settlement Procedure."

36 Robert O. Keohane, Andrew Moravcsik, and Anne-Marie Slaughter, "Legalized Dispute Resolution: Interstate and Transnational," *International Organization*,

vol. 54, no. 3 (2000), pp. 457–88. Daniel Esty, "Non-Governmental Organizations at the World Trade Organization," *Journal of International Economic Law*, vol. 123 (1998).

37 Stephen Schwebel, "The Performance and Prospects of the International Court of Justice," in Karl-Heinz Boeckstiegel, ed., *Perspectives of Air Law, Space Law and International Business Law for the Next Century* (Köln: Carl Heymanns Verlag, 1996).

38 This point was made by Sylvia Ostry at the conference where an earlier version of this chapter was presented.

39 Karen J. Alter, "Who Are the 'Masters of the Treaty'? European Governments and the European Court of Justice," *International Organization*, vol. 52, no. 1 (1998), p. 123.

40 Joseph S. Schumpeter, *Capitalism, Socialism, and Democracy* (1942; Harper Torchbook edition, 1962), p. 269. For a sophisticated analysis of input and output legitimacy in Europe, see Fritz Scharpf, *Governing in Europe* (Oxford University Press, 1999).

41 Pippa Norris, "Global Governance and Cosmopolitan Citizens," in Joseph S. Nye Jr and John Donahue, eds, *Governance in a Globalizing World* (Brookings, 2000).

42 Here we rely on a synthesis by Professor Anne-Marie Slaughter of a number of points made by herself and others at a conference on accountability and international institutions, Duke University, May 7–8, 1999.

43 Lisa L. Martin, *Democratic Commitments: Legislatures and International Cooperation* (Princeton University Press, 2000).

44 Arthur Applebaum, *Ethics for Adversaries: The Morality of Roles in Public and Professional Life* (Princeton University Press, 1999).

45 Peter M. Haas, "Introduction: Epistemic Communities and International Policy Coordination," *International Organization*, vol. 46, no. 1 (1992), pp. 1–36. See also Margaret E. Keck and Kathryn Sikkink, *Activists beyond Borders: Advocacy Networks in International Politics* (Cornell University Press, 1998).

46 For a particularly biting critique, see Joseph Stiglitz, "The Insider: What I Learned at the World Economic Crisis," *New Republic*, April 17, 2000, pp. 56–60.

47 Reply to Stiglitz by Rudiger Dornbush, *New Republic*, May 29, 2000, pp. 4–5.

48 Anne-Marie Slaughter, "Governing the Global Economy through Government Networks," in Michael Byers, ed., *The Role of Law in International Politics: Essays in International Relations and International Law* (Oxford University Press, 2000), pp. 193–94.

49 Wolfgang Reinicke, "The Other World Wide Web: Global Public Policy Networks," *Foreign Policy*, no. 117 (Winter 1999–2000), pp. 44–57.

50 See Sylvia Ostry's, "World Trade Organization: Institutional Design for Better Governance," in Roger B. Purter *et. al.*, eds, *Efficiency, Equity, Legitimacy: The Multilateral Trading System at the Millennium* (Washington: Brookings, 2001), pp. 361–91.

51 For an interesting discussion of the effects of information on trade negotiations, see Judith Goldstein and Lisa L. Martin, "Legalization, Trade Liberalization, and Domestic Politics," *International Organization*, vol. 54, no. 3 (2000), pp. 603–32.

52 "The Non-Governmental Order," *The Economist*, December 11, 1999, p. 21.

53 Robert O. Keohane and Joseph S. Nye Jr, "Governance in a Globalizing World," in Nye and Donahue, *Governance in a Globalizing World*.

11 Governance in a partially globalized world

Robert O. Keohane
(2000)

Facing globalization, the challenge for political science resembles that of the founders of the United States: how to design institutions for a polity of unprecedented size and diversity. Globalization produces discord and requires effective governance, but effective institutions are difficult to create and maintain. Liberal-democratic institutions must also meet standards of accountability and participation, and should foster persuasion rather than rely on coercion and interest-based bargaining. Effective institutions must rely on self-interest rather than altruism, yet both liberal-democratic legitimacy and the meaning of self-interest depend on people's values and beliefs. The analysis of beliefs, and their effect on institutional outcomes, must therefore be integrated into institutional analysis. Insights from branches of political science as diverse as game theory, rational-choice institutionalism, historical institutionalism, and democratic theory can help political scientists understand how to design institutions on a world – and human – scale.

Talk of globalization is common today in the press and increasingly in political science. Broadly speaking, globalization means the shrinkage of distance on a world scale through the emergence and thickening of networks of connections – environmental and social as well as economic (Held *et al.* 1999; Keohane and Nye [1977] 2001). Forms of limited globalization have existed for centuries, as exemplified by the Silk Road. Globalization took place during the last decades of the nineteenth century, only to be reversed sharply during the thirty years after World War I. It has returned even more strongly recently, although it remains far from complete. We live in a partially globalized world.

Globalization depends on effective governance, now as in the past. Effective governance is not inevitable. If it occurs, it is more likely to take place through interstate cooperation and transnational networks than through a world state. But even if national states retain many of their present functions, effective governance of a partially – and increasingly – globalized world will require more extensive international institutions. Governance arrangements to promote cooperation and help resolve conflict must be developed if globalization is not to stall or go into reverse.

Not all patterns of globalization would be beneficial. It is easy to conjure up nightmare scenarios of a globalized world controlled by self-serving elites working to depress wages and suppress local political autonomy. So we need to engage in normative as well as positive analysis. To make a partially globalized world benign, we need not just effective governance but the *right kind* of governance.

My analysis begins with two premises. The first is that increased interdependence among human beings produces discord, since self-regarding actions affect the welfare of others. At worst, the effects of international interdependence include war. As international relations "realists" have long recognized, interdependence and lack of governance make a deadly mixture. This Hobbesian premise can be stated in a more positive form: Globalization creates potential gains from cooperation. This argument is often seen as "liberal" and is associated with Adam Smith and David Ricardo, but it is actually complementary to Hobbes's point. The gains of cooperation loom larger relative to the alternative of unregulated conflict. Both realists and liberals agree that under conditions of interdependence, institutions are essential if people are to have opportunities to pursue the good life (Hobbes [1651] 1967; Keohane 1984; Keohane and Nye [1977] 2001).

My second premise is that institutions can foster exploitation or even oppression. As Judith Shklar (1984, 244) expresses it, "no liberal ever forgets that governments are coercive." The result is what I will call the governance dilemma: Although institutions are essential for human life, they are also dangerous. Pessimistic about voluntary cooperation, Hobbes firmly grasped the authoritarian horn of the governance dilemma. We who are unwilling to accept Hobbes's solution incur an obligation to try to explain how effective institutions that serve human interests can be designed and maintained. We must ask the question that Plato propounded more than two millenia ago: Who guards the guardians?

Clearly, the stakes are high: no less than peace, prosperity, and freedom. Political science as a profession should accept the challenge of discovering how well-structured institutions could enable the *world* to have "a new birth of freedom" (Lincoln 1863). We need to reflect on what we, as political scientists, know that could help actors in global society design and maintain institutions that would make possible the good life for our descendants.

In the first section of this essay I sketch what might be called the "ideal world." What normative standards should institutions meet, and what categories should we use to evaluate institutions according to those standards? I turn next to what we know about real institutions – why they exist, how they are created and maintained, and what this implies about their actual operation. In the concluding section I try to bring ideal and reality together to discuss institutional design. Are there ways by which we can resolve the governance dilemma, using institutions to promote cooperation and create order, without succumbing to exploitation or tyranny?

Desirable institutions for a partially globalized world

Democratic theorists emphasize that citizens should reflect on politics and exercise their collective will (Rousseau [1762] 1978), based on what Jurgen Habermas (1996, 296) has called "a culturally established background consensus shared by the citizenry." Governments derive their just powers from the consent of the governed, as the American Declaration of Independence proclaims, and also from their reflective participation.

To the potential utopianism of democratic thought I juxtapose what a former president of this association, who was also my teacher, called the liberalism of fear (Shklar 1984). In the tradition of realistic liberalism, I believe that the people require institutional protection both from self-serving elites and from their worst impulses, from what James Madison ([1787] 1961) in *Federalist 10* called the "violence of faction." Madison and Shklar demonstrate that liberalism need not be optimistic about human nature. Indeed, at the global scale the supply of rogues may be expected to expand with the extent of the market. Institutional protection from the arbitrary exercise of coercion, or authoritative exploitation, will be as important at the global level as at the level of the national state.

The discourse theory of Habermas restates liberal arguments in the language of communicative rationality. Legitimacy, in this view, rests on institutionalized procedures for open communication and collective reflection. Or, as Habermas (1996, 304) quotes John Dewey ([1927] 1954, 208), "the essential need is the improvement of the methods and conditions of debate, discussion, and persuasion." The ideal that Habermas, John Rawls (1971), Robert Dahl (1976, 45–6), and many other political philosophers have upheld is that of rational persuasion – changing others' minds on the basis of reason, not coercion, manipulation, or material sanctions. Persuasion in practice is much more complex than this ideal type, but seeking to move toward this ideal seems to me to be crucial for acceptable governance in a partially globalized world.

With these normative considerations in mind, we can ask: What political institutions would be appropriate for a partially globalized world? Political institutions are persistent and connected sets of formal and informal rules within which attempts at influence take place. In evaluating institutions, I am interested in their *consequences, functions, and procedures*. On all three dimensions, it would be quixotic to expect global governance to reach the standard of modern democracies or polyarchies, which Dahl (1989) has analyzed so thoroughly. Instead, we should aspire to a more loosely coupled system at the global level that attains the major objectives for which liberal democracy, or polyarchy, is designed at the national level.

Consequences

We can think of outcomes in terms of how global governance affects the life situations of individuals. In outlining these outcome-related objectives, I combine Amartya Sen's concept of capabilities with Rawls's conception of justice. Sen (1999, 75) begins with the Aristotelian concept of "human functioning" and defines a person's "capability" as "the alternative combinations of functionings that are feasible for her to achieve." A person's "capability set represents the freedom to achieve: the alternative functioning combinations from which this person can choose" (p. 75). Governance should enhance the capability sets of the people being governed, leading to enhancements in their personal security, freedom to make choices, and welfare as measured by such indices as the UN Human Development Index. And it should do so in a just way, which I think of in the terms made famous by Rawls (1971). Behind the "veil of ignorance," not knowing one's future situation, people should regard the arrangements for determining the distribution of capabilities as just. As a summary set of indicators, J. Roland Pennock's (1966) list holds up quite well: security, liberty, welfare, and justice.

Functions

The world for which we need to design institutions will be culturally and politically so diverse that most functions of governance should be performed at local and national levels, on the principle familiar to students of federalism or of the European Union's notion of "subsidiarity." Five key functions, however, should be handled at least to some extent by regional or global institutions.

The first of these functions is to limit the use of large-scale violence. Warfare has been endemic in modern world politics, and modern "total warfare" all but obliterates the distinction between combatants and noncombatants, rendering the "hard shell" of the state permeable (Herz 1959). All plans for global governance, from the incremental to the utopian, begin with the determination, in the opening words of the United Nations Charter (1945), "to save succeeding generations from the scourge of war."

The second function is a generalization of the first. Institutions for global governance will need to limit the negative externalities of decentralized action. A major implication of interdependence is that it provides opportunities for actors to externalize the costs of their actions onto others. Examples include "beggar thy neighbor" monetary policies, air pollution by upwind countries, and the harboring of transnational criminals, terrorists, or former dictators. Much international conflict and discord can be interpreted as resulting from such negative externalities; much international cooperation takes the form of mutual adjustment of policy to reduce these externalities or internalize some of their costs (Keohane 1984). Following the convention in the international relations literature, I will refer to these situations, which resemble classic prisoners' dilemmas, as collaboration games (Martin 1992; Stein 1983).

The third function of governance institutions is to provide *focal points* in coordination games (Fearon 1998; Krasner 1991; Martin 1992; Schelling 1960). In situations with a clear focal point, no one has an incentive to defect. Great efficiency gains can be achieved by agreeing on a single standard – for measurement, technical specifications, or language communication. Actors may find it difficult, for distributional reasons, to reach such an agreement, but after an institutionalized solution has been found, it will be self-enforcing.

The fourth major function of governance institutions for a partially globalized world is to deal with system disruptions. As global networks have become tighter and more complex, they have generated systemic effects that are often unanticipated (Jervis 1997). Examples include the Great Depression (Kindleberger 1978); global climate change; the world financial crisis of 1997–98, with its various panics culminating in the panic of August 1998 following the Russian devaluation; and the Melissa and Lovebug viruses that hit the Internet in 2000. Some of these systemic effects arise from situations that have the structure of collaboration games in which incentives exist for defection. In the future, biotechnology, genetic manipulation, and powerful technologies of which we are as yet unaware may, like market capitalism, combine great opportunity with systemic risk.

The fifth major function of global governance is to provide a guarantee against the worst forms of abuse, particularly involving violence and deprivation, so that people can use their capabilities for productive purposes. Tyrants who murder their own people may need to be restrained or removed by outsiders. Global inequality leads to differences in capabilities that are so great as to be morally indefensible and to which concerted international action is an appropriate response. Yet, the effects of globalization on inequality are much more complicated than they are often portrayed. Whereas average per-capita income has vastly increased during the last forty years, cross-national inequality in such income does not seem to have changed dramatically during the same period, although some countries have become enormously more wealthy, and others have become poorer (Firebaugh 1999). Meanwhile, inequality within countries varies enormously. Some globalizing societies have a relatively egalitarian income distribution, whereas in others it is highly unequal. Inequality seems to be complex and conditional on many features of politics and society other than degree of globalization, and effective action to enhance human functioning will require domestic as well as international efforts.

Whatever the economic effects of globalization, social globalization certainly increases the attention paid to events in distant places, highlighting abuses that are widely abhorrent. Such issue advocacy is not new: the transnational antislavery movement between 1833 and 1865 is an important historical example. Yet, the expansion of concern about human rights during the past two decades has been extraordinary, both in the scope of rights claimed – and frequently codified in UN agreements – and in the breadth of transnational advocacy movements and coalitions promoting such rights (Keck and Sikkink 1998). Concern about poverty, however, has not been matched by effective action to eliminate the source of human misery (World Bank 2000).

Procedures

Liberal democrats are concerned not only with outcomes but also with procedures. I will put forward three procedural criteria for an acceptable global governance system. The first is *accountability*: publics need to have ways to hold elites accountable for their actions. The second is *participation*: democratic principles require that some level of participation in making collective decisions be open to all competent adults in the society. The third is *persuasion*, facilitated by the existence of institutionalized procedures for communication, insulated to a significant extent from the use and threats of force and sanctions, and sufficiently open to hinder manipulation.

Our standards of accountability, participation, and persuasion will have to be quite minimal to be realistic in a polity of perhaps ten billion people. Because I assume the maintenance of national societies and state or state-like governance arrangements, I do not presume that global governance will benefit from consensus on deep substantive principles. Global governance will have to be limited and somewhat shallow if it is to be sustainable. Overly ambitious attempts at global governance would necessarily rely too much on material sanctions and coercion. The degree of consensus on principles – even procedural principles, such as those of accountability, participation, and persuasion – would be too weak to support decisions that reach deeply into people's lives and the meanings that they construct for themselves. The point of presenting ideal criteria is to portray a *direction*, not a blueprint.

Now that these normative cards are on the table, I turn to some of the positive contributions of political science. In the next section I ask how we can use our knowledge as political scientists to design sustainable institutions that would perform the functions I have listed. In the final section I explore how these institutions could facilitate the democratic procedural virtues of accountability, participation, and persuasion. These issues are all part of one overriding question: How can we design institutions that would facilitate human functioning, in the sense of Aristotle or Sen?

Institutional existence and power

How can authoritative institutions exist at all? This is a question that Rousseau ([1762] 1978, I, 1) claimed not to know how to answer and that students of international politics have recently debated. No student of international relations is likely to forget that institutions are fragile and that institutional success is problematic.

To address this issue, I begin with the contributions of rational-choice institutionalism, which has insistently sought to raise the question of institutional existence and has addressed it with the tools of equilibrium analysis (Shepsle 1986). To design appropriate and legitimate global institutions, we need to fashion a rich version of institutionalist theory, which uses the power of the rationality assumption without being hobbled by a crude psychology of material self-interest. But before discussing such a theory, it is important to indicate briefly why a simple functional answer is not sufficient.

The inadequacy of functional theories

One can imagine a simple functional theory of global institutions by which the demand for governance, generated by globalism, creates its own supply. Such an account has the defining characteristic that the real or anticipated effects of a process play a causal role (Cohen 1978). A functional account can only be convincing if the causal mechanism for adaptation is clearly specified. In biology, one such mechanism is Darwinian evolution, which in its strong form implies environmental determinism. The selection environment determines which individual organisms, or other units, survive. Although the individual units may undergo random mutations, they do not act in a goal-directed fashion, and they do not fundamentally affect the environment that selects them. But environmental determinism and the absence of goal-seeking behavior are not assumptions that seem to fit human social and political reality (Kahler 1999). Hence, evolutionary arguments in the social sciences have mostly stayed at the level of metaphor. They certainly do not provide us with a warrant for a functionalist account of how governance arrangements for globalization would emerge, since the causal mechanism for selection seems even weaker at the global level than with respect to competition among states.

The other causal mechanism for functional theories involves rational anticipation. Agents, seeing the expected consequences of various courses of action, plan their actions and design institutions in order to maximize the net benefits that they receive. Ronald Coase (1960) and Oliver Williamson (1985) use functional theory in Cohen's sense to explain why firms exist at all. "Transactional economies" account for choices of markets or hierarchies (Williamson 1975, 248). That is, the more efficient organizational arrangement will somehow be selected.

But there is a micro-macro problem here, since arrangements most efficient for society are not necessarily optimal for the leaders of the organization. At the level of societies, as Douglass North has pointed out, the history of real economies is one of persistent *inefficiency*, which he explains essentially in terms of the free rider problem. Even if an institutional innovation would increase efficiency, no one may have the incentive to develop it, since institutional innovation is a public good (North 1981, 68; 1990, 93).

Indeed, rent-seeking coalitions have incentives to resist socially beneficial institutional innovations that would reduce their own advantages (Olson 1982).

Functional solutions to the problem of institutional existence are therefore incomplete. There must be political entrepreneurs with both the capacity and the incentives to invest in the creation of institutions and the monitoring and enforcement of rules. Unless the entrepreneurs can capture selective benefits from their activities, they will not create institutions. And these institutions will not be effective unless sufficient compliance is induced by a combination of material and normative incentives. To use economic language, problems of supply (Bates 1988; Shepsle and Weingast 1995) as well as demand have to be solved.

Mancur Olson's (1965) analysis of the logic of collective action has two major implications for the governance of a globalized world. First, there is no guarantee that governance arrangements will be created that will sustain high levels of globalism. As Western history reveals, notably in the collapse of the Roman Empire and in World War I, extensive social and economic relations can be undermined by a collapse of governance. At the global as well as national level, political scientists need to be as concerned with degrees of governance as with forms of governance (Huntington 1968, 1).

The second implication of Olson's insight is that we cannot understand why institutions vary so much in their degree of effectiveness simply by studying institutions. To focus only on existing institutions is to select on the dependent variable, giving us no variance and no leverage on our problem. On the contrary, we need to explore situations in which institutions have *not* been created, despite a widespread belief that if such institutions were created, they would be beneficial. Or we can compare situations in which institutions exist to earlier ones in which they were absent (cf. Tilly 1975, 1990).

Institutional theory and bargaining equilibria

Rational-choice institutionalism in political science insists that institutions, to persist, must reflect bargaining equilibria of games in which actors seek to pursue their own interests, as they define them. This perspective, stated elegantly by Kenneth Shepsle (1986), is not new in its essentials. Indeed, in investigating the effects of constitutions, Aristotle held that vesting authority in the middle class will promote rationality and the protection of property rights (*Politics* IV, xi, 4–15).[1] He sought to explain variations in constitutional forms by referring to variations in social conditions (*Politics* IV, iii, 1–6). And he argued that a stable constitution is not only one that a majority seeks to maintain but also one for which "there is no single section in all the state which would favor a change to a different constitution" (IV, ix, 10).

In the terms of rational-choice institutionalism, Aristotle was interested both in institutional equilibrium and equilibrium institutions. So were Smith (1776) and Madison ([1787] 1961). The eighteenth century view, which resonates with rational-choice institutionalism, was that the "passions" of people in bourgeois society can be interpreted in terms of their interests (Hirschman 1977, 110) and can be moderated by wise institutions.

Yet, rational-choice institutionalism has been more rigorous and more relentless than its predecessors in insisting on explaining, by reference to incentives, why institutions exist. Because rational-choice theorists seek to explain in formal terms why institutions exist, they have to confront directly two critical questions. (1) Under what conditions will political entrepreneurs have incentives to create institutions? (2) What makes such institutions stable?

Since institutions are public goods, they are likely to be underproduced and, at the limit, not produced at all. Hence there must be selective incentives for politicians to invest in institutional innovations (Aldrich 1995). In addition, significant advantages must accrue to institutional innovators, such as conferring on them control over future rules or creating barriers to entry to potential competitors. Otherwise, latecomers could free ride on the accomplishments of their predecessors, and anticipation of such free riding would discourage institutional innovation. Another barrier to entry for latecomers may be ideology. Insofar as only a few ideologies, quite distinct from one another, can exist, first movers would gain an advantage by seizing favorable ideological ground (cf. Hinich and Munger 1994). The implication for our problem of institutional design is that first-mover advantages are essential if institutional innovation is to occur.

The European Union (EU) provides a compelling example of first-mover advantages in international organizations. New members of the EU have to accept, in their entirety, the rules already established by their predecessors. As a result, the innovators of the European Community – the six founding members – gain persistent and cumulative advantages from having written the original rules. These rules are important. Even if implementation is often slow, during the 1990s all members of the EU had implemented more than 75% of EU directives, and more than half had implemented more than 85% (Martin 2000, 174). First-mover advantages are also evident in the processes of writing national electoral rules: those who win an earlier election create rules that subsequently favor their party, policy positions, and personal careers (Bawn 1993; Remington and Smith 1996).

The second key question is that of stability. If institutional rules constrain majorities, why do these majorities not simply change the institutional rules to remove the constraint? If they do, what happens to the "structure-induced equilibrium" that solves Arrow's paradox of social choice (Riker 1980)? In other words, why do institutions not simply "inherit" rather than solve Arrow's paradox (Aldrich 1993)?

The general answer seems to be that institutions generate rules that resolve Arrow's paradox, for example, by giving agenda-setting power to particular agents (Shepsle 1986) or by requiring supermajorities to change institutional arrangements. These rules ensure that majorities cannot alter them easily when the median voter's preferences change.

First-mover advantages and agenda control provide incentives for institutional innovation and help to stabilize institutions. They operate somewhat differently, however, in coordination and collaboration situations, as described above. In situations of coordination, institutions, once accepted, are in equilibrium. Participants do not have incentives to deviate unilaterally from widely accepted standards for Internet connectivity or airline traffic control. Institutions to solve collaboration problems are much more fragile. After an agreement on institutions to solve collaboration problems is reached, participants typically have incentives to defect if they expect to avoid retaliation from others (Martin 1992).

Students of international relations have used this distinction to show how much more difficult it is to maintain collaboration institutions: monitoring and enforcement are essential. Furthermore, during the bargaining process "hold-outs" may be able to negotiate better terms for themselves in collaboration than in coordination situations, since threats to remain outside collaboration-oriented institutions are more credible than threats to remain outside a widely accepted coordination equilibrium. In international relations, the side-payments negotiated by China and India to join the ozone regime, and the refusal so far of developing countries to be bound by emissions restrictions in a climate change regime, illustrate this point.

If we keep our normative as well as positive lenses in focus, we will see that this apparent advantage of coordination institutions has a dark side. Initiators of coordination institutions can exercise great influence over the choice of focal points, thereby gaining an enduring first-mover advantage over their rivals (Krasner 1991). Collaboration institutions do not offer such first-mover advantages, since participants can defect at lower cost. Collaboration institutions therefore provide fewer opportunities, as compared to coordination institutions, for coercion of latecomers. Real institutions usually combine coordination and collaboration functions, and therefore also contain a mixture of destabilizing (or liberating) elements and stabilizing (or potentially oppressive) ones.

Institutions, whether emphasizing coordination or collaboration, necessarily institutionalize bias, in favor of groups that have agenda control or wish to maintain the status quo. It is therefore not surprising that advocates of social equality, such as Thomas Jefferson, and democrats such as Rousseau, are often suspicious of institutions. Barriers to competition confer monopolistic privileges and therefore create normative problems. Yet, institutions are essential for the good life.

Normatively, those of us who believe in Shklar's (1984) "liberalism of fear" both support institutions and are cautious about them. We support them because we know that without well-functioning political institutions, life is indeed "nasty, brutish, and short." But we are suspicious, since we understand how self-serving elites can use institutions to engage in theft and oppression. In a partially globalized world, we will need institutions of broader scope. But as in national democracies, eternal vigilance will be the price of liberty.

Rational-choice theory has led to fruitful inquiries into the issue of why institutions exist, because it relentlessly questions any apparent equilibrium. The skeptical question – why should institutions exist at all? – has ironically led to a deeper understanding of institutions than has the assumption that we could take their existence for granted and focus on how they work.

The limits of rational egoism

Commenting on Toqueville, Albert Hirschman (1977, 125) has pointed out a normative problem with the emphasis on self-interest that I have thus far emphasized: "Social arrangements that substitute the interests for the passions as the guiding principle of human action for the many can have the side effect of killing the civic spirit." There is also an analytical problem: we know from a variety of work that this egoistic picture is seriously incomplete.

Rationalist theory often carries with it the heavy baggage of egoism. People are viewed as self-interested individuals whose incentives are strictly shaped by their environment, including the rules of the institutions in which they are located. The most sophisticated version of this argument does not make the essentialist claim that "human nature" is fundamentally egoistic but gives priority instead to an instrumentalist logic. Hans J. Morgenthau (1967, Chap. 1), for example, argues that since power is a necessary means to other goals in international politics, we can analyze leaders' behavior in terms of power even if they do not seek power for its own sake (see also Wolfers 1962, Chap. 7). For rationalist students of American and comparative politics, political leaders may have a multiplicity of goals, but since continuation in office is a necessary means to achieve any of them, it can be regarded as a universal objective of politicians, whether purely instrumental or consummatory (Geddes 1994; Mayhew 1974).

Thoughtful theorists of rational choice recognize that the assumption of egoism oversimplifies social reality. Norms of reciprocity and fairness often affect social behavior (Levi 1997; Ostrom 1990). The theoretical predictions derived from the assumption of egoism encounter serious predictive failure in experimental settings (Ostrom 1998). And survey research shows that citizens evaluate the legitimacy of the legal system on the basis not only of their own success in dealing with it but also of their perceptions of its procedural fairness (Tyler 1990).

Sometimes the assumption of egoism is defended on the ground that only with such simple models can solutions be found to strategic games. But the folk theorem of game theory demonstrates that an essentially unlimited number of equilibria appear in all interesting games. When the equilibrium rabbit is to be pulled from the hat, we are as likely to get a thousand rabbits as one. Equilibria multiply like rabbits in Australia and are about as useful. As

Elinor Ostrom (1998, 4) commented in her address to this association three years ago, the assumptions of rationality, amoral self-interest, and lack of influence from social norms lead to explanatory chaos: "Everything is predicted: optimal outcomes, the Pareto-inferior Nash equilibria, and everything in between."

In addressing the problems of institutional design, it is a good thing that people are not purely egotistical. It would be difficult to understand the creation of major political institutions – from the US Constitution to UN-sponsored human rights agreements – if we took egotism and the free-rider problem too seriously. We are indeed wise to assume that institutions, to be in long-term equilibrium, must be broadly consistent with the self-interest of powerful actors. But we cannot understand the origins of institutions if we banish principled action from our analytic world.

Egoists have a hard time overcoming problems of mistrust, because they know that everyone has an incentive to disguise his or her preferences. Only costly signals will be credible; but the cost of signalling reduces the prospective value of cooperation and limits the agreements that can be reached. Egoists also have difficulty solving bargaining problems, since they do not recognize norms of fairness that can provide focal points for agreement. Cool practitioners of self-interest, known to be such, may be less able to cooperate productively than individuals who are governed by emotions that send reliable signals, such as love or sympathy (Frank 1988). In Sen's (1977, 336) phrase, people in purely rational-choice models are "rational fools," incapable of distinguishing among egoistic preferences, sympathy, and commitments.

As Sen makes clear, rejecting the premise of egoism does not imply rejecting the assumption of rationality – more or less bounded in Herbert Simon's (1985) sense. Nor does it imply altruism: people can empathize with others without being self-sacrificing. What it does is demand that norms and values be brought back into the picture. Committed individuals, seeking policy goals as well as office for its own sake, and constrained by norms of fairness or even by more transcendental values, can nevertheless calculate as rationally as the egoists of economic theory.

In thinking about a partially globalized world, one might be tempted to dismiss half the governance dilemma by pointing out that because international institutions are very weak, they are unlikely to be oppressive. For example, contemporary opponents of globalization and associated international institutions have sought to portray the World Trade Organization (WTO) as some sort of bureaucratic monster, although my own university's budget allocates more money in two weeks than WTO spends in a year.[2]

True as it is, this appeal to institutional weakness is not fully convincing. The problem is not that international organizations are huge and oppressive but that they are seen as serving the vested interests of the powerful and privileged. And they do. Indeed, they are institutions of the privileged, by the privileged, and all too often for the privileged. There are severe restraints on the powers of the international civil servants who lead these organizations, but few such checks limit the ability of the strongest states, such as the United States, to dictate policies and veto personnel. Yet, in the absence of such institutions, dictation by strong states would be even more direct, less encumbered by rules. Like Churchill's aphorism about democracy, an institutionalized world is probably the worst form of governance – except for the alternatives.

Ironically, it is the privileged who often appeal to altruism – their own, of course – as the guarantee against the abuse of power. Political scientists have spent too much time debunking altruism as a general motivating factor in politics to be detained long by such claims. Anyone my age has lived through the disastrous failures of social systems, notably in Russia and China, based on the premise that human nature can be remolded. The reality is that the worst people thrive under the cover of such grand visions. In any event, the heterogeneity of the world's population makes it impossible to imagine any single ideology providing the basis for a coherent, value-based system of global governance. The answer to global governance problems does not lie in revelation.

Faced with the governance dilemma, those of us interested in governance on a world scale could retreat to the pure self-interest model. With that set of assumptions, we would probably limit world governance. We would sacrifice gains that could result from better cooperation in order to guard against rule by undemocratic, self-serving institutions responsive, in opaque ways, to powerful elites. If we were successful, the result would be to limit global governance, even at the expense of greater poverty and more violent conflict. We might think ourselves wise, but the results would be sad. Due to excessive fear, we would have sacrificed the liberal vision of progress.

Institutions, expectations, and beliefs

It may seem that we are at an impasse. Sober reliance on limited institutions based on pure self-interest could lead to a low-level "equilibrium trap." But we may be tempted to settle for such an equilibrium rather than accept oppressive global institutions.

There may be a way out of this impasse. That path is to pay more attention than we have to expectations of how others will behave and, therefore, to underlying values and beliefs. Expectations are critical determinants of action. They depend heavily on trust, reputation, and reciprocity, which depend in turn on networks of civic engagement, or social capital. Building such networks is an incremental process. Engagement in a just set of social relations helps create personal integrity, which is the basis for consistent principled action (Grant 1997). Networks of civic engagement are not easily divided into "international" and "domestic" but, rather, cross those lines (Keck and Sikkink 1998). Rational strategic action depends on the expectations and incentives that these networks create.

Until recently, students of international politics paid too little attention to beliefs. The realists insisted on the dominance of interests and power, which they traced to material factors. Marxist and neoclassical political economists also relied on material forces for their explanations. Students of institutions, such as I, sought to gain credibility by showing that our theories are as realistically based in interests and power as those of our realist adversaries, that we are not tainted by the idealist brush. Ironically enough, however, the theory of strategic interaction on which we all rely has insistently argued that beliefs are crucial to understanding any game-theoretic situation (Morrow 1994; Wendt 1999).

The fact that strategic action depends on expectations means that understanding historical and cultural context is critical to any analysis of how institutions operate. Peter Katzenstein (1993, 1996) has used the differing responses of Germany and Japan to military defeat and economic revival to make this point in a cogent and forceful way. Historical explorations of institutional phenomena and negotiations may draw effectively on rational-choice theory, but they must go well beyond its premises to describe multi-dimensional human behavior (Bates *et al.* 1998). Indeed, political scientists have quite a bit to learn from international law, which studies rational strategic action in the context of rules and rule making, deeply structured by interests and power but also reflecting the influence of ideas on interests and on how power is exercised (Grewe 2000).

A major task before our discipline is how to connect rational strategic action with beliefs and values. In her presidential address three years ago, Ostrom (1998) linked rational-choice theory with the laboratory experiments of cognitive science to show that institutional incentives, fundamental norms of trust, and the practice of reciprocity (Axelord 1984; Ostrom 1990) all provide crucial foundations of cooperation. "At the core of a behavioral explanation," Ostrom (1998, 12) said, "are the links between the trust that individuals have in others, the investment others make in trustworthy reputations, and the probability that participants will use reciprocity norms." That is, principled values, "congealed" in institutions, provide the basis for meaningful rational actions and direct such actions in ways that we can describe and explain (Riker 1980).

Robert Putnam's *Making Democracy Work* exemplifies a productive analysis of the connections among values, social norms, and rational behavior. Putnam argues that "networks of civic engagement" produce better government. Why does he think so? Not because engaged people necessarily work altruistically for the common good but because these networks increase costs of defection, facilitate communication, and create favorable expectations of others' likely actions (Putnam 1993, 173–4).

Understanding beliefs is not opposed to understanding interests. On the contrary, interests are incomprehensible without an awareness of the beliefs that lie behind them. Indeed, even the financial self-interest so dear to political economists implies acceptance of norms that would be incomprehensible in many societies, whether those imagined by Jean-Jacques Rousseau or studied by twentieth-century anthropologists. The values and beliefs that are dominant within a society provide the foundations for rational strategy.

Even beliefs about beliefs can be as solid as any material interests. As Barry O'Neill shows brilliantly in a book awarded the Woodrow Wilson Prize, prestige refers to "beliefs about beliefs" – whether people think that others hold a high opinion of someone (O'Neill 1999, 193). Prestige is a "social fact," like a dollar bill (Searle 1995): Although it is genuinely real, its importance does not lie in its material manifestation but in the beliefs people hold. Both money and prestige matter a great deal in politics, but only insofar as people hold beliefs about others' beliefs.

To see how beliefs relate to issues of institutional design, think about two possible worlds of the future. In one of them, the "normative anarchy" portrayed by the "political realism" of the late twentieth century (Waltz 1979) prevails. That is, there is no consensus about principled beliefs on the basis of which governance across national boundaries can take place, and transnational networks of people with similar beliefs are virtually nonexistant. The only norm on which there is general agreement is the "antinorm" of sovereignty: the principle that the rulers of each state are supreme internally and independent from external authority (Bull 1977). Since I expect self-interested agents to continue to dominate among politicians, I would expect, in this world, familiar patterns of modern Western international politics to persist. Rationally egoistic politicians would have few incentives to fight for principles of human rights, since to do so they would have to overcome both collective action problems and ridicule from "realistic" statesmen and academics.

Now consider another world, in which certain principles have become generally accepted – as opposition to slavery became generally accepted in the nineteenth century and as certain human rights seem to be becoming accepted now (Keck and Sikkink 1998). In this world, transnational advocacy networks would be active. Behavior in this world would, of course, be different from that in the first world. Even those who do not subscribe to these principles would have to calculate the costs of acting counter to them.

Now let us go a step farther and imagine that the principled innovators of the new principles, and the value-based transnational networks, disappear, to be replaced by purely rational egoists. Would the egoists seek immediately to overturn these norms of human rights? Probably not, unless they had compelling internal reasons, as tyrants, to do so. Ordinary egoists, governing nontyrannically, would have interests in mimicking the principled leaders whom they succeed. Furthermore, the egoists would face serious collective action problems in overturning norms of human rights: their counterpart egoists would have an interest in defending those rights in order to enhance their reputation as principled agents. As a result, egoistic self-interest would counsel them to uphold the norms established and even to bear some costs in order to send credible signals that they believe in the norms (even though, by assumption, they do not). The effect of former principles would persist for a while, although it would eventually fade.

What this thought-experiment illustrates is a simple but fundamental point. Beliefs in norms and principles – even beliefs only held in the past – can profoundly affect rational action in the present. Joseph Schumpeter ([1942] 1950, 137) made the famous argument sixty years ago that capitalism requires precapitalist values: "The stock exchange is a poor substitute for the Holy Grail." The facile response to his argument at millennium's end could be: "Yes, but he didn't take into account NASDAQ." More seriously, however, the varieties of capitalism in the world today, from Japanese corporatism to American legalism to Russian organized theft, make it clear that what is economically rational in each context varies enormously. Schumpeter was wrong about the staying power of capitalism but right about the dependence of institutions, capitalism included, on beliefs.

Institutional design: bringing ideals and reality together

I began by sketching an ideal vision – a liberal and democratic vision – of how institutions should work. On the liberal side, it includes what one might call the liberalism of progress, represented by such eighteenth-century thinkers as Smith and Madison. But it also includes Shklar's liberalism of fear, which emphasizes the potential depravities of human nature and the pathologies of human institutions and is deeply cognizant of imperialism, totalitarianism, and the Holocaust (Arendt [1951] 1958). The liberalism of fear is horrified by the atrocities of Rwanda and Bosnia, but these atrocities do not shake its liberalism, which was forged in the searing recognition that human action can be horrible.

The liberalism of progress and the liberalism of fear are two sides of the same coin. They both seek to understand how otherwise unattractive human passions can nevertheless promote the general good. Madison is the American father of such a realistic liberalism, but it has deep roots both in English utilitarianism, going back to Hobbes, and in French thought (Hirschman 1977; Keohane 1980). Neither Madison nor Smith indulged in the more utopian dreams of the liberalism of progress. Even though potential gains from trade, combined with advancing technology, make it possible for all economies to prosper simultaneously, the Hobbesian desire for "power after power" gets in the way. So does greed. People often seek to gain distributional advantages not by being more productive but by gaining control of public policies in order to capture rents. Nevertheless, mercantilist theory has been proved bankrupt, and the institutions of liberal democracy have limited, although they have not eliminated, the success of rent-seeking. Smith and Madison would not be fully satisfied, but they would be gratified by the partially successful institutionalization of their ideas.

Together the liberalism of progress and the liberalism of fear emphasize the need for institutions. Smith's liberalism calls for institutions to promote exchange; Shklar's for institutions to control human vices and those individuals among us whose vices are most dangerous to others. For these institutions to be morally acceptable, they must rest both on humane beliefs and substantial mutual trust. The Mafia is not better than anarchy; the people who live under either find themselves impaled on one horn or the other of the governance dilemma.

Democratic theory is even more demanding. From a democratic standpoint it is not enough to have nonoppressive institutions that enforce rules. Accountability, participation, and persuasion are also essential. International institutions will probably never meet the standards of electoral accountability and participation that we expect of domestic democracies (Dahl 1999), so at best they will be low on a democratic scale. It is unfair to demand too much of them. But in the liberal-democratic tradition that I embrace, voluntary cooperation based on honest communication and rational persuasion provides the strongest guarantee of a legitimate process. In this section, I return to the issues of accountability, participation, and persuasion that I introduced earlier.

Accountability is not necessarily electoral, so it is essential to explore other forms of it if we are to increase accountability in global governance. Participation will probably continue to be largely local, so global governance implies viable forms of local self-governance. Finally, for global governance to be legitimate, global institutions must facilitate persuasion rather than coercion or reliance on sanctions as a means of influence. Here there seems to be considerable scope for improvement, so I will emphasize persuasion in the following discussion.

Accountability

The partially globalized world that I imagine would not be governed by a representative electoral democracy. States will remain important; and one state/one vote is not a democratic principle. National identities are unlikely to dissolve into the sense of a larger community that is necessary for democracy to thrive.

Accountability, however, can be indirectly linked to elections without a global representative democracy. Control by democratic states over international institutions can be exerted through chains of delegation. A complementary measure is to strengthen mechanisms of domestic accountability of governments to their publics. Such practices can reinforce accountability insofar as transparency ensures that people within the several states can make judgments about their own governments' performance.

Nonelectoral dimensions of accountability also exist.[3] Some international regimes seek to regulate the activities of firms and of governments, although they are weaker than their domestic counterparts, and they do not meet democratic standards as well as the "best practices" domestically. Global governance, combined with modern communications technology (including technologies for linguistic translations), can begin to generate a public space in which some people communicate with one another about public policy without regard to distance. Criticism, heard and responded to in a public space, can help generate accountability. Professional standards comprise another form of nonelectoral accountability.

Finally, markets provide a third dimension of nonelectoral accountability. Since people do not bring equal wealth to the marketplace, markets are not democratic. But they do hold firms and other institutions with hard budget constraints accountable to their consumers and investors in ways that are often more rapid and effective than electoral democracy. Advocates of principle-based change have learned to use markets on issues as diverse as promotion of infant formula in poor countries, environmental protection, and labor standards.

These mechanisms of accountability exist, in fragmented ways, at the global level, but they are *disarticulated*. They do not come together in a clear pathway by which laws are enacted and implemented. Chains of delegation are long, and some of their links are hidden behind a veil of secrecy. Incentives for politicians to hold leaders of other governments accountable are lacking. Publics, professional groups, and advocacy networks can only punish leaders inconsistently. Governments, nongovernmental organizations, and firms that do not rely on brand names may be immune from market-based sanctions. In devising acceptable institutions for global governance, accountability needs to be built into the mechanisms of rule making and rule implementation.

Participation

Individual participation is essential to democratic governance. In the past, meaningful participation has only been feasible on a face-to-face basis, as in the New England town meeting, and it has been argued that, "in its deepest and richest sense, community must always remain a matter of face-to-face intercourse" (Dewey [1927] 1954, 211). Yet the costs of communication between any two points of the world no longer depend on distance, and within 50 years we can expect the forms of such communication to change in extraordinary ways. Although it is difficult to imagine good substitutes for the multiple dimensions – verbal, visual, and tactile – by which communication occurs when people are close to one another, the potential of communications technology should not be underestimated.

More serious barriers to global democratic participation can be found in numbers and cultural diversity. Meaningful collective participation in global governance in a world of perhaps ten billion people will surely have to occur through smaller units, but these may not need to be geographically based. In the partially globalized world that I am imagining, participation will occur in the first instance among people who can understand one another, although they may be dispersed around the world in "disaporic public spheres," which

Arjun Appuradai (1996, 22) calls "the crucibles of a postnational political order."

Whatever the geographical quality of the units that emerge, democratic legitimacy for such a governance system will depend on the democratic character of these smaller units of governance. It will also depend on the maintenance of sufficient autonomy and authority for those units, if participation at this level is to remain meaningful.

Persuasion and institutions

Since the global institutions that I imagine do not have superior coercive force to that of states, the influence processes that they authorize will have to be legitimate. Legitimacy is, of course, a classic subject of political philosophy and political science (Rousseau [1762] 1978, book 1, Chap. 1; see also Hobbes [1651] 1967, Chaps. 17–18; Locke [1689] 1967, Chap. 9; Weber [1920] 1978, 214). In the liberal tradition that I embrace, voluntary cooperation based on honest communication and rational persuasion provides the strongest guarantee of a legitimate process (Habermas 1996; Rawls 1971). To understand the potential for legitimate governance in a partially globalized world, we need to understand how institutions can facilitate rational persuasion. How do we design institutions of governance so as to increase the scope for reflection and persuasion, as opposed to force, material incentives, and fraud?

"Persuasion" means many things to many political scientists. I will define it with reference to two other processes, *bargaining* and *signalling*. In a bargaining situation, actors know their interests and interact reciprocally to seek to realize them. In a signalling situation, a set of actors communicates to an audience, seeking to make credible promises or threats (Hinich and Munger 1994). Both processes essentially involve flows of information. If successful, these flows enable actors to overcome informational asymmetries (Akerlof 1970) as well as private information (Fearon 1995) and therefore reach mutually beneficial solutions. Neither bargaining nor signalling as such involves any changes in *preferences over attributes*, that is, over the values involved in choices.

If targets of influence change their choices as a result of bargaining and signalling, they do so by recalculating their own strategies as a result of new information they receive about the strategies of others. That is, they become aware that others will not behave as they had previously expected. In bargaining, a quid pro quo is involved; in signalling, threats and promises may be unilateral.

Persuasion, as I will use it, involves changing people's choices of alternatives *independently of their calculations about the strategies of other players*. People who are persuaded, in my sense of the word, change their minds for reasons other than a recalculation of advantageous choices in light of new information about others' behavior. They may do so because they change their preferences about the underlying attributes. They may consider new attributes during processes of choice. Or they may alter their conceptions of how attributes are linked to alternatives.

Unlike bargaining on the basis of specific reciprocity, persuasion must appeal to norms, principles, and values that are shared by participants in a conversation. Persuasion requires giving reasons for actions, reasons that go beyond assertions about power, interests, and resolve (Elster 1998; Risse 2000). Karl Deutsch (1953, 52) argued long ago that to be susceptible to persuasion, people "must already be inwardly divided in their thought," that there must be "some contradictions, actual or implied, among their habits or values." These contradictions, sharpened by discussion, may lead to reflection and even attitude change.

Persuasion is a major subject of study in social psychology (McGuire 1985; Petty and Wegener 1998). Thousands of experiments later, the essential message from this field is that, even in the laboratory, it is difficult to find strong and consistent relationships that explain attitude change. As William McGuire (1985, 304) puts it, "human motivation is sufficiently complex so that multiple and even contradictory needs may underlie any act."

What we do know about persuasion in politics indicates that it consistently involves various degrees of agenda control and manipulation. Rational or open persuasion, which occurs when people change their choices of alternatives voluntarily under conditions of frank communication, is an interesting ideal type but does not describe many major political processes. Yet, the ideal is important, since it is so central to the liberal-democratic vision of politics. Indeed, thinking about persuasion helps restate the central normative question of this address: How can institutions of governance be designed so as to increase the scope for reflection, and therefore persuasion, as opposed to force, material incentives, and fraud?

If governance were exercised only by those with direct stakes in issues, such a question might have no answer. Actors could be expected to use their resources and their guile to achieve their desired objectives. And the institutions would themselves "inherit" the inequalities prevalent in the societies that produced them, as Rousseau and many successors have pointed out (Aldrich 1993; Riker 1980). Indeed, choices of electoral institutions can often be traced to the policy, party, and personal preferences of the politicians who created them (Bawn 1993; Remington and Smith 1996).

One feature of both democratic governance and contemporary international institutions, however, is that decision making is not limited to the parties to a dispute. On the contrary, actors without a direct stake in the issues under consideration may play important roles, as members of the mass public in democracies and legislators often do on issues arising for decision through voting. In general, the legalization of rules – domestically, and more recently in international politics – requires the formation of durable rules that apply to classes of cases and puts interpretation and rule-application into the hands of third parties, whose authority depends on maintaining a reputation for impartiality (Goldstein *et al.* 2000). Legalization also increases the role of precedents. Precedents matter, not because loopholes are impossible to find or because they cannot be overruled, but because the status quo will prevail in the absence of a decision to overturn it.

Some third parties will have calculable interests that closely parallel those of the principal disputants or advocates. Others may have strongly held beliefs that determine their positions. Some may accept side-payments or succumb to coercive pressure. But still others may lack both intense beliefs and direct stakes in the outcome. Legal requirements or internalized normative standards may inhibit them from accepting inducements for their votes. Even more important, uncertainty about the effect of future rules may make it difficult for them to calculate their own interests. Rule makers face a peculiar form of "winner's curse": they risk constructing durable rules that suit them in the immediate instance but will operate against their interests in the unknown future.

Insofar as uncertainty is high, actors face a situation similar to one covered by a "veil of ignorance" (Rawls 1971). In game-theoretic terms, the actors may still have preferences over outcomes, but these preferences over outcomes do not directly imply preferences over strategies, since actors do not know their future situations. In experiments, introducing a veil of ignorance in prisoners' dilemma games without communication induces a dramatic increase in the willingness of subjects to cooperate (Frohlich and Oppenheimer 1996). It is reasonable to hypothesize that under conditions of uncertainty in the real world, the chain of "inheritability" will be broken, and actors' preferences about future outcomes will not dictate their choices of alternatives in the present.

Under conditions of authority for impartial third parties, or high uncertainty about future interests, opportunities for persuasion are likely to appear, even if everyone is a rational egoist. Egoists have a long-term interest in rules that will correspond to an acceptable general principle, since they may be subject to these rules in the future. Various principles could be chosen – expected utility maximization, the maximum principle (Rawls 1971, 152), minimax regret (Riker 1996), or utility maximization subject to a floor minimum, which is the prevailing choice in laboratory experiments (Frohlich and Oppenheimer 1992). Insofar as the consequences and functions of institutions are not seriously degraded, institutions that encourage reflection and persuasion are normatively desirable and should be fostered.

Conclusion

I have asked how we can overcome the governance dilemma on a global scale. That is, how can we gain benefits from institutions without becoming their victims? How can we help design institutions for a partially globalized world that perform valuable functions while respecting democratic values? And how can we foster beliefs that maintain benign institutions? My answers are drawn, mostly implicitly, from various schools of work in political science.

From rational-choice institutionalism, we learn both the value of institutions and the need for incentives for institutional innovation. These incentives imply privileges for the elite, which have troubling implications for popular control.

From a variety of perspectives, including game theory, the study of political culture, and work on the role that ideas play in politics, we learn how important beliefs are in reaching equilibrium solutions, and how institutionalized beliefs structure situations of political choice.

From traditional political theory, we are reminded of the importance of normative beliefs for the practice of politics – and for institutions. It is not sufficient to create institutions that are effective; they must be accompanied by beliefs that respect and foster human freedom.

From historical institutionalism and political sociology, we understand how values and norms operate in society. Without such understanding, we can neither comprehend the varying expectations on which people rationally act nor design institutions based on normative views. We abdicate our responsibility if we simply assume material self-interest, as economists are wont to do.

From democratic theory, we discover the crucial roles of accountability, participation, and especially persuasion in creating legitimate political institutions.

These lessons are in tension with one another. Institutional stability is often at odds with innovation and may conflict with accountability. Protection against oppression can conflict with energetic governance; a practical reliance on self-interest can conflict with the desire to expand the role of persuasion and reflection. Governance, however, is about reconciling tensions; it is Max Weber's ([1919] 1946) "boring of hard boards."

As students of political philosophy, our objective should be to help our students, colleagues, and the broader public understand both the necessity for governance in a partially globalized world and the principles that would make such governance legitimate. As positive political scientists, we need to continue to analyze the conditions under which different forms and levels of governance are feasible. As practitioners of a policy science, we need to offer advice about how institutions for global governance should be constituted. This advice must be realistic, not romantic. We must begin with real people, not some mythological beings of higher moral capability. But we need also to recognize, and seek to expand, the scope for reflection and the normative principles that reflective individuals may espouse. We should seek to design institutions so that persuasion, not merely interests and bargaining, plays an important role.

The stakes in the mission I propose are high, for the world and for political science. If global institutions are designed well, they will promote human welfare. But if we bungle the job, the results could be disastrous. Either oppression or ineptitude would likely lead to conflict and a renewed fragmentation of global politics. Effective and humane global governance arrangements are not inevitable. They will depend on human effort and on deep thinking about politics.

As we face globalization, our challenge resembles that of the founders of this country: how to design working institutions for a polity of unprecedented size and diversity. Only if we rise to that challenge will we be doing our part to ensure Lincoln's "rebirth of freedom" on a world – and human – scale.

Notes

1 All references to Aristotle's *Politics* are to Barker's (1948) translation.
2 The budget of the WTO for 2000 is 127,697,010 Swiss francs, or approximately $73.8 million, at September 2000 exchange rates ($.578 per Swiss franc, September 26, 2000). The total operating expenses of Duke University for the last year available (1998–99) were $1,989,929,000, or approximately $38.2 million *per week*. For the WTO budget, see http://www.wto.org. For the Duke budget, see the *Annual Report of Duke University*, 1998–99.
3 For a very sophisticated discussion of different forms of accountability, see Scharpf 1999, especially Chapter 1.

References

Akerlof, George A. 1970. "The Market for Lemons." *Quarterly Journal of Economics* 84 (August): 488–500.

Aldrich, John. 1993. "On William Riker's 'Inheritability' Problem: Preferences, Institutions, and Context." Paper presented at the Southern Political Science Association, Savannah, Georgia.

Aldrich, John. 1995. *Why Parties? The Origin and Transformation of Party Politics in America*. Chicago: University of Chicago Press.

Appuradai, Arjun. 1996. *Modernity at Large*. Minneapolis: University of Minnesota Press.

Arendt, Hannah. 1951/1958. *The Origins of Totalitarianism*. Cleveland: World Publishing.

Axelrod, Robert M. 1984. *The Evolution of Cooperation*. New York: Basic Books.

Barker, Ernest. 1948. *The Politics of Aristotle*, trans. Ernest Barker. Oxford: Clarendon.

Bates, Robert H. 1988. "Contra Contractarianism: Some Reflections on the New Institutionalism." *Politics and Society* 16 (June–September): 387–401.

Bates, Robert H., Avner Grief, Margaret Levi, Jean-Laurent Rosenthal, and Barry R. Weingast. 1998. *Analytic Narratives*. Princeton, NJ: Princeton University Press.

Bawn, Kathleen. 1993. "The Logic of Institutional Preferences: German Electoral Law as a Social Choice Outcome." *American Journal of Political Science* 37 (November): 965–89.

Bull, Hedley. 1977. *The Anarchical Society: A Study of Order in World Politics*. New York: Columbia University Press.

Coase, Ronald H. 1960. "The Problem of Social Cost." *Journal of Law and Economics* 3 (October): 1–44.

Cohen, G. A. 1978. *Karl Marx's Theory of History: A Defense*. Princeton, NJ: Princeton University Press.

Dahl, Robert A. 1976. *Modern Political Analysis*. 3rd ed. Englewood Cliffs, NJ: Prentice-Hall.

Dahl, Robert A. 1989. *Democracy and Its Critics*. New Haven, CT: Yale University Press.

Dahl, Robert A. 1999. "Can International Organizations Be Democratic?" In *Democracy's Edges*, ed. Ian Shapiro and Casiano Hacker-Cordon. Cambridge: Cambridge University Press. Pp. 19–36.

Deutsch, Karl W. 1953. *Nationalism and Social Communication*. Cambridge: MIT Press.

Dewey, John. [1927] 1954. *The Public and Its Problems*. Chicago: Swallow Press.

Elster, Jon. 1998. "Deliberation and Constitution Making." In *Deliberative Democracy*, ed. Jon Elster. Cambridge: Cambridge University Press. Pp. 97–122.

Fearon, James D. 1995. "Rationalist Explanations for War." *International Organization* 49 (Summer): 379–414.

Fearon, James D. 1998. "Bargaining, Enforcement and International Cooperation." *International Organization* 52 (Spring): 269–305.

Firebaugh, Glen. 1999. "Empirics of World Income Inequality." *American Journal of Sociology* 104 (May): 1597–631.

Frank, Robert H. 1988. *Passions within Reason: The Strategic Role of the Emotions*. New York: W. W. Norton.

Frohlich, Norman, and Joe A. Oppenheimer. 1992. *Choosing Justice: An Experimental Approach to Ethical Theory*. Berkeley: University of California Press.

Frohlich, Norman, and Joe A. Oppenheimer. 1996. "Experiencing Impartiality to Invoke Fairness in the n-PD: Some Experimental Results." *Public Choice* 86 (1–2): 117–35.

Geddes, Barbara. 1994. *Politician's Dilemma: Building State Capacity in Latin America*. Berkeley: University of California Press.

Goldstein, Judith, Miles Kahler, Robert O. Keohane, and Anne-Marie Slaughter. 2000. *Legalization and World Politics*. Special issue of *International Organization*, vol. 54, no. 3 (Summer).

Grant, Ruth W. 1997. *Hypocrisy and Integrity: Machiavelli, Rousseau, and the Ethics of Politics*. Chicago: University of Chicago Press.

Grewe, Wilhelm G. 2000. *The Epochs of International Law*, trans. Michael Byers. The Hague: De Gruyter.

Habermas, Jurgen. 1996. *Between Facts and Norms: Contributions to a Discourse Theory of Law and Democracy*. Cambridge: MIT Press.

Held, David, Anthony McGrew, David Goldblatt, and Jonathan Perraton. 1999. *Global Transformations: Politics, Economics and Culture*. Stanford, CA: Stanford University Press.

Herz, John H. 1959. *International Politics in the Atomic Age*. New York: Columbia University Press.

Hinich, Melvin J., and Michael Munger. 1994. *Ideology and the Theory of Political Choice*. Ann Arbor: University of Michigan Press.

Hirschman, Albert O. 1977. *The Passions and the Interests: Political Arguments for Capitalism Before its Triumph*. Princeton, NJ: Princeton University Press.

Hobbes, Thomas. [1651] 1967. *Leviathan: or the Matter, Forme and Power of a Commonwealth, Ecclesisticall and Civil*, ed. Michael Oakeshott. Oxford: Basil Blackwell.

Huntington, Samuel P. 1968. *Political Order in Changing Societies*. New Haven, CT: Yale University Press.

Jervis, Robert. 1997. *System Effects: Complexity in Political and Social Life*. Princeton, NJ: Princeton University Press.

Kahler, Miles. 1999. "Evolution, Choice and International Change." In *Strategic Choice and International Relations*, ed. David A. Lake and Robert Powell. Princeton, NJ: Princeton University Press. Pp. 165–96.

Katzenstein, Peter J. 1993. "Coping with Terrorism: Norms and Internal Security in Germany and Japan." In *Ideas and Foreign Policy*, ed. Judith Goldstein and Robert O. Keohane. Ithaca, NY: Cornell University Press, Pp. 265–95.

Katzenstein, Peter J., ed. 1996. *The Culture of National Security: Norms and Identity in World Politics*. New York: Columbia University Press.

Keck, Margaret, and Kathryn Sikkink. 1998. *Activists beyond Borders: Advocacy Networks in International Politics*. Ithaca, NY: Cornell University Press.

Keohane, Nannerl O. 1980. *Philosophy and the State in France: The Renaissance to the Enlightenment*. Princeton, NJ: Princeton University Press.

Keohane, Robert O. 1984. *After Hegemony: Cooperation and Discord in the World Political Economy*. Princeton, NJ: Princeton University Press.

Keohane, Robert O., and Joseph S. Nye, Jr. [1977] 2001. *Power and Interdependence*. 3rd ed. New York: Addison-Wesley.

Kindleberger, Charles P. 1973. *The World in Depression, 1929–1939*. Berkeley: University of California Press.

Krasner, Stephen D. 1991. "Global Communications and National Power: Life on the Pareto Frontier." *World Politics* 43 (April): 336–66.

Levi, Margaret. 1997. *Consent, Dissent and Patriotism*. Cambridge: Cambridge University Press.

Lincoln, Abraham. 1863. *The Gettysburg Address* (November 19, 1863).

Locke, John. [1689] 1967. *Second Treatise of Government*, ed. Peter Laslett. Cambridge: Cambridge University Press.

Madison, James. [1787] 1961. *Federalist No. 10*. In *The Federalist Papers*, by Alexander Hamilton, John Jay, and James Madison, ed. Jacob E. Cooke. Middletown, CT: Wesleyan University Press. Pp. 56–65.

Martin, Lisa M. 1992. "Interests, Power and Multilateralism." *International Organization* 46 (Autumn): 765–92.

Martin, Lisa M. 2000. *Democratic Commitments: Legislatures and International Cooperation*. Princeton, NJ: Princeton University Press.

Mayhew, David. 1974. *Congress: The Electoral Connection*. New Haven, CT: Yale University Press.

McGuire, William J. 1985. "Attitudes and Attitude Change." In *Handbook of Social Psychology*, 3rd ed., ed. Gardner Lindzey and Elliott Aronson. New York: Random House. Pp. 233–346.

Morgenthau, Hans J. 1967. *Politics among Nations: The Struggle for Power and Peace*. New York: Knopf.

Morrow, James D. 1994. *Game Theory for Political Scientists*. Princeton, NJ: Princeton University Press.

North, Douglass. 1981. *Structure and Change in Economic History*. New York: Norton.

North, Douglass. 1990. *Institutions, Institutional Change and Economic Performance*. New York: Cambridge University Press.

Olson, Mancur, Jr. 1965. *The Logic of Collective Action*. Cambridge, MA: Harvard University Press.

Olson, Mancur, Jr. 1982. *The Rise and Decline of Nations: Economic Growth, Stagflation and Social Rigidities*. New Haven, CT: Yale University Press.

O'Neill, Barry. 1999. *Honor, Symbols and War*. Ann Arbor: University of Michigan Press.

Ostrom, Elinor. 1990. *Governing the Commons: The Evolution of Institutions for Collective Action*. New York: Cambridge University Press.

Ostrom, Elinor. 1998. "A Behavioral Approach to the Rational Choice Theory of Collective Action." *American Political Science Review* 92 (March): 1–22.

Pennock, J. Roland. 1966. "Political Development, Political Systems and Political Goods." *World Politics* 18 (April): 415–34.

Petty, Richard E., and Duane T. Wegener. 1998. "Attitude Change: Multiple Roles for Persuasion Variables." In *Handbook of Social Psychology*, 4th ed. vol. 1, ed. Daniel T. Gilbert, Susan T. Risk, and Gardner Lindzey. Boston: McGraw-Hill. Pp. 323–90.

Putnam, Robert D. 1993. *Making Democracy Work: Civic Traditions in Modern Italy*. Princeton, NJ: Princeton University Press.

Rawls, John. 1971. *A Theory of Justice*. Cambridge, MA: Harvard University Press.

Remington, Thomas F., and Steven S. Smith. 1996. "Political Goals, Institutional Context, and the Choice of an Electoral System: The Russian Parliamentary Election Law." *American Journal of Political Science* 40 (November): 1253–79.

Riker, William H. 1980. "Implications from the Disequilibrium of Majority Rule for the Study of Institutions." *American Political Science Review* 74 (June): 432–46.

Risse, Thomas. 2000. "'Let's Argue!' Communicative Action in World Politics." *International Organization* 54 (Winter): 1–40.

Rousseau, Jean-Jacques. [1762] 1978. *On the Social Contract*, ed. Roger D. Masters. New York: St. Martin's.

Scharpf, Fritz. 1999. *Governing in Europe*. Oxford: Oxford University Press.

Schelling, Thomas C. 1960. *The Strategy of Conflict*. Cambridge, MA: Harvard University Press.

Schumpeter, Joseph A. [1942] 1950. *Capitalism, Socialism and Democracy*. 3rd ed. New York: Harper and Row.

Searle, John. 1995. *The Construction of Social Reality*. New York: Free Press.

Sen, Amartya K. 1977. "Rational Fools: A Critique of the Behavioral Foundations of Economic Theory." *Philosophy and Public Affairs* 6 (Summer): 317–44.

Sen, Amartya K. 1999. *Development as Freedom*. New York: Knopf.

Shepsle, Kenneth A. 1986. "Institutional Equilibrium and Equilibrium Institutions." In *Political Science: The Science of Politics*, ed. Herbert F. Weisberg. New York: Agathon. Pp. 51–81.

Shepsle, Kenneth A., and Barry R. Weingast. 1995. *Positive Theories of Congressional Institutions*. Ann Arbor: University of Michigan Press.

Shklar, Judith N. 1984. *Ordinary Vices*. Cambridge, MA: Harvard University Press.

Simon, Herbert A. 1985. "Human Nature in Politics: The Dialogue of Psychology with Political Science." *American Political Science Review* 79 (June): 293–304.

Smith, Adam. [1776] 1976. *The Wealth of Nations*. Chicago: University of Chicago Press.

Stein, Arthur A. 1983. "Coordination and Collaboration: Regimes in an Anarchic World." In *International Regimes*, ed. Stephen D. Krasner. Ithaca, NY: Cornell University Press. Pp. 115–40.

Tilly, Charles. 1975. "Reflections on the History of European State-Making." In *The Formation of National States in Western Europe*. Princeton, NJ: Princeton University Press. Pp. 3–83.

Tilly, Charles. 1990. *Coercion, Capital and European States AD 990–1990*. Oxford: Basil Blackwell.

Tyler, Tom R. 1990. *Why People Obey the Law*. New Haven, CT: Yale University Press.

Waltz, Kenneth N. 1979. *Theory of International Politics*. Reading, MA: Addison-Wesley.

Weber, Max. [1919] 1946. "Politics as a Vocation." In *From Max Weber: Essays in Sociology*, ed. H. H. Gerth and C. Wright Mills. Oxford, Oxford University Press. Pp. 77–128.

Weber, Max. [1920] 1978. *Economy and Society*, ed. Guenther Roth and Claus Wittich. Berkeley: University of California Press.

Wendt, Alexander E. 1999. *Social Theory of International Politics*. Cambridge: Cambridge University Press.

Williamson, Oliver. 1975. *Markets and Hierarchies*. New York: Free Press.

Williamson, Oliver. 1985. *The Economic Institutions of Capitalism*. New York: Free Press.

Wolfers, Arnold. 1962. *Discord and Collaboration*. Baltimore, MD: Johns Hopkins University Press.

World Bank. 2000. *Entering the 21st Century: World Development Report 1999–2000*. Oxford: Oxford University Press.

12 The globalization of informal violence, theories of world politics, and the "liberalism of fear"[1]

Robert O. Keohane

(2002)

The attacks on the United States on September 11, 2001, have incalculable consequences for domestic politics and world affairs. Reliable predictions about these consequences are impossible. However, it may be worthwhile, even at this early point, to reflect on what these acts of violence reveal about the adequacy of our theories of world politics. In what respects have our assumptions and our analytical models helped us to understand these events, and responses to them? And in what ways have we been misled by our theories?

In this chapter, I will not attempt to be comprehensive. Instead, I will focus instead on specific issues on which my commentary may be of some value, without presuming that these are the most important issues to address. For instance, the attacks of September 11 reveal that all mainstream theories of world politics are relentlessly secular with respect to motivation. They ignore the impact of religion, despite the fact that world-shaking political movements have so often been fueled by religious fervor. None of them takes very seriously the human desire to dominate or to hate – both so strong in history and in classical realist thought. Most of them tend to assume that the world is run by those whom Joseph Schumpeter (1950 [1942]: 137) called "rational and unheroic" members of the bourgeoisie. After September 11 we need also to keep in mind another motivation: the belief, as expressed by Osama bin Laden, that terrorism against "infidels" will assure one "a supreme place in heaven."[2] However, since I have few insights into religious motivations in world politics, I will leave this subject to whose who are more qualified to address it.

In the next section of this article I define the phrase, "the globalization of informal violence." In referring to a general category of action, I substitute this phrase for "terrorism," since the latter concept has such negative connotations that it is very difficult to define in an analytically neutral and consistent way that commands general acceptance.[3] Even as the United Nations Security Council has passed resolutions against terrorism, it has been unable to define the term. Since everyone is against terrorism, the debate shifts to its definition, as each party seeks to define its enemy's acts, but not its own, as terrorist. Nevertheless, deliberately targeted surprise attacks on arbitrarily chosen civilians, designed to frighten other people, are clearly acts of terror. The attacks on the World Trade Center of September 11, 2001, were therefore terrorist acts and I refer to them as such.

This paper has three themes. First, the events of September 11 illustrate starkly how our assumptions about security are conceived in terms of increasingly obsolescent views of geographical space. Second, the globalization of informal violence can be analyzed by exploring patterns of asymmetrical interdependence and their implications for power. Third, United States responses to the attacks tell us quite a bit about the role of multilateral institutions in contemporary world politics.

My argument is that our theories provide important components of an adequate post-September 11 conceptualization of world politics, but that we need to alter some of our assumptions in order to rearrange these components into a viable theoretical framework. Effective wielding of large-scale violence by non-state actors reflects new patterns of asymmetrical interdependence, and calls into question some of our assumptions about geographical space as a barrier. Responses to these actions reveal the significance of international institutions as well as the continuing central role of states. In thinking about these issues, students of world politics can be usefully reminded of Judith N. Shklar's concept of the "liberalism of fear," and her argument that the most basic function of a liberal state is to protect its citizens from the fear of cruelty.

The globalization of informal violence and the reconceptualization of space

The various definitions of globalization in social science all converge on the notion that human activities across regions and continents are being increasingly linked together, as a result both of technological and social change (Held *et al.*: 15). Globalism as a state of affairs has been defined as "a state of the world involving networks of interdependence at multicontinental distances, linked through flows of capital and goods, information and ideas, people and force, as well as environmentally and biologically relevant substances" (Keohane and Nye 2001: 229).

When globalism is characterized as multidimensional, as in these definitions, the expansion of terrorism's global reach is an instance of globalization (Held *et al.* 1999: 80; Keohane and Nye 2001: 237). Often, globalism and globalization have been defined narrowly as economic integration on a global scale; but whatever appeal such a definition may have had, it has surely disappeared after September 11. To adopt it would be to imply that globalized informal violence, which takes advantage of modern technologies of communication, transportation, explosives, and potentially biology, somehow threatens to *hinder* or *reduce the level of* globalism. But like military technology between 1914 and 1945, globalized informal violence strengthens one dimension of globalism – the networks through which means of violence flow – while potentially weakening globalism along other dimensions, such as economic and social exchange. As in the past, not all aspects of globalization go together.

I define informal violence as violence by non-state actors, capitalizing on secrecy and surprise to inflict great harm with small material capabilities. Such violence is "informal" because it is not wielded by formal state institutions and it is typically not announced in advance, as in a declaration of war. Such violence becomes globalized when the networks of non-state actors operate on an intercontinental basis, so that acts of force in one society can be initiated and controlled from very distant points of the globe.

The implications of the globalization of *formal* violence were profound for traditional conceptions of foreign policy in an earlier generation, particularly in the United States, which had so long been insulated by distance from invasion and major direct attack. The great expositors of classical realist theories of foreign policy in the United States, such as Walter Lippmann, began with the premise that defense of the "continental homeland" is "a universally recognized vital interest." Before World War II, threats to the homeland could only stem from other states that secured territory contiguous to that of the United States or that controlled ocean approaches to it. Hence the Monroe Doctrine of 1823 was the cornerstone of American national security policy. As Lippmann recognized in 1943, changes in the technologies of formal violence meant that security policy needed to be more ambitious: the United States would have to maintain coalitions with other great powers that would "form a combination of indisputably preponderant power" (Lippmann 1943: 88, 101). Nevertheless, Lippmann was able to retain a key traditional concept: that of a geographically defined defensive perimeter, which can be thought of as a set of concentric circles. If the United States were to control not only its own area but the circle surrounding that area, comprising littoral regions of Europe and Asia, its homeland would be secure.

The American strategists of the 1950s – led by Bernard Brodie, Thomas Schelling, and Albert Wohlstetter – had to rethink the concept of a defensive perimeter, as intercontinental ballistic missiles reduced the significance of distance: that is, as formal violence became globalized. John Herz (1959: 107–108) argued that nuclear weapons forced students of international politics to rethink sovereignty, territoriality, and the protective function of the state:

> With the advent of the atomic weapon, whatever remained of the impermeability of states seems to have gone for good. . . . Mencius, in ancient China, when asked for guidance in matters of defense and foreign policy by the ruler of a small state, is said to have counseled: 'dig deeper your moats; build higher your walls; guard them along with your people.' This remained the classical posture up to our age, when a Western sage,

Bertrand Russell, could still, even in the interwar period, define power as a force radiating from one center and diminishing with the distance from that center until it finds an equilibrium with that of similar geographically anchored units. Now that power can destroy power from center to center everything is different.

September 11 signifies that informal violence has become globalized, just as formal, state-controlled violence became globalized, for the superpowers, during the 1950s. The globalization of informal violence was not *created* by September 11. Indeed, earlier examples, extending back to piracy in the 17th century, can be easily found. But the significance of globalization – of violence as well as economically and socially – is not its absolute newness but its increasing magnitude as a result of sharp declines in the costs of global communications and transportation (Keohane and Nye 2001: 243–45).

Contemporary theorists of world politics face a challenge similar to that of this earlier generation: to understand the nature of world politics, and its connections to domestic politics, when what Herz called the "hard shell" of the state (Herz 1959: 22) has been shattered. Geographic space, which has been seen as a natural *barrier* and a locus for human barriers, now must be seen as a *carrier* as well.

The obsolescence of the barrier conception of geographic space has troubling implications for foreign policy. One of the strengths of realism in the United States has always been that it imposed limitations on American intervention abroad. By asking questions about whether vital national interests are involved in a particular situation abroad, realists have sought to counter the moralistic and messianic tendencies that periodically recur in American thinking. For Lippmann, the key to a successful foreign policy was achieving a "balance, with a comfortable surplus of power in reserve, [between] the nation's commitment and the nation's power" (Lippmann 1943: 9). Going abroad "in search of monsters to destroy" upset that balance.[4] Realism provided a rationale for "just saying no" to advocates of intervening, for their own ideological or self-interested reasons, in areas of conflict far from the United States. It is worthwhile to be reminded that Lippmann, Hans J. Morgenthau and Kenneth N. Waltz were all early opponents of the war in Vietnam. Unfortunately, this realist caution, salutary as it has been, is premised on the barrier conception of geographical space. In the absence of clear and defensible criteria that American leaders can use to distinguish vital from non-vital interests, the United States is at risk of intervening throughout the world in a variety of conflicts bearing only tangential relationships to "terrorism with a global reach."

The globalization of informal violence, carried out by networks of non-state actors, defined by commitments rather than by territory, has profoundly changed these fundamental foreign policy assumptions.[5] On traditional grounds of national interest, Afghanistan should be one of the least important places in the world for American foreign policy – and until the Soviet invasion of 1979, and again after the collapse of the Soviet Union in 1991 until September 11, the United States all but ignored it. Yet in October 2001 it became the theatre of war. Globalization means, among other things, that threats of violence to our homeland can occur from anywhere. The barrier conception of geographical space, already anachronistic with respect to thermonuclear war and called into question by earlier acts of globalized informal violence, was finally shown to be thoroughly obsolete on September 11.

Interdependence and power

Another way to express the argument made above is that networks of inter-dependence, involving transmission of informal violence, have now taken a genuinely global form. Using this language helps us to see the relevance for the globalization of informal violence of the literature on interdependence and power, which was originally developed to understand international polit-ical economy. In that literature, interdependence is conceptualized as mutual dependence, and power is conceptualized in terms of *asymmetrical inter-dependence*.[6] This literature has also long been clear that "military power dominates economic power in the sense that economic means alone are likely to be ineffective against the serious use of military force" (Keohane and Nye 2001: 14).

September 11 revealed how much the United States could be hurt by informal violence, to an extent that had been anticipated by some government reports but that had not been incorporated into the plans of the government.[7] The long-term vulnerability of the United States is not entirely clear, but the availability of means of mass destruction, the extent of hatred for the United States, and the ease of entering the United States from almost anywhere in the world, all suggest that vulnerability may be quite high.

If the United States were facing a territorial state with conventional object-ives, this vulnerability might not be a source of worry. After all, the United States has long been much more vulnerable, in technological terms, to a nuclear attack from Russia. But the United States was not *asymmetrically vulnerable*. On the contrary, the United States either had superior nuclear capability or "mutual assured destruction" (MAD) kept vulnerability more or less symmetrical. Russia has controlled great *force*, but has not acquired power over the United States from its arsenal.

With respect to terrorism, however, two asymmetries, which do not nor-mally characterize relationships between states, favored wielders of informal violence in September 2001. First, there was an *asymmetry of information*. It seems paradoxical that an "information society" such as that of the con-temporary United States would be at an informational disadvantage with respect to networks of individuals whose communications seem to occur largely through hand-written messages and face-to-face contacts. But an information society is also an open society. Potential terrorists had good information about their targets, while before September 11 the United States had poor information about the identity and location of terrorist networks within the United States and other Western societies. Perhaps equally important, the United States was unable coherently to process the information that its various agencies had gathered. Second, there is an *asymmetry in beliefs*. Some of Osama bin Laden's followers apparently believed that they would be rewarded in the afterlife for committing suicidal attacks on civilians. Others were duped into participating in the attacks without being told of their suicidal purpose. Clearly, the suicidal nature of the attacks made them more difficult to prevent and magnified their potential destructive power. Neither volunteering for suicide missions nor deliberately targeting civilians is consistent with secular beliefs widely shared in the societies attacked by al-Qaeda.

The United States and its allies have enormous advantages in resources, including military power, economic resources, political influence, and technological capabilities. Furthermore, communications media, largely based in the West, give greater weight to the voices of people in the wealthy democracies than to those of the dispossessed in developing countries. Hence the asymmetries in information and beliefs that I have mentioned are, in a sense, exceptional. They do not confer a permanent advantage on the wielders of informal violence. Yet they were sufficient to give the terrorists at least a short-term advantage, and they make terrorism a long-term threat.

Our failure to anticipate the impact of terrorist attacks does not derive from a fundamental conceptual failure in thinking about power. On the contrary, the power of terrorists, like that of states, derives from asymmetrical patterns of interdependence. Our fault has rather been our failure to understand that the most powerful state ever to exist on this planet could be vulnerable to small bands of terrorists due to patterns of asymmetrical interdependence. *We have overemphasized states and we have over-aggregated power.*

Power comes not simply out of the barrel of a gun, but from asymmetries in vulnerability interdependence – some of which, it turns out, favor certain non-state actors more than most observers anticipated. The networks of interdependence along which power can travel are multiple, and they do not cancel one another out. Even a state that is overwhelmingly powerful on many dimensions can be highly vulnerable on others. We learned this lesson in the 1970s with respect to oil power; we are re-learning it now with respect to terrorism.

Institutions and legitimacy

Institutionalist theory implies that multilateral institutions should play significant roles wherever interstate cooperation is extensive in world politics. Yet a reader of the American press immediately after the September 11, 2001 attack on the World Trade Center and the Pentagon, might well have thought this claim weirdly divorced from reality. Immediate reactions centered on domestic security, military responses, and the creation of a broad international coalition against terrorism. Although the United Nations Security Council did act on September 12, passing resolution 1368, its response attracted relatively little attention. Indeed, President Bush's speech to Congress of September 20 did not mention the United Nations, although the President did praise NATO and made a generic reference to international organizations. And coverage of the United Nations was virtually nonexistent in the *New York Times*.

But theory is not tested by the immediate reactions of policymakers, much less by those of the press. Social science theory purports to elucidate underlying structures of social reality, which generate incentives for action. Kenneth Waltz rightly looks for confirmation of his theory of the balance of power "through observation of difficult cases." The theory is confirmed, he claims, where states ally with each other, "in accordance with the expectations the theory gives rise to, even though they have strong reasons not to cooperate with one another" (Waltz 1979: 125). Realists rightly argue that if leaders seem to be compelled toward actions that theory suggests – as, for instance, Winston Churchill was when Britain allied with the Soviet Union in 1941 and American leaders when they built NATO after World War II – this counts for their theory. Indeed, the most demanding test of theory comes when policymakers are initially unreceptive to the arguments on which the theory is based. If they nevertheless turn to the policy measures that the theory anticipates, it gains support.

The terrorist attacks of September 11 therefore pose a fruitful test for institutionalist theory. Before September 11, the Bush Administration had been pursuing a notably unilateralist policy with respect to several issues, including global warming, trade in small arms, money laundering, and tax evasion. Its leading policymakers all had realist proclivities: they emphasized the decisive use of force and had not been public supporters of international institutions. Their initial inclinations, if their public statements and those of the President are any guide, did not lead them to emphasize the role of the United Nations.

Nevertheless, the United States returned to the Security Council. On September 28, 2001, the Security Council unanimously adopted Resolution 1373, on the motion of the United States. This resolution used the mandatory provisions of Chapter VII of the United Nations Charter to require all states to "deny safe haven" both to terrorists and to those who "provide safe haven" to terrorists. Resolution 1373 also demanded that states prevent potential terrorists from using their territories, and "prevent and suppress the financing of terrorist acts." It did not, as noted above, define terrorism. Furthermore, the United States continued to engage the United Nations, indeed delegating to it the task of bringing Afghan factions together in Germany in a meeting that culminated in an agreement in December 2001.

Why should the United States have relied so extensively on the United Nations? The UN, in Stalin's famous phrase, has no divisions. The United States, not the UN, carried out the significant military actions. Transnational banks, central banks, and states in their capacities as bank regulators, froze funds allegedly belonging to terrorists. Even before the September 28 Security Council resolution, allies of the United States had already invoked Article 5 of NATO's Charter.

Inis L. Claude proposed one answer almost 35 years ago (Claude 1967). States seek "collective legitimation" for their policies in the United Nations. Only the UN can provide the breadth of support for an action that can elevate it from the policy of one country or a limited set of countries, to a policy endorsed on a global basis. In contemporary jargon, the "transaction costs" of seeking support from over 150 countries around the world are higher than those of going to the Security Council, ready to meet at a moment's notice. But more important than these costs is the fact that the institution of the United Nations can confer a certain degree of legitimacy on a policy favored by the United States.

What does legitimacy mean in this context? Legally, decisions of the United Nations Security Council on issues of involving the use of violence are legitimate since members of the United Nations, through the Charter, have authorized such decisions. In a broader popular and normative sense, decisions are legitimate for a given public insofar as members of that public believe that they should be obeyed. As Weber pointed out, the sources of such legitimacy may include tradition, charisma or rational–legal authority (Weber 1978: 954); they may also include appeal to widely accepted norms. People in various parts of the world may believe that their governments should obey decisions of the Security Council because they were made through a process that is normatively as well as legally acceptable. Or they may regard its decisions as legitimate insofar as they are justified on the basis of principles – such as collective opposition to aggression – that they regard as valid.

Why is legitimacy important? In part, because people will voluntarily support a legitimate policy, without requiring material inducements.[8] But it would be naive to believe that leaders of most countries will be persuaded, by Security Council action, of the wisdom or righteousness of the policy and will therefore support it for normative reasons. To explain the impact of Security Council resolutions, we need also to look for self-interested benefits for leaders.

Even if the leaders are entirely cynical, the adoption of a legitimate UN resolution will change their calculations. If they lead democratic societies in which publics accept the legitimacy of UN action, they will benefit more politically from supporting policies endorsed by the United Nations, than from supporting policies not so endorsed. If they exercise rule over people who are unsympathetic to the policies and who do not accept them merely due to UN endorsement, the legal status of Security Council resolutions may change their calculations. Chapter VII decisions are mandatory, which means that states defying the Security Council run the risk of facing sanctions themselves, as in the Gulf War. Leaders of countries with unsympathetic populations can point out that, however distasteful it may be to take action against Osama bin Laden and his network, it could be more costly to be cut off from essential supplies and markets, to suffer disruption of transportation and banking services, or even to become a target of military action.

The general point is one that has often been made by institutional theory: international institutions work largely by altering the costs of state strategies. Of course, there is no guarantee that institutions will be sufficiently important to ensure that strategies change: they are only one element in a mixture of calculations. Yet, as the use of the United Nations by the United States indicates, they are an element that should not be overlooked.

How important multilateral institutions will in fact be is another question – one that was much debated during the early months of 2002. Several factors seem to work in favor of more reliance on multilateral institutions in the wake of 9/11. As noted, the United States seeks legitimacy for its military actions. Furthermore, it needs help from more different countries, from Pakistan to the Philippines. Even the very powerful United States needs to negotiate for access to sovereign territory, and must provide some reciprocal benefits in return for access and cooperation. Some of these benefits may be provided through concessions in multilateral institutions on a variety of issues, ranging from money-laundering to controls on trade in weapons.

On the other hand, the war against terrorism also increases incentives for unilateral action and bilateral diplomacy. Threats of terrorism generate incentives to retain the ability to act decisively, without long deliberation or efforts at persuasion. The United States government in February 2002 signalled that it might renew its war on Iraq, with or without the endorsement of the United Nations Security Council or even its traditional allies. In the conduct of its war in Afghanistan during the fall of 2001, the United States was notably reluctant to permit the United Nations, or its own allies, to restrict its military freedom of action. In fact, requests by Great Britain to send in troops to protect relief operations were rebuffed by the United States on the advice of its military commanders. A cynical interpretation of United States policy toward multilateral institutions would suggest that American policymakers want to retain freedom of military action for themselves, but to delegate tedious political issues – such as reconstructing Afghanistan – to the United Nations. When the inevitable political failures become evident, blame can be placed at the door of the UN.

One can easily imagine an even more pessimistic scenario for the next few years. The United States government could decide that its security required radical measures that would not be supported even by many of its NATO allies, such as an attack on Iraq without strong evidence of Iraqi complicity in prior attacks on the United States. In such an eventuality, American actions would not be legitimised either by the United Nations or by NATO. Having acted unilaterally, the United States would not be moved to rely more heavily on international institutions, and multilateralism could suffer a serious blow.

Even if the multilateral path is chosen, it is hardly likely to be sufficient. It is unlikely that multilateral organizations will be the key *operating agencies* in dealing with the globalization of informal violence: they are too cumbersome for that. The state, with its capacity for decisive, forceful action and the loyalty it commands from citizens, will remain a necessary part of the solution to threats of informal violence. *Jejeune* declarations of the "death of the state" are surely among the casualties of the terrorist offensive, but multilateral organizations will be an essential part of the process of legitimizing action by states.

It should be evident that these arguments about multilateral institutions and networks are not "anti-realist." On the contrary, they rest on an appreciation of the role of power, and of state action, in world politics; on an understanding that new threats create new alliances; and on a belief that structures matter. Analysts who are sensitive to the role of multilateral institutions need not regard them as operating *independently* from states, nor should they see such institutions as a panacea for our new ills. But sensitivity to the role of multilateral institutions helps us see how these institutions can play a role: not only by reducing transaction costs but also by generating opportunities for signalling commitments and providing collective legitimacy for effective action.

The "liberalism of fear"

Judith N. Shklar's "liberalism of fear" envisages liberal democracy as "more a recipe for survival than a project for the perfectibility of mankind." It seeks to avoid the worst outcomes, and therefore declares that "the first right is to be protected against the fear of cruelty" (Shklar 1984: 4; 237). The liberalism of fear certainly speaks to our condition today, as it did to that of victims of the Nazis such as Judith Shklar. It raises both an analytical and a normative issue. Analytically, it leads us to ask about the protective role of the state, facing the globalization of informal violence. Normatively, it should make us think about our own role as students of world politics.

The erosion of the concept of a protected homeland within a defensive perimeter, discussed above, makes the "liberalism of fear" more relevant to Americans than it has been in almost two centuries. Suddenly, the task of protecting citizens from the fear of cruelty has become a demanding project for the state, not one that a superpower can take for granted.

Judith Shklar looked to the state as the chief threat. "No liberal," she declared, "ever forgets that governments are coercive" (Shklar 1984: 244). In this respect, the "liberalism of fear" shares a blind spot with the most popular theories of world politics, including realism, institutionalism and some forms of constructivism. All of these views share a common fault: they do not sufficiently take account of how globalization facilitates the agency of non-state entities and networks. After September 11 no liberal should be able to forget that non-state actors, operating within the borders of liberal states, can be as coercive and fear-inducing as states.

Recognition of the dangers of informal violence may lead the United States toward a broader vision of its global interests. As we have seen, classical realist thinking drew a bright line between geographical areas important to the national interest and those parts of the world that were insignificant from the standpoint of interests. Now that attacks against the United States can be planned and fostered within countries formerly viewed as insignificant, this bright line has been blurred.

One of the implications of this blurring of lines is that the distinction between self-defense and humanitarian intervention may become less clear. Future military actions in failed states, or attempts to bolster states that are in danger of failing, may be more likely to be described *both* as self-defense and as humanitarian or public-spirited. When the only arguments for such policies were essentially altruistic ones, they commanded little support, so the human and material price that American leaders were willing to pay to attain them was low. Now, however, such policies can be framed in terms of American self-interest, properly understood. Sound arguments from self-interest are more persuasive than arguments from responsibility or altruism.

More generally, recognition of the dangers of informal violence will force a redefinition of American national interests, which could take different forms. Such a redefinition could lead Americans to support measures to reduce poverty, inequality and injustice in poor countries. The Marshall Plan is a useful if imperfect analogy. In 1947 the United States redefined its self-interest, taking responsibility for helping to build a democratic and capitalist Europe, open to other capitalist democracies. The United States invested very large resources in this project, with great success. The task now in the less developed countries is much more daunting, both in sheer magnitude and since the political systems of most of these countries are weaker than those of European countries in 1947.[9] But the resources available to the United States and other democratic countries are also much greater than they were in 1947.

Any widely appealing vision of American interests will need to be based on core values that can be generalized. Individual freedom, economic opportunity, and representative democracy constitute such values. The ability to derive gas-guzzling sports utility vehicles (SUVs) does not. In the end, "soft power" (Nye 1990) depends not merely on the desire of people in one country to imitate the institutions and practices prevailing in another, but also their ability to do so. Exhibiting a glamorous lifestyle that others have no possibility of attaining is more likely to generate hostility and a feeling of "sour grapes" than support. To relate successfully to people in poor countries during the twenty-first century, Americans will have to distinguish between their values and their privileges.

The attachment of Americans to a privileged lifestyle raises the prospect of a defensive and reactionary broadening of American national interests. Recall that a virtue of classical realism was to link commitments to a relatively limited set of interests, defined partly by geography. Ideology and a self-serving attempt to preserve privileges could define a different set of interests. Opponents – not merely those who have attacked the United States – would be demonized. Deals would continue to be cut with corrupt and repressive regimes to keep cheap oil flowing to the United States. The United States would rely exclusively on military power and bilateral deals rather than also on economic assistance, trade benefits, and efforts at cultural understanding. The costs would include estrangement from our democratic allies and hatred of the United States in much of the world. Ultimately, such a vision of national interest is a recipe for isolation and continual conflict – an environment in which liberal democracy could be threatened by the emergence of a garrison state at home.

Normatively, thinking about the "liberalism of fear" reminds our generation that in a globalized world, we cannot take liberal societies for granted. People such as Judith Shklar, who experienced Nazism, understood the fear of cruelty in their bones. Those of us who grew up in the United States during the Cold War experienced such fear only in our imaginations, although nuclear threats and wars such as those in Korea and Vietnam gave our imaginations plenty to work with. The generations that have come of age in the United States since the mid-to-late 1980s – essentially, those people under 35 – have been able to take the basics of liberalism for granted, as if the United States were insulated from the despair of much of the world's population. The globalization of informal violence means that we are not so insulated. We are linked with hateful killers by real physical connections, not merely those of cyberspace. Neither isolationism nor unilateralism is a viable option.

Hence, the liberalism of fear means that we who study international interdependence and multilateral institutions will need to redouble our efforts. We should pay less attention to differentiating our views from those of other schools of international relations; more to both synthesis and disaggregation. We need to synthesize insights from classical realism, institutionalism, and constructivism, but we also need to take alternative worldviews – including religious worldviews – more seriously. We need to examine how purposes are shaped by ideas and how calculations of power interact with institutions, to produce outcomes in world politics. We need, at the same time, to disaggregate strands of asymmetrical interdependence, with their different implications for power; and to differentiate international institutions and networks from one another, in their effects and their potential for good or ill.

Conclusion

The terrorist attacks on New York and Washington force us to rethink our theories of world politics. Globalism should not be equated with economic integration. The agents of globalization are not simply the high-tech creators of the internet, or multinational corporations, but also small bands of fanatics, travelling on jet aircraft and inspired by fundamentalist religion. The globalization of informal violence has rendered problematic our conventional assumptions about security threats. It should also lead us to question the classical realist distinction between important parts of the world, in which great powers have interests, and insignificant places, which were thought to present no security threats although they may raise moral dilemmas. Indeed, we need to reconceptualize the significance for homeland security of geographical space, which can be as much a carrier of malign informal violence as a barrier to it.

Most problematic are the assumptions in international relations theory about the roles played by states. There has been too much "international relations," and too little "world politics," not only in work on security but also in much work on international institutions. States no longer have a monopoly on the means of mass destruction: more people died in the attacks on the World Trade Center and the Pentagon than in the Japanese attack on Pearl Harbor in 1941. Indeed, it would be salutary for us to change the name of our field, from "international relations" to "world politics."[10] The language of "international" relations enables us to slip back into state-centric assumptions too easily. Asymmetrical interdependence is not merely an interstate phenomenon.

Yet as the state loses its monopoly on means of mass destruction, the response to terrorism is strengthening the powers of states, and the reliance of people on government. Even as states acquire more authority, they are likely to cooperate more extensively with each other on security issues, using international institutions to do so. Ironically, as states acquire more authority, they will be forced to learn better how to relate to networks – both hostile networks and networks that they may use instrumentally – and to rely more heavily on multilateral institutions. These institutions, in turn, will have to define their tasks in ways that emphasize their advantages – in conferring collective legitimacy on actions – while minimizing the impact of their liabilities, as cumbersome organizations without unity of command.

One result of these apparently paradoxical changes is closer linkages between traditional security issues and other issues. The artificial but convenient separation of the field into security and political economy may be one of the casualties of the struggle against terrorism. Areas formerly seen as "non-security areas," such as air transport, transnational finance, and migration, have become more important to security, and more tightly subject therefore to state regulation.

Finally, the globalization of informal violence indicates how parochial have been some of the disputes among various schools of international relations theory. Analysis of the ramifications of the attacks on the United States must come to grips not only with structures of power, but also with changing subjective ideas and their impact on strategies. It must be concerned with international institutions, and with non-state actors and networks – elements of world politics emphasized by different schools of thought. And it must probe the connections between domestic politics and world politics. We do not face a *choice* between these perspectives, but rather the task of *synthesizing* them into a comprehensive, yet coherent, view.

Our understanding of world politics has often advanced under the pressure of events, such as those of World War II, the Nuclear Revolution, and the growth of economic interdependence over the last fifty years. Perhaps the globalization of informal violence will refocus our attention for a new period of intellectual creativity, as sober thinking about global governance and classic political realism converge on problems identified so well by the "liberalism of fear."

Notes

1 Paper prepared for *Dialog IO*, the online version of *International Organization*, and scheduled to be posted, February 2002; and for *Understanding September 11*, edited by Craig Calhoun, Paul Price and Ashley Timmer, published by the New Press and the Social Science Research Council, September 2002. I am grateful for comments on earlier versions of this paper to Carol Atkinson, Hein Goemans, Peter Gourevitch, Nannerl O. Keohane, Lisa L. Martin, Joseph S. Nye, John Gerard Ruggie, and Anne-Marie Slaughter, as well as to participants at seminars at the University of Pennsylvania, October 18, 2001; at the University of Amsterdam, November 2, 2001; at Duke University, November 16, 2001; and at the University of Tokyo, December 10, 2001. At the Amsterdam colloquium I benefited particularly from the comments of Gerd Junne and at the Tokyo colloquium from the comments of Yasuaki Osuma.
2 Statement by Osama bin Laden, *New York Times*, October 8, 2001, p. B7.
3 The best definitional discussion of terrorism that I know of us by Alex Schmid, who defines it as "an anxiety-inspiring method of repeated violent action, employed by (semi)clandestine individual, group or state actors, for idiosyncratic, criminal or political reasons, whereby – in contrast to assassination – the direct targets of violence are not the main targets" (Schmid 1993: 8, 12).
4 From a Fourth of July oration by John Quincy Adamas at the Capitol in 1821. Perkins 1993: 149–50.
5 A few pessimistic and prescient observers understood that terrorism could pose a threat to the United States homeland despite our dominance in military power. See Carter and Perry 1999, and the Hart–Rudman Report, Phase I, September 15, 1999, Conclusion 1.
6 In 1977 Joseph Nye and I distinguished between two types of dependence, which

we labeled (following the contemporary literature on economic interdependence) sensitivity and vulnerability dependence. Sensitivity dependence refers to "liability to costly effects imposed from outside before policies are altered to try to change the situation." Vulnerability dependence, in contrast, refers to "an actor's liability to suffer costs imposed by external events even after policies have been altered." This language seems inappropriate in the contemporary situation, since in ordinary language, the attacks on an unprepared United States on September 11 demonstrated how vulnerable the country was. But the distinction between levels of dependence before and after policy change remains important. See Keohane and Nye 2001: 11; the text is unchanged from the 1st edition, 1977.

7 My colleague Ole Holsti has pointed out to me that in surveys conducted by the Chicago Council on Foreign Relations in 1994 and 1998, the public more often regarded international terrorism as a "critical" foreign policy issue than did leaders. Indeed, 69% and 84%, respectively, of the public regarded terrorism as a critical issue in those years, compared to 33% and 61% of the elites. See Holsti 2000: 21.

8 Douglas North links legitimacy to the costs of enforcing rules. "The costs of maintenance of an existing order are inversely related to the perceived legitimacy of the existing system. To the extent that the participants believe the system fair, the costs of enforcing the rules and property rights are enormously reduced." North 1981: 53.

9 It is tempting in hindsight to forget that the political systems of European countries were not terribly strong in 1947. Germany was still under occupation, Italy had recently been Fascist, and France and Italy had very large, pro-Soviet communist parties. Nevertheless, these countries had relatively highly-educated populations, they had some history of democratic or at least liberal politics, and their administrative bureaucracies were quite effective.

10 This is a point that the late Susan Strange repeatedly emphasized.

References

Carter, Ashton B. and William Perry. 1999. *Preventive Defense: A New Security Strategy for America*. Washington, DC: Brookings.

Claude, Inis L. 1967. *The Changing United Nations*. New York: Random House.

Hart, Gary, Warren Rudman, *et al.* 1999. *Phase I Report on the Emerging Global Security Environment for the First Quarter of the 21st Century*, United States Commission on National Security/21st Century (Washington: September 15). "Hart–Rudman Report."

Held, David and Anthony McGrew, David Goldblatt, and Jonathan Perraton. 1999. *Global Transformations*. Stanford: Stanford University Press.

Herz, John H. 1959. *International Politics in the Atomic Age*. New York: Columbia University Press.

Holsti, Ole. 2002. "Public Opinion and Foreign Policy." In Robert Lieber, ed., *Eagle Rules?* (New York: Longman): 16–46.

Keohane, Robert O. and Joseph S. Nye. 2001. *Power and Interdependence. 3rd edition*. New York: Addison Wesley Longman.

Lippmann, Walter. 1943. *US Foreign Policy: Shield of the Republic*. Boston: Little, Brown.

North, Douglas C. 1981. *Structure and Change in Economic History*. New York: W. W. Norton.

Nye, Joseph S. 1990. *Bound to Lead: The Changing Nature of American Power*. New York: Basic Books.

Perkins, Bradford. 1993. *The Creation of a Republican Empire, 1776–1865*. Volume I of *The Cambridge History of American Foreign Relations*. Cambridge: Cambridge University Press.

Schmid, Alex P. 1993. "The Response Problem as a Definition Problem," in Schmid and Crelinsten, 1993: 7–13.

Schmid, Alex P. and Ronald D. Crelinsten. 1993. *Western Responses to Terrorism*. London: Frank Cass.

Schumpeter, Joseph. 1950 [1942]. *Capitalism, Socialism and Democracy*. New York: Harper and Row.

Shklar, Judith N. *Ordinary Vices*. 1984. Cambridge: the Belknap Press of Harvard University Press.

Waltz, Kenneth N. 1979. *Theory of International Politics*. Reading, MA: Addison-Wesley.

Weber, Max. 1978. *Economy and Society*, edited by Guenther Roth and Claus Wittich. Berkeley: University of California Press.

Index